JOSEPH R. MANCUSO is an internationally known entrepreneur and author. He is the founder and director of the Center for Entrepreneurial Management, Inc., an affiliate of the American Management Associations, in Worcester, Massachusetts. He has launched seven businesses and serves as a board member and advisor for a score of entrepreneurial ventures. Dr. Mancuso holds a B.S.E.E. from Worcester Polytechnic Institute and an M.B.A. from Harvard Business School. He earned his Doctorate in Education from Boston University. In addition he has written and edited nine books in the field of small business management including *402 Things You Must Know Before Starting a New Business* and *How to Start, Finance, and Manage Your Own Small Business*, also published by Prentice-Hall, Inc.

The Small Business Survival Guide

sources of help for entrepreneurs

Joseph R. Mancuso

A SPECTRUM BOOK

PRENTICE-HALL, INC., *Englewood Cliffs, New Jersey 07632*

Library of Congress Cataloging in Publication Data

Mancuso, Joseph R
  The small business survival guide.

  (A Spectrum Book)
  Includes index.
  1. Small business—Information services—United
States. 2. Small business—Information services.
I. Title.
HD2346.U5M36   658'.022'072   80-19061
ISBN 0-13-814228-9
ISBN 0-13-814210-6 (pbk.)

To Karl Schulz, the retired owner/operator of the general store in Elroy, Wisconsin (population 1500), who knows the value of being independent.

Editorial/production supervision by Louise M. Marcewicz
Interior design by Norma Miller Karlin
Cover design by Tony Ferrara Studios, Inc.
Manufacturing buyer: Cathie Lenard

A SPECTRUM BOOK

10 9 8 7 6 5 4 3 2 1

Printed in the United States of America

PRENTICE-HALL INTERNATIONAL, INC., *London*
PRENTICE-HALL OF AUSTRALIA PTY. LIMITED, *Sydney*
PRENTICE-HALL OF CANADA, LTD., *Toronto*
PRENTICE-HALL OF INDIA PRIVATE LIMITED, *New Delhi*
PRENTICE-HALL OF JAPAN, INC., *Tokyo*
PRENTICE-HALL OF SOUTHEAST ASIA PTE. LTD., *Singapore*
WHITEHALL BOOKS LIMITED, WELLINGTON, *New Zealand*

Contents

Introduction

My secret desire has always been to have available to all small-business-owners an 800 (toll-free) telephone number which would be an entrepreneur's lifeline to sources of help.* While I still fantasize about this, I have come to realize that it would soon become a security blanket. It's often so lonely in an entrepreneurial venture that the need to talk to someone who can understand, empathize, or share the burden might cause people to use this number much as we "dial a prayer."

The best idea is to dial a friend who can give help and understanding. The cost of just *one* 800 number would be about $5,000 per month—that's the monthly fee for one line, and it doesn't include the person who answers the telephone, and so on.

In fact, I envision this 800 number to be so wonderful that we'd need more than one telephone line. While I haven't calculated how many lines would be needed, I realize one line wouldn't be enough. But in my daydreaming, this issue of the number of telephone lines kept nagging at me.

So, I did what any sensible entrepreneur would do—made a rough estimate. To start, I knew there were 9½ million small businesses in the U.S. because I had read such a statistic published by the Small Business Administration. Second, I concluded that not every

*The Small Business Administration has installed a toll-free number in order to provide quick delivery of free SBA pamphlets, but it's really not the same thing: (800)433-7302, or if a resident of Texas (800)792-8901.

small-business owner would use the toll-free number, so I guessed one-third would use it and two-thirds would ignore it. But then I realized that people other than small-business owners would use the service. In fact, its greatest users were likely to be would-be entrepreneurs. I didn't really know of any published statistics on how many would-be entrepreneurs existed, so I checked again with the SBA and discovered that they only know "it is a lot." I asked the friends in my universe and concluded that more would-be entrepreneurs existed than practicing entrepreneurs—at a ratio of at least 3:1. So now, the number of potential users was back to my original estimate of about 9.5 million people.

But of course they wouldn't all use the toll-free number every day. Even so, the 800 number could be receiving a million calls a day, if it were a quality service. Do you know how much it would cost to staff an 800 number that handled a million calls a day? The cost would be staggering—beyond any individual's financial reach, surely infinitely beyond mine.

But it still seemed like a great idea—a really sound concept. Then it occurred to me that the only entity able to deal in such large numbers would be the United States government. Maybe this was the solution! The government could foot the bill for the toll-free number to offer help and advice to entrepreneurs.

This "solution" could have fearful consequences—the cure could turn out to be worse than the disease! Not only would entrepreneurs discover that the telephone lines were always busy, they'd probably get bad advice, which is worse than no advice at all. How could the people who brought us social security and the swine flu vaccine help my little business?

At that point in my daydreaming, an old joke flashed through my mind which put the government's effectiveness into a revealing perspective:

> The Lord's Prayer is composed of 50 words. The Gettysburg Address is composed of 266 words. The Ten Commandments have 297 words. And a recent government proclamation setting the price of cabbage had 26,911.

That settled it—my dreams wouldn't work. That's when I decided to compile this book—I hope you like it!

May I suggest you start this source book by reading Chapter 20, "Sources of Help," first; it is worth an early, independent reading.

1

Advertising and Public Relations

Resources contained in this chapter concern promoting and advertising both products and services for an entrepreneurial venture. The entrepreneur's strategy is almost always to obtain as much *free* advertising and public relations as possible before spending money for them. The problem that always confronts an entrepreneur is how to obtain free publicity, free new-product releases, and free information to promote the business. This section should be analyzed along with Chapter 25, "Magazines and Periodicals," for information that will be helpful to the small-business owner or potential entrepreneur.

My advice about advertising is very simple: Get help early and often. People tend to believe that they are experts on advertising and, therefore, try to do it themselves. This is often a disaster, if not a classic mistake.

One enterprising company I worked with had a fascinating and successful philosophy—it was determined to obtain every ounce of free advertising possible before placing even one paid advertisement in a trade journal. During its first million or two of sales, nothing was paid for advertising. Rather, the company hired an individual to research all the trade journals and various media to secure new-product releases, new-literature releases, and news stories. That person was paid about $15,000 annually and obtained close to $1,000,000 worth of free publicity and information.

Many entrepreneurs avoid hiring advertising agencies because they consider them too expensive. They refuse to pay for advertis-

1

ing help or advice until an impasse develops in the marketing plans—then it's too late to solve what may be a fundamental problem.

I believe in finding a good small advertising agency early in the game. It can be an important member of your entrepreneurial team. I suggest a small agency because here you'll probably get the attention of the top executives. Possibly a firm of a dozen or so people is the proper size to work with you in developing an entrepreneurial venture.

The agency may be a junior member of your team, but it should be selected early. An integrated corporate communications concept for letterheads, business cards, envelopes, and logos will establish a valuable corporate identity. It makes a big difference when all the corporate communications are well coordinated from the beginning. In this way your company can avoid the embarrassment of looking unprofessional or not being taken seriously.

Once you've found the right advertising agency, let it do its job. Be candid and honest, and give the agency all the information you can about your product and your markets—but don't try to impose your artistic tastes. The more solid the information you give the agency, the more effectively it can serve you.

When it comes to agency compensation, don't rely on the old 15-percent-of-the-media-costs method. This method of compensating for agency efforts is very simple. Most approved media will allow an accredited agency to deduct a 15 percent discount very much like the airlines allows a travel agency a 7 percent discount. Hence, an advertising agency that annually places $100,000 of media billing for a client can be indirectly compensated by paying the various media $85,000 while billing the client the published rates of $100,000. But it's impossible for an agency to work profitably on a straight commission basis unless the media expenditures are considerable. Remember, the agency is in business to make a profit too. Furthermore, this method tends to create a conflict of interest for the agency, since it is to its advantage if your advertising dollars go into "commissionable" media. The best course for your company may be direct mail or some other noncommissionable media. Do you want the agency working for your company or for the commissionable advertising media?

Then too, there is a possible conflict between what is good for the media and what is good for the client. An agency that is reimbursed only for print or electronic media may be unreceptive to

designing brochures or trade literature. An estimate of the annual advertising budget should be the foundation for determining an agency's compensation. This allows a fuller, fairer choice of the optimal allocations between commissionable and non-commissionable activities.

The most practical and fairest method of agency compensation is a monthly retainer fee which amounts to about 10 percent more than the commissions the agency would receive on an annual forecasted commissionable media expenditure. This method eliminates the conflict of interest and lets the agency worry about what's best for *you*, not about what's best for itself. These resources are offered to complement your advertising agency selection, not to supplement it.

ADVERTISING: NEWSPAPERS AND NEWSLETTERS

1. The leading weekly newspaper serving the advertising industry is *Advertising Age.* It features current news on advertising and public relations. Weekly issues are in excess of 100 pages in a large format. The magazine focuses on advertising in the broadest sense; it claims to be the international newspaper of marketing. Write:

Advertising Age
Crain Communicates
740 Rush Street
Chicago, IL 60611
(312)649-5200
Circulation: about 70,000

2. The *Business Ideas Newsletter* is of interest to people in advertising, merchandising, or promotion. The focus is on selling ideas, premium suggestions, and direct-mail promotions. Write:

Business Ideas Newsletter
57 Lakeview Avenue
Clifton, NJ 07013
Circulation: 5,000
Published by:

The Dan Newman Company, Inc.
930 Clifton Avenue
Clifton, NJ 07013
(201)473-3262

3. *AD Day/USA* is a six-page weekly newsletter published every Thursday. The first two pages contain bulletin news about changes in marketing products, advertising, etc. The next four pages are feature pages (e.g., editorials, marketing studies). All information covers the entire United States. Write:

AD Day/USA
400 East 54th Street
New York, NY 10022
(212)421-3713
Circulation: about 10,000

PUBLICITY AND ADVERTISING IDEAS

1. *How to Create Your Own Publicity—And Get it For Free!*, by Steve Berman (1977) is a comprehensive guide for those who want to create their own publicity, whether in a letter to the editor of the local newspaper or as a guest on a radio or TV show. This book tells you where to start and how to go about it. Includes sample questionnaires for talk-show hosts, sample press kits, sample interviews, sample advertising, and ways of preparing materials for instant interest. An invaluable aid in receiving free publicity. Write:

Frederick Fell Publishers, Inc.
386 Park Avenue, South
New York, NY 10016
(212)685-9017

2. The *Advertising Illustration Clip Book* contains over 1,000 fine drawings of almost every subject conceivable, all ready to reproduce for your circulars, letterheads, ads, brochures, etc. This treasure trove of art is available from:

Magiera & Associates
1917 Xerxes Avenue, North
Minneapolis, MN 55411
(612)521-6561

3. *Media Decisions* is a monthly magazine focusing on the value of various media for various advertising messages. Write:

Media Decisions
342 Madison Avenue
New York, NY 10017
(212)953-1888
Circulation: about 30,000

4. *The Effective ECHO—A Dictionary of Advertising Slogans,* edited by Valerie Nobel (1970), classifies and identifies more than 2,000 advertising slogans. It is indexed alphabetically by subject classification and by service. A brief essay on the history of each slogan is offered. This is a useful book in developing slogans and ideas for your small business, especially in coming up with a name for your business. Write:

Special Library Association
235 Park Avenue, South
New York, NY 10003
(212)777-8136

PUBLIC RELATIONS

To find assistance with publicity and public relations, consult the following publications:

1. *Apollo Handbook of Practical Public Relations,* by Alexander B. Adams. Write:

Apollo Editions
666 Fifth Avenue
New York, NY 10019
(212)489-2200

2. *Building Customer Confidence in Your Service Shop* is a free booklet you can get by writing:

Small Business Administration
Washington, DC 20417

3. *How to Handle Your Own Public Relations,* by H. G. Lewis is available from:

Nelson-Hall
325 W. Jackson Boulevard
Chicago, IL 60606
(312)922-0856

4. *Knowing Your Image* is a free booklet. Write:

Small Business Administration
Washington, DC 20417

5. *Lesly's Public Relations Handbook,* by Philip Lesly is published by:

Prentice-Hall, Inc.
Englewood Cliffs, NJ 07632
(201)592-2000

6. *News Releases: How to Write and Where to Place Them,* by J.L.
Angel & June L. Aulick (1980), is published by:

World Trade Academy Press
50 East 42nd Street
New York, NY 10017
(212)697-4999

7. *Professional's Guide to Public Relations* is published by:

Richard Weiner, Inc.
888 7th Avenue, 28th Floor
New York, NY 10019
(212)582-7373

8. *Profitable Community Relations for Small Business* is available
from:

Small Business Management Series No. 27
Small Business Administration
Washington, DC 20417

9. *Public Relations Handbook,* by Richard Darrow, is published
by:

Dartnell Corporation
4660 Ravenswood Avenue
Chicago, IL 60640

10. *What You Should Know about Public Relations,* by Edward
Starr, is published by:

Oceana Publications, Inc.
Dobbs Ferry, NY 10522
(914)693-1394 (editor)
(914)693-5944 (sales)
(914)693-1320 (orders)

RATES AND DATA: PUBLICATIONS AND SERVICES

Standard Rate and Data Service, Inc.

Some sections include "market data summary" estimates and
Standard Metropolitan Statistical Area (SMSA) rankings. Included
are data for state, county, and metropolitan areas. They also offer a

guide to magazines and periodicals for publicity and promotion. SRDS is one of the fundamental services for the advertising industry because it provides numerous publications that contain all the information necessary to place an advertisement. For information on these, write:

Standard Rate and Data Service
5201 Old Orchard Road
Skokie, IL 60076
(312)966-8560

1. *Spot Television, Rates and Data.* Published on the 15th of every month.
2. *Spot Radio Small Markets Edition.* Published semiannually in May and November.
3. *Spot Radio, Rates and Data.* Published on the first of every month.
4. *Network, Rates and Data.* Published bimonthly in January, March, May, July, September, and November.
5. *Newspaper, Rates and Data.* Published on the 12th of every month.
6. *Newspaper Circulation Analysis.* Published annually in August. Included in subscription to *Newspaper Rates and Data* (above).
7. *Business Publication, Rates and Data.* Published on the 24th of every month.
8. *Consumer Magazine and Farm Publication, Rates and Data.* Published on the 27th of every month.
9. *Weekly Newspaper and Shopping Guide, Rates and Data.* Published semiannually in March and September.
10. *Print Media, Production Data.* Published quarterly in March, June, September, and December.
11. *Transit Advertising, Rates and Data.* Published quarterly in February, May, August, and November.
12. *Canadian Advertising, Rates and Data.* Published monthly by Maclean-Hunter, Toronto, Canada in collaboration with SRDS.
13. *International, Rates and Data.* To compete effectively in world markets, use the list below as a source of help:

British Rates and Data. 4,075 listings published monthly.

Dati E Tariffe Pubblicitarie (Italy). 2,000 listings published bimonthly.

Media Daten (Fed. Rep. Germany). 4,902 listings published bimonthly.

Media Daten (Austria). Published semiannually.

Media Daten (Switzerland). Published semiannually.

Medios Publicitarios Mexicanos (Mexico). 748 listings published quarterly.

Tarif Media (France). 3,387 listings, 5 issues per year.

14. *Direct Mail List, Rates and Data.* Published semiannually in January and July.

Information on Premium and Incentive Buying

There are many products that can be sold to people or organizations that will use them as premiums or giveaways or in incentive buying programs. Perhaps your product(s) can be used this way. For a list of such buyers, there are several sources you can contact:

The Salesman's Guide
1182 Broadway
New York, NY 10001
(212)684-2985

Incentive Marketing
633 Third Avenue
New York, NY 10017
(212)986-4800
Circulation: about 35,000

Premium/Incentive Business
1515 Broadway
New York, NY 10036
(212)869-1300
Circulation: about 24,000

NPSE (Nation Premium Sales Executives) Newsletter
1600 Route 22
Union, NY 07083
(201)687-3090
Circulation: about 2,000

FREE PUBLICITY

Rather than launching a marketing program with a series of paid advertisements, you may want to consider a free publicity release program. Your firm may be eligible for news releases or product releases or literature releases, all of which are free. Doesn't it make sense to have all initial effort directed toward using free material? Good managers obtain all the available free product releases before they pay for advertisements.

Directories and Publicity Release Programs

The procedure for contacting the various trade journals varies from industry to industry. Some journals require black-and-white photographs, others require color photographs, and others accept no photographs. To obtain specific information on how to obtain publicity and to obtain a list of relevant trade journals, these four publishers offer you directories and publicity release programs. Also see *Gebbie House Magazine Directory*.

1. The most comprehensive source of newspaper information is *Ayer's Directory of Newspapers and Periodicals*. Write:

Ayer Press
210 West Washington Square
Philadelphia, PA 19106
(215)829-4472

2. For the finest overall source of publicity in the country, contact:

Bacon's Publicity Checker
14 East Jackson Boulevard
Chicago, IL 60604
(800)621-0561

3. For an excellent overall list of periodicals, use the *Standard Periodical Directory,* published by:

Oxbridge Publishing Company
183 Madison Avenue, Room 1108
New York, NY 10016
(212)189-8524

4. *Ulrich's Directory of Periodicals* is most often available in libraries and as a reference in college libraries. It is published by:

R. Bowker Company
1180 Avenue of the Americas
New York, NY 10036
(212)764-5100

Clipping Services

Below is a partial list of services that will clip newspaper and magazine articles about your company or about a product area. This can be a valuable service to keep you posted on advertising and

public relations efforts of your competitors as well as your own company's programs.

Note: This list is not complete because no organization keeps this information on a national basis. Inspect your local yellow pages to determine whether such an organization exists within your geographical area.

> Allen's Press Clipping Bureau
> 657 Mission Street
> San Francisco, CA 94105
> (415)392-2353
>
> Bacon's Clipping Service
> 14 East Jackson Boulevard
> Chicago, IL 60604
> (312)922-8419
>
> Florida Clipping Service
> Box 10278
> Tampa, FL 33679
> (813)831-0962
>
> Luce Press Clipping Service
> 912 Kansas Avenue
> Topeka, KS 66612
> (913)232-0201
>
> New England Newsclip Service
> 5 Auburn Street
> Framingham, MA 01701
> (617)879-4460

MARKETING SOURCES

1. The National Research Bureau is a subsidiary of the Automated Marketing Systems, Inc. It offers the *Gebbie House Magazine Directory,* which lists company house organs, newsletters, and internal company information. It is an often overlooked source of publicity—this directory is a part of the *Working Press of Nations,* a five-volume set of invaluable aids to over 100,000 prime media contacts (available from NRB, Burlington, IA 52601). Contact:

> National Research Bureau Headquarters
> 104 South Michigan Avenue
> Chicago, IL 60603
> (312)641-2655

Washington National Research Bureau
1141 National Press Building
Washington, DC 20045
(202)638-4746

2. John Jay Daily Associates has prepared a series of booklets, memos, and other information on various types of services offered to business people. One such booklet is *Eighteen Principles of Direct Mailing*. It covers the various types of direct-mail and direct-marketing techniques. There is also a memo called *Forty Questions to Answer When Planning and/or Evaluating Your Program or Project*. Write:

Daily Associates, Inc.
Suite 702, World Center Building
918 Sixteenth Street, N.W.
Washington, DC 20006

3. Conventions and trade show listings are compiled and offered by the following sources:

Exhibits Schedule
144 East 44th Street
New York, NY 10017

The Hendrickson Publishing Company
91 North Franklin Street
Hempstead, NY 11550
(516)483-6883

International Association of Fairs and Exhibits
77 Arbor Road
Winston-Salem, NC 27104

Sales Meeting Magazines
633 Third Avenue
New York, NY 10017
(212)986-4800

Trade Show Week
1605 Cahuenga Boulevard
Los Angeles, CA 90028
(213)463-4891

2

Barter
and Grants

Two areas of help often overlooked by entrepreneurs are the opportunities to obtain grants from foundations and government agencies, or the possibility of bartering for services with other entrepreneurial ventures.

BARTER

A growing interest has developed in bartering, and many publications and services have emerged. These services and publications are entrepreneurial in their own way; the claim is made that several billion dollars annually are exchanged through barter. Bartering has an obvious advantage because it avoids taxes. In other words, if a doctor gives you $100 worth of medical service and you do $100 worth of labor for him in his home, neither of you has really declared income of $100. Actually, all you have done is swap services, and this is not a taxable transaction.

It's interesting to note that the government maintains accurate figures on its Gross National Product (GNP), which is the aggregate of the country's output on the basis of products and services that are sold for cash. Barter never enters into the gross national product picture. Goods that are bartered back and forth, and not individually exchanged for cash, are not recorded in government statistics.

The other aspect of barter which has appeal involves the possibility of a good bargain. Unfortunately, a good bargain isn't always attainable because people who are bartering services for goods or goods for services often tend to inflate the price. Consequently, in examining barter alternatives, you must be wary of unscrupulous buyers and sellers.

The sources of information on barter provided in this chapter could be helpful in securing new products or services for your firm, or in offering your firm's services or products in the same manner. Unfortunately, the connotation of low quality is often associated with barter. Since it's a fact of small-business life, you must not ignore it.

Barter Clubs

The barter clubs listed below are geared primarily to the self-employed person or small-business owner and offer an alternative to increasing cash outlay. For exchanges with subsidiary offices in several states, the address of the exchange's headquarters is listed. These offices can be contacted for more information about barter clubs in your area.

Business Exchange, Inc.
4716 Vineland Avenue
North Hollywood, CA 91602

Business Owners' Exchange
4901 W. 77th Street, Suite 123-B
Minneapolis, MN 55435

Exchange Enterprises
159 West Haven Avenue
Salt Lake City, UT 84115

Hilton Exchange
5032 Lankersheim Boulevard
North Hollywood, CA 91601

International Trade Exchange, Inc.
7656 Burford Drive
McLean, VA 22101

Mutual Credit Buying
6420 Wilshire Boulevard
Los Angeles, CA 90048

Barter Communique
6500 Midnight Pass Road
Penthouse Suite 504
Sarasota, FL 33581
(813)349-2242
Circulation: 50,000

The Learning Exchange
Box 920
Evanston, IL 60204

Useful Services Exchange
c/o Wellborn Company
1614 Washington Plaza
Reston, VA 22090

Atwood Richards, Inc.
99 Park Avenue
New York, NY 10016

Barter Billionaire
Lock Box 983
Department E-1
W. Caldwell, NJ 07006

GRANTS

In 1979, 27,000 United States foundations gave away just over $3.0 billion in grants. And the federal government, mostly through the Department of Health, Education and Welfare (HEW), gave away $59 billion. Very little of such grants goes to small business, but it does not have to be that way. Although 95 percent of the grant proposals submitted are rejected, the fact is that small businesses seldom seek grant support.

Most entrepreneurial ventures never attempt to receive grants. The government and private foundations hand out millions of dollars annually to causes you might judge less worthy than your own. Even though your venture may not be eligible for a grant, it may make sense for you to consider an affiliation with a local non-profit organization, such as a college or chamber of commerce, to tackle any project you feel worthwhile. These affiliations will allow the non-profit agency to receive the grant and to hire you or your business as a subcontractor.

14

While a special exemption letter is needed to win a grant for any profit-seeking business, it is not uncommon to award the grant to a nonprofit organization and for the entrepreneur to be a subcontractor on the grant. This is becoming an increasingly popular alternative. The process can be aided by contacting the following sources:

1. The Foundation Center is an information clearinghouse that maintains national libraries in Chicago, New York City, and Washington, D.C., as well as 62 regional libraries in 48 states, plus Mexico and Puerto Rico. These libraries are open to the public at no charge.

The Foundation Directory lists 2,800 foundations that awarded $1.8 billion in 1976. The data in the directory includes:

1. Name and address (by state)
2. Founders
3. Total assets
4. Official's names
5. Foundation purposes and activities
6. Number and dollar amount of grants awarded during the year

This directory is available at any large library.

2. The *Foundation Grants Index*, which is unlike the *Foundation Directory*, lists the grants made by the 300 major foundations of more than $5,000 each. It lists the name of the recipient, the purpose of the grant, and the dollar amount awarded. A separate "Key Word & Phrase" index is especially useful in determining the current real interests of the foundation. This is also available in most large libraries.

3. The *Catalog of Federal Domestic Assistance and the Annual Register of Grant Support* are good starting points for a search for grants. The *Register* lists:

1. Procedures
2. Programs
3. Names of agency officers
4. Total number of applications received and awarded by program by year

To obtain the Register and the Catalog, write:

Marquis Who's Who
4300 West 62nd Street
Indianapolis, IN 46206

3

Bankruptcy

Bankruptcy is a process created by law to solve in a fair way the interest of both the creditor who is owed the money and the debtor who is not able to pay his debts. In 1978, President Carter signed a major amendment to the bankruptcy law and bankruptcy laws have changed dramatically. And the changes were all fundamental improvements. While bankruptcy may be a depressing subject, this source guide would really not be complete without a section devoted to it.

Bankruptcy tends to sneak up on entrepreneurs like a summer cold—and once you get it, it's hard to get rid of. Just like the common cold, there are no real cures, only ways to help relieve the symptoms.

The sources of help listed here will familiarize you with the various issues in bankruptcy. Many small businesses find themselves, their customers, or their suppliers in bankruptcy and are totally unable to cope with the problem. Unfortunately, roughly half of the entrepreneurial ventures that go bankrupt do not survive. But keep in mind that Henry Ford, the premier entrepreneur, who started the Ford Motor Company, failed twice before he succeeded. Bankruptcy is really not a bad thing, but it does hold bad connotations.

1. Kits of bankruptcy forms are available from:

American Bankruptcy Council
2525 Van Ness Avenue
San Francisco, CA 94109

17

2. *Bankruptcy and Insolvency Accounting: Practice and Procedure,* by Grant W. Newton (1975), puts bankruptcy issues in fairly easy-to-read and understandable accounting language. Publisher:

Ronald Press
79 Madison Avenue
New York, NY 10016

3. *Bankruptcy: Problems, Process & Reform,* by David T. Stanley and Marjorie Girth (1971), is a book that integrates bankruptcy with other economic and social events, setting bankruptcy into proper perspective in the American business scene. The Brookings Institution, which publishes the book, is a high-quality source of original information about economic issues. Write:

The Brookings Institution
1775 Massachusetts Avenue, N.W.
Washington, DC 20036

4. *The Complete Guide to Getting Yourself Out of Debt,* by Lewis M. Finley (1975), is a practical manual for everyone who urgently needs relief from the tensions of debt. The author explains how to stop bill collectors, suits, garnishments, and wage attachments; how to wipe out old debts without borrowing or bankruptcy and still retain AAA credit; how to set up a workable family budget; and much more. Write:

Frederick Fell Publishers, Inc.
386 Park Avenue, South
New York, NY 10016
(212)685-9017

5. A magazine called *Credit Executive* is published by the New York Credit & Financial Management Association exclusively for its members; the subscription charge is included in the membership fee. Occasionally, special provisions are made so that universities, government agencies, or even an interested individual can receive the magazine. The publication features articles of interest to middle and top executives in commercial credit and finance.

The Association also publishes a number of handbooks, available to the general public. Current titles are:

1. *A Practical Guide to Chapter XI of the Bankruptcy Act*
2. *What the Businessman Should Know About Commercial Arbitration*

3. *What the Business Executive Should Know About the Uniform Commercial Code*

4. *Guarantees and Subordinations*

For information on these publications, write:

Credit Executive
71 West 23rd Street
New York, NY 10010
(212)741-4743

6. *The Guide to Personal Bankruptcy,* by John T. Slavicek and Robert E. Burger (1975), is a workbook outlining the bankruptcy process. It is complete with sample forms and copies of actual forms. Its down-to-earth language makes it worth reading. Publisher:

Crown Publishing Company
419 Park Avenue, South
New York, NY 10016

7. *How to Get Out If You're In Over Your Head,* by Ted Nicholas (1976), is a large workbook with practical advice on how to get out of debt. Write:

Enterprise Publishing
1300 Market Street
Wilmington, DE 19801
(302)575-0440

8. *National Bankruptcy Reporter* is an interesting newsletter that will inform you of the vital data of business bankruptcy filings all across the country. It's expensive—over \$1,000 annually—but it provides useful facts on a subject that can be hard to acquire information about. Write:

Andrews Publications, Inc.
1634 Latimer Street
Philadelphia, PA 19103
(215)353-2565

9. *Strategies and Techniques for Saving the Financially Distressed Small Business,* by Arnold Goldstein (1975), a practicing attorney, shows business people how to protect themselves from overzealous creditors and how to turn their business adversity around. It offers an overview of some of the remedies that are available. Write:

Pilot Books
347 Fifth Avenue
New York, NY 10016
(212)685-0736

10. *Ten Cents on the Dollar,* by Sidney Rutberg (1973), is an extremely easy-to-read, understandable book on the ins and outs of bankruptcy. Offers insight into why "10 cents on the dollar" is a common slogan for bankruptcy. Publisher:

Simon & Schuster
Rockefeller Center
630 Fifth Avenue
New York, NY 10020
(212)615-6400

4
Books

Books covering the range of small business are among the best-selling books in the country; our listing here cannot be complete because the topic is so immense. What we have attempted in compiling this list of books is to offer both variety and depth. Beside some specific topics, we have given special attention to entrepreneurs and entrepreneurial ventures. May we suggest you consult the master directory, known as *Books In Print* (published by R. Bowker and Company) if you are interested in additional books on entrepreneurship and small business. The books we categorize here are selected because of their breadth of appeal and because we consider them valuable reading.

1. *The Basic Book of Business,* by John R. Klug (1977) is divided into four parts: (1) "How to Organize Your Own Business," (2) "How to Operate Your Own Business," (3) "How to Buy or Sell Your Business," and (4) "Retirement, Life Insurance and Estate Planning." Publisher:

Cahners Books International, Inc.
89 Franklin Street
Boston, MA
(617)423-4310

2. A more conceptual book on the subject of blending business and academia, is *The Effective Entrepreneur,* by Charles Swayne and William Tucker (1973), published by:

General Learning Corp.
250 James Street
Morristown, NJ 07960
(201)538-0400

3. Corporate strategy first for large companies, successful strategies for entrepreneurs second, but a good blend of ideas, *The Entrepreneurs,* by Richard Bruce (1976). Publisher:

Folium Press, Ltd.
18 Regent Parade
Birmingham 1, England

4. Another helpful book is *The Entrepreneurial Function,* by W. Arnold Hosmer, Arnold C. Cooper, and Karl Vesper (1967). Publisher:

Prentice-Hall, Inc.
Englewood Cliffs, NJ 07632
(201)592-2000

5. *Entrepreneurial Management,* by Charles A. Dailey, is a book on management first and entrepreneurs second, which may be a good sequence. Publisher:

McGraw-Hill Book Company
1221 Ave. of the Americas
New York, NY 10020
(212)997-1221

6. *The Entrepreneur's Handbook* (2 vol.), edited by Joseph Mancuso (1974), is designed as a permanent reference for the business person who wants immediate access to answers as questions arise. Heralded as one of the most complete sources of pertinent data in the entrepreneurial field, these two volumes contain 50 articles. Information is presented in practical, hands-on, how-to language, and arranged for fast location of the desired facts. Publisher:

Artech House Inc.
Department E
610 Washington Street
Dedham, MA 02026
(617)326-8220

7. *Entrepreneurship and Venture Management,* by Joseph Mancuso and Clifford Baumback (1975), has become a standard reference for courses dealing with small-business management, venture manage-

22

ment, and entrepreneurship. Many schools and colleges have adopted it as a supplemental reading requirement. Publisher:

Prentice-Hall, Inc.
Englewood Cliffs, NJ 07632
(201)592-2000

8. *Fun and Guts,* by Joseph Mancusco (3rd ed., 1977), is a quick and painless way to gather the core ideas of entrepreneurship. Provides the background you need through a mixture of humorous and serious messages about the process of managing a small venture. Contains invaluable information on the characteristics of an entrepreneur, the life cycle of a small business, marketing your product, and much more. Publisher:

The Center for Entrepreneurial Management, Inc.
One of the American Management Association
311 Main Street, Suite #402
Worcester, Mass. 01608
(617)755-0770

9. *How to Start, Finance, and Manage Your Own Small Business,* by Joseph R. Mancuso (1978), has been a featured book club selection. One unique element is the "Entrepreneur's Quiz," designed to help you identify the degree of your natural entrepreneurial ability. The book covers everything from raising capital and preparing an effective business plan to profit disbursement and public stock issue. Five actual business plans and commentaries are included. Publisher:

Prentice-Hall, Inc.
Englewood Cliffs, NJ 07632
(201)592-2000

10. In *Managing Technology Products* and *Marketing Technology Products* (1975), Joseph Mancuso has compiled over 50 significant readings that will be essential for entrepreneurs launching new products. This set of books applies not only to the independent entrepreneur but also to the "international entrepreneur," often a product manager charged with the planning, development, and introduction of a new product.

Artech House, Inc.
Department E
610 Washington Street
Dedham, MA 02026
(617)326-8220

11.* *No Guts, No Glory . . . Or, How to Fight Dirty Against Management,* by Joseph Mancuso (1976) is a provocative little book that introduces humor to the field of corporate politics. It was created especially for the internal entrepreneur, who has to develop a business while working for someone else. The author tells this struggling individual how to survive management baloney, how to succeed more than fail. Fighting dirty, it turns out, is not all bad. Publisher:

The Center for Entrepreneurial Management, Inc.
311 Main Street, Suite #402
Worcester, MA 01608
(617)755-0770

12. *The Entrepreneur's Manual: Business Start-Ups, Spin-Offs, and Innovative Management,* by Richard M. White, is a basic information manual on how to start a new business with special emphasis on manufacturing, industrial services, retail sales or retail services, and franchises. Publisher:

Chilton Book Company
201 King of Prussia Way
Radnor, PA 19089
(215)687-9828

13. The Executive Program is a book club focusing on business-related books. It has a favorable bias toward small business and some of its selections are excellent. Beside being a convenient method of keeping current on new books, the club allows a savings on original publisher prices. Write:

The Executive Program
Box 503
Riverside, NJ 08075

14. *How to Be Self-Employed,* by Bert Fregly (1977), covers virtually every aspect of small-business operation that confronts owners

---

*The books described in paragraphs 6 to 11 can also be obtained by contacting:

The Center for Entrepreneurial Management, Inc.
311 Main Street
Worcester, MA 01608
(617)755-0770

daily—from inception of the business to retirement plans for the self-employed. Write:

Bert Fregly Publications
2850 Reynard Way
Suite 9
San Diego, CA 92103

15. E. Joseph Cossman, author of several best-selling books, including *How I Made A Million Dollars in the Mail Order Business* (1971), also has several excellent sets of material for small-business owners. His course at Pepperdyne University is available on an audio cassette and the handouts are worth the price of the course alone. Write:

E. Joseph Cossman
1838 Barona Road
Palm Springs, CA 92262
(714)327-0550

16. *How to Get $100,000 Worth of Services Free Each Year from the United States Government,* by E. Joseph Cossman (1973), lists the wide range of inexpensive and free services and publications the government makes available. The author has selected publications from various agencies and departments which he thinks offer the best and most helpful types of materials. There are ten chapters, each concerned with a particular special-interest group (such as inventors, home owners, students, and owners of small businesses). His selections are good, and he covers a wide range of subjects. Publisher:

Frederick Fell Publishers, Inc.
386 Park Avenue, South
New York, NY 10016
(212)685-9017

17. *The New Encyclopedia of Little-Known, Highly Profitable Business Opportunities,* by Jack W. Payne (1974), shows you the way to opportunity through several hundred sources that provide keys to thousands of new business opportunities. The author gives complete instructions for developing money-making opportunities through finder's fees, unusual franchises, distributorships and dealerships, import opportunities, speculative investments, mergers, and acquisitions. Sources for financial, managerial, manufacturing, and sales help for your business venture are provided along with helpful tips

and suggestions in each category. The publisher of this book is
Frederick Fell (see address above). The author also publishes a newsletter, *Opportunities Unlimited.* To obtain this, write:

Opportunities Unlimited Publications
Box AA
Magalia, CA 95954

18. Frederick Fell Publishers also offers a very interesting and
useful source of "how to do" anything books. Send for free 25-page
catalog of books; many will be helpful to entrepreneurs. Among the
books available from the publisher are the following:

The Complete Guide to Getting Yourself Out of Debt, by Lewis Finley
    (1975).
The Greatest Salesmen in the World, by Og Mandino (1968).
How to Create Your Own Publicity—And Get It for Free, by Steve Berman
    (1977).
How to Finance a Growing Business, by Royce Diener (1973).

19. *How to Form Your Own Corporation Without a Lawyer for Under
$50.00,* by Ted Nicholas (1977), is an interesting book about small
business and venture capital published by:

Enterprise Publishing Company
1300 Market Street
Wilmington, DE 19801
(302)575-0440

20. *How to Organize and Operate a Small Business,* 5th ed., by
Clifford M. Baumback, Kenneth Lawyer, Pearce C. Kelley (1973), is
a four-part book stressing the importance of good management and
the impact of small business in the nation's economy. It is published
by:

Prentice-Hall, Inc.
Englewood Cliffs, NJ 07632

21. *How to Start Your Own Business,* ed. William Putt (1974), is a
group of readings by MIT alumni and faculty. Publisher:

MIT Press
28 Carleton Street
Cambridge, MA 02142

22. *Inc. Yourself,* by Judith H. McQuown (1977) is a good book on the advantages of incorporating a business. The author does a fine job of differentiating among the various forms of business enterprises and of articulating the features of a corporation, especially of a professional corporation. Publisher:

Macmillan Publishing Co.
866 3rd Avenue
New York, NY 10022
(212)935-2000

23. *Legal Handbook for Small Business,* by Marc J. Lane (1977), is a small book, quick reading, and good, on lawyers. It is fairly broad in coverage and has a good index. Publisher:

American Management Association
135 West 50th Street
New York, NY 10020

24. An interesting collection of readings is available in a book called *Managing the Dynamic Small Firm,* by Lawrence A. Klatt (1974). Publisher:

Wadsworth Publishing Co., Inc.
Belmont, CA 94002
(415)592-1300

25. *Managing the Small Business,* rev. ed., by Donald P. Stegall, Lawrence L. Steinmetz, and John B. Kline (1976), offers information on small-business management and lists various categories of help for the entrepreneur. Publisher:

Richard D. Irwin
Homewood, IL 60430

26. *New Business Ventures and the Entrepreneur,* by Patrick R. Liles (1974), covers seven basic sections for new business development. Publisher:

Richard D. Irwin
1818 Ridge Road
Homewood, IL 60430
(312)548-6000

27. The Research Department of International Entrepreneurs Association offers complete start-up manuals on 115 businesses, giving detailed instruction and market studies on each. Write:

Research Department
International Entrepreneurs Association
631 Wilshire Boulevard
Santa Monica, CA 90401

28. *Small Business Management,* 4th ed., by Halsey N. Broom and Justin C. Longenecker (1975), is a basic text. The latest edition adds concerns for environment, public relations, consumerism, and business ethics. Publisher:

Southwestern Publishing Co.
5101 Madison Road
Cincinnati, OH
(513)271-8811

29. Classic academic text with cases and writeups are contained in *Small Business Management: A Guide to Entrepreneurship,* by Nicholas C. Siropolis (1977). Publisher:

Houghton Mifflin Co.
1 Beacon Street
Boston, MA 02107

30. *Small Business and the Quality of American Life* is a compilation of source material on the relationship between small business and the quality of life from 1946 to 1976. It was prepared for the first session of the 95th Congress and printed in 1977 for use by the Select Committee on Small Business, Senator Gaylord Nelson, Chairman. No. 052-070-04295-8. Write:

Superintendent of Documents
U.S. Government Printing Office
Washington, DC 20402

31. *Venture Capital,* by John R. Dominiguez (1974), provides worthwhile reading. Publisher:

Lexington Books
7 Oakland Street
Lexington, MA 02173
(617)862-8900

32. *Venture Capital in the 70's,* by Milton Stewart (1973), is a good collection of readings, checklists, sample forms and guides— the articles are well grouped in two volumes. Write:

Practicing Law Institute
1133 Avenue of the Americas
New York, NY 10036

The following three books have been written so as to complement each other with minimum overlap.*

33. *Up Your OWN Organization! A Handbook on How to Start and Finance a New Business,* by Donald M. Dible (1974) has three sections, which cover: (1) a realistic view of small business startup and operating problems, (2) a four-chapter "cookbook" for preparing a business plan, and (3) a detailed analysis of forty generic money sources from closed-end investment companies to Veterans Administration loans. Additionally, six appendixes provide an extensive small-business bibliography of books and periodicals, lists of organizations providing help, venture capital directory, numerous checklists, plus a full index.

34. *The Pure Joy of Making More Money,* by Donald M. Dible, (1976), is based on three small-business seminars that the author presents in cooperation with numerous universities across the United States. More than 100 seminars are offered each year. Material in this book includes techniques for stimulating new-product ideas, establishing channels of distribution, product sales and promotion, techniques for starting businesses with extremely modest financial resources (including case examples), and a bibliography of marketing information sources.

35. *Winning the Money Game—How to Plan and Finance a Growing Business* by Donald M. Dible (1975), contains the proceedings of a two-day small-business seminar. Fourteen contributors including attorneys, accountant, commercial banker, investment banker, market researcher, equipment leasing specialists, management consultant, founder of several technology-related firms, commercial finance expert, and several venture capitalists provide sixteen chapters on small-business topics within their specialty areas.

36. *The Woman's Guide to Starting a Business,* by Claudia Jessup and Genie Chipps, is a two-part guide is concerned with the special problems that women face when establishing a business. Part I consists of basic information on getting started, and Part II is a collection of interviews of successful women entrepreneurs.

Holt, Rinehart & Winston
383 Madison Avenue
New York, NY 10017

*If you have trouble finding these books, you can write:

The Entrepreneur Press
3422 Astoria Circle
Fairfield, CA 94533
(707)422-6822

ADDITIONAL BOOKS OF VALUE TO
THE ENTREPRENEUR

The ABC's of Borrowing
by SBA Financial Assistance Staff
(SBA, Washington, DC, 1971)

The Art of Negotiating
by G. Nierenberg
(Hawthorne Books, Inc., 1976)

Basic Business Finance
by G. Donaldson, C. M. Williams, and P. Hunt
(Richard D. Irwin, 1961)

Entrepreneurship: Playing to Win
by Gordon Baty
(Reston Publishing Co., 1974)

Financing Business Firms
by J.E. Wert and C.L. Prather
(Richard D. Irwin, 1975)

Financing—Short and Long Term Needs
by SBA Administrative Management Course Program
(SBA, Washington, DC, 1975)

Guide to Venture Capital Sources
by S.M. Rubel
(Capital Publishing Corporation, 1977)

How to Raise Money to Make Money
by W.J. Casey, et al.
(Institute for Business Planning, 1976)

Managerial Finance
by J.F. Weston and E.F. Brigham
(Holt, Rinehart & Winston, 1969)

New Venture Creation: A Guide to Small Business Development
by J.A. Timmons, L.E. Smollen, A.L.M. Dingee
(Richard D. Irwin, 1977)

ALL-TIME BEST-SELLING
SELF-DEVELOPMENT BOOKS

Think and Grow Rich, by Napoleon Hill
Laws of Success, by Napoleon Hill
Psycho-Cybernetics, by Maxwell Maltz, M.D.

Success Through a Positive Mental Attitude, by Napoleon Hill and W. Clement Stone

The Success System that Never Fails, by W. Clement Stone

The Power of Positive Thinking, by Dr. Norman Vincent Peale

The Greatest Salesman in the World, by Og Mandino

How to Win Friends and Influence People, by Dale Carnegie

Your Greatest Power, by J. Martin Kohn

How I Raised Myself from Failure to Success in Selling, by Frank Bettger

HOW TO SELL BY MAIL ORDER

I recently came across a very effective manual on "How to Sell via the Established Mail Order Houses." Should your product have the necessary appeal for mail order distribution, it may make sense for you to consider trying to interest some of the big mail order distributors into offering it as one of their catalog items.

Here are some of the large mail order houses:

Sunset House

Miles Kimball

Hanover House

Foster & Gallagher

Bruce Bolind

The basic business of a mail order house such as the above is to sell specialty items direct to the consumer via a mass mailing of a promotional catalog. Do you realize that sixty million of these mail order catalogs are distributed annually? Yet few entrepreneurial ventures consider this unique distribution channel. Very few, in practice, and mostly because they are unaware of how to tap this potential.

The unique manual I recommend is: *The $25.00 50 page Book Worth $50,000* by Ron Playle. It is a manual on how to do it and its title is self-explanatory. Write:

Ron Playle

R & D Series

Box 644

Des Moines, Iowa 50303

Business Associations

There are two basic categories of associations that are of value to entrepreneurs: international or national associations such as the International Council for Small Business Management Development (ICSBMD), and regional associations. The ICSBMD headquarters is at the University of Wisconsin extension in Milwaukee. This is an international organization serving small businesses around the world.

Regional organizations, such as the Smaller Business Association of New England (SBANE), cater to local small-business clientele. SBANE has been in operation for over forty years, and is one of the strongest regional associations of small businesses in the country. Such groups provide valuable services to their local entrepreneurial clientele. You should examine the merits of the small-business association in your region as well as the national and international associations. Each of these can mail you information concerning the benefits of membership.

There is also a federation of eight regional smaller business associations: the Council of Small and Independent Business Associations (COSIBA). These are identified below:

1. Council of Smaller Enterprises of the Greater Cleveland
   Growth Association
   690 Union Square Building
   Cleveland, OH 44115

2. Independent Business Association of Wisconsin
   11050 West Bluemound Road
   Milwaukee, WI 53226

3. National Association of Small Business Investment Companies
512 Washington Building
Washington, DC 20005

4. National Business League
4324 Georgia Avenue, N.W.
Washington, DC 20011

5. National Federation of Independent Business
150 West 20th Avenue
San Mateo, CA 94402

6. National Small Business Association
1225 19th Street, N.W.
Washington, DC 20036

7. Smaller Business Association of New England
69 Hickory Drive
Waltham, MA 02154

8. Smaller Manufacturers Council
339 Boulevard of Allies
Pittsburgh, PA 15222

ASSOCIATIONS PROVIDING INFORMATION AND SERVICES FOR SMALL-BUSINESS OWNERS AND MANAGERS

Consulting Services

1. If you need specialized professional help, lists of consultants are available from:

Association of Management Consultants
811 East Wisconsin Avenue
Milwaukee, WI 53202

2. A list of university-based consultants is available from:

Academy of Management
College of Business
University of South Florida
Tampa, FL 33620

3. Directory of Members, is a list of individual management consultants certified by the Institute of Management Consultants, along with capsule descriptions of their areas of competence/fields

of practice. There are no firm memberships in the Institute—every member must qualify on his or her individual merits.

Directory of Members
Institute of Management Consultants, Inc.
347 Madison Avenue
New York, NY 10017
(212)687-2503

General Services

1. The American Management Association provides the training, research, publications, and information services required by managers to do a better job. It offers educational programs for managers through meetings, seminars, workshops, conferences, books, reports, etc. Write:

American Management Association
The American Management Associations Building
135 West 50th Street
New York, NY 10020
(212)586-8100

I recently had the opportunity to meet with the members of the office of the President of the American Management Association headquarters in New York City. This not-for-profit management association is easily the largest of its kind in America. Under the dynamic leadership of Jim Hayes, it has gone from being the American Management Association in the singular, to the American Management Associations in the plural.

The AMA is a membership organization with about 70,000 members and about $70,000,000 annual revenue. It has offices all across the country. It is unique in its service to large companies because of its ability to offer seminars and training. Within the AMA, the 2,000 members who are in the President's Association (P/A) are an especially elite group. This organization is headed up by Mr. Ron Myers, a dynamic 43 year old executive, and a former owner of a family business. The P/A runs very effective five-and-a-half day workshops for chief executive officers (CEO's) of entrepreneurial ventures. I'd suggest you contact Ron Myers at the AMA's New York headquarters to determine your possible interest in these kinds of programs.

An interesting sub-organization, which is headed by Mr. Steve

Cummings, is a division of the American Management Associations and it's known as the National Association of Corporate Directors. This organization provides information for corporate directors. It's the only organization we could find of its kind. It provides a newsletter, special reports, monographs, alerts, quality news digests, corporate governance reviews, executive compensation service, a bookstore, libraries, director's information service, briefings and seminars, annual conferences, NACD Institute, and a director's register.

Thus far, it has been one of the most effective organizations in helping pick, select, and work with corporate directors. May I suggest that you contact them? Write to:

Mr. Steve Cummings
National Association of Corporate Directors
1800 K St., N.W.
Suite 1124
Washington, DC 20006
(202)466-8540

2. The Council of Independent Managers has four chapters located in Milwaukee and Madison, Wisconsin; and Minneapolis and St. Cloud, Minnesota. Write:

Council of Independent Managers
7603 West State Street
Milwaukee, WI 53213

3. The American Society of Association Executives (ASAE), consisting of professional associations and nonprofit organizations in technical, educational, business, civic, and trade fields, provides the public with information on the functions of associations and the names and addresses of organizations in particular areas of interest. It offers *Association Management,* a forum among association executives for the exchange of ideas about how to successfully operate a trade or professional association. The magazine offers a diverse range of articles ranging from basic reminders and checklists on handling association activities to thought-provoking and forward-looking articles on trends in small-business associations.

Another service this group offers is *Finding the Right Speaker,* a directory of the professional speakers who work providing seminars and lectures to associations. Name, address, phone number, subject, and reference are provided for more than 700 speakers. The listings are cross-referenced by geographical home base and by subject. Editorial materials on working with speakers are included. Write:

Director of Information
American Society of Association Executives
1101 16th Street, N.W.
Washington, DC 20036
(202)659-3333

4. The International Council for Small Business (ICSB) is a nonprofit organization devoted to continuing management education for small-business owners and managers. Membership in this group is open to all persons interested in improving administration and operating management knowledge and skills. All members receive the ICSB publications, including the Journal of Small Business Management (JSBM). Many colleges, universities, and businesses are also members; student memberships are also welcomed. Write:

International Council for Small Business
c/o University of Wisconsin—Extension
929 North 6th Street
Milwaukee, WI 53203

5. Course offerings for academic managers and faculty who are concerned with course and program design and contents, texts, and reference materials in small-business management and entrepreneurship are available from:

General Secretary
International Council for Small Business
929 North 6th Street
Milwaukee, WI 53203
(414)224-1816

6. The National Retail Merchants Association, a nonprofit organization, represents 35,000 stores in the United States, Canada, and 50 other countries with a combined annual sales volume of $80 billion. It offers numerous services and information, outlined in a 66-page general catalog. The association also publishes newsletters, periodicals, films, and directories of value. Write:

National Retail Merchants Association
100 West 31st Street
New York, NY 10001

7. The National Federation of Independent Business is a nonprofit organization representing over 525,000 independent businesspeople. Members vote on proposed legislative measures on current issues that affect independent business through a newsletter/

ballot, *Mandate.*NFIB presents members' views to the Congress, White House, and federal agencies, as well as to state legislators through a separate state ballot. Other publications available from NFIB are: *Quarterly Economic Report for Small Business;* an economic poster, *What's the Difference,* comparing the standard of living between the US/USSR/UK; and Public Policy Discussion papers, such as *The Forgotten Consumer: Hidden Costs of Government Regulation.* Single complimentary copies are available. Write:

Education Department
National Federation of Independent Business
150 West 20th Avenue
San Mateo, CA 94402
(415)341-7441

8. The Smaller Business Association of New England, Inc. (SBANE) is an association of some 1,200 New England small businesses. Services offered include an active government liaison program in Washington and numerous educational seminars geared to the executive in a small, growing enterprise. SBANE also publishes a monthly newsletter and has cost-savings benefits in insurance, auto leasing, and auto rental. Write:

Small Business News
69 Hickory Drive
Waltham, MA 02154
(617)890-9070
Circulation: 2,150

9. The Small Business Service Bureau is a national association that seeks to help small-business owners and managers. It is effective in the retail trades and in assisting very small (less than five employee) businesses. The organization offers excellent insurance packages for small companies, as well as a monthly magazine. Write:

Small Business Service Bureau
544 Main Street
Box 1441
Worcester, MA 01601
(617)756-3513

10. The Smaller Manufacturers Council is an association of business people involved in manufacturing who have combined their experience, knowledge, and energies to become an effective force for progress through private enterprise. (A manufacturer is

someone who produces 60 percent of his own sales volume.) Since the organization's formation by 16 small manufacturers in 1945, membership has grown to 600 companies. Eleven times a year the SMC produces a newsletter that is circulated to the 600 members and 3,000 nonmembers. In addition, a well-organized directory of (a) members, (b) purchasing agents, (c) engineering departments, and (d) manufacturers and buyers is available. This is a worthwhile and extremely active association. Write:

> The Smaller Manufacturer
> 339 Boulevard of the Allies
> Pittsburgh, PA 15222
> (412)391-1624

11. Business partners in search of partners. I spent a fascinating two days in New York City with Ms. Beverly Rivers, the female version of the entrepreneurial species. This energetic and gracious hostess has launched a fascinating business which seeks to match business partners. Her idea for a business is to "marry" people with ideas and those with money. It's a neat idea, but the reason it works is the style of Ms. Rivers, who is the consummate hostess.

She has several franchises in other parts of the country serving the same purpose, so check with her if you are seeking a business partner in territories other than New York. Her business works like a big cocktail party. Everyone pays $50 to gather in a rented ballroom of a hotel. Then all the guests mix over coffee and cookies. The fun maximizes an hour or so later.

The system initially reminded me of a version of "the gong show," except no one is gonged. Each person has three minutes at a microphone to tell inner secrets and display personal desires. It's fun and everyone is identified by a number. Finally, the bell rings and everyone rushes about the room to talk to the so-called "good looking" prospective partners.

Honestly, it's better than a movie or a play, even if you attend just to be a spectator. Now, should you honestly want to locate a business partner, it becomes all business. And, as far as I can tell, it's the only dating service in town. Write:

> Ms. Beverly Rivers
> Business Partners in Search of Partners
> 663 Fifth Avenue
> New York, NY 10022
> (212)355-5633

Publications

In addition to the publications listed in discussions of the organizations above, these are some more helpful publications:

1. A monthly newsletter, *COSE Update,* is offered by:

Council of Smaller Enterprises of the Greater
Cleveland Growth Association
690 Union Commerce Building
Cleveland, OH 44115
(216)621-3300
Circulation: 3,500

2. The *Family Business Forum* is the newsletter of the National Family Business Council. As the "voice of family business," this publication voices important issues which affect the small-business owner/manager. It also keeps its membership informed of the happenings within the organization on a local and national level. Write:

National Family Business Council
3916 Detroit Boulevard
W. Bloomfield, MI 48033
(313)553-1000, ext. 381

3. The *National Memo* is a monthly newsletter of the National Business League that provides timely information on economic and business issues and events. *The Corporate Guide to Minority Vendors* is a resource manual for use by corporate executives and minority entrepreneurs to strengthen the communications network between the two sectors. NBL also maintains a file of minority vendors and a comprehensive list of corporate procurement and purchasing agents for constituents. Write:

National Business League
4324 Georgia Avenue, N.W.
Washington, DC 20011
(202)829-5900
Circulation: 15,000

4. *The Voice of Small Business* is a monthly newsletter for small-business owners/managers in all industries, trades, or professions. It deals generally with news of interest to small business relating to legislative and governmental activities in Washington. It is the membership newsletter of the National Small Business Association, a non-profit and non-partisan organization dedicated to the preserva-

tion and expansion of the small-business sector of the economy. Write:

Voice of Small Business
1605 K Street, N.W.
Washington, DC 20006
(202)296-7400
Circulation: 55,000

5. The newsletter of the Chamber of Commerce* of the United States is called *Washington Report.* Most of its subscribers are business people, and the majority of its articles provide information about federal policies and programs that can affect their firms and the economy. Write:

Washington Report
Chamber of Commerce of the United States
1615 H Street, N.W.
Washington, DC 20062
(202)659-6000
Circulation: 330,000

6. The Center for Venture Management, a nonprofit organization devoted to serving small-business owners and managers, has provided a number of very helpful publications that can be obtained by writing:

Center for Venture Management
207 E. Buffalo Street, Suite 508
Milwaukee, WI 53202

Following are some of these publications:

The Entrepreneur and New Enterprise Formation: A Resource Guide, by James W. Schreier and John L. Komives (1975), contains well over 900 separate items and is extensively cross-referenced with special-interest listings for the potential entrepreneur and the educator. In addition, many of the items are annotated and special notations have been made on the relevance and availability of the items. The Resource Guide's entries (people, games, books, articles, films, and research reports) should be of interest to anyone working or studying the subjects of entrepreneurship, new enterprise formation, and small-business management.

---

*Your local chamber of commerce can also be a source of valuable assistance, providing information about plant or storage locations, and financing. It is most quickly located via the local telephone directory.

The Female Entrepreneur, A Pilot Study, by James W. Schreier (1975), is a pilot study of women who have started their own businesses. The study was undertaken to provide data on the personality of female entrepreneurs, to discover the extent of entrepreneurial activity among women, and to provide a basis for the encouragement of women who are interested in starting their own businesses.

Consulting for Black Enterprise (Vol. I—A Challenge to the Business Establishment; Vol. II—Experience During the Second Year) report the efforts of an MBA program at the University of Wisconsin—Madison to provide consulting services to struggling black-owned and operated enterprises. Each volume contains detailed case studies of the various business clients. These cases have been used by other schools in which the teaching of minority enterprise is part of the curriculum.

The Entrepreneur and New Enterprise Formation: Venture Initiation Teaching State of the Art, by Karl H. Vesper (1976), is the second compilation of descriptions of collegiate-level courses in venture initiation throughout the United States. The study was compiled as a project for the Society for Entrepreneurship Research and Application (Milwaukee, Wisconsin).

The Founding of Technology-Based Firms is a detailed report of the study conducted by Dr. Arnold Cooper in 1970 and 1971 of ten years of enterprise formation in and near Palo Alto, California. It contains descriptions of entrepreneur backgrounds and sources of ideas and information for starting a business. There is information about rates of spinoff from established companies and some ideas about regional efforts to induce entrepreneurship in high technology areas.

ADDRESSES OF OTHER HELPFUL ASSOCIATIONS

The Executive Committee
1201 North Prospect Avenue
Milwaukee, WI 53202

Presidents Association
135 West 50th Street
New York, NY 10020

National Council for Small Business Management Development
c/o University of Wisconsin—Ext.
Civic Center Campus
600 West Kilbourn Avenue
Milwaukee, WI 53203

National Retail Hardware Association
964 North Penn Street
Indianapolis, IN 46204

6

Business
Plans

A document written to raise money for growing entrepreneurial venture is known as a business plan. The most common types are written by entrepreneurs attempting to raise money to expand a business; however, internal entrepreneurs within venture management teams with larger companies also write business plans. A business plan offers several unique ingredients. Most of all, it describes the philosophy and operating nature of the business. The heart of a business plan is its financial projection. It predicts what's going to happen financially to the business over a sequence of years. The preparation of a business plan is one of the crucial elements in any entrepreneurial venture. Once the prediction is on paper, it becomes a written goal or objective, and performance can then be judged against this criteria.

Writing a business plan is a very personal matter and one each person likes to individualize. This is good. It would be boring if everyone wrote a business plan in the identical manner.

These sources of help offer guidance, but your business plan should be singularly your creation.

1. *The Entrepreneur's Handbook* is a two-volume book of readings for entrepreneurs. It contains many good articles on business plans (plus other entrepreneurial subjects). Write:

Artech House
610 Washington Street
Dedham, MA 02026
(617)326-8220

or

The Center for Entrepreneurial Management
311 Main Street
Worcester, MA 01608
(617)755-0770

2. *The Business Planning Guide* by David Bangs and William Osgood (1976) is one of the better documents available on this subject. It was originally offered free by the Federal Reserve Bank of Boston, and received wide distribution. Write:

Country Business Brokers
225 Main Street
Brattleboro, VT 05301
(802)254-4504

or

David Bangs and William Osgood*
Upstart Publishing Company
366 Islington Street
Portsmouth, NH 03801
(603)436-0219

3. Several excellent articles on developing a business plan are contained within *Source Guide to Borrowing Capital* (1976) and *Venture Capital Sources* (1977), offered by the most professional source of venture capital information: Capital Publishing Company. Although expensive, these excellent books provide practical, worthwhile information. Write:

Capital Publishing Company
2 Laurel Street, Box 348
Wellesley Hills, MA 02181
(617)235-5405

4. *The Business Plan* by Len Smollen (1976) is a two-part document on preparing a business plan. Write:

Institute for New Enterprise Development
385 Concord Avenue
Belmont, MA 02178
(617)489-3950

5. *Understanding Financial Statements* is a fine booklet offered

---

*Osgood also publishes *Common Sense,* a monthly newsletter that discusses forecasting, marketing, cash flow, and other pertinent small-business subjects.

free by the world's largest securities firm, Merrill Lynch, Pierce, Fenner & Smith. This booklet is often used in graduate-level college finance courses. It discusses the three basic financial tools: (1) balance sheet, (2) cash-flow statement, and (3) profit and loss statement. This booklet can be obtained from your local Merrill Lynch office.

6. The Small Business Administration offers several excellent inexpensive pamphlets on writing a business plan:

Small Marketeer Aid 153
(Business plan for small service firm)

Small Marketeer Aid 150
(Business plan for retailer)

Management Aid for Small Manufacturers 218
(Business plan for small manufacturer)

Contact your local SBA field office for further current information, or write:

The Small Business Administration
Box 15434
Fort Worth, TX 76119

7

Canada

Canada is treated much like the United States in this source book, but there are several sources of help specifically for Canada that are comprehensive and unique. For instance, the Canadian government offers a number of services for small business, and so do some Canadian banks. The material presented in this chapter offers brief glimpses of what is available to Canadian small businesses. Also, you should contact local chambers of commerce for further information on what is available in particular regions of Canada. The information that follows is largely excerpted from a booklet describing the Federal Business Development Bank of Canada.

THE FEDERAL BUSINESS DEVELOPMENT
BANK OF CANADA

Canada's Federal Business Development Bank assists in the establishment and development of business enterprises in the country by providing firms with financial and management services.

FBDB extends financial assistance to new or existing businesses of almost every type in Canada which do not have other sources of financing available to them on reasonable terms and conditions. The qualifications for FBDB financing are:

1. That the amount and character of investment in such a business by persons other than FBDB may reasonably be expected to ensure the continuing commitment of these persons to the business, and
2. That the business may reasonably be expected to prove successful.

FBDB financing is available by means of loans, loan guarantees, equity financing, or leasing, or by any combination of these methods, in whatever manner best suits the particular needs of the business. Loans are made at interest rates in line with those generally available to businesses. Most loans are repaid within ten years. Where equity is involved, FBDB normally takes a minority interest and is prepared to have its investment repurchased on suitable terms.

Most of the customers of the bank use FBDB funds to acquire land, buildings, or equipment. Others use them to strengthen the working capital of a business, to establish new businesses, for metric conversion, and other purposes.

FBDB also offers a counseling service called CASE (Counseling Assistance to Small Enterprise). This service completed 5,000 counseling assignments to small businesses in 1978 by using its roster of over 1,600 retired business people.

There are also new owner/manager courses entitled "Retailing: An Introduction" and "An Introduction to Marketing," which are available to Canada's Provincial Departments of Education for distribution to community colleges.

Helpful Bank Publications

1. The International Business Exchange publishes *Business Encyclopedia*, edited and published by Peter G. Jovanovich (1976), containing dozens of powerful money-making ideas that will help you increase your business skills and profits. The encyclopedia presents the latest business and financial information so vital to the success of your present (or future) business. It also provides helpful practical solutions to major problems encountered in starting/running a successful business. Unusual advertising/promotional methods currently being used by successful entrepreneurs to increase profits are shown. Write:

International Business Exchange
17 Front Street, W.
Box 6449
Toronto, Ontario
M5W 1K3, Canada, 766-7435
Circulation: 20,569

2. An ongoing series of free pamphlets called *Minding Your Own Business** (edited by Dennis A. Cavendish) is published by the Federal Business Development Bank to help promote sound management practices in small business.

Small Business News is a newsletter published by the Federal Business Development Bank to help smaller Canadian firms keep in touch with business developments.†

For the pamphlets and the newsletter, write:

Federal Business Development Bank
P.O. Box 6021
Montreal, Quebec
Canada
(514)283-4195

British Columbia Regional Office

900 West Hastings Street
Vancouver, B.C. V6C 1E7
(604)666-8631

Cranbrook	30 South 11th Avenue Cranbrook, B.C. V1C 2P1 (604)426-7241
Kelowna	260 Harvey Avenue Kelowna, B.C. V1Y 7S5 (604)762-2035
Vernon	3303 Coldstream Avenue Vernon, B.C. V1T 1Y1 (604)545-7215
Kamloops	235 First Avenue Kamloops, B.C. V2C 3J4 (604)374-2121

*Available in French as *Votre affaire, c'est notre affaire.*

†Available in French as *Nouvelles de la petite enterprise.*

48

Williams Lake	30A North, Third Avenue Williams Lake, B.C. V2G 2A2 (604)398-8233
Prince George	1320 Fifth Avenue Prince George, B.C. V2L 3L5 (604)563-0641
Terrace	4548 Lakelse Avenue Terrace, B.C. V8G 1P8 (604)635-4951
Chilliwack	Kamar Plaza 45850 Yale Road West Chilliwack, B.C. V2P 2N9 (604)792-6621
Abbotsford	2467 Pauline Street Abbotsford, B.C. V2S 3S1 (604)853-5561
Langley	20316-56th Avenue Langley, B.C. V3A 3Y7 (604)533-1221
New Westminster	227-6th Street New Westminster, B.C. V3L 3A5 (604)525-1011

FBDB Branch Office Locations

Burnaby	4240 Manor Street Burnaby, B.C. V5G 3X5 (604)438-3581
Richmond	3751 Shell Road Richmond, B.C. V6X 2W2 (604)273-8611
Vancouver	885 Dunsmuir Street Vancouver, B.C. V6C 1N7 (604)681-7484
Vancouver East	3369 Fraser Street Vancouver, B.C. V5V 4C2 (604)873-6391
North Vancouver	145 West 15th Street North Vancouver, B.C. V7M 1R9 (604)980-6571

Victoria	850 Fort Street Victoria, B.C. V8W 1H8 (604)385-3375
Nanaimo	190 Wallace Street Nanaimo, B.C. V9R 5B1 (604)753-2471
Courtenay	497 Fitzgerald Avenue Courtenay, B.C. V9N 2R1 (604)338-6232
Campbell River	906 Island Highway Campbell River, B.C. V9W 2C3 (604)287-9236

Atlantic Regional Office

1400 Cogswell Tower, Scotia Square
Halifax, N.S. B3J 3K1
(902)426-7860

St. John's	Viking Building, Crosbie Road St. John's, Newfoundland A1B 3K4 (709)737-5505
Grand Falls	42 High Street Grand Falls, Newfoundland A2A 1C6 (709)489-2181
Corner Brook	Corner Brook Plaza Trans Canada Highway Corner Brook, Newfoundland (709)639-9186
Halifax	Trade Mart 2021 Brunswick Street Halifax, N.S. B3K 2Y5 (902)426-7850
Sydney	48-50 Dorchester Street Sydney, N.S. B1P 5Z1 (902)539-4556
Bridgewater	655 King Street Bridgewater, N.S. B4V 1B5 (902)543-7821

Truro	CN Commercial Centre 34 Esplanade Street Truro, N.S. B2N 2K3 (902)895-6377
Saint John	75 Prince William Street Saint John, N.B. E2L 2B2 (506)658-4751
Fredericton	Kings Place Complex 440 King Street Fredericton, N.B. E3B 5H8 (506)455-7745
Moncton	860 Main Street Moncton, N.B. E1C 1G2 (506)858-2370
Bathurst	270 Douglas Avenue Bathurst, N.B. E2A 1M9 (506)548-3345
Charlottetown	137 Kent Street Charlottetown, P.E.I. C1A 1N3 (902)892-9151

Quebec Regional Office

4600 Place Victoria,
800 Victoria Square,
Montreal, P.Q.
H4Z 1C8
(514)283-3657

Sept-Iles	690 Laure Boulevard Sept-Iles, P.Q. G4R 1X9 (418)968-1420
Rimouski	320 St. Germain Street, East Rimouski, P.Q. G5L 1C2 (418)724-4461
Chicoutimi	475 des Champs Elysees Street Chicoutimi, P.Q. G7H 5V7 (418)545-1580
Quebec	925 Chemin St. Louis, Quebec, P.Q. G1S 1C1 (418)681-6341

Levis	113 St. Georges Street, West Levis, P.Q. G6V 4L2 (418)837-0282
Trois-Rivieres	1410 Des Cypres Street Trois-Rivieres, P.Q. G8Y 4S3 (819)375-1621
Drummondville	288 Heriot Street Drummondville, P.Q. J2C 1K1 (819)478-4951
Sherbrooke	2532 ouest, rue King Sherbrooke, P.Q. J1J 2E8 (819)565-4740
Granby	161 rue Principale Granby, P.Q. J2G 2V5 (514)372-5202
Longueuil	Complexe Bienville 1000 de Serigny Street Longueuil, P.Q. J4K 5B1 (514)670-9550
Valleyfield	85 Champlain Street Valleyfield, P.Q. J6T 1W4 (514)371-0611
Montreal	1008 Place Victoria 800 Victoria Square Montreal, P.Q. H4Z 1C8 (514)878-9571
	205 Place Frontenac 2600 Ontario Street, East Montreal, P.Q. H2K 4K4 (514)524-1188
LaSalle	1550 Dollard Avenue LaSalle, P.Q. H8N 1T6 (514)364-4410
St. Laurent	750 Laurentien Boulevard St. Laurent, P.Q. H4M 2M4 (514)748-7323
St. Leonard	5960 Jean-Talon Street, East St. Leonard, P.Q. H1S 1M2 (514)254-6073

Laval	2525 Marois Boulevard Chomeday, Laval, P.Q. H7T 1S9 (514)681-9289
St. Jerome	Galeries des Laurentides St. Antoine des Laurentides, P.Q. (514)436-6441
Rouyn-Noranda	147 Mercier Avenue Rouyn, P.Q. J9X 4X4 (819)764-6701
Hull	Plaza Val Tetreau 400 Alexandre Tache Boulevard Hull, P.Q. J9A 1M5 (819)997-4434

Ontario Regional Office

250 University Avenue
Toronto, Ont.
M5H 3E5
(416)368-4874

Ottawa	151 Sparks Street Ottawa, Ont. K1P 5E3 (613)237-8430
Kingston	797 Princess Street Kingston, Ont. K7L 1G1 (613)549-1531
Peterborough	340 George Street, N. Peterborough, Ont. K9H 7E8 (705)748-3241
Oshawa	22 King Street, West Oshawa, Ont. L1H 1A3 (416)576-6800
Toronto	204 Richmond Street, W. Toronto, Ont. M5V 1V6 (416)598-0341
Etobicoke	Valhalla Executive Centre 302 The East Mall Islington, Ont. M9B 6C7 (416)239-4804

Scarborough	2978 Eglington Avenue, East Scarborough, Ont. M1J 2E7 (416)431-5410
Toronto-North	4430 Bathurst Street Downsview, Ont. M3H 3S3 (416)638-0823
Barrie	70 Collier Street Barrie, Ont. L4M 1G8 (705)728-6072
Oakville	345 Lakeshore Road, East Oakville, Ont. L6J 1J5 (416)844-0911
Hamilton	8 Main Street, East Hamilton, Ont. L8N 1E8 (416)528-0471
St. Catharines	71 King Street St. Catharines, Ont. L2R 3H6 (416)684-1153
Kitchener-Waterloo	305 King Street, West Kitchener, Ont. N2G 1B9 (519)744-4186
Owen Sound	1139 Second Avenue, East Owen Sound, Ont. N4K 2J1 (519)376-4431
London	197 York Street London, Ont. N6A 1B2 (519)434-2144
Woodstock	430 Dundas Street Woodstock, Ont. (519)537-5846
Stratford	1036 Ontario Street Stratford, Ont. N5A 6Z3 (519)271-5650
Chatham	59 Adelaide Street, South Chatham, Ont. N7M 4R1 (519)354-8833
Windsor	500 Ouellette Avenue Windsor, Ont. N9A 1B3 (519)254-8626

Northern Ontario District Office

421 Bay Street
Sault Ste. Marie, Ont., P6A 5N7
(705)949-1983

Sudbury	96 Larch Street Sudbury, Ont. P3E 1C1 (705)674-8347
Timmins	83 Algonquin Boulevard, West Timmins, Ont. P4N 2R4 (705)264-9432
Sault Ste. Marie	452 Albert Street, East Sault Ste. Marie, Ont. P6A 2J8 (705)949-3680
Thunder Bay	106 Centennial Square Thunder Bay, Ont. P7E 1H3 (807)623-2745
Kenora	20 Main Street, South Kenora, Ont. P9N 1S7 (807)468-5575

Prairie and Northern Regional Office

161 Portage Avenue
Winnipeg, Man. R3B 0Y4
(204)943-8581

Winnipeg	386 Broadway Avenue Winnipeg, Man. R3C 3R6 (204)944-9991
St. Boniface	851 Lagimodiere Boulevard Winnipeg, Man. R2J 3K4 (204)233-6791
Brandon	136-11th Street Brandon, Man. R7A 4J4 (204)727-8415
Regina	2220-12th Avenue Regina, Sask. S4P 0M8 (306)569-6478

Saskatoon	1102 CN Towers, Midtown Plaza Saskatoon, Sask. S7K 1J5 (306)665-4822
Prince Albert	1100-1st Avenue, East Prince Albert, Sask. S6V 2A7 (306)764-6448
Lethbridge	740-4th Avenue, South Lethbridge, Alta. T1J 0N9 (403)328-9681
Calgary	404 Sixth Avenue, S.W. Calgary, Alta. T2P 0R9 (403)269-6981
Calgary South	5940 Macleod Trail, S.W. Calgary, Alta. T2H 2G4 (403)253-6501
Red Deer	4909 Gaetz Avenue Red Deer, Alta. T4N 4A7 (403)346-8821
Edmonton	10150-100th Street Edmonton, Alta. T5J 0P6 (403)429-4926
Edmonton South	11044-51st Avenue Edmonton, Alta. T6H 5B4 (403)436-6533
Edmonton West	11574-149th Street Edmonton, Alta. T5M 1W7 (403)452-3232
Yellowknife	5010-50th Avenue Yellowknife, N.W.T. (403)873-3566
Grande Prairie	10135-101st Avenue Grande Prairie, Alta. T8V OY4 (403)532-8875
Whitehorse	Travelodge Commercial Mall Whitehorse, Y.T. (403)667-7333

CANADIAN PUBLICATIONS & ORGANIZATIONS

1. An organization was formed in 1965 to promote small business in the Manitoba province. It conducts seminars, offers workbooks and counseling, and claims to be a center of excellence for management development. Write:

The Manitoba Institute of Management, Inc.
193 Sherbrook Street
Winnipeg R3C 2B7
CANADA

2. The Canadian Department of Industry, Trade and Commerce publishes a newsletter in both French and English entitled *Small Business World.* Write:

Small Business Secretariat
Dept. of Industry, Trade and Commerce
235 Queen Street
Ottawa, Canada K1A 0H5

3. A non-profit organization dedicated to improving the skills of the independent business person and the professional manager is known as Business Warriors. Affiliated with the Lakehill Management Center of Boston, Massachusetts, this is a membership organization to help entrepreneurs. As their name suggests, they are rebels who are independent of the Canadian government. This group of young, energetic upstarts helps package loan proposals and assists businesses that are in trouble. Write:

The Business Warriors
Suite 506
122 St. Patrick St.
Toronto, Ontario M5T 2X8
(416)597-1749

4. A thorough and informative booklet entitled a *Guide to Small Business Management* was prepared by Ryerson Polytechnic Institute on behalf of the Canadian Federation of Independent Business. Both these organizations are of considerable value to Canadian entrepreneurs. The Canadian Federation of Independent Business is

57

the largest small business membership organization in all of Canada. Write either:

Ryerson Polytechnic Institute
285 Victoria St.
Toronto, Ontario
Canada M5B1E8

or

The Canadian Federation of Independent Business
15 Coldwater Road
Don-Mills
Ontario CFIB
CANADA M3B BJ1
(416)445-9214

8

Data Processing

The list of data-processing information in this chapter is far from complete. This is one of the most dynamic and changing fields in the entire U.S. business economy. However, the need for data-processing and word-processing information in the small-company office is immense. A fine source of current information is the advertisements in the popular periodicals such as *Business Week, Fortune,* and *Forbes.* In addition, many other periodicals that focus specifically on small business carry information on the newest data-processing and word-processing equipment for your office. The list of sources provided in this chapter should help you get started.

Given the pace of technological changes owing largely to the advent of micro processors, a complete list is simply impossible. The best overall source for hardware selection is Datapro, a research company whose surveys you should read before purchasing equipment for your office.

1. A list of data processing and time-sharing services that serve small and medium-sized businesses, *Directory of Members and Profile Listings,* is available from:

Association of Data Processing Service Organizations, Inc.
210 Summit Avenue
Montvale, NJ 07645
(201)391-0870

Also available from the same source are:

Directory of Data Processing Service Centers
Annual Industry Survey of Computer Services Industry
A Recommended Uniform Accounting System for the
   Computer Services Industry
Wage and Salary Study
Survey of State Taxation

2. A 66-page report evaluating the pluses and minuses of 228 small computer systems has recently been published by the Datapro Research Corporation. This organization publishes excellent independent reports, ratings, analyses, and news about commercially available information-processing systems. Write:

Datapro Research Corporation
1805 Underwood Boulevard
Delran, NJ 08075
(609)764-0100
Circulation: 35,000

3. Management Information Corporation was formed in May 1971 as a consulting and information service company dedicated to data entry, small-business computer systems, EDP management, and data communications. This company offers monthly publications, reports, seminars, and consulting services. For information, write:

Management Information Corporation
140 Barclay Center
Cherry Hill, NJ 08034

Data-Processing Automation for the Office

There are a number of publications that you may find helpful in your search for data-processing equipment for your office.

1. *Automation for Small Offices* is a management aid booklet. Write:

Small Business Administration
Washington, DC 20417
Small Business Bibliographies 58, free.

2. *Basic of Data Communications*, ed. Harry R. Karp (1976), is published by:

McGraw-Hill Book Company
1221 Avenue of the Americas
New York, NY 10020

3. *Computer Applications in Management,* by John R. Birkle and Ronald Yearsly (1976), is published by:

Associated Business Programmes
London, England

4. *Computer Organization and Programming,* by C. William Gear (1974), is published by:

McGraw-Hill Book Company
1221 Avenue of the Americas
New York, NY 10020

5. *Computers and Information Systems in Business,* by George J. Brabb (1975), is published by:

Houghton Mifflin
One Beacon Street
Boston, MA 02108

6. *Digital Computer Fundamentals,* by Jefferson C. Boyce (1977), is published by:

Prentice-Hall, Inc.
Englewood Cliffs, NJ 07632

7. *Management Standards for Developing Information Systems,* by Norman L. Enger (1976), is published by:

American Management Association
135 West 50th Street
New York, NY 10020

8. *Operating Data Entry Systems,* by Peggy Hanson (1977), is published by:

Prentice-Hall, Inc.
Englewood Cliffs, NJ 07632

9. *What the Manager Should Know about the Computer* can be obtained from:

Business Education Division
Dun & Bradstreet, Inc.
T.Y. Crowell Company
99 Church Street
New York, NY 10007

Entrepreneurial Education

There are several major trends occurring across the country to promote the interchange of information between the academic world and small businesses. College courses related to small business have increased. While student enrollment in colleges is generally falling across the country, the enrollment related to entrepreneurship and small business has been generally increasing. The typical college student's anti-big business feelings often propel him or her to start a small business.

In the early 1970s the Small Business Administration launched the Small Business Institute, involving close to 500 colleges which help small companies within specified geographic regions. The SBI provides the name of a company needing assistance and a small stipend to the assisting college. The college provides faculty members and student teams that assist the small companies. Many small-business cases have been written and many small businesses have been helped by this program.

The Small Business Administration has more recently provided several large grants to certain colleges for the establishment of University Business Development Centers to promote interaction between students, small companies, and faculty members. The interaction is generally a very healthy process because it encourages entrepreneurship on campus at the same time that it provides small companies with assistance.

You, as a small-business owner or manager (or a potential one), can attend some of the courses offered by the UBDC in your area.

You can also take advantage of free labor in the form of college students to help your small company.

Often an individual making a transition from a salaried position to an entrepreneurial venture benefits from a total change of pace and environment. These schools for entrepreneurs are useful in helping such a person during the transitional phase. Research conducted by Professor Albert Shapiro of Ohio State University concludes that entrepreneurial tendencies may be heightened when a person is displaced from one business to another. For example, when a person is returning from the military service and coming back into the workforce, or when a person leaves one job and prepares to move on to another, latent entrepreneurial tendencies may suddenly develop. These schools for entrepreneurs can be invaluable when a person is in such a transitional period. They provide an opportunity to reflect and learn and they also provide a network of people who can help to start your venture or to expand an already going concern.

1. Karl Vesper of the University of Washington in Seattle has the enviable record of being three professors in one: mechanical engineering, business administration, and marine biology. However, he is best known for his work as scorekeeper of academic courses of small business and entrepreneurship. He recently surveyed 610 schools of business and 243 schools of engineering and based upon a response of 61 percent and 48 percent, respectively, here is what he found!

Year	1968	1970	1972	1974	1976	1978	Planned
Total number of schools offering courses in new ventures	8	29	47	75	105	137	215

These are data for teaching new ventures, not the more popular small business management type courses. There are about thirty schools of engineering teaching entrepreneurship, according to Vesper, the remainder are business schools. He distributes a detailed list of schools and course descriptions. Write:

The Center for Venture
  Management
207 E. Buffalo Street
Milwaukee, WI 53202

Further, as the scorekeeper, Karl has begun keeping score of

the emergence of academic chairs in dual fields of entrepreneurship and free enterprise. This emerging topic is close to my heart because we have our own close affiliation with academic chairs. They are on the cover of many of our books and brochures. And, the entrepreneur's chair is a special animal which gives comfort and solace just where and when it's needed most. According to Vesper's early data, the endowed chairs are primarily in the field of private (free) enterprise, with a minority in the field of entrepreneurship.

Colleges and Universities with Established Chairs and Programs:

American International College
Appalachian State University
Augusta College
Babson Institute
Baylor University
Birmingham-Southern College
Brescia College
Brunswick Junior College
George Peabody College
Georgia State University
Harding College
John Carroll University
Kent State University
Lamar University
Lambuth College
Loyola University of Chicago
North Georgia College
Northeast Louisiana University
Ohio State University
Purdue University
Regis College
St. Mary's University
Samford University
Southwest Baptist College
Texas A&M University
Texas Christian University

University of Akron
University of Indiana
University of Oklahoma
University of Tennessee, Chattanooga
University of Texas, Austin
University of Wisconsin, Madison
Washington University
Wharton School
Wichita State University

Further information about endowed chairs like these is available from two sources. Richard Emerson and John L. Ward, School of Business, Loyola University, 820 North Michigan Avenue, Chicago IL, 60611, have prepared a paper summarizing chairs in existence or planned at 59 colleges and universities. Craig Aranoff is President of the Association for Chairs of Private Enterprise, centered at the School of Business, Georgia State University, Atlanta, GA, 30303.

PRIVATE SCHOOLS AND SEMINARS

1. A small but fascinating school, the Country Business Brokers, for entrepreneurs is housed in various quaint country inns in the beautiful state of Vermont. James Howard is the founder of the Country Business Brokers, and a former public relations executive on Madison Avenue. With the help of Brian Smith, head of the Management Department at Franklin Pierce College, and Virginia Page, an expert on women entrepreneurs, this young organization is making itself known in the entrepreneurial world with weekend seminars held in Vermont.

The seminar program is often couple-oriented, and classes are small. The clients are recruited primarily through newspaper advertisements, and the operations of an inn are often cited as an example of a small business. For further information, write:

The Country Business Brokers
225 Main Street
Brattleboro, VT 05301
(802)254-4504

2. Another school for entrepreneurs, The Entrepreneurship Institute, is headed by William J. McCrea. This institute has an annual budget of close to $1 million; about 20 percent of the revenue is derived from seminars and the remainder from corporate contributions and work done for developing countries. This school moves from city to city and offers weekend training seminars entitled "How to Create and Manage Your Own Business." For information, contact:

The Entrepreneurship Institute
90 East Wilson Bridge Road
Suite 247
Worthington, OH 43085
(614)855-0585

3. Bob Schwarz is the counter-cultural "New Age" entrepreneur and the sole owner of the Tarrytown Conference Center, a magnificent 26-acre estate in New York.

His School for Entrepreneurs meets over two consecutive weekends, several times a year. These two weekends are event-filled and action-packed. Besides all the good things which come from the "how to start your own business" program, this group has a special sense of community and sharing. The classes are offered in New York, and in California. Write:

The School for Entrepreneurs
Tarrytown House
East Sunnyside Lane
Tarrytown, NY 10591
(212)933-1232
(914)591-8200

4. "Transforming the Experiences of Business into the Celebration of Life", by Marshall Thurber. I recently spent a lovely weekend in the only state which has more cows than people—Vermont. This time the weekend was spent in the northeast kingdom, supposedly the most beautiful country in the world. East Burke, Vermont, is really not near anything, unless you call Saint Johnsbury, Vermont, something. It's four hours north of Boston, at the upper end of the state of New Hampshire, an hour south of the Canadian border, and hours from civilization. It's only accessible through long winding back roads that were obviously originally engineered by cows.

This rural setting is the home of the Burklyn Conference Cen-

ter, the newly acquired, one-thousand acre estate, now owned by Marshall Thurber. This estate was created in 1908 by a wealthy New York businessman who owned one of Fifth Avenue's more successful hotels, and sold to Thurber a few years ago. The decor of the estate reflects the creator's unusual Fifth Avenue tastes, as it is elegant. It includes horses, stables, barns, and Vermont-type buildings, plus the palatial home on the hill. The grounds, however, are the reasons to go there, not the buildings.

Who is this Marshall Thurber and why has he turned it into a conference center? Marshall Thurber and his group are one of a new breed of entrepreneurial managers. Marshall is a lawyer who grew up in Vermont, fifteen minutes away from the Burklyn Estates. He was extremely successful in San Francisco real estate and he returned to purchase the big estate in his home town. Marshall Thurber, William F. Raymond, and Robert Cassill were the founders of Hawthorne/Stone, an entrepreneurial venture in San Francisco which bought and sold properties. They have all become millionaires in three years and they claim that their net worth is increasing at a rate of over one million dollars annually. The firm has thirty-four staff members and six employees, not including the partners, and earns over $200,000 each year, according to their published brochures.

Their basic business was buying and selling speculative real estate in the San Francisco area. Renovating brownstones, converting condominiums, and capitalizing on the dramatic growth in the California real estate market, has been the pattern of this company.

Two new executives, Jean Obry and Bobby Deporter, joined Hawthorne/Stone in the past few years. But the interesting person is the leader of the pack, Marshall Thurber. Marshall has a baby face, curly hair, and looks like one of the Beatles. His manner and action put him clearly in the new-age category. He had earlier started a newspaper in central Vermont, not far from the Burklyn estate, but his real success came in the development of his people orientation at Hawthorne/Stone. Marshall has two phrases that repeat themselves in any interview. The first is "life is good" and the second is "business can be a win/win proposition." The first concept, that life is good, absolutely flows from his mouth every five minutes independent of whether or not he is engaged in a conversation. The second, "win/win," describes his philosophy of business "that a loser is an unnecessary part of the process, only winners need exist."

Based on his philosophy, Marshall established the Burklyn Bus-

iness School which is a six-week course which meets at the Burklyn Estate every summer through July and August. Last year, tuition was $2,500 a member and they enrolled between fifty and sixty students. This year, tuition will be $5,000 a member, and they expect just under one hundred students. The faculty and the stars that attract this high priced audience include not only a former Babson College Professor of entrepreneurship, Terry Allan who, by the way, is now full-time on Thurber's staff, it also includes the most famous philosopher of all, Buckminster Fuller.

During these six intense weeks, the business school concentrates on both the mind and body by waking the students at 6:30 in the morning and keeping them "running" until midnight, working hard at both body and mind improvements.

Thurber says, "We don't have a track record long enough to establish our performance in this school, but I know it's going to work better than any other method of teaching business in the country."

Thurber also promotes and sells a personal support system, which is a very complicated but efficient notebook. In the beginning of the notebook are pictures of his family and friends, things that he loves and cherishes and his sources of support. In the middle of the book are appointment books, calendars, and a methodical system of keeping track of his time. The notebook has notes and scribblings of things to do and appointments to keep. He sells the system for one hundred dollars. In addition, he provides cassettes explaining how it works. He revolves his life around his notebook, which tells him what to do and how to do it.

Marshall has a strong people orientation. He's a bit of a dreamer, a visionary. He's inspirational and he attracts to him individuals who are captivated by this kind of personality. He is truly an entrepreneur/starter of things, as his own entrepreneurial traits are very strong. The interesting question, which I mused but never answered, is, is his system of management better or was he smart enough to ride a winning horse? In other words, does love and money really go together like it does in Burklyn, Vermont? Or, did the San Francisco real estate market boom occur so fast that anybody caught in its wake was swept along? As yet, I don't know the answer, but it is apparent that Hawthorne/Stone and Marshall Thurber are big winners. And now they have enough capital and talent to try again. And it could be that even if his business methods are not the reason for his initial success, they still may be solid and prove to be the long term win in his favorite win/win game.

Marshall is a lawyer who graduated from California's Hasting College of Law in 1969 and practiced law in San Francisco as a trust buster and expert in real estate investments. Not only does he sponsor the six-week summer course, he also conducts a one-week, "Money and You" course that is a condensation of the six-week course. The six-week course has a rigid admission policy, according to Thurber, but the one-week course will take anybody. This emerging school is another example of the entrepreneurial movement across the country and the exploding interest in the entrepreneurial manager as a species.

Why not send a note to:

Burklyn Enterprises
1700 Montgomery
Suite 230
San Francisco, CA 94111
(415)376-2827

or

Marshall Thurber
1288 Rimer Drive
Morage, Calif. 94556

I went to see what happens at this new business school in Vermont, and it's a little different from The Harvard Business School. The program is as surprising as its tuition of $5,000 for six weeks of sunshine and Marshall Thurber. It's a different kind of school, set on the magnificent 1,000 acre estate of Burklyn, recently purchased from the State of Vermont by Marshall Thurber. The setting is storybook and the school is visionary.

Here's a typical school day—one that I attended. The sixty-seven eager beavers rise at 6:30 a.m. to greet the sunshine by jogging with Marshall. After jogging, it's calisthenics at the Nautilis until 7:30 a.m., and then it's a breakfast feast of wild honey and protein—that is, if you're not on the pristine diet—about a dozen were on this diet. It must be a real good diet because the food tasted awful. Then school starts at 9:00 a.m. on the castle on the hill.

The class holds hands together to begin the day. They don't say the Lord's prayer, but they do begin by breathing deeply and singing a little together. Then it's class time. Philosophy of life is the essence of a typical day's work and Marshall is the philosopher. Terry Allen, a former entrepreneurship professor at Babson College, teaches the "hard" stuff. Terry was a doctoral student in Virginia, but he decieed to give up academics to join the inner circle of

the Marshall Thurber group. He even bought one of the many houses on the Burklyn estate. It's his home now. But, lunch soon arrives and it too is elegant, a collection of natural food wonders.

Then super learning occurs from 2:00 p.m. to 5:00 p.m. every day after lunch. The whole group learns and studies French 'til dinner. I never figured out really what super learning was all about, but I'm told that you can learn French in six weeks. If that's the case, it must be super! Dinner is an extravaganza of delight. A real treat. Then it's back to the classroom after dinner to hear Marshall and his friends talk about business.

A day ends at 10:00 p.m., and the serious students head either to the bar or to the hot tub, or first to one and then the other. It's a new world in Vermont, and East Burke could blow your mind if you're traditional. This is an unusual cast of students and teachers, not built on the traditions of academia and not centered in history. The students were young (late twenties) and old (late fifties), about equally divided between men and women. They were bright and energetic and uniformly committed to both their leader and the message. One was from Seoul, Korea, others were real estate people from California, and others had read about the school from "New Realities" magazine.

To add to the excitement and confusion of whether Marshall Thurber is smart or lucky—after I visited the Burklyn Business School, I ran across the following Associated Press story on July 27, 1979. Rather than paraphrase it, I'll reproduce it:

BURKLYN INVESTORS PROMISED REIMBURSEMENT

(The Associated Press). EAST BURKE. An investment management service directed by Marshall Thurber, part-owner of the Burklyn Conference Center in East Burke, has lost about $2 million.

But Thurber, 36, said Wednesday that he will attempt to reimburse all investors, including an undetermined number of Vermonters, who lost money through his transactions.

"Investors are guaranteed to be covered to the extent of my assets," he said. "The whole point is that my assets would go first."

Thurber, a St. Johnsbury native and self-made millionaire, said the losses are connected with an investment business he runs with another Burklyn owner, Roberta DePorter.

Thurber said he and DePorter will make full financial disclosures after they meet with investors in San Francisco.

The Burklyn Center is scheduled to close next week. The buildings and 700 acres are up for sale, with a $2 million asking price.

5. The University Services Institute in Cleveland, Ohio offers a host of interesting family-oriented business seminars. Its head, Dr. Leon Danco, is one of the finest authorities on the father-son team and of issues of families within small business. For further information, write:

University Services Institute
5862 Mayfield Road
Box 24197
Cleveland, OH 44124
(216)442-0800

6. The East-West Center is a resource systems institute that assists small-business owners in identifying and developing their entrepreneurial capabilities and in originating or finding new enterprise opportunities suited to local conditions.

This is one of the international meeting places for entrepreneurs of varying cultures and backgrounds. An excellent report published by this organization is entitled *Entrepreneurial Discovery and Development.*

The East-West Center
1777 East-West Road
Honolulu, HI 96848
Cable: EASWESCEN
Telex: 7430331

7. Babson College's Entrepreneurial Hall of Fame. Below are the members of Babson College's entrepreneurial Hall of Fame.

Recipients for 1978

Kenneth H. Olsen is the president of Digital Equipment Corporation which was founded in 1957. It was a new idea to start a company at this time of recession when a number of new companies were in trouble. With only $70,000 to work with, every dollar was carefully watched and most of the work from cleaning the floors to making their own tools was done by Olsen and his associates. He started with the ideas of no government funding for their research and they sought to make a profit from day one.

Berry Gordy, the president and chairman of Motown Industries, Inc. loved writing and creating songs. His first record store in Detroit was opened in 1953, and by 1955 he was bankrupt. After not being able to collect from a publisher who owed him $1,000, he decided to start a company for young writers. He was told that he could not do it and that was all he needed to hear and Motown was born. He believes that you must first consider happiness before success in order that success does not destroy you later.

Royal Little is the former chairman of Textron, Inc. He used his textile business to expand into more diversified areas of industry. He believed that if one business is not performing, get out—sell it; and then buy another one. His idea worked and this started the conglomerate trend in the United States.

Ray Kroc, chairman of the McDonald Corporation, started out with the Lily Cup Company selling paper cups for about 17 years. As a salesman for a multiple milkshake mixer, the Multi-Mixer, he heard of an operation in California run by the McDonald brothers. Their stand was using eight of these mixers, making up to 40 milkshakes at one time. After his association with the McDonalds, he felt that he was growing faster than they were, and in 1954, he opened his first "McDonalds," and in 1960, he bought the business for $1.5 million. His theory is "part of being an entrepreneur (is) knowing what to give and when to give it."

Soichiro Honda founded the Honda Motor Company 30 years ago. He first brought motorcycles to the U.S. 20 years ago, and thus created a new market with an original product. His first task was to sell the U.S. on motorcycling, then he had to sell Honda. He is not sure that he is an entrepreneur, only that he is a man with imagination, creativity, and desire behind him.

1979 Recipients

John Eric Jonsson, 77, is the founder and former chairman of Texas Instruments. After graduating from Rensselaer Polytechnic Institute in 1922, he became interested in Texas Instruments, then Geophysical Services, Inc., in Newark, New Jersey. The outfit moved to Texas in 1934, and he and Eugene McDermott bought out what is now a billion dollar concern.

Diane Von Furstenburg, president of DVF, Inc., came to the United States in 1969 and saw a great need in the fashion industry. She designed a basic dress, in a basic material called jersey. Her

claim to success is that you can be a woman, mother, and be in business if you are willing to work, plan, and discipline yourself.

John H. Johnson is the founder of *Ebony* magazine. Poverty drove him to work harder in high school, this earned him a scholarship to the University of Chicago. In his junior year, he worked on a company magazine, which gave him the idea to publish a Negro Digest similar to the Reader's Digest. The profits he received from this magazine enabled him to start *Ebony* magazine.

Thomas Mellon Evans is the chairman of Crane Company, which manufactures everything from steel to anti-pollution gear. He took over Crane Company in 1959, and more recently purchased 7.3% of the outstanding common stock of MacMillan, Inc., the broadly-based purchaser. He has always shown a profit and companies usually succeed under his management.

Byung Chull Lee, chairman of Samsung Group, started a rice cleaning plant in S. Korea in 1935. After deciding that his country could only prosper through trade, he established the Samsung (Three-Start) export-import company in 1952. Today, as Korea's richest man, his fortune is over $500 million and Samsung has become a 24 company conglomerate with sales of $2 billion per year.

UNIVERSITY BUSINESS DEVELOPMENT CENTERS

1. In addition to the Small Business Administration, which sponsors the University Business Development Centers, other government agencies have university-based programs designed to help the entrepreneur. The National Science Foundation has been a pioneer in this regard. The NSF has sponsored a number of university-based innovation centers. While these centers have an engineering overtone, they do indeed assist the entrepreneur.

A copy of the evaluation of the three existing innovation centers can be obtained from:

Research Triangle Institute
P.O. Box 12194
Research Triangle Park
North Carolina, 27709
(919)541-6000

Following are the innovation centers that are currently operating:

University of Oregon
Eugene, OR 97403
(503)686-3326

MIT, School of Engineering
77 Massachusetts Avenue
Cambridge, MA 02139
(617)253-1000

Carnegie-Mellon University
Frew Avenue
Pittsburgh, PA 15213
(412)578-2000

2. University Business Development Centers (UBDC's) are funded by government agencies (usually the Small Business Administration) and are affiliated with local universities. They are charged with helping small businesses grow and prosper within a specific region. They can be of very specific assistance, especially in the development of a business plan, and they are currently operational at the colleges listed below. Other colleges are currently launching SBDC's, so be sure to inquire in your area. This is an outgrowth of the SBA's Small Business Institute college program. Under the SBI program, local colleges and the SBA send 5,000 to 10,000 student teams to help small businesses annually. They can help and they are free, so it may pay to inquire about the SBI college serving your area. An excellent newsletter exists on the SBI program and provides continuing help for entrepreneurs:

Small Business Institute
    Directors Association
University of Northern Colorado
School of Business
Greeley, CO 80639

Addresses of university correspondents for the nine UBDC schools are listed below. The first address for each school is the key contact; the second address is the secondary contact; and the third address is the SBA contact.

California State Polytechnic University

School of Business Administration
California State Polytechnic University
3801 West Temple Avenue
Pomona, CA 91768
(714)598-4211

SBA-WAE
California State Polytechnic University
3801 West Temple Avenue
Pomona, CA 91768
(714)598-4211

SBA District Office
3500 South Figueroa Street
Los Angeles, CA 90071
(213)688-2900, FTS 798-2800

University of West Florida

Director, Small Business Development Center
University of West Florida
Eglin-Ft. Walton Beach Center
P.O. Box 1492
Eglin AFB, FL 34542
(904)882-5409

Faculty of Management Studies
University of West Florida
Pensacola, FL 32504
(904)476-9500, ext. 425

SBA District Office
Federal Building, Room 261
400 W. Bay Street
Jacksonville, FL 32202
(904)791-4787, FTS 946-3787

California State University

Dean, School of Business
California State University
Chico, CA 95209
(916)895-6271

Center for Business and Economic Development
Yuba Hall
California State University
Chico, CA 95929
(916)895-5938

SBA Regional Office
Federal Building, Box 36044
450 Golden Gate Avenue
San Francisco, CA 94102
(415)556-7647, FTS 556-7647

University of Maine at Portland-Gorham

New Enterprise Institute
Center for Research and Advanced Study
622 Research Center
University of Maine at Portland-Gorham
96 Falmouth Street
Portland, ME 04103
(207)773-2981

School of Business
96 Falmouth Street
Portland, ME 04103
(207)773-2981

SBA District Office
40 Western Avenue
Augusta, ME 04330
(207)622-6171, ext. 225, FTS 833-6225

University of Nebraska at Omaha

College of Business Administration
University of Nebraska at Omaha
Box 688
Omaha, NE 68101
(402)554-2303

College of Business Administration
(402)554-2521

SBA District Office
Room 3209
215 North 7th Street
Omaha, NE 68102
(402)221-3604, FTS 864-3604

University of Missouri–St. Louis

School of Business Administration
University of Missouri–St. Louis
8001 Natural Bridge Road
St. Louis, MO 63121
(314)453-5881

8001 Natural Bridge Road
Room 461, SSB Building
St. Louis, MO 63121
(314)453-5621

Robert Andrews, ADDMA
SBA District Office
Suite 2500, Mercantile Tower
One Mercantile Center
St. Louis, MO 63101
(314)425-4516, FTS 279-4516

Rutgers University

Rutgers University School of Business
Conklin Hall
Newark, NJ 07102
(201)648-5287

SBA District Office
970 Broad Street
Federal Building, Room 1635
Newark, NJ 07102
(201)645-3832, FTS 341-3832

University of Georgia at Athens

College of Business Administration
University of Georgia at Athens
Athens, GA 30602
(404)542-8100

UBDC Director
Division of Services
College of Business Administration
University of Georgia
Athens, GA 30602
(404)542-5760

SBA District Office
1720 Peachtree Road, N.W.
Atlanta, GA 30309
(404)881-2441, FTS 257-2441

Howard University

Institute for Minority Business Education
School of Business and Public Administration
Howard University
P.O. Box 748
Washington, DC 20059
(202)636-7187

SBA District Office
1030 15th Street, N.W.
Suite 250
Washington, DC 20005
(202)653-6980, FTS 653-6980

National contact for UBDC at the SBA:

Chief, UBDC Division
The Small Business Administration
Washington, DC 20416

SMALL BUSINESS DEVELOPMENT CENTER

Small Business Development Centers (SBDCs) are sources of management assistance for persons who are operating a small business or contemplating launching a new business. They are located on university campuses and are funded by the Small Business Administration. There are presently eleven operational SBDCs located throughout the country. Five new locations have been funded and will bring the total of SBDCs to sixteen. Those already in existence are located at:

California State Polytechnic University
Pomona, CA

California State University
Chico, CA

Rutgers University
New Brunswick, NJ

University of Georgia
Athens, GA

University of Missouri
St. Louis, MO

University of Nebraska
Omaha, NE

University of Southern Maine
Portland, ME

University of West Florida
Pensacola, FL

Howard University
Washington, DC

University of Wisconsin
Madison, WI

University of S. Carolina
Columbia, SC

The five new locations are:

Wharton School of Finance
University of Pennsylvania
Philadelphia, PA

St. Cloud University
St. Cloud, MN

University of Arkansas
Fayetteville, AR

University of Utah
Salt Lake City, UT

Washington State University
Pullman, WA

According to A. Vernon Weaver, Administrator of the SBA, the five new university sites were selected in a competitive process based upon submission of state bids.

10
Franchising

Franchises exist in many industries: fast foods, motels, automobiles and parts, infrared heating, business services, dry cleaning, home repair, health clubs, industrial supplies, building products, schools, vending operations, and so on. Although franchise operations are not new, they have expanded greatly since the middle of the 1950s. By the 1980s there will be some million outlets doing upwards of $300 billion in sales.

A franchising operation is a legal contractual relationship between a franchisor (the company offering the franchise) and a franchisee (the individual who will own the business). Usually the franchisor is obligated to maintain a continuing interest in the business of the franchisee in such areas as site location, management training, financing, marketing, promotion, and record keeping. In addition, the franchisor offers the use of a store motif, standardized operating procedures, prescribed territory, and a trade name. The franchisee, in return, agrees to operate under the conditions set forth by the franchisor. For the help and services provided, the franchisee is usually expected to make a capital investment in the business. In addition, the franchisee agrees to pay a commission on all of the franchisee's sales and/or agrees to buy from the franchisor all of his product needs.

Franchising allows a manufacturer to conserve capital while at the same time establishing a distribution system in the shortest time possible. It takes many dollars and much time to develop a major

distribution system. Using franchisees can cut down on both, because the franchisee finances part of the system through his initial franchise fee and because it is many times easier and faster to enlist entrepreneurs committed to doing a good job than it is to sign up independent firms. Also, franchising makes lower marketing costs possible for the manufacturer. Franchising substantially cuts down on the maintenance of company-owned branch units or stores and on the subsequent commitment to fixed overhead expenses such as for personnel administration. For the franchisee, a franchise can facilitate going into business because it cuts down on the amount of capital required and provides a sense of security through the guidance offered by the franchisor. Franchising is a way for the small-business owner to overcome problems that can ruin a business.

Prospective franchisees should enter a franchise agreement cautiously. Some considerations include the following: (1) the strength of his or her financial position; (2) how long the franchisor has been in business; and (3) how the franchisor selects franchisees. Reference checks should be made, particularly regarding financial considerations. Inquiries about the product should be made concerning its quality, seasonal appeal, exclusiveness, competitiveness, and effectiveness in bringing in repeat customers. Questions should be asked concerning territory exclusiveness and site-location assistance. Is the area well defined, and does it allow for growth? Is it large enough to support predicted sales? Are other of the firm's franchise operations distant enough so that they do not compete? Below are some of the issues to research:

1. Are all financial arrangements listed, including payment of fee, royalty, and promotion? Are these amounts fixed or variable?
2. Does the contract permit the franchisee to return unsalable merchandise?
3. Does the contract provide for responsibility if a lawsuit arises over the product?
4. Is it possible to sell, terminate, or transfer the franchise? Is there a commission?
5. Is the franchise renewable, and is there a renewal fee?
6. Does the contract require the purchase of company products?
7. What restrictions does the franchisee have outside of business interests?
8. Is there a quota set on sales? What is the penalty?

Prospective franchisees should also question their own qualifications and motives before signing a contract. They should have enough capital to operate and buy the franchise, and they should be capable of supervision. They should also be capable of accepting the rules and regulations of the franchisor. If the franchisee can couple these requirements with drive, ambition, character, good health, and some business experience, he or she probably will succeed in this type of business.

1. *Buyerism Newsletter* helps you get a decent break when you are buying or starting a small business. It pinpoints small businesses with potential, those ideally suited to absentee ownership, those requiring a minimal capital investment, etc. Good for franchising and retailing business. Write:

Buyerism Newsletter
WWWWW/Information Services, Inc.
Box 3660
Rochester, NY 14609
(716)461-1888
Circulation: 500

2. *Closeout Report* is an eagle-eyed bulletin of national and international genuine closeout opportunities. Independent, it has no connection with any offering presented. It reveals type of closeout, quantity, price, terms, name, address, and telephone number of seller. It offers free write-up service for offerings of subscribers. Good for retailers. Write:

Closeout Report
15 West 38th Street
New York, NY 10018
(212)840-2423

3. The *Continental Franchise Review* is an independent publication offering comprehensive, current coverage of consumer, economic, and industry trends, legal/legislative activity, and interpretation of events affecting the franchise system of distribution. Write:

Continental Franchise Review
National Research Publications
P.O. Box 6360
Denver, CO 80206
(303)750-7150

4. The *Franchise Annual* lists over 1,200 franchise headquarters, including full descriptions, number of units, how long estab-

lished, and required investments. A complete "Handbook" section details how to investigate the franchise field and any specific franchisor.

Info Press, which publishes *Franchise Annual,* also offers *1979 Franchise Annual Directory.* Write:

The Franchise Annual
Info Press, Inc.
736 Center Street
Lewiston, NY 14092
(716)754-4669

5. The *Franchise Review* provides authoritative information on franchising in Australia and around the world. It is published by International Franchising Pty, Ltd., the largest franchise consulting organization in the southern hemisphere. Write:

Franchise Review
Kiplings Newsletter Service
150 Albert Road, S. Melbourne
Victoria, Australia, 3205
03/699 3166
Circulation: 750

6. *Franchiser,* by Stanley Elkin (1976) is published by:

Farrar, Strauss & Giroux, Inc.
19 Union Square
New York, NY 10003
(212)741-6900

7. Franchising, Bank of America
Small Business Reporter
Business Operations, Vol. 9, No. 9
1975, free

8. *Franchising,* by Charles L. Vaughn (1974), is published by:

Lexington Books
125 Spring Street
Lexington, MA 02173

9. *Franchising Today,* 5th ed., Charles L. Vaughn, editor (1970), is published by:

Farnsworth Publishing Co., Inc.
89 Randall Avenue
Rockville Center, NY 11570
(516)536-8400

10. *Business Building Ideas for Franchises and Small Business* (1978) describes one of the most important operations in any business—a well-planned and executed promotion program. This is what brings in the customers. By successfully implementing only one of the ideas presented, you can earn the cost of the book many times over. This book, and the next four listings, are published by:

Pilot Books
347 Fifth Avenue
New York, NY 10016
(212)685-0736

11. *Directory of Franchising Organizations* (revised annually) comprehensively lists the nation's top money-making franchises, giving concise descriptions and approximate investment. It includes important facts about franchising, and an evaluation checklist. This directory is highly recommended by America's leading business publications.

12. *Financial Security and Independence through a Small Business Franchise* (1978) is a practical, useful guide to a successful future in franchising—with limited investment and minimum risk. It shows where to find opportunities, how to raise capital, how to protect your investment, pitfalls to avoid, plus hundreds of other vital facts.

13. *A Franchising Guide for Blacks* (1978) is a down-to-earth guide to owning a franchised business. It suggests specific businesses, required investment, and explains how the black community can profit from black ownership.

14. *Franchise Investigation and Contract Negotiation* (1978) explains how to select, analyze, and investigate a franchise; then what to look for in negotiating the franchise contract. The authors, an attorney and an accountant, who are impartial and experienced in franchising, show you what facts *must* be obtained, what money-saving factors should be considered, how to read the available financial information, how to project sales costs, and what to look for in the franchise contract.

15. If you've been thinking of buying a franchise, a new government publication, *Franchise Opportunities*, tells you how much capital is typically required (for example, a $50,000 cash down payment for a Shakey's Pizza Parlor). The publication lists 750 franchisors in fields from auto parts to water conditioning. Write:

Government Printing Office
Washington, DC 20402
Publication No. 003-009-00241-9

16. Further information on franchising may be obtained from the U.S. Government Printing Office at minimal expense in such booklets as:

Franchise Business Risks, 1975. Presents detailed information on how to evaluate a franchise opportunity.

Franchise Opportunity Handbook, 1976.

Franchising in the Economy, 1975-1977

Write:

Superintendent of Documents
U.S. Government Printing Office
Washington, DC 20402

17. *How to Franchise Your Own Business* (1977), describes how a proven successful business, even though small, can expand on a sound basis through franchising without sacrificing ownership or control. Step-by-step procedures are given for establishing a franchising system. Included in the discussion is information on pilot operations, site selection, franchise package, profit potential, marketing, advertising, and selling the franchise. Other topics covered are: profile of the franchisee, training programs, preparing a dealer's manual, legal points in a franchise contract, legislation, and regulation of franchises. This book, and the next four listings, are published by:

Pilot Books
347 Fifth Avenue
New York, NY 10016
(212)685-0736

18. *How to Start a Profitable Retirement Business* (1977) is a useful guide to business success after retirement. It includes a selective list of proven businesses requiring a minimum investment (many for $500 or less), which can be operated from your home, often on a part-time basis.

19. *Pilot's Question and Answer Guide to Successful Franchising* (1977) shows how to avert failure in a franchise. It provides the right questions to ask, and indicates what the right answers should be.

20. *Starting a Business after 50* tells you how to establish (1) a small business, (2) a franchised business, and (3) a business at home. It lists over 175 franchise opportunities, and tells how to use your lifetime experience and contacts in establishing a business requiring

modest capital investment, with adjustable hours, possibly sharing responsibilities with your husband or wife.

21. *A Woman's Guide to Her Own Franchised Business* (1977) is addressed to women of all ages—from women whose children are grown to widowed, divorced, and single women. Franchising, the author points out, is a field peculiarly adaptable to women.

22. *Security Management* is geared to those people who are concerned with reducing the loss of profits and property. Eliminating the risks or minimizing the costs of crimes and natural or human-caused disasters are among the few ways remaining to increase profit margins. In this publication, security professionals share their experiences—successful and unsuccessful—for others' education. Write:

Security Management
2000 K Street, N.W.
Washington, DC 20006
(202)331-7887

23. *Tomorrow's Convenience Stores* is a combination trade news summary and thought-provoker on trends in the retailing of convenience items to the general public (food, drink, gas, and other daily needs and impulse wants). It is written to and for the top managements of the country's over 600 convenience store chains (approximately 35,000 retail stores); it includes a tip sheet for field supervisors. Write:

Tomorrow's Convenience Stores
Convenience Stores Research
29-A Estancia Drive
Marana, AZ 85238
(602)682-4500
Circulation: 1,000

24. The following are some sources that claim to help an individual succeed in franchising:

American Business
8404-FE Stohldrehen, N.W.
Massilon, OH 44646

Franchise Concepts, Inc.
920 Ash Street
Flossmoor, IL 60422
(312)957-9300

Information Press
736 Center Street
Lewiston, NY 14092

National Association of Franchised
    Businesswomen and Businessmen
1067 National Press Building
Washington, DC 20045

11

Financial Publications

One of the most dynamic areas of growth among the sources of help for entrepreneurs is that of the financial journals and newsletters. The need for capital and the ability to raise capital is a vital concern in a small business; these publications provide a valuable source of information. In addition, you should examine Chapter 20, "Sources of Help."

1. *American Banker,* the only daily newspaper serving the banking industry, was established in 1836. Its reprint service is outstanding, it offers, at modest prices, listings of banks and all types of fundamental financial institutions. It is an excellent source of information. Write:

American Banker
525 West 42nd Street
New York, NY 10036
(212)563-1900

2. The *American Journal of Small Business* offers academic views and practical information on small business. Included are book reviews of concern to the entrepreneur or manager, but it is a scholarly journal. Write:

American Journal of Small Business
University of Baltimore
847 No. Howard Street
Baltimore, MD 21201

3. *Finders International* is a newsletter which finds capital for small-business ventures. Write:

Finders International
Star Route 2
Box 26
Hawley, PA 18428

4. The leading *weekly* newspaper for the financial community is *Barrons*—it's simply the best. Write:

Barron's
22 Cortlandt Street
New York, NY 10007
(212)285-5374

5. *Bits & Pieces* is a monthly mixture of horse sense and common sense about working with people. This small booklet is widely read and enjoyed for its plain talk about people-related issues.

Bits & Pieces
The Economics Press, Inc.
12 Daniel Road
Fairfield, NJ 07006

6. An eight-page newsletter is published every two weeks under the title *The Business Borrower*. It is under the editorial direction of Howard and Company and the publisher is Philip Glick. Write:

The Business Borrower
Suite 500
1529 Walnut Street
Philadelphia, PA 19102
(215)563-8032

7. *Business Monthly* is a publication that simplifies complicated management techniques, and also contains a question-and-answer section. It is one of the most widely read newsletters on business. Write:

Business Monthly
United Media International, Inc.
306 Dartmouth Street
Boston, MA 02116
(617)267-7100

8. *Business Owner* is a journal offering current information on accounting, insurance, taxation, corporate law, etc. It is published monthly. (More description of this journal is offered in Chapter 20.) It also publishes a monthly newsletter entitled *Capital Markets.*

Business Owner
Business Owner, Inc.
50 Jericho Turnpike
Jericho, NY 11753

9. *CASHCO* is an upbeat newsletter for finance. It is an interesting compilation of ideas for making money. The newsletter is part of a package of financial services to small businesses. Write:

CASHCO
2232 Arrowhead Avenue
Brooksville, FL 33512

10. *Corporate Communications Report* is a bimonthly newsletter on current trends in investor relations and accounting. Write:

Corporate Communications Report
112 East 31st Street
New York, NY 10016
(212)889-2450
Circulation: 1,000

11. *Corporate Financing Week* is published weekly by Institutional Investor magazine, as is CFW's sister newsletters, *Wall Street Letter, Bank Letter, Trust News,* and *Options Letter.* CFW covers long-term financing (public offerings of debt and equity securities as well as private placements of same), bank financing, money-market trends, innovative financing, working with commercial and investment bankers, cash management, and other subjects of interest to corporate financial executives and financial intermediaries (banks, etc.). Write:

Corporate Financing Week
488 Madison Avenue
New York, NY 10020
(212)832-8888

12. The *Directory of Operating Small Business Companies* is a free directory that will help you find small-business financing information. Write:

Directory of Operating Small Business
   Investment Companies
U.S. Small Business Administration
Washington, DC 20417

13. *Money Maker Newsletter* is an unusual and colorful source of financial information. Write:

DuVall Press Financial Publications
920 W. Grand River
Williamstown, MI 48895
(517)655-3333

14. *The Entrepreneurial Manager's Newsletter* is a concise review of news. It weeds out the unnecessary and gets right down to basics; new sources of information, case histories of entrepreneurial success, clarification of new laws and regulations—a host of valuable information you'd spend months searching for if you tried to collect it alone. This newsletter contains a variety of topics: business trends, special market information, sources of help for entrepreneurs, employee relations from the entrepreneurial point of view. Write:

The Center for Entrepreneurial Management, Inc.
Joseph R. Mancuso, Director
311 Main Street
Worcester, MA 01608
(617)755-0770

15. *Finderhood Report* lists opportunities to earn finder's fees. It is sent only to members of Finderhood, a world-wide finder's club. Every listing is backed by a signed payment agreement offering a specific finder's fee. Write:

Finderhood Report
Finderhood, Inc.
15 W. 38th Street
New York, NY 10018
(212)840-2423

16. *The Guide to Selling a Business* is a directory that covers corporate acquirers and merger intermediaries. Sales figures, acquisition criteria, and recently acquired companies are listed. The same publisher offers *Guide to Venture Capital Sources,* listing some 600 venture capital companies. Write:

Capital Publishing Corporation
2 Laurel Street
Box 348
Wellesley Hills, MA 02181
(617)235-5405

17. *International Wealth Success* is a monthly newsletter that lets subscribers place free advertisements. Other books and pamphlets are available on money and borrowing sources. Write:

International Wealth Success
24 Canterbury Road
Rockville Centre, NY 11570
(516)766-5850

18. The *Journal of Commercial Bank Lending* is a monthly publication that goes to 20,000 subscribers interested in the field of commercial lending and credit. It has been published by Robert Morris Associates since 1914. RMA offers many other publications on this topic as well as cassettes, films, and training manuals.

In addition, this industry association has a financial form available which is widely used by commercial loan officers. This single spread sheet neatly packages an income statement, cash flow, and balance sheet. On this form, the interrelationship of these three basic financial statements makes it a great deal easier to interpret pro forma statements. It's especially useful in preparing a business plan and in making the financial statements in the business plan easier to read and understand.

Journal of Commercial Bank Lending
PNB Building
Philadelphia, PA 19107
(215)563-0267

19. *The Journal of Small Business Management* publishes quarterly editions, each of which deals with a specific area of interest to the small-business owner. Write:

Journal of Small Business Management
National Council for Small Business Management and the
Bureau of Business Research of West Virginia University
Morgantown, WV 26505

20. An *MMC* subscription promises a year of surprises immediately in the opportunity world. This source packages a variety of newsletters on a trial basis. Write:

MMC
P.O. Box 849
Carlsbad, CA 92008

21. The Alexander Hamilton Institute publishes a biweekly newsletter focusing on investments and the stock markets entitled *Money Strategies.* Write:

Money Strategies
Alexander Hamilton Institute
605 Third Avenue
New York, NY 10016

22. *Annual Statement Studies* gives financial data on 306 industries based on information compiled on 45,000 bank borrowers. It includes sixteen commonly used balance sheet and operating ratios. Write:

Robert Morris Associates
1432 Philadelphia National Bank Building
Philadelphia, PA 19107
(215)563-0267

23. *NASBIC News* is a semimonthly newsletter of current information on government activity of concern to small business. Write:

NASBIC News
National Association of Small Business
    Investment Companies
618 Washington Building
Washington, DC 20005

24. Nubrenetics, Inc. publishes *Nubrenetics,* or "How to Build an Instant Fortune." The company also publishes a quarterly newsletter called *Prosperity Now.* Write:

NUBREN
Box 2201
Fort Myers, FL 33902

25. The *Quarterly Economic Report for Small Business* gives U.S. economic conditions as well as results of questionnaires sent to a sample membership by the National Federation of Independent Business. Write:

Quarterly Economic Report for Small Business
National Federation of Independent Business
Washington, DC

26. *Business Opportunities Digest* is a high-energy source of help for entrepreneurs. Also available from the same source are:

1. *Raising Speculative Capital*
2. *Capital Sources*
3. *Financing Sources*
4. *Business Intelligence Network* (monthly newsletter)

Business Opportunities Digest
Suite 114
3110 Maple Drive, N.E.
Atlanta, GA 30305
(404)237-9678

27. *Success Orientation* is a business management and personal improvement newsletter which contains many short articles to help business executives and professional leaders improve their personal and professional skills. This same source offers an unusual selection of speakers for business functions.

Success Orientation
c/o Success Publications, Inc.
3121 Maple Drive, Suite One
Atlanta, GA 30305
(404)261-1122

28. *Stull & Company* is an association dedicated to success education and benefit for all interested in the financial field. It offers newsletters and information on other sources of mortgage money, lecturers, counselors, and publishers. It may be worth getting on this mail list if you are interested in investments or venture capital. Below is a capsule of some of their services:

1. *Stull Financial News*
2. *How and Where to Obtain Capital*
3. *Stull Golden Rule Observer* (monthly newspaper)
4. *News of the Business and Financial World*

Write:

Stull & Company
79 Wall Street, Suite 501
New York, NY 10005
(212)344-6676

or

Stull & Company
615 Union Building
1836 Euclid Avenue
Cleveland, OH 44115
(216)687-1471

29. *Think Yourself Rich,* by E. Joseph Cossman (1970) is a classic book on mail-order selling. Cossman, a self-made millionaire, also holds action-packed seminars—he is an infinite source of ideas and energy. Cossman also offers books and newsletters on where to get free sources of help.

Think Yourself Rich
Cossman International, Inc.
P.O. Box 4203
Palm Springs, CA 92262
(714)327-0550

30. The leading daily newspaper for the financial community is the *Wall Street Journal*—it's simply the best. Write:

The Wall Street Journal
Eastern Edition
22 Cortlandt Street
New York, NY 10007
(212)285-5000

31. Jerry Buchanan offers a unique newsletter, inspirational and valuable to writers and entrepreneurs. Write:

Jerry Buchanan
Towers Clubs, USA
Box 2038
Vancouver, WA 98661

For more information on financial journals, books, and newsletters, refer to the *Business Periodicals Index* available in most librar-

ies. This publication cites magazines and periodicals concerned with small business management.

32. *Organizations Providing Business & Economic Education Information* is a very useful directory published by the Public and Government Affairs Division of Standard Oil Company. It's a soft cover, 8½ × 11 directory of 200 pages which was published in January 1979. It's a very comprehensive guidebook, presenting unusually diverse levels of information. It can be obtained two ways:

Public & Government Affairs
Standard Oil Company of Indiana
200 East Randolph Drive
Chicago, IL 60601
Free (while supplies last)

or

Eric Document Reproduction
  Service
Box 190
Arlington, VA 22210
Hard Copy, $9.50
Microfiche, $0.90

33. *The Corporate Finance Sourcebook 1979,* offers profiles of 1,500 banks, plus insurance companies and consultants throughout the U.S.A. It supplies key names of Security and Exchange Commission personnel (SEC), Employee Stock Ownership Plans (ESOP), and a directory of U.S. based foreign banks. These foreign-owned banks can offer unusual banking advantages to entrepreneurs. The *Sourcebook* also offers data on insurance companies, investment banking, and commercial banks. Write:

McGraw-Hill Book Company
1221 Avenue of the Americas
New York, NY 10020

12

Government
Sources
of Information

There is a great deal of information about small business available from Washington, DC on both U.S. and international sources. However, getting that information is sometimes more difficult than tackling the original problem the information intended to solve. There are a number of organizations and associations that help small-business owners. This chapter lists some of the fundamental sources of help. In addition, you might want to try your local, city, and state governments for other sources of help. The chamber of commerce in each of these areas is especially important. Moreover, state and regional government associations can also provide some of the information that is available in Washington.

Information about selling your product overseas or buying products from overseas markets is equally important. Two yellow-page directories—those of New York City and Los Angeles—list most of the import-export offices of major companies. These directories are invaluable.

The Small Business Administration is the arm of the federal government charged with helping entrepreneurs; it is treated in Chapter 18 of this source book. In addition to all the sources listed here, there is a champion of the entrepreneur in Washington who can help you.

If you have ever felt that penetrating the U.S. government was like kicking a 200-foot sponge, help is now available. The Small Business Administration has created an office for small-business ad-

vocacy. This taxpayer-funded job is to champion entrepreneurial causes. Write:

Chief of Advocacy
Small Business Administration
1441 L Street, N.W.
Washington, DC 20416

There is a wealth of information that can be used by small-business owners, but much of it goes unused because too few know about it. Next time, when you need information or are trying to solve a problem, try the National Referral Service of the Library of Congress ([202]426-5467), a good starting point for most information searches. The Library routinely conducts searches free of charge and handles most queries in less than five days. The Federal Information Center ([202]755-8660) can direct you to the right government agency to get the information you need. The Commerce Department's Industrial Trade Administration ([202]377-2000) will compile business profiles on your foreign competitors at a cost as low as $25.00.

SOURCES OF U.S. INFORMATION

1. *Regulation* is published by American Enterprise Institute for Public Policy in Washington, DC. It is a bi-monthly magazine that provides an overview of domestic social and economic issues in scholarly articles and commentaries. Write:

American Enterprise Institute for Public Policy
1150 17th Street, N.W.
Washington, DC 20036
(202)862-5800
Circulation: 6,000

2. *Bulletin to Management* provides fast notification about activities dealing with rules, regulations, litigation, etc., relevant to small businesses. It has down-to-earth discussions of real-life work situations; it presents valuable charts and graphs showing wage levels, living costs, benefit plans, job absence, and turnover rates. It provides policy guides on the techniques used by companies in dealing with specific areas of personnel and labor relations management. Write:

Bulletin to Management
The Bureau of National Affairs, Inc.
1231 25th Street, N.W.
Washington, DC 20037

3. *The Code of Federal Regulation,* available from U.S. Government Printing Office, is well indexed and composed of 50 sections of broad interest. It is a compilation of regulations still in effect, plus new regulations going into effect. This code is most effective when it's used in conjunction with the *Federal Register,* also available from the U.S. Government Printing Office. This publishes proposed and final federal agency regulations. It also offers schedules and timetables for hearings and such. The outcome of pending legislation can be affected and an entrepreneur concerned with the impact of any proposed legislation should consult the *Federal Register* to determine an appropriate course of action.

4. *The Daily Report for Executives* is a daily service, available from the Bureau of National Affairs in Washington, DC (202)452-4200.

5. The *Weekly Regulatory Monitor* offers a calendar of future hearings and proposals. This can be obtained from the *Washington Monitor,* Washington, D.C.

6. The *Congressional Directory* provides information on all senators and congressmen, with home addresses; also data on the Washington Press Corps. Write:

Congressional Directory
Government Printing Office
Washington, DC 20402

7. The *Congressional Staff Directory* covers congress, committees, and the executive branch. Write:

The Congressional Staff Directory
Box 62
Mount Vernon, VA 22121

8. *The Congressional Yellow Book* is a looseleaf directory of members of congress, their committees, and their key aides. It is updated quarterly. Write:

The Congressional Yellow Book
Washington Monitor, Inc.
National Press Building
529 14th St. N.W.
Washington, DC 20045

9. *The Devices and Diagnostics Letter* is designed for executives and concerned with government regulation of medical devices and diagnostic products. Write:

Devices and Diagnostics Letter
National Press Building
529 14th St. N.W.
Washington, DC 20045
(202)737-3830

10. The *Federal Executive Telephone Directory* is a telephone book that is updated every other month. Write:

Federal Executive Telephone Directory
Carroll Publishing Company
1058 Thomas Jefferson Street, N.W.
Washington, DC 20007

11. The Federal Organizational and Personal Service provides detailed organizational charts of federal agencies, a custom research service, and monthly bulletins to update information. Write:

The Federal Organizational and Personal Service
Carroll Publishing Company
1058 Thomas Jefferson Street, N.W.
Washington, DC 20007

12. The *Federal Yellow Book* is a looseleaf directory of the 25,000 top federal officials and managers. It includes names, title, address, room, and telephone number; and all listings are arranged by organization. It is updated every two months. Write:

The Federal Yellow Book
Washington Monitor, Inc.
National Press Building
Washington, DC 20045
(202)347-7757

13. The *Gallagher Presidents' Report* is a weekly newsletter for company presidents covering topics like government legislation, economic investment, management trends, social movements affecting business, environmental problems, the stock market, opportunities for new businesses, and corporate expansion. Write:

The Gallagher Presidents' Report
230 Park Avenue
New York, NY 10017
(212)661-4400

14. The Government Industry Data Exchange Program (GIDEP) is a cooperative activity between government and industry participants seeking to reduce or eliminate expenditures of time and money by making maximum use of existing knowledge. The program is limited to technology transfer among program participants only. It provides a means to exchange certain types of technical data essential in the research, design, development, production, and operational phases of the life cycle of systems and equipment. Any activity that uses and generates the types of data GIDEP exchanges may be considered for membership. Participants are provided access to four major data banks: (1) engineering; (2) metrology; (3) reliability-maintainability; and (4) failure experience. Each data bank is available on 16 mm microfilm. Participation requirements or additional information about GIDEP may be obtained by contacting:

Director
GIDEP Operations Center
Corona, CA 91720
(714)736-4677
Circulation: 600

15. The *Kiplinger Washington Letter* provides crisp, concise weekly briefings on business trends, with analyses, forecasts, and judgments of what lies ahead. It describes new government policies and programs, political moves and their real meaning, also union plans and tactics—anything that will affect you, your job, your personal finances in the future. Write:

Kiplinger Washington Letter
1729 H Street, N.W.
Washington, DC 20006
(202)298-6400

16. The National Technical Information Service of the U.S. Department of Commerce offers a professional report announcement service for new information in many fields: administration, agriculture and food, behavior and society, biomedical technology and human factors engineering, building industry technology, business and economics, chemistry, civil engineering, communication, computers, control and information theory, electrotechnology, energy, environmental pollution and control, government inventions for licensing, health planning, industrial and mechanical engineering, library and information sciences, materials science, medicine and biology, NASA Earth Resources Survey Program,

natural resources and earth sciences, ocean technology and engineering, physics, problem-solving information for state and local governments, transportation, urban and regional technology and development. Write:

National Technical Information Service
U.S. Department of Commerce
5285 Port Royal Road
Springfield, VA 22161
(703)557-4642

17. The *Product Safety and Liability Reporter* is a comprehensive weekly information service reporting on significant developments in the field of consumer product safety, including legislative, regulatory, judicial and product liability developments. Includes a reference file, regularly updated, with full text of consumer product safety laws, standards, regulations, and other pertinent material. Write:

Product Safety and Liability Reporter
The Bureau of National Affairs, Inc.
1231 25th Street, N.W.
Washington, DC 20037
(202)452-4200

18. First in its field, *Product Safety Letter* monitors the activities of the U.S. Consumer Product Safety Commission. PSL gives you inside information about major regulatory trends, actions, opinions, and ideas. The perceptive weekly offers vital advance notice of tough new rules that hit production, marketing, and sale of consumer products ranging from TV's to toys and cleansers to clothing. Write:

Product Safety Letter
Washington Business Information, Inc.
1080 National Press Building
Washington, DC 20045
(202)393-3830

19. *Regulations of Brokers, Dealers, and Security Markets,* by Nicholas Wolfson, Thomas A. Russo and Richard M. Phillips (1977), is an excellent source book on the securities market regulations. It is comprehensive and well indexed and a must for any entrepreneurial venture planning a public stock offering. It is published by:

Warren Gorham & Lamont, Inc.
210 South Street
Boston, MA 02111
(617)423-2020

20. Business and professional leaders get a unique overview of what government is doing from the biweekly magazine, *The Regulators,* edited by Pulitzer Prize winner Louis Kohlmeier, the authority in Washington on government regulation and its economic consequences for business. Providing timely forecasts and analyses, *The Regulators* deciphers the complex economic pressures, political forces, and legal trends—in congress, the White House, the Supreme Court, and major federal agencies—affecting regulation of energy, communications, transportation, insurance, labor, advertising, and product safety. Write:

The Regulators
235 National Press Building
Washington, DC 20045
(202)737-3830

21. The Regulatory Watchdog Service is an information/alert system that saves you the time and frustration of trying to discover and obtain documents in the bureaucratic mazes. The service provides a weekly bulletin describing pertinent materials from the Consumer Product Safety Commission, Food and Drug Administration, Congress, Federal Trade Commission, and other agencies. Subscribers select the documents they need and Watchdog Service rushes them by first-class mail—within 24 hours of receipt of an order. Write:

Regulatory Watchdog Service
235 National Press Building
Washington, DC 20045

22. *Report* is a Chamber of Commerce Membership Newsletter regarding news on travel, conventions, economic development, and internal chamber news. Write:

Report
P.O. Box 1011
Asheville, NC 28802
(704)254-1981
Circulation: 1,600

23. The *U.S. Government Manual* lists each federal agency, plus regional offices along with names of top echelon offices. Write:

The U.S. Government Manual
Government Printing Office
Washington, DC 20402

24. Bidders Early Alert Message (BEAM), a service of the Small Business Administration, offers a new computerized system to facilitate accessibility of small businesses to government contracts. Under the new system, called Procurement Automated Source System (PASS), a company submits to its local SBA office a description of its products and manufacturing/production capabilities. This information is fed into the computer where it is easily recalled when the SBA is notified that a government agency is calling for bids on a contract. Qualifying companies are then notified of the opportunity to submit bids.

Local SBA offices will assist small companies in preparing bids and guide them through government red tape. It is anticipated that approximately 150,000 small companies will be served by PASS in the next few years.

Contact your regional SBA office for application forms for PASS. Or write:

Office of Procurement
Small Business Administration
1441 L Street, N.W.
Washington, DC 20416

25. *The Information Report—Compendium of Back Issues* is a complete collection of back issues of *The Information Report* from winter 1975 to spring 1977. For this, and the next three listings, write:

Washington Researchers
910 Seventeenth Street, N.W.
Washington, DC 20006
(202)452-0025

26. The *List of Industry Analysts in the Federal Government* (1977) covers industry analysts at the Department of Commerce and industry specialists at the Bureau of Census. The list is arranged by industry and product giving the name, address, and telephone number of over 100 analysts and specialists.

27. *Sources of State Information on Corporations* (1977) provides background information on those companies that are *not* required to

file with the Securities and Exchange Commission. Every state requires companies doing business in its state to file company information which is made available to the public. Through various departments within the state governments, companies are required to file information ranging from articles of incorporation and yearly profit-and-loss statements to balance sheet information filed under the Uniform Commercial Code. Now, for the first time, a single reference source is available from each of the states. Also supplied are the name, address, and telephone number of the source to contact for copies of specific documents pertaining to a company.

28. *Sources of Information for Selling to the Federal Government* (1977) is aimed at identifying the abundance of information that is all available (free or for the price of a telephone call) to those who wish to sell to the federal government. Sections include: how to use the Freedom of Information Act, how to monitor legislation over the telephone, how to find a free expert on any topic, and how to obtain listings from the federal government of those who are current contractors. Hundreds of names, addresses, and telephone numbers are also provided which will prove to be invaluable tools for getting around Washington.

Consumer Information Sources

The following is a list of offices in the federal government established for handling consumer problems or for directing consumers to others who may solve their problems. If you have a problem, start with an office you think is relevant.

Agriculture, Department of	(202)447-3165
Civil Aeronautics Board	(202)673-5526
Commerce, Department of	(202)377-3176
Comptroller of the Currency	(202)447-1600
Consumer Product Safety Commission-National	(301)492-6504
Product Safety Hotline	(800)638-2666
Hotline(800)638-2666	
in Washington, D.C.	(202)492-2937
Defense, Department of	(202)697-9192
Environmental Protection Agency	(202)755-0707
Federal Aviation Administration	(202)426-1960

Federal Communications Commission	(202)632-7000
Federal Deposit Insurance Corporation	(202)389-4295
Federal Energy Administration	(202)566-9021
Federal Insurance Administration Flood Insurance	(800)424-8872
Federal Home Loan Bank Board	(202)376-3249
Federal Power Commission	(202)275-4006
Federal Reserve System	(202)452-3667
Federal Trade Commission	(202)523-3543
Food and Drug Administration	(301)443-3170
General Services Administration	
Consumer Information Center	(202)566-1794
Government Printing Office	(202)275-3050
Health, Education, and Welfare	(202)245-6401
Housing and Urban Development	(202)755-5353
Housing Discrimination Hotline	(800)424-8590
In Washington, D.C.	(202) 755-5490
Interior, Department of	(202)343-8331
Interstate Commerce Commission	(202)275-7252
Justice, Department of	(202)739-4174
Labor, Department of	(202)523-6951
Moving Hotline	(800)424-9312
in Washington, D.C.	(202)275-7301
in Florida	(800)432-4537
National Highway Traffic Safety Admin.	(800)424-9393
in Washington, D.C.	(202)426-0123
Postal Service, U.S.	(202)245-4514
Securities and Exchange Commission	(202)755-1114

Small Business Administration   (202)653-6840
State, Department of   (202)632-9818
Transportation, Department of   (202)426-4518
Treasury, Department of   (202)566-5487

Latest Economic Indicators

There is no reason for getting economic news late, or for making decisions without the latest data. The following is a list of the major indicators published on a quarterly, monthly, or weekly basis. Along with each category name is the name and telephone number of the office producing the information with the telephone number, where applicable, of the publishing office.

Census, to order publications: (202)763-5853

Construction Expenditures (C-30)
Construction Statistics Office, (202)763-7163

Manufacturers Shipments, Inventories, and Orders (M3-1)
Industry Division, (202)763-5850

Advance Monthly Retail Sales
Business Division, (202)763-7564

Housing Starts (C-20)
Construction Statistics Division, (202)763-7163

Advance Report on Durable Goods, Manufacturers Shipments, and Orders (M3-1)
Industry Division, (202)763-5850

Export and Import Merchandise Trade
Business Division, (202)763-7564

Monthly Wholesale Trade
Business Division, (202)763-5294

Federal Reserve, to order publications: (202)452-3245

Money Stock Measures (H.6)
Research and Statistics Division, (202)452-3591

Consumer Credit (G.19)
Research and Statistics Division, (202)452-2458

Industrial Production and Related Data (G.12.3)
Industrial Production, (202)452-3153

Capacity Utilization in Manufacturing (G.3)
Research and Statistics Division, (202)452-3197

Bureau of Labor Statistics, to order publications: (202)523-1221

The Employment Situation
Office of Current Employment Analysis, (202)523-1944

Wholesale Price Index
Wholesale Price Division, (202)523-1080

Consumer Price Index
Consumer Price Division, (202)523-7827

Bureau of Economic Analysis

Gross National Product (Preliminary)
National Income and Wealth Division, (202)523-0669

Personal Income
National Income and Wealth Division, (202)523-0669

Merchandise Trade Balance, Balance of Payments Basis
Balance of Payment Division, (202)523-0668

Advance Business Conditions Digest
Statistical Indicators Division, (202)523-0535

Defense Indicators
Agriculture, to order publications: (202)447-4021

Agriculture, to order publications: (202)447-4021

Agricultural Prices
Prices and Labor Branch, (202)447-3570

Key to Agency Listing

CPSC	Consumer Product Safety Commission
CSC	Civil Service Commission
CWPS	Council on Wage and Price Stability

DOC	Department of Commerce
DOE	Department of Energy
DOJ	Department of Justice
DOL	Department of Labor
DOT	Department of Transportation
EEOC	Equal Employment Opportunity Commission
EPA	Environmental Protection Agency
FCC	Federal Communications Commission
FDA	Food and Drug Administration
FEC	Federal Election Commission
FTC	Federal Trade Commission
GAO	General Accounting Office
GSA	General Services Administration
HEW	Department of Health, Education and Welfare
ICC	Interstate Commerce Commission
NIOSH	National Institute for Occupational Safety and Health
OMB	Office of Management and Budget
OSAHRC	Occupational Safety and Health Review Commission
OSHA	Occupational Safety and Health Administration
PBGC	Pension Benefit Guaranty Corporation
SBA	Small Business Administration
SEC	Securities and Exchange Commission
USPS	United States Postal Service

SOURCES OF INTERNATIONAL INFORMATION

1. *The Business Idea,* or *Die Geschaeftsidee,* is a publication written in German. It is a report on profitable small businesses in West Germany. Each issue contains two complete reports about profitable small businesses and several pages of other business and marketing ideas. Write:

Die Geschaeftsidee (The Business Idea)
Verlag Norman Rentrop, Langenbergsweg
72, 5300 Bonn-Bad Godesberg
W. Germany, 0-222-1/34 34 50

2. A monthly report on international opportunities, including U.S. government aid to business, specific foreign trade leads, opportunities to buy, sell, and exchange are found in the *Government Marketing News.*

Government Marketing News, Inc., is a successful publisher of newsletters, books, and reports on many different subjects, most of them concerned with how to make more money, either as extra income or as a full-time business. *Buyer's and Seller's Exchange* and the *BSE Associates* plan are also offered by this publisher. Write:

Government Marketing News, Inc.
Suite 1019
1001 Connecticut Avenue, N.W.
Washington, DC 20036
(301)340-3010

3. Some international trade services are in the list below:

American Import and Export Bulletin
North American Publishing Company
401 N. Broad Street
Philadelphia, PA 19108
(215)574-9600

Commerce America
U.S. Department of Commerce
c/o Superintendent of Documents
Government Printing Office
Washington, DC 10402
(202)377-2066

Custom House Guide
North American Publishing Company
401 N. Broad Street
Philadelphia, PA 19108
(215)574-9600

Export Administration Regulations
(Directory with updating service)
Superintendent of Documents
Government Printing Office
Washington, DC 20402
(202)783-3238

4. The *International Development Review* is a quarterly publication. It is free to the Society for International Development members. It contains articles on economic and social development by scholars and practitioners, also contains book and media review sections, and a roundup of news in the development profession. Write:

International Development Review
1346 Connecticut Avenue, N.W.
Washington, DC 20036
(202)296-3810
Circulation: 6,000

5. The *International Intertrade Index* lists the many new products that will soon be available for import to the U.S. Foreign manufacturers inform this publication directly and then the data is translated and compiled without charge (because no advertising is accepted). You are assured of honest, unbiased trade reports. Write:

International Intertrade Index
744 Broad Street, Suite 3400
Box 636
Newark, NJ 07101
(201)623-2864

6. The *International Market Bulletin* buys and sells news for brokers, finders, principals, importers, exporters, and manufacturers. For more information on subscriptions and advertising, write:

J. Godfrey H. Childers Enterprises
International Market Bulletin
P.O. Box 762
Cupertino, CA 95014

7. The *International Marketing Report* is devoted to an interpretive role. It does not aim to report the international trade news of the day, although it includes much exclusive international marketing, advertising, and public relations news in the course of a year. The aim is to report on techniques, strategies, tactics to help you do your job better. Write:

International Marketing Report
144 The Lane
Hinsdale, IL 60521
(312)986-0064

8. The Marketmatch program can bring you foreign business.

A new computerized service puts prospective buyers and sellers in the United States in touch with sellers and buyers abroad. The program is run by the World Trade Center in New York City in cooperation with 99 other trade groups in 40 countries. For an annual fee, a company can list up to 15 products to sell and 15 to buy, find out whom to contact, and give a brief advertising message. For a small additional fee, a product catalog can be distributed at many foreign trade centers. Every month, a subscriber gets the names and addresses of trading prospects found by the computer. For information on the program, contact:

Marketmatch
World Trade Information Center
One World Trade Center
New York, NY 10048
(212)466-3067

9. The *Normandy Express Newsletter* contains monthly tips on Canadian business. Write:

Normandy Express Enterprises
P.O. Box 1154
Station A
Toronto, Canada M5W 1G6

10. *Trade Channel Journal* allows you to expose your product to buyers in 150 countries every month or be the first to hear of new products being placed on the world market, or be able to obtain exclusive representation from overseas firms anxious to do business in the USA. Write:

Trade Channel Journal
Trade Channel Organization
Helmholtzstraat 61
Amsterdam 1006, The Netherlands

11. A subscription to the *UNIDO Newsletter* is free. It is an eight-page publication available in Arabic, English, French, Russian, or Spanish containing information about the work of the United Nations Industrial Development Organization. Contents include news items, publications available, industrial opportunities, technical information files available to requestors in developing countries, information about technologies available from developing countries, and a calendar of meetings. Circulation is controlled. Write:

UNIDO Newsletter
Room C114 UNIDO
P.O. Box 707
A-1011
Vienna, Austria
Telephone: 43 50 889
Circulation: about 23,000

12. The *United States Herald* is a report of what is happening in the U.S., designed primarily for overseas readers. Write:

United States Herald
Herald Enterprises, Ltd.
P.O. Box 27021
Philadelphia, PA 19118
(215)242-4779
Circulation: 350

13. The Washington Diplomatic Corp of the State Department is available in the *Washington Information Directory,* with complete names, titles, home addresses, and telephone numbers. Information is arranged by subject. Write:

The Washington Information Directory
Congressional Quarterly, Inc.
1414 22nd Street, N.W.
Washington, DC 20037

14. Washington Researchers provides a list of international experts in the State, Commerce and Agriculture Departments who specialize in developing international trade, or a list of over 100 domestic industry analysis experts working at the Commerce Department and the Census Bureau. Write:

Washington Researchers
910 Seventeenth Street, N.W.
Washington, DC 20006
(202)452-0025

15. *World Wide MOD* is a monthly publication listing buyers and sellers around the world who are looking for merchandise. You can get a subscription by writing:

International Commercial Network, Ltd.
17 Victoria Avenue
Harrogate HG1 5RE
N. Yorkshire, England

16. *The Worldwide Marketing Opportunities Digest* brings together both companies that desire to purchase products and those that want to sell products. It also covers international agency opportunities and product licensing. (Formerly Pan American Airways *Marketing Horizons.*) Write:

A.D.C. Suite 302
291 S. LaCienega Boulevard
Beverly Hills, CA 90211
(213)655-7890
Circulation: 20,000

Those interested in international trade and finance can write:

Worldwide Business Opportunities
Takawir Mafukidze
International Trade & Finance Consultants
61 Bates Street
Pittsburgh, PA 15213

17. Staff–House Small Business Committee. A reference list of people in government who play major roles in the everyday operation of a smaller enterprise.

General Counsel
2361 Rayburn House Office Bldg.
(202)225-5821

Communications Specialist
2361 Rayburn House Office Bldg.
(202)225-6020

Minority Counsel
B-343 Rayburn House Office Bldg.
(202)225-4038

Subcommittee on SBA and SBIC Authority and General Small Business Problems

General Counsel (see above)

Minority Subcommittee Counsel
2361 Rayburn House Office Bldg.
(202)225-4038

Subcommittee on General Oversight and Minority Enterprises

Subcommittee Counsel
2361 Rayburn House Office Bldg.
(202)225-9321

Minority Subcommittee
Professional Staff Member
2361 Rayburn House Office Bldg.
(202)225-4601

Subcommittee on Antitrust and Restraint of Trade Activities Affecting Small Business

Subcommittee Professional Staff
 Member
B-363 Rayburn House Office Bldg.
(202)225-8944

Minority Subcommittee Professional
Staff Member
B-363 Rayburn House Office Bldg.
(202)225-4541

Subcommittee on Energy, Environment, Safety, and Research

Subcommittee Counsel
B-363 Rayburn House Office Bldg.
(202)225-6026

Minority Subcommittee Counsel
B-363 Rayburn House Office Bldg.
(202)225-4541

Subcommittee on Access to Equity Capital and Business Opportunities

Subcommittee Counsel
B-363 Rayburn Building
(202)225-7797

Minority Subcommittee Counsel
B-363 Rayburn House Office Bldg.
(202)225-4541

Subcommittee on Special Small Business Problems

Subcommittee Professional Staff
  Member
B-363 Rayburn House Office Bldg.
(202)225-9368

Minority Subcommittee
Professional Staff Member
B-363 Rayburn House Office Bldg.
(202)225-4541

(All addresses are Washington, DC 20515)

18. If you, as a venturesome entrepreneur, are considering the foreign market, the following sources of information can be utilized to explore most areas of such an undertaking.

Director
Bureau of Export Development
U.S. Department of Commerce
Washington, D.C. 20230

Programs to write for from the Dept. of Commerce:

Foreign Trader's Index

Trade Opportunities Program (TOP)

Export Contact List Service

Agent Distributor Service

World Traders Report

Commerce Business Daily

Export-Import Bank of the
  United States
811 Vermont Avenue NW
Washington, D.C. 20571
Toll-free, Hotline Number:
(800)424-5201

Director
Export Trade Services Div.
Foreign Agricultural Service
U.S. Dept. of Agriculture
Washington, D.C. 20250
(202)447-6343

Federal Trade Commission
Public Reference Branch
6th Street & Pennsylvania
   Avenue
Room 130
Washington, D.C. 20580
(202)523-3830

Department of the Treasury
U.S. Customs Service
1303 Constitution Ave. NW
Washington, D.C. 20520
(202)566-8195

Office of Commercial Affairs
Bureau of Economic and Business Affairs
Room 33-34
U.S. State Department
Washington, D.C. 20520
(202)632-8097

World Trade Center
New York, NY 10048
(212)466-3067

Publications

Government and Business: A Joint Venture in International Trade (free booklet published by the U.S. State Department's Office of Commercial Affairs). To order, write to:

Office of Public Communication
Bureau of Public Affairs
U.S. State Department
Room 48-27A
Washington, D.C. 20520
(202)632-6575

Guide to United Nations Conference of Trade and Development (UN-CTAD) Publications (free catalog published by UNCTAD). Write:

United Nations Sales Section
Editorial & Document Section
Palais Des Nations 1211
Geneva 10, Switzerland

Lorna M. Daniells, *Business Information Sources,* (Berkeley, California: University of California Press, 1976) p. 258. List of reference data sources for exporters.

> *Quarterly Economic Review* (London, England: Economist Intelligence Unit), reviews 45 countries quarterly.
>
> *OECD Economic Surveys* (Paris, France: Organization for Economic Cooperation and Development), individual, annual reviews listed by country.
>
> *Investing, Licensing and Trading Conditions Abroad,* (New York, NY: Business International), two volumes.

The Department of Commerce provides free consultation with an expert trade specialist who can help answer questions about the feasibility of exporting your product to other countries, government regulations, cultural mores, and competition. Bankers in the international departments of major city banks are also good contacts to help assess a foreign market. A third source of information about export possibilities is foreign students at your local universities who can suggest marketing potential and possible cultural and governmental limitations.

19. Ombudsman. Entrepreneurs can call on the Ombudsman:

—Selling to the Government

—Domestic or world markets

—Federal policies and programs

—Commodity supply situations

—Financial assistance programs

—Consumer expectations

For personal attention and action on problems affecting business—particularly those arising from Government action—

Call: (202)377-3176

Write: The Ombudsman for Business
      U.S. Department of Commerce
      Washington, DC 20230

Visit: Room 3800
      Main Commerce Building
      14th and E Street, N.W.
      Washington, D.C.

To receive Situation Reports on various topics of interest to business, ask to be put on the list for this free service.

20. Federal Laboratory Consortium (FLC). In each of the 180 federal research and development laboratories, there is a person with the title "technical transfer representative." This job is to respond to questions from businesses. The good news is that there is no charge.

A directory is available from:

FLC Headquarters
Federal Laboratory Program Manager
National Science Foundation ISPT
Washington, DC 20550
(202)634-7996

21. Washington Information Sources.

Division of Information Services
   Bureau of Labor Statistics
441 G Street, N.W.
Washington, DC 20212
(202)523-1239

—has data available on employment, living conditions, prices, productivity, and occupational safety and health.

Bill Status Office
3669 HOBA#2
The LEGIS Office
Washington, DC 20515
(202)225-1772

—will provide you with current status of any legislation or tell you if legislation has been introduced on a topic.

National Referral Center
Library of Congress
10 First Street, S.E.
Washington, DC 20540
(202)426-5670

—will find an organization willing to provide free information on any topic, for free.

Federal Information Center
General Services Administration
7th and D Streets, S.W.
Washington, DC 20407
(202)755-8660

—will locate an expert in the federal government to tell you how the federal government can help you.

Reference Section, Science and Technology Division
Library of Congress
10 First Street, S.E.
Washington, DC 20540
(202)426-5639

—offers both free and fee reference and bibliographic services.

Data Users Services Division
Bureau of the Census
U.S. Department of Commerce
Washington, DC 20233
(301)763-7662

—will identify census data on your topic.

Economics, Statistics, and Cooperative Service
U.S. Department of Agriculture
Information Staff
Washington, DC 20250
(202)447-4230

—can provide the latest production and stock estimates for agricultural products as well as the supply-demand-price relationships and other economic factors.

Bureau of Domestic Business Development
U.S. Department of Commerce
Washington, DC 20230
(202)377-2786

—100 industry analysts can provide or guide you to information on a company or industry.

Information Central
American Society of Association Executives
1101 16th Street, N.W.
Washington, DC 20036
(202)659-3333

—will identify an association that can help with your problem, if you cannot find help in Gale's "Encyclopedia of Associations."

Energy Information Sources
National Energy Information Center
Energy Information Administration
1726 M Street, N.W.
Washington, DC 20461
(202)566-9820

National Solar Heating and Cooling Information Center
P.O. Box 1607
Rockville, MD 20850
(800)523-2929

Technical Information Center
U.S. Department of Energy
Oak Ridge, TN 37830
615-483-8611, ext. 34271

U.S. Civil Service Commission
Bureau of Manpower Information Systems
Manpower Statistics Division
1900 E Street, N.W.
Washington, DC 20415
(202)655-4000

—material available: Civil Service employment, payroll information, and paydays (particularly useful in scheduling campaigns for consumer goods in Washington).

U.S. Department of Commerce, Census Bureau
Social and Economic Statistics Administration
Washington, DC 20233
(202)655-4000

—material available: General Census statistics, Census of Business, educational demographics, statistics on construction and other businesses in the Washington area.

U.S. Department of Labor
Bureau of Labor Statistics
441 G Street, N.W.
Washington, DC 20210
(202)393-2420

—material available: Cost of Living Index, monthly reports on employment by state and metro area, and general labor statistics.

District of Columbia Government
Department of Manpower
Community Relations and Information Division
500 C Street, N.W.
Washington, DC 20011
(202)393-6151

—material available: General employment information and occupational make-up of the District of Columbia.

Metropolitan Washington Council of Governments
Information Services
1225 Connecticut Avenue, N.W.
Washington, DC 20036
(202)223-6800

—material available: General statistical data and planned development information for the metropolitan Washington area.

Washington Center for Metropolitan Studies
1717 Massachusetts Avenue, N.W.
Washington, DC 20036
(202)462-4868

—material available: Population demographics and updated 1970 Census information.

22. Useful Government Data. Materials that can be very beneficial to you are published by all the various Nader groups. A wide variety of reports and publications are available. To obtain copies of the following free citizen action materials, send a *self-addressed, stamped envelope* to P.O. Box 19404, Washington, DC, 20036 (unless another address is indicated).

1. Public Citizen, Reports and Publications: A complete list of all reports and publications by Ralph Nader and other well-known consumer advocates.

2. Public Citizen Action Projects: A list of many citizen action projects that can be undertaken by any interested group.

3. Public Citizen Health Research Group's list of reports and publications includes information in the areas of food and drugs, occupational safety and health, pesticides, product safety, health care delivery and how to get a copy of your health records.

4. Toll Free Hotline numbers: A complete guide to all federal agencies designed to help and inform consumers.

5. Airline Passenger Rights: Information on your rights as an airline passenger, including how to deal with an airline-related prob-

lem. Write to ACAP (Aviation Consumer Action Project), P.O. Box 19029, Washington, DC, 20036.

6. Freedom of Information: Pamphlet on the Freedom of Information Act and how to use it. Send SASE to Freedom of Information Clearinghouse, P.O. Box 19367, Washington, DC, 20036.

7. Pension Rights: Information on the rights of employees, retirees, and spouses under the new private pension reform law. Send SASE to the Pension Rights Center, 1346 Connecticut Avenue, N.W., Room 1019, Washington, DC, 20036.

8. Human Rights and the Elderly: Information on Programs involved with agism and other special projects. Send a first-class stamp to the Gray Panthers, 3700 Chestnut Street, Philadelphia, PA, 19104.

9. People and Taxes: Monthly newspaper of the Public Citizen's Tax Reform Research Group. Please include a first-class stamp.

10. Critical Mass: Nesspaper covering nuclear power information and activity. Write to Critical Mass, P.O. Box 1538, Washington, DC, 20013. Please include a first-class stamp.

11. People and Energy, CPSI Quarterly, The Nutrition Newsletter, and publications list: Newsletter from The Center for Science in the Public Interest. Send SASE to Center for Science in the Public Interest, 1757 S Street, N.W., Washington, DC, 20009.

23. The White House Conference on Small Business. The White House Conference on Small Business was to be held in Washington, DC on January 17 through 20, 1980. So far, about sixty regional meetings have been attended by just under 40,000 people to elect 2,500 delegates to this first-of-its-kind conference. It's too early to speculate on what to expect, but it is proper to state that this is the biggest event of its kind ever. Delegates were elected and appointed on a state by state basis and they voted on certain proposals at the conference. Contact the Small Business Administration (SBA) in your area to be sure your delegates have represented your views.

Select Staff, SBA Office of Advocacy

Advocacy staffers can be reached through:

Office of Advocacy
Small Business Administration
1441 L. St. N.W. Room 1010
Washington, DC 20416

Chief Counsel for Advocacy
(202)653-6984

Executive Assistant
(202)653-6984

Administrative Officer
(202)653-6808

Director
Office of Interagency Policy
(202)653-6216

Director
Office of Small Business
  Services Management
(202)653-6579

Director
Office of Economic Research
(202)634-4886

Director
Office of Women in Business
(202)634-6087

Chief Economist
(202)634-4886

Advocate for Energy & Natural Resources
(202)653-6986

Advocate for Government
  Industry Relations
(202)653-6840

Assistant Chief Counsel for
  State & Local Affairs
(202)653-6808

Field Activities Coordinator
(202)653-6808

Trade Assoc. Coordinator
(202)653-6808

13

Management and Planning

A wide range of sources of management assistance exists to help an entrepreneurial manager plan the growth of a small enterprise. This topic category is so broad that almost any other topic category could reasonably fit under it. Consequently, the dividing line between this category of information and other categories is blurred. However, managing the small enterprise is the art of accomplishing tasks through other people. Consequently, this group of sources lists information that can help to plan the growth of your enterprise. These sources are especially helpful in establishing a degree of professional entrepreneurial management as the mode of operation in your company. Our definition of a professional is someone who has attained a level of proficiency and daily seeks to improve.

The Small Business Administration has a separate division entitled Management Assistance. Under this division, a wide range of assistance is offered to small companies. Please see Chapter 18 of this book, which offers this information.

1. *Behavioral Sciences Newsletter* is a newsletter for top management, line managers, management development directors, and personnel directors dealing with the latest developments in the behavioral sciences as applied to business and industry. Write:

Behavioral Sciences Newsletter
Roy W. Waters & Associates
60 Glen Avenue
Glen Rock, NJ 10452
(201)652-8200
Circulation: 4,500

2. Management consultants, users and practitioners alike, devour *Consultants' News,* a lively monthly newsletter for exclusive news of an enigmatic emerging profession. Write:

Consultants' News
Box 84
Fitzwilliam, NH 03447
(603)585-2200
Circulation: several thousand

3. If you are a corporate officer or director, you are vulnerable to lawsuits. The *Corporate Director's Guide* deals with questions about, for example, bribes, sales and purchases of major assets, securities law, and product liability. Write:

Finance Office
Government and Public Affairs Communicators
Suite 520, 1629 K Street, N.W.
Washington, DC 20006
(202)832-3242, (202)296-3174

This same source offers two newsletters containing a monthly compendium of relevant SEC actions: *Disclosure Digest* and *Bondholders Newsletter.* The *Disclosure Handbook,* an excellent source of SEC information, and another directory, entitled *Analysis of Shareholders Proposals,* are two more publications of this source.

4. The official monthly newsletter of the National Association of Corporate Directors is known as *Director's Monthly.* This is a profit-motivated organization dedicated to the preservation of the free enterprise system. It focuses on information of value to members of boards of directors. It is 15–20 pages per issue. Write:

National Association of Corporate Directors
777 Fourteenth Street, N.W.
Washington, DC 20005
(202)466-4474

5. *The Doctor's Management Report* is published for the medical profession. Write:

The Doctor's Management Report
Institute for Management, Inc.
Old Saybrook, CT 06475

6. *Digest of Executive Opportunities* contains completely new listings of job opportunities obtained by research staff from 61 national

and international periodicals, and from over 1,200 recruiters throughout the world. The parent company, General Executives Services, has provided both recruitment and placement services for corporate clients since 1961.

Digest of Executive Opportunities
General Executive Sources
72 Park Street
New Canaan, CT 06840
(203)966-1673
Circulation: 1,500

7. *The Executive's Personal Development Letter* is a monthly newsletter for the development of personal skills and managerial expertise for the executive. Write:

Alexander Hamilton Institute, Inc.
605 Third Avenue
New York, NY 10016
(212)557-5200
Circulation: 4,000

8. *Foremanship* contains practical articles to help supervisors. Write:

The Dartnell Corp.
4660 Ravenswood Avenue
Chicago, IL 60640
(312)561-4000

9. A monthly report on people and business entitled *The Effective Manager* is an 8-page newsletter. It stresses the people or personnel side of management. Write:

Warren, Gorham, and Lamont
210 South Street
Boston, MA 02111
(617)423-2020

10. A monthly newsletter designed to cut costs, increase sales, reduce taxes, and boost profits and personal wealth is known as the *Management Action Letter*. It also features an idea exchange; it offers one of the broadest coverages of any newsletter. Write:

Management Action Letter
176 Sutton Manor Road
New Rochelle, NY 10805

11. To keep abreast of what is being published in current periodicals in marketing, management, economics, and general business, you can subscribe to a relatively new publication, *Management Contents.* Each biweekly issue contains the contents tables of the finest business/management periodicals and the publication intends to fill the needs for current information. It provides listings of what has just been published in your own field and related areas.

The same publisher also offers *Business Alert,* which is custom-tailored to the subscriber's business and management information needs. Each month this magazine automatically compares a subscriber's interests against all the current articles in the *Management Contents* data base. A custom printout is produced giving the article name, author(s), publication name, date, pages, subject terms, and a concise abstract of the article. Write:

Management Contents
P.O. Box 1054
Skokie, IL 60077

12. An excellent source of strategic planning information is available through membership in the Strategic Planning Institute. Through an analysis of the actual operating expenses of 1,800 businesses, a unique data base allows these strategies to claim to be actually "business-tested." The Institute has its historical roots in General Electric and the Harvard Business School. In 1975, the participating companies established SPI as an independent, nonprofit corporation. The Institute's limited information report is extremely helpful in evaluating startups and acquisitions. The Institute can also help entrepreneurs identify appropriate recovery on survival strategies.

The major emphasis of this 150-member tax-exempt organization, representing about 1,000 products, is the PIMS letter. This newsletter is published every week and is quite interesting and informative. This organization especially enjoys working with venture capital investment decisions. For information, write:

The Strategic Planning Institute
1 Broadway
Cambridge, MA 02142
(617)492-3810

13. The same source publishes an interesting venture capital study. Venture Capital Investing letter stock funds versus venture groups. A study in techniques with recommendations. Lucien Ruby

also has a venture capital study which contrasts letter stock with venture stock. This is a 78-page report published in August 1977 and available by writing c/o:

Lucien Ruby
Box 656
Madisonville, KY 42431

14

Manufacturer's Representatives

How to select the proper manufacturer's representative for your product line is one of the most difficult questions facing an entrepreneurial venture. The following sources list several organizations and directories that will help small businesses find competent sales representatives.

FINDING MANUFACTURER'S REPRESENTATIVES: SEARCH ORGANIZATIONS

Below is a list of organizations which specialize in helping small entrepreneurial ventures find competent sales representatives. The process of locating qualified manufacturer's representatives is a crucial element of the marketing efforts. Write one of the following:

Albee-Campbell
806 Penn Avenue
Sinking Springs, PA 19608
(215)678-3361

Representative Resources, Inc.
Drower Avenue
Thorndale, PA 19372
(215)383-1177

L. H. Simmonds, Inc.
60 East 42nd Street
New York, NY 10017
(212)889-1530

United Association of Manufacturers' Agents
808 Broadway
Kansas City, MO 64105
(816)842-8130

Anthony J. Zinno Associates
2 Park Avenue
Manhasset, NY 11030
(516)627-2642

FINDING MANUFACTURER'S REPRESENTATIVES: SOURCES OF INFORMATION

1. The Direct Selling Association is composed of about 100 firms engaged in selling products and services to consumers primarily in their homes. Several directories of members are available to member firms. Write:

Direct Selling Association
1730 M Street, N.W.
Suite 610
Washington, DC 20036
(202)293-5760

2. A 30-year old industry association of manufacturers' agents and an excellent source of information is:

Manufacturers Agents National Association
2021 Business Center Drive, Box 16878
Irvine, CA 92713

3. The New England Manufacturing Exchange (NEMEX) is a clearinghouse that maintains up-to-date computerized information on products offered by some 1,400 suppliers. Both buyers and suppliers can obtain information on this nationwide free service by writing:

NEMEX
10 Moulton Street
Cambridge, MA 02138
(617)354-1150

4. Pacific International takes the guesswork out of appointing reps. This company has in its files a list of reps and rep companies in 42 major marketing areas in the United States and all foreign countries. Write:

Pacific International
P.O. Box 894
Escondido, CA 92025
(714)745-7361

5. The Electronic Representatives Association publishes a directory listing more than 2,000 U.S. electronic representative firms and branches, indexed by geographical region and cross-indexed alphabetically. The association also offers a service including a listing in the ERA *Lines Available Bulletin,* issued monthly to some 1,500 members, and designed to help manufacturers establish representation. In addition, there is a hotline service which enables manufacturers looking for reps in one or two markets to get their messages, within 36 hours, to representatives serving the defined territories. Write:

Electronic Representatives Association
233 East Erie Street
Chicago, IL 60611
$10.00 for the directory

6. Your low-cost ad in the *Manufacturers Agents Newsletter* reaches manufacturers throughout the United States and Canada and in some foreign countries whose principal method of selling their products is through manufacturers' representatives. Your ad in the newsletter can let these manufacturers know who you are, where you are, which territory you cover, and which product lines you are looking for. Write:

Manufacturers Agents Newsletter, Inc.
23573 Prospect Avenue
Farmington, MI 48024

7. Rep Information Service offers a wide range of assistance in securing manufacturers' representatives. Its three fundamental publications are listed below. The service is an excellent source of lines or products for manufacturers' agents. Write:

Rep Information Service
5521 Reseda Boulevard, Suite 17
Tarzana, CA 91356
(213)705-1222

Agent Edition—Rep Information Service is a published biweekly lead service giving sales agents over 1,000 "agents wanted" leads during the life of subscription, plus personal assistance in locating new product lines.

Manufacturers' Edition—Rep Information Service is a service that helps manufacturers find agents, manufacturers' representatives, and trading companies on a worldwide basis, plus regular mailings of published "lines wanted" listings, plus personal referral services to assist in locating agents in specific territories.

Directory of 1,235 Opportunity Offers is a directory listing 1,235 money-making opportunity advertisements, complete with explanation of what was received in experience of answering all these offers, plus detailed explanation of illegal offers, postal regulations, schemes, chain letters, and how money-making opportunity offers work.

8. *Rep World* is a quarterly publication to about 5,000 subscribers; it focuses on manufacturers' representatives. Write:

Rep World
578 Penn Avenue
Sinking Spring, PA 19608
(215)678-3361

9. *Specialty Salesmen and Business Opportunities* is a monthly magazine on direct mailing and direct-to-consumer selling. A directory of agents is also available. Write c/o:

Specialty Salesmen and Business Opportunities
307 North Michigan Avenue
Chicago, IL 60601
(312)726-0743

10. For a free ad in a weekly bulletin which goes to rep members in all fields, worldwide, write:

United Association Manufacturers' Reps
808 Broadway
Kansas City, MO 64105
(816)842-8130

11. *Verified Directory of Manufacturers' Representatives* is published biennially by Manufacturers' Agent Publishing Company. It

presents a geographic listing of about 15,000 manufacturers' representatives (domestic and export) serving all industries, except food products, for the U.S. and Canada. It gives the principal lines carried and trading area covered.

The company also publishes *Manufacturers' Agents' Guide,* containing more than 11,500 manufacturers who distribute through agents. Classification is by industry, and includes name, address of manufacturer, principal products, credit ratings, and name and title of sales executives.

National Association Diversified Manufacturers Representatives
Manufacturers Agents Publishing Company, Inc.
663 Fifth Avenue
New York, NY 10022
(212)682-0326

12. *Who's Who in Electronics* (1977) lists 7,500 electronic manufacturers, 2,500 industrial electronic parts and equipment distributors, 3,500 independent electronic representative firms together with a separate product index section with 1,600 product breakdowns, their manufacturers and distributors. It has information of products, sales volume, marketing areas, key personnel, research facilities, telephone numbers, plant sizes, and new firms and information concerned with the electronics field. Write:

B. Klein Publications
Box 8503
Coral Springs, FL 33065
(305)752-1708

13. *National Directory of Manufacturers' Representatives,* Herbert F. Holtje, will help you find reps on your own. The alphabetical listing of reps includes size of staff, geographic territories, products represented, markets served, and special services. A second section, listed by state, indicates the Standard Industrial Classification (SIC) codes for all the industries called on by reps in that state. Write:

McGraw-Hill Publishing Company
1221 Avenue of the Americas
New York, NY 10020

14. Another good source of information about manufacturers' representatives is:

National Council of Salesmen's Organizations
96 Fulton Street
New York, NY 10038
(212)349-1707

15

Marketing

This chapter offers sources of marketing information that fall into several categories: marketing directories and publications, organizations that exist to help the entrepreneur with the marketing function, and marketing research agencies.

The group of directories offered in this chapter are exceptionally worthwhile because they offer statistics and information of markets and market sizes. In addition, the Small Business Administration offers a guide book called *Library Sources for Information that You May Want to Look At,* which lists many of the marketing directories. This is available at any of the regional SBA offices. Your local library will be helpful in locating directories of marketing for you. Further, college libraries should be investigated as well.

These organizations and publications listed here can be helpful in either selling your product or understanding how your product is sold. On the premise that all entrepreneurial problems will vanish if you sell enough of your product at the right price, these journals and organizations focus on how to expand your sales. You should also examine the other marketing categories and the marketing information available from manufacturer's representatives.

There are a number of agencies which nationally specialize in marketing research for small companies. These agencies and informational sources are listed here. They are especially helpful on an industry-by-industry basis to find your specific source of help within your industry. (This information is particularly vital to the new-product decision process.)

1. *Audits & Surveys* contains a 17 × 22″ retail map of the USA which shows retail sales in nine regional areas. Write:

Audits & Surveys
One Park Avenue
New York, NY 10016

2. *Data Publications* offers a wide range of zip code services. By five-digit zip codes, they offer county and city maps, and income and population data. They also list media sources, newspapers, TV, radio, county codes, which include zip code boundaries on census tract maps, demographic maps, worksheets, postal marketing data, wall maps, sales maps, and population and age projections. Write:

Data Publications
24 East Wesley Street
South Hackensack, NJ 07606

3. The *Directory of National Trade and Professional Associations* provides contacts for information in industry, private companies, governmental agencies, and also tells what individuals to reach regarding specialty projects. Write:

Potomac Books, Inc.
1518 K Street, N.W.
Washington, DC 20005

4. Dun & Bradstreet lists business enterprises in the United States with an indicated worth over $500,000 but less than $1,000,000; a listing of over 30,000 small businesses. For information on the directories listed below, write:

Dun & Bradstreet
99 Church Street
New York, NY 10007

Million Dollar Directory (1978)—contains marketing information on approximately 44,000 businesses, each with a net worth of $1,000,000 or more.

Middle Market Directory (1978)—contains marketing information on approximately 30,000 companies with a net worth of $500,000 to $1,000,000.

Metalworking Directory (1978)—contains information on approximately 42,000 metalworking plants and metal producing plants in the United States.

5. One of the most useful sources of help for all business people is The Gale Research Company which offers a 48-page catalog of all its reference books. Some are invaluable for small businesses. Below are just a few of the more helpful reference books available.

> *Encyclopedia of Business Information Sources,* 3rd ed. (1979), has 17,000 entries in 1,280 subject areas. It can direct you to the best sources of information such as sourcebooks, periodicals, organizations, directories, handbooks, bibliographies, etc.
>
> *Directory Information Service* (1977), which has 500 listings per issue and is issued three times a year, is a periodic reference guide to directories, lists, periodical special issues, rosters, and other guides.
>
> *Encyclopedia of Associations,* 11th ed. (1979), lists 46,000 items, and is a directory of associations indexed by key word, subject, and proper name. Write:

Encyclopedia of Associations
Gale Research Company
Book Tower
Detroit, MI 48226

6. The *Klein Guide to American Directories* is a directory of directories. Indexing is by specific name, and broken down by general industry and associated categories. It is also an excellent mail-order directory. For information, write:

B. Klein Publishing, Inc.
11 Third Street
Rye, NY 10581

The company also offers the following directories:

Directory of Mailing List Houses

*Guide to American Scientific and
    Technical Directories*

*American Register of Exporters and
    Importers*

Business Capital Sources

Directory of Management Consultants

Encyclopedia of U.S. Government Benefits

How and Where to Get Capital

Madison Avenue Handbook

*National Trade and Professional Association
  of the U.S., Canada, and Labor Unions*

News Bureaus in the U.S.

990 Successful Little One-Man Businesses

*Professional's Guide to Public Relations
  Services*

*Small Business Investment Company
  Directory and Handbook*

Syndicated Columnists

Who's Who in Electronics

Worldwide Riches Opportunities

7. *MacRae's Blue Book* is a corporate index which contains an alphabetical product listing identifying manufacturers of each product. Write:

MacRae's Blue Book
100 Shore Drive
Hinsdale, IL 60521

8. The *Manual of Electronic Business Research: A Guide for Marketing and Business Planning* lists 500 publications and organizations which offer information of value to electronic business planners. Information includes frequency of publication, editorial content and scope, special issues or features, primary audience, scope of organization activities and services, including U.S. government publications. It describes indexes, abstracts, bibliographies, directories, guides, periodicals, associations, consultants, etc. Write:

Venture Development Corp.
1 Washington Street
Wellesley, MA 02181

9. *Map Collection in the U.S.A. and Canada,* 3rd ed., ed., David K. Carrington ed. (1978), is a useful marketing tool. Write:

Special Library Association
235 Park Avenue, South
New York, NY 10003
(212)777-8136

10. *Population Profile of the United States: 1976* is a cheap but invaluable marketing tool. This 42-page report contains a wide variety of figures and statistics on changing trends, age groups, etc. (Census Bureau Population Reports, Series P-20, No. 307) write:

Superintendent of Documents
Government Printing Office
Washington, DC 20402

11. *Rand McNally's Commercial Atlas & Manual Guide* provides population, growth, and commercial information on individual states. Write:

Rand McNally
Western Road
Ossining, NY 10562

12. The *Sources of State Information and State Industrial Directories* contain the names and addresses of private and public agencies which furnish information about their states. Under each state are listed industrial directories and directories of manufacturers published by state agencies or private organizations. Write:

Chamber of Commerce of the U.S.A.
1615 H Street, N.W.
Washington, DC 20006
(202)659-6191

13. *Standard & Poor's Register* lists American corporations, directors, and executives with general product classifications. It is an annual directory which lists the products and business listings of 37,000 companies plus the names of 390,000 company officials. The three volumes also list brief biographies of 75,000 officers and directors. This is a classic directory in wide use. Write:

Standard & Poor's Register
345 Hudson Street
New York, NY 10014
(212)924-6400

14. The State Industrial Directories Corporation offers a wide range of state-by-state directories. These directories offer an alphabetical list of companies from A to Z. They are also indexed by geography and by product category. This corporation claims to be America's largest publisher and distributor of state industrial directories. In addition, a business change service is provided in selected areas that identifies businesses that have changed their status of location in the past 12 weeks. Write:

State Industrial Directories Corp.
2 Penn Plaza
New York, NY 10001
(212)564-0304

15. For the most extensive and descriptive listing of American manufacturers and their products, write:

Thomas Register of American Manufacturers
1 Penn Plaza
New York, NY 10001

16. In the *Zip Code Marketing Business Atlas,* various maps and marketing information provide the basis for limitless market research and sales functions. This Atlas includes data on 465 U.S. cities and metropolitan markets, 5 digit county maps, regional sectional center wall map, postal region state maps, demographic information as well as zip code marketing and advertising information plus numeric and alphabetic USPO directory. For information, write:

National Demographic Research
24 E. Wesley Street
So. Hackensack, NJ 07606

17. The *American Marketing Association* has 68 local chapters, mostly in the larger cities, and provides conferences, seminars, and a wide range of services to marketing professionals. It is one of the more broad-based and wide-ranging associations, with 233 collegiate chapters. It publishes several journals, including the *Journal of Marketing* (circulation is about 18,000), which blends applied and academic material; the *Journal of Marketing Research,* which is primarily a quantitative academic journal; and the biweekly newspaper, *Marketing News.* This newspaper offers items of current interest in marketing. The prices and subscription rates for these services are a function of membership, dues, and subscription prices. Write:

American Marketing Association
Suite 606
222 South Riverside Plaza
Chicago, IL 60602
(312)648-0536

18. There are many trade associations, organized to promote the ideas and to coordinate action for the mutual benefit of mem-

bers. Each association can provide information and statistics relevant to its particular trade. For information on either of the two following directories, write:

Columbia Books, Inc.
Room 601
734 15th Street, N.W.
Washington, DC 20005
(202)737-3777

National Trade and Professional Associations of the United States and Canada, and Labor Unions lists 6,000 organizations alphabetically by name. Information is updated by means of annual questionnaires and continuous screening of association literature. This directory includes key word, geographic, budget and executives indexes. A mailing list is also available based on this directory. Each entry in the directory gives the association's full name, address, telephone, name and title of chief executive, date established, number of members, staff size, budget size, information on publications and annual meetings, and historical data.

Washington Representatives of American Associations and Industry lists more than 5,000 individuals, 500 law and PR firms, and more than 4,000 organizations throughout the U.S. which retain representation in Washington. It consists of an alphabetical list of the representatives themselves, showing for whom they work; an alphabetical list of companies and organizations showing who works for them; and a list of companies and organizations by the key word of their titles, by industry category, by the subject of their legislative concerns, or by country groupings.

19. *Direct Marketing* was originally founded by Henry Reed Hoke in 1938 as the *Reporter of Direct Mail Advertising.* In addition to independent subscribers, all members of the Direct Mail Marketing Association receive the magazine as an association service. Write:

Direct Mail Marketing Association
6 East 43rd Street
New York, NY 10017

20. *Growth Industry News* is a newsletter of 8 to 10 pages which focuses on developments within the classic growth industries. It often discusses the emerging areas of new business opportunities. Write:

Growth Industry News
Business Communications Corp., Inc.
Box 20706, 9 Viaduct Road
Stanford, CT 06906

21. The annual edition of *Industrial Marketing,* which is a monthly publication, provides market data arranged by specific industry. It is one of the better sources of marketing information on industrial products. Write:

Industrial Marketing, Inc.
Craine Communication, Inc.
740 Rush Street
Chicago, IL 60611
(212)986-5050

22. Marketing Digests, Inc., publishes a number of marketing publications, including a capsule of what is being said and done in the field in an annotated fashion on a monthly basis. Write:

Marketing Digests, Inc.
466 Central Avenue
Northfield, IL 60093
(312)446-0709

23. The *Marketing Information Guide* is an annotated bibliography of pertinent and timely publications. It is issued bimonthly and serves the marketplace—domestic and foreign—to satisfy the marketing/management information needs of business, academia, and government. It includes semiannual indexes issued in July and December. Write:

The Marketing Information Guide
224 Seventh Street
Garden City, NY 11530
(516)746-6700

24. The National Mail Order Association provides extensive literature on doing business by mail. It is a source of continuing information if your product can be sold by mail. Write:

National Mail Order Association
5818 Venice Boulevard
Los Angeles, CA 90019
(213)934-7986

25. *Selected Business Ventures* is published by the General Electric Company, and presents new and established products, processes, and businesses that are available for purchase or license. It is published monthly in six business categories. Published information includes product advantages, potential applications, and market potential.

New Business Digest lists descriptions of over 500 products, processes, and businesses along with the names and addresses to contact for follow-up. These are items that have been announced previously in the monthly *Selected Business Venture Newsletter* and are still available when the *Digest* is updated. Write:

New Product/New Business Digest
General Electric Company
120 Erie Boulevard
Schenectady, NY 12305
(518)385-2577

26. *Potentials in Marketing* is a marketing-oriented magazine. Write:

Potentials in Marketing
731 Hennepin Avenue
Minneapolis, MN 55403
(612)333-0471

27. If you need a reliable source for talent and materials needed for marketing and sales promotion, there is a unique service available. Promotion Finders can supply writers, artists, printers, direct-mail and communications specialists, package designers, conference leaders, manufacturers of exhibit materials, etc. There is no fee for the client; a finder's fee is paid by the supplier whose services or products are utilized. An up-to-date file of suppliers and experts is maintained at the offices of:

Promotion Finders
1 World Trade Center
Suite 86155
New York, NY 10048
(212)466-1100

28. Sales and Marketing Executives International is a professional association of sales and marketing executives with 22,000 members in 49 nations. These associations are usually focused around a geographic area (city) and listed in local telephone direc-

tories. The company publishes a magazine every other month entitled *Marketing Times*. It also offers sales and marketing courses, seminars, institutes, and workshops. Write:

Sales and Marketing Executives International
380 Lexington Avenue
New York, NY 10017
(212)661-0088, (212)986-9300

29. *Sales Management Magazine* provides estimates for population, effective buying income, and retail sales for U.S. states, counties, and cities; also per capita and per household income. This is a monthly magazine which offers valuable data on market size by product and by region. The annual issue is published in July and is widely used to determine geographic market size data. Write:

Sales Management Magazine
630 Third Avenue
New York, NY 10017

30. *Salesman's Opportunity Magazine* specializes in direct sales of home or consumer product by direct salespeople. Write:

Opportunity Publishing Company
General Advertising and Editorial Offices
John Hancock Center, Suite 1460
875 N. Michigan Avenue
Chicago, IL 60611
(312)337-3350

31. *Bradford's Directory* is a very useful compilation of both marketing research agencies and management consultants in the USA and the world. This is a useful tool to locate sources of marketing and management assistance. Write:

Bradford's Directory
Box 276
Fairfax, VA 22030

32. Creative Strategies, Inc., is a research and consulting firm specializing in high-growth, advanced technology industries. It publishes specialized reports on growth markets; these reports are available as either individual reports or on a subscription basis by the company industry analysis service. A few reports are offered on each subject. Write:

Creative Strategies, Inc.
4340 Stevens Creek Boulevard
Suite 275
San Jose, CA 95129
(408)249-7550

33. *The Marketing Directory* is a valuable source of industry-by-industry analysis which is available from Kline and Company. It is a directory of U.S. and Canadian Marketing surveys and services. Studies in the following industries are also offered: paint industry, paper and pulp industry, packaging industry, and chemical industry. Write:

Charles H. Kline and Company
330 Passaic Avenue
Fairchild, NJ 07006
(201)227-6262

34. A source of market-by-market and industry-by-industry analysis is available from The Morton Research Corporation. It offers a free general brochure of reports and marketing services. Write:

Morton Research Corporation
1745 Merrick Avenue
Merrick, NY 11566

35. Predicasts, Inc. is an integrated business information, market and consumer research firm. Business and economic information is published in various forms, for the diverse needs of management, corporate and market planners, researchers, librarians, and information specialists. The company releases 14 publications and about 30 industry studies each year, offer educational and custom information services and compile and maintain Predicasts Terminal System (PTS), a computerized on-line data base presently containing over 2 million worldwide statistical, market abstract, index, and bibliographic records.

Marketing Ideas is the biweekly newsletter of Predicasts, designed to keep marketing executives supplied with "tips and techniques from around the world." This single newsletter summarizes information from 200 publications. This same source of information also offers a wide range of reviews to entrepreneurs. Write:

Predicasts, Inc.
200 University Circle Research Center
11001 Cedar Avenue
Cleveland, OH 44106
(216)795-3000

36. *Mainly Marketing* is a monthly report on the techniques of marketing highly technical products, especially within the electronics industry. Crash courses are offered for engineers on marketing in a series of "how-to" manuals. Several excellent hardbook series are available.

For information on other services, including consulting, speaking, and the like, ask for the leaflet *When the Written Word Is Not Enough.*

Brochures on these publications and two free samples of *Mainly Marketing* are available to those who send a stamped, self-addressed envelope to:

Warren K. Schoonmaker
Mainly Marketing
P.O. Drawer M
Coram, NY 11727
(516)473-8741

Handbook on Marketing for Electronic Engineers (1979)

Handbook for Principals of Manufacturers Representatives (1979)

Selling through Distributors (1979)

Handbook on Market Research for the Electronics Industry (1979)

The Advertising and Promotion Handbook for the Electronics Industry (1979)

The Handbook on Corporate Criteria for Electronic Companies and Update (1979)

37. Special industry reports are offered by a research firm called Specialists in Business Information, Inc. Reports include a variety of subjects and economics. Write:

Specialists in Business Information, Inc.
3375 Park Avenue
Wantagh, NY 11793
(516)781-7277

38. A research and publications firm, Theta Technology Corporation offers a wide variety of studies on specific industries. The studies are in technical industries, especially medical and instrumentation, but they are very comprehensive. This is an excellent source of marketing research information. Write:

Theta Technology Corporation
462 Ridge Road
Wethersfield, CT 06109
(203)563-9400

39. Listed below are sources of industry data in various miscellaneous areas:

Aircrafts:
Forecast Associates, Inc.
Box 606
Ridgefield, CT 06877
(203)743-0212

Automobiles:
Arthur D. Little, Inc.
25 Acorn Park
Cambridge, MA 02140
(617)864-5770

Clothing:
R. H. Brunswick Associates
303 Georges Street
New Brunswick, NJ 08903
(201)249-1800, (212)349-0781

Fairchild Books
7 East 12th Street
New York, NY 10003

Computers:
International Data Corporation
214 Third Avenue
Waltham, MA 02154
(617)890-3700

Electronics:
International Reserve Development, Inc.
125 Elm Street, Box 1131
New Canaan, CT 06840
(203)966-5615

Warren K. Schoonmaker
Drawer M
Coram, NY 11727
(516)473-8741

Venture Development Corporation
One Washington Street
Wellesley, MA 02181

Energy:
B. J. Esposito
Eastern Research Analysis Corporation
Box 110
Farmington, CT 06032
(203)677-2190

Furniture:
Frost & Sullivan
106 Fulton Street
New York, NY 10038
(212)233-1080

Plastics:
Metra Consulting Group, Ltd.
23 Lower Belgrave Street
London SWIW ONS
UK Phone 01-730-0855
Telex 919173 MCGLDN

Business Communication Company
9 Viaduct Road
Stamford, CT 06906
(203)325-2208

Trade Journals: Annual Issues

The following annual issues, which are published by a number of American trade journals, run in length from a few pages of statistics up to entire issues of useful facts, current trends, and developments.

These trade journals, with their special issues, can be found in many large public libraries as well as in most business-school libraries. Personal copies can be purchased from each publisher or by personal subscription.

Advertising

Advertising Age, "Marketing Profiles of Leaders," includes useful facts
about sales and earnings, leading product lines and brands, and
advertising expenditures as well as names of marketing personnel.
It also publishes annual issues giving "Newspaper Advertising Expenditures for 30 Top Markets" and "100 Markets Section," which
profiles recent significant business developments in each of the top
100 SMSA's. Write:

Advertising Age
Crain Communications
740 Rush Street
Chicago, IL 60611

Air Transport

Air Transport World, "Annual Market Development Issue," gives all
types of airline statistics on vacation markets, charter traffic, U.S.
local, regional, and all-cargo carriers, commuter airlines, etc., and a
section for each continent giving developments for specific airlines.
Write:

Air Transport World
Reinhold Publishing Corp.
600 Summer Street
Stamford, CT 06904

Appliances, Household

Merchandising, "Statistical & Marketing Report," includes ten-year tables for manufacturer sales and retail value of major appliances,
home and automobile electronics, personal communications, tape
audio and hi-fi, and electric and nonelectric housewares industries.
Four other special issues of interest are also offered:

"Statistical & Marketing Forecast"

"Annual Electronics Statistical & Marketing Report"

"Annual Housewares Statistical & Marketing Report"

"Annual Major Appliance Statistical & Marketing Report"

Write:

Merchandising
Billboard Publications, Inc.
1515 Broadway
New York, NY 10036

Chemicals

Chemical & Engineering News, "Facts and Figures for the Chemical Industry," includes production data on top chemicals, financial data for companies, as well as a ranking of the 50 top chemicals and the 50 top chemical producers. Other special issues are "Salary Survey" and "World Chemical Outlook." Write:

Chemical & Engineering News
American Chemical Society
1155 Sixteenth Street, N.W.
Washington, DC 20036

Chemical Week, "Chemical Week 300," gives sales, profits, profit ratios, and per-share data for leading companies in each of 20 chemical-processing industry categories. Write:

Chemical Week
McGraw-Hill
1221 Avenue of the Americas
New York, NY 10020

Electronics

Electronic News, "Looking at the Leaders," provides financial information on the 50 leading U.S. companies and 9 leading foreign ones in the electronics industry. Write:

Electronic News
Fairchild Publications
7 East 12 Street
New York, NY 10003

Food and Food Stores

Beverage World, "Beverage Market Index," lists consumption estimates (in gallons) in 209 local markets, by broad type of beverage (packaged or bulk soft drinks, soft drink mixes, fruit drinks, packaged or draft beer, wines, and distilled spirits). Tables are given for each of these kinds of beverages, showing state consumption, production, and manufacturers' costs. Write:

Beverage World
Keller Publishing
150 Great Neck Road
Great Neck, NY 11021

Chain Store Age Supermarkets, "Sales Manual," contains a product-by-product analysis of supermarket industry sales within 35 categories. Also given is a short "Census of Supermarket Growth" which includes a ranking of the top 100 food chains, the 50 largest co-ops and voluntaries, the 50 local chain pacesetters, and the top convenience stores. Write:

Chain Store Age Supermarkets
Lebhan–Friedman, Inc.
425 Park Avenue
New York, NY 10022

Progressive Grocer, "Annual Report of the Grocery Industry," includes charts and statistics on a wide variety of topics in the grocery industry. Write:

Progressive Grocer
708 Third Avenue
New York, NY 10017

Quick Frozen Foods, "Frozen Foods Almanac," gives retail and institutional poundage and dollar values for types of frozen foods. Write:

Quick Frozen Foods
Harcourt Brace Jovanovich, Inc.
757 Third Avenue
New York, NY 10017

Supermarketing, "Annual Consumer Expenditures Study," includes a three-year summary of the amount of money spent in grocery stores for 455 product lines and data on percentages of total store sales. Write:

Supermarketing
Gralla Publications
1515 Broadway
New York, NY 10036

Marketing Data

Sales and Marketing Management, "Survey of Buying Power," is a special issue that is usually the first place checked by marketing and economic researchers when they seek current estimates showing U.S. and Canadian geographic variations in population, income, and retail business. Write:

Sales and Marketing Management
Bill Communications
633 Third Avenue
New York, NY 10017

Metals and Minerals

Chilton's Iron Age, "Annual Statistical Review," shows statistical trends in metal prices and production. Write:

Chilton's Iron Age
Chilton Book Company
Chilton Way
Radnor, PA 19089

Engineering and Mining Journal, "Annual Review and Outlook for Mineral Commodities," gives surveys for 49 commodities, each written by an authority. Also gives tables of average metal prices, starting from 1910, at the front. Write:

Engineering and Mining Journal
McGraw-Hill
1221 Avenue of the Americas
New York, NY 10020

Motor Vehicles

Automobile News, "Market Data Book Issue," contains useful statistics on U.S. automobiles. Write:

Crain Automotive Group, Inc.
965 E. Jefferson Avenue
Detroit, MI 48207

Paper

Paperboard Packaging, "Annual Industry Statistical Review," reviews paperboard in the economy. Write:

Magazines for Industry, Inc.
777 Third Avenue
New York, NY 10017

Pulp and Paper, "North American Profile," gives statistics on the U.S. and Canadian paper industries. Write:

Miller–Freeman Publications
500 Howard Street
San Francisco, CA 94105

Petroleum

National Petroleum News, "Factbook Issue," features information on petroleum marketing trends, capital spending for marketing, and other useful facts. It also includes a directory with key marketing executives, and a directory of associations. Write:

National Petroleum News
McGraw-Hill
1221 Avenue of the Americas
New York, NY 10020

Oil and Gas Journal, "Forecast/Review," includes statistics that cover U.S. production of crude oil and lease condensate, forecast of supply and demand, and so forth. Write:

Petroleum Publishing
P.O. Box 1260
Tulsa, OK 74101

World Oil, "Forecast-Review Issue," provides statistics and short-range forecasts on such topics as supply and demand, production, and world crude oil production. "International Outlook Issue" discusses trends in exploration, drilling, and production, by region and by country. Write:

World Oil
Gulf Publishing Company
3301 Allen Parkway
P.O. Box 2608
Houston, TX 77001

SIC MARKETING

One of the most useful marketing tools is the federal government's unique Standard Industrial Classification (SIC) numerical

system, which subdivides all of the U.S.'s businesses into finer and more detailed product industries or market segments.

The SIC coding system first divides the nation's overall economy into 10 Basic Industries, each of which is given a range of 2-digit classification codes. Manufacturing, for example, has 20 2-digit codes (20-39) each representing a Major Group, such as Food: SIC 20. These, in turn, are subdivided into 143 3-digit Industry Groups, such as dairy products: SIC 202. At the next level of detail, they are subdivided into 454 4-digit Specific Industries, such as creamery butter: SIC 2021; and natural and processed cheese: SIC 2022.

A complete list of industries, and their definitions, appears in the Standard Industrial Classification Manual: 1972, available from the U.S. Government Printing Office, Washington, DC 20402. A second helpful source for data on shipments and employment is the General Summary Report, 1972 Census of Manufacturers, MC72(1)-1, Census Bureau, Washington, DC 20230.

A helpful explanation of SIC and its drawbacks is contained in "SIC: The Increasing Misapplication of a Useful Tool," by Machinery & Allied Products Institute, Washington, DC.

CHANNELS OF DISTRIBUTION

Many entrepreneurial ventures do not utilize traditional or well established distribution channels to reach their customers. This creates a double problem, one is slower sales and the second is the high cost of sales. Consequently, with an unorthodox product, it's often wise to search for an unusual distribution channel. CEM has found one that looks good to us.

Firms offering products to mail order firms, resident buyers, trading companies, catalog distributors, and agencies who contact government facilities can find value in this sales contact service. Write:

Sales Contact Service
Division of J. E. Distributing Inc.
5521 Reseda Blvd.
P.O. Box "L"
Tarzana, CA 91356
(213)705-1222

AREA CODE 800-THE DIRECTORY OF TOLL FREE NUMBERS

With *Area Code 800,* you can make toll-free long distance calls to hotels, airlines, government agencies, and hundreds of businesses ranging from auto parts dealers to yacht brokers. You may also dial 1-800-555-1212 to discover the toll free number, but this directory often speeds and sharpens the process.

For each organization, the book provides the toll free number, the main office address, the local phone number, and additional descriptive information that is helpful.

The body of the book is organized like the yellow pages of your local telephone book. A comprehensive index is provided as well.

This publication is sold only through the mail. Payments must accompany orders from individuals.

To order your copy of *Area Code 800,* write to Department T3, Lansford Publishing Co., Inc., P.O. Box 8711, San Jose, CA, 95155.

16

Minority Businesses

A minority business, or a business owned by a disadvantaged minority person, is offered special assistance from government programs. The Minority Business Small Business Investment Company (MESBIC) is an example of the government's help in business owned or controlled by minority groups. The information sources here are in addition to those listed elsewhere. These sources, in addition to the others, should be helpful for a minority business enterprise seeking to grow. The reader should also refer to the relevant sections of Chapter 10, "Franchising."

1. A listing of all *Minority Enterprise Small Business Investment Companies* (MESBIC) is available via a monthly newsletter called *AAMESBIC News.* Write:

AAMESBIC News
1413 K Street, N.W., 13th Floor
Washington, DC 20005
(202)347-8600
Circulation: 1,000

2. A list of the largest black owned or operated businesses is published by *Black Enterprise,* a monthly magazine for black business executives. Write:

Black Enterprise
295 Madison Avenue
New York, NY 10017
(212)889-8220
Circulation: 217,000

3. The Minority Business Information Institute, Inc. is a research and reference center in New York City, partially funded by the U.S. Department of Commerce, Office of Minority Business Enterprise. MBII was formed in June 1971 to answer the need for a specialized reference center focusing on minority economic development.

The MBII library's holdings consist of approximately 1,500 volumes, subscriptions to about 130 periodicals and newspapers, 30 newsletters, and 17 vertical file drawers of clippings, pamphlets, and other nonbook materials.

Although the emphasis is on minority business, related areas such as history of the black movement, the Caribbean and Africa, and relevant biographies, are also in its scope of coverage.

The library is open by appointment to qualified researchers working in the field of minority economic development. The staff also answers brief written and telephoned reference inquiries. An MBII newsletter (circulation about 4,000) is published quarterly and distributed to OMBE-funded organizations and other public agencies. It is most effective in the New York region. There is no charge for the services of the library. Write:

The Minority Business Information Institute, Inc.
295 Madison Avenue, 19th Floor
New York, NY 10017
(212)889-8220

4. *The Minority Executive Newsletter* is published to aid black business owners and executives. Write:

Minority Executive Newsletter
Resource, Placement, and Development
77 Maple Street
Springfield, MA 01105
(413)733-3121
Circulation: 250

5. The *National Memo* is a monthly newsletter that provides timely information on economic and business issues and events. *The Corporate Guide to Minority Vendors* is a resource manual for use by corporate executives and minority entrepreneurs to strengthen the communications network between the two sectors. National Business League also maintains a file of minority vendors and a comprehensive list of corporate procurement and purchasing agents for constituents. Subscription fee is included in the League membership dues. Write:

National Memo
Corporate Guide to Minority Vendors
4324 Georgia Avenue, N.W.
Washington, DC 20011
(202)829-5900
Circulation: 15,000

National Business League
4324 Georgia Avenue, N.W.
Washington, DC 20011

6. The U.S. Government Printing Office, Washington, DC, 20402, offers the following publications for minority businesspeople:

Minority Business Development Administration Hearings, 94th Congress, 2nd Session on S. 2617 to Establish an Office for Minority Business Development and Assistance in the Department of Commerce, April 13, 1976.

Minority Markets (1975), a report that analyzes recent trends in minority consumer expenditures and the factors influencing these expenditures and makes projections of future market trends and minority spending.

Minority Owned Businesses: Blacks (1974) contains data on businesses owned by blacks. Statistics are given on the number of firms, gross receipts, and numbers of paid employees distributed geographically by industry, size of firm, and legal form of firm organization. Maps and tables are included.

ORGANIZATIONS ASSISTING CORPORATIONS IN DOING BUSINESS WITH MINORITY-OWNED COMPANIES

1. The National Minority Purchasing Council has profiles of about 10,000 minority enterprises and also provides information about minority purchasing programs of large corporations. Write:

National Minority Purchasing Council
1925 K Street, N.W.
Washington, DC 20006
(202)466-7077

2. Office of Minority Business Enterprise funds organizations familiar with minority-owned companies in specialized areas such as

construction and manufacturing. The agency and its six regional offices also keep lists of companies. Write:

Office of Minority Business Enterprise
14th and Constitution, N.W.
Washington, DC 20230
(202)377-2654

3. The Interagency Council for Minority Business Enterprise can provide information on minority set-aside programs within the federal bureaucracy; it also has a computerized list of about 30,000 minority-owned companies. Write:

Interagency Council for Minority Business Enterprise
Department of Commerce
14th and Pennsylvania, N.W., Room 6627
Washington, DC 20230
(202)377-4625

4. The Small Business Administration maintains lists of minority small businesses. Write:

U.S. Small Business Administration
1441 L Street, N.W.
Washington, DC 20416
(202)653-6407

5. Other venture capital organizations specializing in minority companies include:

Urban National Corp.
177 Milk Street
Boston, MA 02109
(617)482-3651

Presbyterian Economic Development Corp.
475 Riverside Drive
New York, NY 10027
(212)870-2125

Opportunity Funding Corp.
2021 K Street, N.W., Suite 701
Washington, DC 20006
(202)833-9580

12

Patents and Inventions

The information and sources in this chapter comprise one of the most complete lists compiled on this subject. While there are some additional books on how to obtain patents and how to protect trademarks and inventions, this source guide should offer most of the fundamental information for inventors.

THE NATIONAL TECHNICAL INFORMATION SERVICE

The National Technical Information Service of the U.S. Department of Commerce is the central source for the public sale of U.S. and foreign government-sponsored research, development, and engineering reports, and other analyses prepared by national and local governmental agencies, their contractors or grantees, or by special technology groups. NTIS also is a central source for federally generated machine-processable data files and manages the Federal Software Exchange Center.

NTIS ships about 20,000 information-products daily as one of the world's leading processors of specialty information. It supplies its customers with about 4 million documents and microforms annually. The NTIS information collection exceeds one million titles and all are available for sale. About 105,000 titles are stocked in multiple

161

copies. Current lists of best-selling reports describe those most in demand. About 150,000 of NTIS's million research report titles are of foreign origin.

NTIS sells technical reports and other information products of specialized interest under provisions of Title 15 U.S. Code 1151-7. This law, which established a clearinghouse for scientific, technical, and engineering information, also directs NTIS to recover its costs from the sales of its products and services.

NTIS, therefore, is a unique government agency operating very much as a business; it is sustained only by its customers. All the costs of its products and services, including salaries, marketing, promotion, and postage are paid from sales income, not by tax-supported congressional appropriation.

Timely and continuous reporting to subscribers is ensured by agreements between NTIS and federal research-sponsoring organizations and special technology groups. NTIS is the marketing coordinator for the latter, for their publications, technical inquiries, and special analyses.

Customers may quickly locate summaries of interest from among some 500,000 federally sponsored research reports completed and published from 1964 to date, using the agency's on-line computer search service (NTISearch) or the more than 1,000 published searches in stock. About 70,000 new technical summaries and reports are added annually. Copies of the whole research reports on which the summaries are based are sold by NTIS in paper or microform. For information write:

National Technical Information Service
U.S. Department of Commerce
5285 Port Royal Road
Springfield, VA 22161
(703)557-4642

The NTIS Bibliographic Data File (on magnetic tape) includes unpublished research summaries and is available for lease. The computer products of other federal agencies are sold or leased by NTIS.

Current summaries of new research reports and other specialized information in various categories of interest are published in some 26 weekly newsletters (weekly government abstracts), and these are indexed. An all-inclusive biweekly journal *(Government Reports Announcements & Index)* is published for librarians, technical

information specialists, and those requiring all the summaries in a single volume.

A standing order microfiche service, *Selected Research in Microfiche* (SRIM), automatically provides subscribers with the full texts of research reports specially selected to satisfy their individual requirements. Automatic distribution of paper copies also is available.

NTIS is the central source for information about government inventions. It handles the promotion, licensing, and foreign patent filing for those inventions assigned to the Department of Commerce.

Additional services, such as the coordination, packaging, and marketing of unusual information for individuals and organizations, may be specially designed.

The 26 *Weekly Government Abstract* newsletters provide 100,000 readers with timely research summaries within two weeks of their receipt by NTIS from the originating agencies. WGA's ensure maximum coverage of 26 areas of government research in brief and convenient form and at minimal cost. Summaries of special interest are highlighted at the front of each issue.

The last issue of the year is a subject index containing up to ten cross-references for each research summary indexed. The WGA titles are:

Administration

Agriculture and Food

Behavior and Society

Biomedical Technology and Engineering

Building Technology

Business and Economics

Chemistry

Civil Engineering

Communication

Computers, Control and Information Theory

Electrotechnology

Energy

Environmental Pollution and Control

Government Inventions for Licensing

Health Planning

Industrial and Mechanical Engineering
Library and Information Sciences
Materials Sciences
Medicine and Biology
Natural Resources and Earth Sciences
NASA Earth Resources Survey Program
Ocean Technology and Engineering
Physics
*Problem Solving Information for State
    and Local Governments*
Transportation
Urban Technology

Numbers to call:

To Check on Orders	(703)557-4660
Subscriptions	(703)557-4630
Computer Products	(703)557-4763
New Orders for Documents and Reports	(703)557-4650
NTISearches	(703)557-4642
SRIM	(703)557-4640
Pickup Orders, Washington Information Center and Bookstore (9 A.M.–4:30 P.M.):	(202)724-3382
after 4:30 P.M.:	(202)724-3383
At Springfield Operations Center	(703)557-4650
Accounting	(703)557-4970
Fast Ordering	(703)557-4700
Other Information	(703)557-4600
Telecopier or 3M Facsimile Service	(703)321-8199
Telex	89-9405

HELPFUL PUBLICATIONS

1. *How to Get a Patent* is a booklet about America's patent law. For a copy of the booklet, write:

Consumer Information Center
Department 126E
Pueblo, CO 81009

2. *The Inventors News,* published by the Inventors Club of America, offers information on protection before patent, marketing and manufacturing, and development. The Inventors Club of America is a nonprofit organization established to help inventors who are willing to help themselves. They show you ways to develop and market your ideas yourself. Write:

Inventors News
Box 3799
Springfield, MA 01101
(413)737-0670

or

Inventors Club of America
National Headquarters
1562 Main Street
Box 3799
Springfield, MA 01101
(413)737-0670

3. *Action* is published regularly to serve as a medium of communication between members of the Association for the Advancement of Invention and Innovation, open to inventors, entrepreneurs, research directors, businesspeople, scientists, engineers, lawyers, patent attorneys and agents, educators, patent examiners, economists, and others who support the objectives of the Association. Write:

The Association for the Advancement of Invention and Innovation
Suite 301, Crystal Mall 1
1911 Jefferson Davis Highway
Arlington, VA 22202

4. *New Products and Processes Newsletter,* a publication of Newsweek, Inc., is a source for the most comprehensive, timely, and usable new product information available anywhere. Each issue contains reviews of 75 to 100 new products and processes including complete product descriptions, many with illustrations, and availability for manufacturing, sales of licensing arrangements. Write:

New Products and Processes
Newsweek International
444 Madison Avenue
New York, NY 10022

5. *New Tech* is a new publication for an entrepreneur or a small businessperson/investor. It will help you to keep up to date on new technology as it relates to entrepreneurial opportunity. Write:

NewTech
1212 Avenue of the Americas
New York, NY 10036

WHERE TO GET HELP ON PATENTS AND LICENSING

Have a good idea? Is it patentable? Where can you turn for help? Here is a comprehensive listing of help available, arranged as follows:

1. Inventors' associations.
2. Invention brokers.
3. Publications.
4. Other.

1. *Inventors' associations.* Arrange meetings with inventors to educate them in aspects of the patenting process and the seeking of licenses:

Institute of American Inventors
635 F Street, NW
Washington, DC 20004
(202)737-6616

Inventors Assistance League, Inc.
1815 W. 6th Street
Los Angeles, CA 90057
(213)483-4850

Mortic Corp.
2030 E. 4th Street
Suite 149
Santa Ana, CA 92705
(714)835-4353

The United Inventors and Scientists of
  America
2503 W. 7th Street
Los Angeles, CA 90057
(213)389-3003

Inventors Club of America
1562 Main Street
Box 3799
Springfield, MA 01101
(413)737-0670

2. *Invention brokers.* Firms specializing in getting licensor and licensee together:

Battelle Development Corp.
505 King Avenue
Columbus, OH 43201
(614)424-6424

Control Data Technotec, Inc.
8100 34th Avenue South
Minneapolis, MN 55440
(612)853-4405

Dr. Dvorkovitz and Associates
P.O. Box 1748
Ormond Beach, FL 32044
(904)677-7033

Eurosearch Marketing, Inc.
663 Fifth Avenue
New York, NY 10022
(212)355-5633

International Inventors, Inc.
Suite 309
4900 Leeburg Pike
Alexandria, VA 22303
(703)931-3130

Invention Marketing, Inc.
701 Smithville Street
12th Floor, Arott Building
Pittsburgh, PA 15222
(412)288-1300

Invention Marketing, Inc.
Suite L-5 The Vendome
160 Commonwealth Avenue
Boston, MA 02116
(617)266-7696

Kessler Sales Corp
Kessler Bldg.
1247 Napoleon Street
Fremont, OH 43420
(419)332-6496

Licensing Management Corp.
80 Park Avenue
New York, NY 10016
(212)682-5944

Arthur D. Little, Inc.
Invention Management Corp.
Acorn Park
Cambridge, MA 02140
(617)864-5770

L and M Product Finders
752 Guinda
Palo Alto, CA 94301
(415)322-7082

Promotional Marketing, Inc.
615 Milwaukee Avenue
Glenview, IL 60025
(312)729-6100

REFAC Technology Development Corp.
122 E. 42nd Street
New York, NY 10017
(212)687-4741

Research Corporation
405 Lexington Avenue
New York, NY 10016
(212)695-9301

University Patents, Inc.
2777 Summer Street
Stamford, CT 08905
(203)325-2285

3. Publications. Several specialized publications seek to match products offered for license with licensors:

American Bulletin of International
   Technology Transfer
International Advancement
5455 Wilshire Blvd.
Suite 1009
Los Angeles, CA 90036
(213)931-7481

International New Product Newsletter
Box 191
390 Stuart Street
Boston, MA 02117
(617)631-3225

New Products and Processes
Newsweek International
444 Madison Avenue
New York, NY 10022
(212)350-2000

Technology Mart
Thomas Publishing Co.
One Penn Plaza
New York, NY 10001
(212)695-0500

Technology Transfer Times
Benwill Publishers
167 Corey Road
Brookline, MA 02146
(617)5470

Institute for Inventions and
   Innovations, Inc.
85 Irving Street
Box 436
Arlington, MA 02174
(617)646-0093

4. Other. One publisher produces two excellent newsletters which may prove of interest to you.

A. *Invention Management.* An informational and educational journal for individuals and companies concerned with intellectual

property. This monthly publication is excellent in the area of patents, technology transfer, and inventions.

B. *Copyright Management,* also published monthly, deals with copyrights, licensing, and trademarks.

For either newsletter, write:

Institute for Invention and
   Innovation, Inc.
85 Irving Street
Arlington, MA 02174
(617)646-0093

5. *Federal Laboratory Consortium (FLC).* In each of the 180 federal research and development laboratories, there is a person with the title "technical transfer representative" whose job is to respond to questions from businesses. The good news is that there is no charge. A directory is available from:

FLC Headquarters
Federal Laboratory Program Manager
National Science Foundation ISPT
Washington, DC 20550
(202)634-7996

6. *Industrial Application Centers.* A more expensive source of information exists at seven university-based technical information centers. A study costs between $5,000 and $10,000, but literature searches are also available. These organizations draw on a vast array of business, government, and trade organizations data. The locations are:

New England Research Applications Center, Mansfield Professional Park, Storrs, CT 06268; North Carolina Science and Technology Research Center, P.O. Box 12235, Research Triangle Park, NC 27709; Knowledge Availability Systems Center, University of Pittsburgh, Pittsburgh, PA 15260; Aerospace Research Application Center, Administration Building, 1201 E. 38 St., Indianapolis, IN 47401; Technology Use Studies Center, Southeastern Oklahoma State University, Durant, OK 74701; Technology Application Center, University of New Mexico, Albuquerque, NM 87131; and Western Research Application Center, University of Southern California, University Park, Los Angeles, CA 90007.

18

The Small Business Administration

The SBA is a government agency focusing on helping small companies throughout the country. It employs 4,000 people and offers a great range of services to entrepreneurs. Recently, the SBA established an Office of Advocacy reporting directly to the president. This office helps and advocates small-business programs throughout the government and the country.

The U.S. Small Business Administration is an independent federal agency created by Congress in 1953 to assist, counsel, and champion American small business. The agency provides prospective, new, and established members of the small-business community with financial assistance, management training and counseling, and help in getting a fair share of government contracts through over 100 offices in all parts of the nation. In order to provide quick service, SBA has delegated decision-making authority in the vast majority of the programs to its field offices. Information about the SBA can be obtained by visiting one of these local field offices. To find the SBA office in your city, look in the telephone directory under "U.S. Government, Small Business Administration." SBA also serves as small-business chief advocate in the halls of the federal government, and administers the government's home, personal property, and business Disaster Loan Recovery Program.

Eligibility For SBA Assistance

Most small independent businesses (except speculative firms, newspapers, radio and television stations, and other forms of the

	ANNUAL RECEIPTS NOT EXCEEDING	AVERAGE ANNUAL NO. OF EMPLOYEES NOT EXCEEDING
A. For Loans		
Service	*$2–$8 million	
Retail	*$2–$7½ million	
Wholesale	*$9½–$22 million	
General Construction	*$9½ million	
Special Trade Construction	*$5 million	
Farming and Related Activities	*$275,000	
Manufacturing		*250–1,500
B. For SBA Help in Winning Government Procurement Contracts		
Service	*$2–$9 million	
General Construction	$12 million	
Manufacturing		500–1,500

C. For Small Business Investment Company (SBIC) or 301 (d) SBICs (formerly called MESBICs) Assistance

All industries: Assests not exceeding $9 million.
Net worth not exceeding $4 million.
Average net income (after taxes) not
exceeding $400,000.

D. For Surety Bonds	
Service	(Same as in Section A above)
Retail	(Same as in Section A above)
Wholesale	(Same as in Section A above)
Manufacturing	(Same as in Section A above)
Special Trade Construction	(Same as in Section A above)
General Construction	$2 million

*Varies by industry (call local SBA office, if specifics are needed).

Note: The size standards listed in Sections A and C increase by 25% if the business is located in a labor surplus area.

media, and, normally, businesses engaged in gambling) are eligible for SBA assistance. Under the Disaster Loan Recovery Program, owners of small and large businesses, homeowners, and renters are eligible to apply for SBA Disaster Loan Assistance. SBA defines a small business as one that is independently owned and operated, is not dominant in its field, and meets the preceding criteria stated in maximums described on page 172.

Financial Assistance

For the small business that needs money and cannot borrow it on reasonable terms from conventional lenders, SBA offers a broad range of loan programs. The agency may either participate with a bank or other lender in a loan, or guarantee up to 90 percent of any loan a bank or other lender agrees to make. By law only if the bank or other lender cannot provide funds under either of these methods may SBA consider lending the entire amount as a direct government loan, if the funds are available. However, the demand for direct loans traditionally exceeds SBA's supply of direct loan monies, and as a result, most of SBA's loans are made in cooperation with banks. SBA loans may be used for:

> Business construction, expansion, or conversion
> The purchase of machinery, equipment, facilities,
>   supplies, or materials
> Working capital

Regular Business Loans

Under *Section 7(a)* of the Small Business Act, as amended, SBA is authorized to make regular business loans to small firms on a direct, participation, or guaranteed basis.

Economic Opportunity Loans

The agency grants economic opportunity loans to help persons who are socially or economically disadvantaged own their own businesses. Both prospective and established small firms are eligible for these loans.

Local Development Company Loans

Local development companies are made up of local citizens whose primary purpose is to improve their area's economy through assisting small business concerns and may apply for SBA loans to help buy land, build new factories, shopping centers, etc., acquire machinery and equipment, and expand or convert existing facilities, provided that the project will assist at least one small business. Local development companies must provide a reasonable share of the cost of the project to be financed, usually 20 percent of the total amount.

State Development Company Loans

State development companies, which are organized by a specific act of a state legislature to assist statewide business growth and development, including small business growth, may apply for SBA state development company loans, the monies from which are then used to supply small business concerns within the state with long-term loans and equity capital.

Pool Loans

Pool loans are made to corporations formed and capitalized by groups of small-business companies for the purchase of raw materials, equipment, inventory, or supplies to be used in their individual businesses. These loans may also be used to obtain the benefits of research and development or establish research and development facilities.

Revolving Line of Credit Guarantees

A small firm that cannot obtain a line of credit from a bank in order to fulfill construction or other contracts may apply to SBA for a revolving line of credit guarantee. The agency can guarantee the credit extended by the bank for a continuous period of up to 18 months.

Displaced Business Loans

Small firms suffering substantial economic injury because they are displaced by federally aided renewal or other construction projects are eligible to apply for SBA displaced business loans to help

relocate or reestablish. Reasonable upgrading of the business while it is being reestablished is permitted.

Handicapped Assistance Loans

Physically handicapped small-business owners and public and private nonprofit organizations which employ and operate in the interests of physically handicapped persons are eligible for handicapped assistance loans.

Physical Damage Natural Disaster Recovery Loans

When the president or the administrator of SBA declares a specific geographical area a disaster area as a result of a natural disaster such as a hurricane, a widespread fire, a tornado, flooding, or earthquake, homeowners, renters, and the owners of small and large businesses within the disaster area may apply to SBA for home, personal property, and business disaster recovery loans to repair or replace their damaged or destroyed property.

Economic Injury Natural Disaster Loans

When the president, the secretary of agriculture, or the administrator of SBA declares a specific geographical area a disaster area as a result of a natural disaster, the owners of small businesses that have suffered economic losses as a result of the disaster may apply to SBA for economic injury disaster loans for working capital and funds to pay financial obligations the owners could have met if the disaster had not occurred.

Product Disaster Loans

SBA makes product disaster loans to small firms that have suffered substantial economic injury because they cannot process or market a product for human consumption because of disease or toxicity resulting from either natural or undetermined causes.

Base Closing Economic Injury Loans

Base closing economic injury loans are made to small firms that have suffered or will suffer substantial economic injury as a result of

the closing of a major federal military installation or a severe reduction in the scope and size of operations of a major military installation. These loans can be used to help a small business continue in business at its existing location, reestablishing its business, purchase a new business, or establish a new business.

Strategic Arms Economic Injury Loans

SBA is authorized to make these loans to assist or refinance the existing indebtedness of any small business concern directly or indirectly affected by a significant reduction in scope or amount of federal support for any project as a result of any international agreement limiting the development of strategic arms or the installation of strategic arms facilities.

Emergency Energy Shortage Loans

These loans were authorized by amendments made to the Small Business Act, as amended in August 1974. Such loans may be made to small businesses that are suffering economic injury as a result of shortages of fuel, electrical energy, or energy-producing resources, or shortages of raw or processed materials resulting from shortages of energy.

Regulatory Economic Injury Loans

Small firms that must make changes in their equipment, facilities, or operations because of new federal laws and regulations, and any ensuing state or local laws and regulations, are eligible for SBA regulatory economic injury loans, if the agency determines that the concerns are likely to suffer substantial economic injury without such loans. Examples of federal regulations and laws which have required major changes in small firms are: the Federal Coal Mine and Safety Act of 1969, the Egg Products Act, the Wholesome Poultry Products Act, the Wholesome Meat Products Act of 1967, the Occupational Safety and Health Act of 1970, the Clean Air Act of 1970, and the Federal Water Pollution Control Act of 1974.

Surety Bonds

SBA is committed to making the binding process accessible to small and emerging contractors who, for whatever reasons, find

bonding unavailable to them. The agency is authorized to guarantee to a qualified surety up to 90 percent of losses incurred under bid, payment, or performance bonds issued to contractors on contracts valued up to $1 million. The contracts may be for construction, supplies, or services provided by either a prime or subcontractor for governmental or nongovernmental work.

Small Business Investment Companies (SBICs)

Another way in which SBA helps finance small firms is through privately owned and operated small business investment companies (SBICs). SBICs are licensed, regulated and, in certain cases, financed by the agency. They supply venture capital and long-term financing to small firms for expansion, modernization, and sound financing for their operations. Some SBICs also provide management assistance to small businesses.

301(d) Small Business Investment Companies [301(d) SBIC's]

In cooperation with the U.S. Department of Commerce, SBA has instituted a specialized application of the SBIC principle in the licensing of 301(d) small business investment companies, formerly called minority enterprise SBICs. The 301(d) SBICs are dedicated solely to assisting small-business concerns owned and managed by socially or economically disadvantaged persons. Such disadvantage may arise from cultural, social, chronic economic circumstances or background, or other similar causes. This category often includes, but is not restricted to, Black Americans, American Indians, Spanish-Americans, Oriental Americans, Eskimos, and Aleuts. Service in the Armed Forces during the Vietnam War may be a contributing factor in establishing social or economic disadvantage. 301(d) SBICs are owned and operated by established industrial or financial concerns, community or business-oriented economic development organizations, or private or public investors who combine money and management resources for assistance to disadvantaged entrepreneurs.

Procurement Assistance

Each year, the federal government contracts with private companies for billions of dollars worth of goods and services. SBA helps small businesses obtain a fair share of this government business. In

recent years, small business' share has added up to about one-third of the total federal procurement.

Federal procurement specialists in SBA offices throughout the country counsel small businesses on how to prepare bids and obtain prime contracts and subcontracts, direct them to government agencies that buy the products or services they supply, help them get their names placed on bidders' lists, assist in obtaining drawings and specifications for proposed purchases, and offer many related services, which include supplying leads on research and development projects, new technology, and assistance in technology transfer.

Prime Contracts

Government purchasing offices "set aside" contracts or portions of contracts for exclusive bidding by small business. SBA procurement center representatives stationed at major military and civilian procurement installations recommend additional "set-asides," refer small-business sources to contracting officers, assist small concerns with contracting problems, and recommend relaxation of unduly restrictive specifications. SBA also checks the effectiveness of small-business programs administered by procurement installations.

Subcontracts

SBA develops subcontracting opportunities for small business by maintaining close contact with prime contractors and referring qualified small firms to them. The agency has developed agreements and close working relationships with the majority of the nation's top 100 prime contractors who cooperate by offering small firms opportunities to compete for their subcontracts.

Certificates of Competency

If a small firm is the low bidder on a federal contract, and the contracting officer questions the firm's ability to perform the contract, the firm may ask SBA for a certificate of competency (COC), which will certify its competency to perform the contract. When a firm applies for a COC, SBA makes an on-site study of its facilities, management, performance record, and production capacity in relationship to the contract in question. If SBA determines that the firm is capable of performing the contract within the required time

period, the agency issues a COC attesting to that fact. The contracting officer must then award the contract to the small firm.

Procurement Source Files

Each of the agency's ten regional offices maintains a list of small businesses which are located within the region and can provide products and services to major private corporations and federal, state, and local government agencies. Large companies and government agencies that want to buy from a small business are referred to the regional procurement source files.

Contract Opportunity Workshops

Federal contracting agencies and prime contractors often present their needs and requirements and discuss bidding opportunities at contracting workshops. SBA participates in these meetings, and SBA field offices can provide information about scheduled workshops to interested small businesses.

Property Sales and Energy-Related Mineral Lease Contracts

Annually, the federal government sells large amounts of surplus real and personal property and natural resources, such as timber. SBA works with the government agencies that are selling the property and resources to assure that small businesses have an opportunity to buy a fair share of them. The agency also insures that small firms operating in energy-related industries obtain an equitable portion of federal energy-related mineral lease contracts.

Technology Assistance

Billions of federal dollars are spent for research and development of new technologies for space and undersea exploration, health and welfare programs, national defense projects, and a broad range of other subjects. In addition to making sure that small businesses get a fair share of federal research and development contracts, SBA sees to it that any produced technology that has or may have commercial utilization is made available to the small-business community. The agency provides advice, counsel, and technology search and retrieval help to small firms requiring technological assis-

tance for production techniques, modernization processes, and new-product development. In cooperation with other government agencies, SBA operates a technology information transfer service through brochures which briefly describe new technology that may be of use to small businesses.

8(a) Business Development

Section 8(a) of the Small Business Act, as amended, authorizes SBA to enter into contracts with any federal department, agency, or office that has procurement powers. This authority, in combination with other financial, technical, and management resources at SBA's disposal, allows the agency to contract with other federal departments and agencies to supply their goods, services, and construction needs and then subcontract the actual performance of the work to small-business concerns that are owned and controlled by socially or economically disadvantaged persons. The *8(a)* program assists in the expansion and development of existing, newly organized, or prospective small firms and helps them gain the ability to compete independently and effectively in the nation's marketplace.

Help for Minority Vendors

SBA's Minority Vendors' Program identifies small businesses that are owned and controlled by socially or economically disadvantaged persons and then can furnish products and services to major private corporations and federal, state, and local government agencies. The agency then refers large corporations or government agencies interested in buying a product or service from such a firm to the minority vendors listed in SBA's computer bank.

Management Assistance

Most businesses fail because of a lack of good management. For this reason, SBA places special emphasis on improving the management ability of small business owners and managers. The agency Management and Technical Assistance Program is extensive and diversified. It includes free individual counseling by retired and active business executives, university students and other professionals, courses, conferences, workshops, and problem clinics, and a wide range of publications.

Counseling

SBA helps small-business owners obtain individual assistance with management problems, and counsels prospective small-business owners who want management information on specific types of business enterprises.

SCORE/ACE and Professional Association Volunteers

In addition to the help provided by SBA management assistance staff, management counseling can be obtained from the members of the Service Corps of Retired Executives/Active Corps of Executives (SCORE/ACE) and numerous national professional associations, all of which have volunteered to help prospective small-business owners and troubled small businesses. SBA tries to match the need of a specific small business with the expertise of one of its thousands of volunteers. Then an assigned counselor visits the small business in question. Through careful observation, a detailed analysis is made of the business and its problems. If the problems are complex, the counselor may call on other volunteer experts to help the small business. Finally, a plan is offered to remedy the trouble and assist the business through its critical period.

Small Business Institute (SBI)

Through the Small Business Institute, senior and graduate students of the nation's leading schools of business provide on-site management counseling to small-business owners. The students are guided by a faculty member and an SBA management assistant officer, and they receive academic credit for their participation in the Institute. Although SBA counseling is usually restricted to SBA clients (loan recipients and small firms performing federal contracts), it is available if there are enough student counselors in the program to assist all small-business owners who want SBI help.

Call Contracts

The Call Contracts Program provides management and technical assistance to small-business entrepreneurs from professional consulting firms under contract with SBA. The kind of assistance provided ranges from junior and senior accounting to complex engineering.

181

Courses

Business management courses concerning planning, organizing, and controlling a business, as distinguished from day-to-day operating activities, are co-sponsored by SBA and public and private educational institutions and business associations. The courses are generally held during the evening, and last from six to eight weeks.

Conferences, Workshops, and Clinics

Conferences covering subjects such as working capital, business forecasting, and diversification of markets are held for established businesses on a regular basis. SBA also conducts prebusiness workshops dealing with capital requirements, sources of financing, types of businesses, business organization, and business site selection for prospective small-business owners. Clinics concerning specific problems of small firms in specific industrial categories are held on an as-needed basis.

Foreign Trade

SBA works closely with the U.S. Department of Commerce and other agencies to help generate small-business export activity and to furnish information on export opportunities to the small business community.

Publications

SBA issues hundreds of management, technical, and marketing publications which have been valuable aids to millions of established or prospective managers of small firms. Most of these management publications are available from the agency free of charge, while others can be obtained for a small fee from the Superintendent of Documents at the U.S. Government Printing Office in Washington, DC. In addition to management assistance publications, brochures explaining each of the agency's areas of assistance are available at all SBA offices.

Minority Small Business

SBA has combined its efforts with those of private industry, banks, local communities, and other federal agencies to increase substantially the number of small businesses that are owned and

182

operated by citizens who are members of socially or economically disadvantaged minority groups. In addition to the Economic Opportunity Loan Program, the 8(a) Business Development Program, the Minority Vendors' Program, and the 301(d) Small Business Investment Company Program mentioned previously, the agency's overall Minority Small Business Program brings all of SBA's services together in a coordinated effort to make more sound business opportunities available to socially and economically disadvantaged individuals. A minority small-business overview staff located in the agency's Washington, DC central office is assisted by minority small-business field representatives stationed in SBA's ten regional offices and many district offices. Minority small-business staff members cooperate with local business development organizations and explain to potential minority entrepreneurs how SBA's services and programs can help them become successful business owners.

Advocacy

SBA actively and forcefully represents the small-business community at national, state, and local government levels and with business, professional, and trade associations and organizations. The agency's Advocacy Office endeavors to find out what problems small businesses are having, calls these problems to the attention of government officials, and attempts to develop solutions to these problems. SBA is the focal point for complaints, criticisms, and suggestions from small businesses about other federal departments and SBA, and the Advocacy Office counsels individual small-business owners and groups of small firms on the best ways to resolve their difficulties with such problems as the burden of complying with government regulations, paperwork requirements, and product liability.

Women in Business

Prospective and established women business owners are eligible for all of SBA's programs and services. The agency understands the unique problems faced by women in business and is on constant alert to see that special attention is given to them. All too many women in business who need help are not coming to SBA for assistance, and the agency has started a major national outreach program to encourage more women to apply for SBA's services and start businesses of their own.

Help for Veterans of the Armed Forces

Veterans of the Armed Forces have fought to keep the freedom that has made our country strong and helped us maintain and improve individualism and free enterprise as the basis of our economic system. Specifically designated SBA veterans' affairs officers assure that veterans receive the benefits of all of the programs the agency provides and that special consideration is given to veterans and their survivors and dependents.

All SBA programs are administered to insure nondiscrimination on the basis of race, color, religion, sex, age, marital status, national origin, or on any other basis not related to credit worthiness or lawful qualifications.

SBA Field Offices

Agana, GU	Concord, NH
Albany, NY	Coral Gables, FL
Albuquerque, NM	Corpus Christi, TX
Anchorage, AK	Dallas, TX
Atlanta, GA	Denver, CO
Augusta, ME	Des Moines, IA
Baltimore, MD	Detroit, MI
Biloxi, MS	Eau Claire, WI
Birmingham, AL	Elmira, NY
Boise, ID	El Paso, TX
Boston, MA	Fairbanks, AK
Buffalo, NY	Fargo, ND
Camden, NJ	Fresno, CA
Casper, WY	Greenville, NC
Charleston, WV	Harrisburg, PA
Charlotte, NC	Hartford, CT
Chicago, IL	Hato Rey, PR
Cincinnati, OH	Helena, MT
Clarksburg, WV	Holyoke, MA
Cleveland, OH	Honolulu, HI
Columbia, SC	Houston, TX
Columbus, OH	Indianapolis, IN

Jackson, MS

Jacksonville, FL

Jericho, NY

Kansas City, MO

Knoxville, TN

Las Vegas, NE

Little Rock, AR

Los Angeles, CA

Louisville, KY

Lower Rio Grande
   Valley, TX

Lubbock, TX

Madison, WI

Marquette, MI

Marshall, TX

Memphis, TN

Milwaukee, WI

Minneapolis, MN

Montpelier, VT

Nashville, TN

Newark, NJ

New Orleans, LA

New York, NY

Oklahoma City, OK

Omaha, NE

Philadelphia, PA

Phoenix, AZ

Pittsburgh, PA

Portland, OR

Providence, RI

Rapid City, SD

Reno, NE

Richmond, VA

Rochester, NY

St. Louis, MO

Sacramento, CA

Salt Lake City, UT

San Antonio, TX

San Diego, CA

San Francisco, CA

Seattle, WA

Shreveport, LA

Sioux Falls, SD

Spokane, WA

Springfield, IL

St. Thomas, VI

Syracuse, NY

Tampa, FL

Washington, D.C.

West Palm Beach, FL

Wichita, KS

Wilkes-Barre, PA

Wilmington, DE

MANAGEMENT ASSISTANCE PUBLICATIONS

Management assistance booklets are published by the Small Business Administration and are sold by the Superintendent of Documents, not by the Small Business Administration. Prices of booklets are subject to change without notice, so write for current listings. A very few of their titles are: *National Mailing-List Houses,*

Tourism and Outdoor Recreation, Basic Library Reference Sources, Statistics and Maps for National Market Analysis, and *National Directories for Use in Marketing.*

Pamphlets and books published by U.S. government agencies, such as the Small Business Administration, should be purchased from:

> Superintendent of Documents
> Government Printing Office
> Washington, DC 20402

To help cut energy costs, consult a 23-page booklet called *Energy Management Guide for Light Industry and Commerce,* published by the U.S. Government Printing Office.

Change in Distribution of SBA Publications

On February 1, 1978, the U.S. Small Business Administration initiated a centralized distribution center to handle national requests from the public for free publications.

Before that time, all public requests for free publications were handled by the nearest SBA district office. With the mounting demands and minimum staff, public requests took as much as three weeks to process. Under the new system, an interested individual can simply fill out a request and mail it to:

> Small Business Administration
> P.O. Box 15434
> Fort Worth, TX 76119

Publications will be mailed within three days of receipt of requests. Each request should be made on an SBA Form 115A, which is a list of the available publications. A copy of this form may be requested from the distribution center. Requests must be limited to no more than five copies per item. If more than five are desired, the request should be sent to the nearest SBA office rather than the distribution center at Forth Worth. The Center will also respond to telephone requests on the same basis as described for written requests. The nationwide toll-free WATTS number is (800)433-7212 except for persons calling from Texas, who should use (800)792-8901. The telephone recording service is available 24 hours per day, 7 days a week.

Small-Business Management Series

The booklets in this series provide discussions of special management problems in small companies.

1. *An Employee Suggestion System for Small Companies* explains the basic principles for starting and operating a suggestion system. It also warns of various pitfalls and gives examples of suggestions submitted by employees.
2. *Human Relations in Small Business* discusses human relations, finding and selecting employees, developing them, and motivating them.
3. *Improving Material Handling in Small Business* has a discussion of the basics of the material-handling function, the method of laying out workplaces, and other factors necessary to setting up an efficient system.
4. *Handbook of Small Business Finance* has been written for the small-business owner who wants to improve his/her financial management skills. It indicates the major areas of financial management and describes a few of the many techniques that can help the small-business owner.
5. *Ratio Analysis for Small Business* is another helpful booklet. Ratio analysis is the process of determining the relationships between certain financial or operating data of a business to provide a basis for managerial control. The purpose of the booklet is to help the owner/manager in detecting favorable or unfavorable trends in his or her business.
6. *Profitable Small Plant Layout* provides help for the small-business owner who is in the predicament of rising costs on finished goods, decreasing net profits, and lowered production because of the lack of economical and orderly movement of production materials from one process to another throughout the shop.
7. *Practical Business Use of Government Statistics* illustrates some practical uses of federal government statistics, discusses what can be done with them, and describes major reference sources.
8. *Guides for Profit Planning* discusses computing and using the break-even point, the level of gross profit, and the rate of return on investment. It is designed for readers who have no specialized training in accounting and economics.
9. *Personnel Management Guides for Small Business* is an introduction to the various aspects of personnel management as they apply to small firms.
10. *Profitable Community Relations for Small Business* provides practical in-

formation on how to build and maintain sound community relations by participation in community affairs.

11. *Small Business and Government Research and Development* provides an introduction for owners of small research and development firms that seek government R&D contracts. It includes a discussion of the procedures necessary to locate and interest government markets.

12. *Management Audit for Small Manufacturers* has a series of questions that will indicate whether the owner-manager of a small manufacturing plant is planning, organizing, directing, and coordinating business activities efficiently.

13. *Insurance and Risk Management for Small Business* has a discussion of what insurance is, the necessity of obtaining professional advice on buying insurance, and the main types of insurance a small business may need.

14. *Management Audit for Small Retailers* is designed to meet the needs of the owner-manager of a small retail enterprise, with 149 questions to guide the owner-manager in an examination of himself and the business operation.

15. *Financial Recordkeeping for Small Stores* is written primarily for the small store owner or prospective owner whose business doesn't justify hiring a full-time bookkeeper.

16. *Small Store Planning for Growth* provides a discussion of the nature of growth, the management skills needed, and some techniques for use in promoting growth. Included is a consideration of merchandising, advertising and display, and checklists for increases in transactions and gross margins.

17. *Franchise Index/Profile* presents an evaluation process that may be used to investigate franchise opportunities. The index tells what to look for in a franchise. The profile is a worksheet for listing the data.

18. *Training Salesmen to Serve Industrial Markets* discusses the role of sales in the marketing program of a small manufacturer and offers suggestions for salespeople to use in servicing customers. It also provides material to use in training program.

19. *Financial Control to Time-Absorption Analysis* includes a profit control technique that can be used by all types of business. A step-by-step approach shows how to establish this method in a particular business.

20. *Management Audit for Small Service Firms* is a do-it-yourself guide for owner-managers of small service firms to help them evaluate and improve their operations. Brief comments explain the importance of each question in thirteen critical management areas.

21. *Decision Points in Developing New Products* provides a path from idea to marketing plan for the small manufacturing or R&D firm that wants

to expand or develop a business around a new product, process, or invention.

Starting and Managing Series

This series is designed to help small entrepreneurs in their effort "to look before they leap" into a business. The first volume in the series—*Starting and Managing a Small Business of Your Own*—deals with the subject in general terms. Each of the other volumes deals with one type of business in detail; their titles are designed to inform of their contents. Available titles are listed below.

1. *Starting and Managing a Small Business of Your Own*
2. *Starting and Managing a Service Station*
3. *Starting and Managing a Carwash*
4. *Starting and Managing a Retail Flower Shop*
5. *Starting and Managing a Pet Shop*
6. *Starting and Managing a Small Retail Music Store*
7. *Starting and Managing a Small Retail Jewelry Store*
8. *Starting and Managing an Employment Agency*
9. *Starting and Managing a Small Drive-In Restaurant*
10. *Starting and Managing a Small Shoestore*

Non-Series Publications

1. *Export Marketing for Smaller Firms* is a manual for owner-managers of smaller firms who seek sales in foreign markets.
2. *U.S. Government Purchasing and Sales Directory* is a directory for businesses that are interested in selling to the U.S. government. It lists the purchasing needs of various agencies.
3. *Managing for Profits* has ten chapters on various aspects of small-business management—for example, marketing, production, and credit.
4. *Buying and Selling a Small Business* deals with the problems that confront buyers and sellers of small businesses. Discusses the buy-sell transaction, sources of information for buyer-seller decision, the buy-sell process, using financial statements in the buy-sell transaction, and analyzing the market position of the company.
5. *Strengthening Small Business Management* contains twenty-one chapters

on small-business management. This collection reflects the experience the author gained in a lifetime of work with the small-business community. A companion form, SBA-115A, lists current free publications and is offered without charge from SBA's Washington and Field Offices.

Free Management Aids

These leaflets deal with functional problems in small manufacturing plants and concentrate on subjects of interest to administrative executives.

170 *The ABC's of Borrowing*

171 *How to Write a Job Description*

174 *Is Your Cash Supply Adequate?*

176 *Financial Audits: A Tool for Better Management*

178 *Effective Industrial Advertising for Small Plants*

179 *Breaking the Barriers to Small Business Planning*

186 *Checklist for Developing a Training Program*

187 *Using Census Data in Small Plant Marketing*

188 *Developing a List of Prospects*

189 *Should You Make or Buy Components?*

190 *Measuring the Performance of Salesmen*

191 *Delegating Work and Responsibility*

192 *Profile Your Customers to Expand Industrial Sales*

193 *What Is the Best Selling Price?*

194 *Marketing Planning Guidelines*

195 *Setting Pay for Your Management Jobs*

197 *Pointers on Preparing an Employee Handbook*

199 *Expand Overseas Sales With Commerce Department Help*

200 *Is the Independent Sales Agent for You?*

201 *Locating or Relocating Your Business*

203 *Are Your Products and Channels Producing Sales?*

204 *Pointers on Negotiating DOD Contracts*

205 *Pointers on Using Temporary-Help Services*

To receive copies of the publications listed, complete and return an order blank available from the nearest SBA office. Your order will be filled as soon as possible. Check only titles pertinent to your needs.

To be placed on a regular mailing list so as to receive, in the future, a continuation of individual copies in any of the Aids Series, a mailing list application may be obtained from your nearest SBA office.

A companion form, SBA 115B, listing Small-Business Management Series booklets, is available from SBA Offices.

BIBLIOGRAPHY*

The purpose of this bibliography is to acquaint the small-business owner with the wealth of business information available through library research. A small-business owner can tap sources of information through a good business library reference service. Some of these sources are similar to the businessperson's trade association, bank, accountant, lawyer, supplier, and management consultant services.

The consulting services of many experts are available to anyone who learns how to use reference sources. Many of the nation's public libraries, such as the Cleveland Public Library and the Public Library of Newark, New Jersey, have become well-known for their services to business.

This bibliography lists books and other publications, including periodicals, that provide information on basic library business reference sources. It includes federal, state, and nongovernment publications and services. Most of the references listed are available at public and university libraries.

Publishers are given for the titles which the businessperson may want to buy for his or her own library. Publishers and others are invited to notify SBA of relevant publications for possible inclusion in future revisions of this bibliography.

Free Federal Publications

Order from issuing agency as described in the selected listing by giving the publication's title and series number (if stated). If the agency has no local office, request the publication from the address given in this Bibliography.

GPO (Government Printing Office) identifies publications that may be purchased. Order these from the Superintendent of Documents, U.S. Government Printing Office, Washington, DC, 20402. Give the publication's title, its series number (if stated), and name of issuing federal agency.

For additional information on how to use a business library, see *How to Use the Business Library: With Sources of Business Information*, 64th ed., by H. Webster Johnson and S. W. McFarland, 1972, South-Western Publishing Company. The major part of this book is

*Bernice T. Clarke and Terry E. Nelson, SBA Library Assistants, prepared the revision of this small-business bibliography.

devoted to specific publications (handbooks, periodicals, business services, government publications), but there are also brief sections on locating information in libraries, writing reports, audio-visual aids, and data processing.

The following list contains the most basic business directories, guides, and reference sources available in many libraries. It is by no means all-inclusive, but is intended to indicate the wealth of information available. Your local librarian can supplement this list with additional reference material.

Business Operating Guides and Handbooks

Handbooks that treat specific phases of business operation often contain practical information. Only a few examples of the many types available are listed below.

1. *Apollo Handbook of Practical Public Relations,* by Alexander B. Adams, 1970, Apollo Editions. This is a guide for the nonspecialist who wants to get his organization's message to the public. Includes suggestions for preparing news releases, making speeches, and other aspects of communications.

2. *CCH Federal Tax Guide—1976* (control edition includes weekly reports). Has authentic information with tax control methods for practical and competent guidance to insure effective tax management. Commerce Clearing House, Inc.

3. *Credit Management Handbook,* 2nd ed., Credit Research Foundation, 1965, Richard D. Irwin, Inc. Explains how to organize and operate a credit department, to make credit decisions on orders and accounts, to collect overdue accounts, and to use credit reporting and rating agencies.

4. *Foreign Commerce Handbook* (3813), 17th ed., 1975, Chamber of Commerce of the United States. A guide to sources of information and services for exporters and importers. Gives types of service of U.S. government, intergovernmental and private organizations in foreign trade and related matters. Information sources under 60 major subjects, includes a bibliography of further references.

5. *Marketing Handbook,* 2nd ed., ed. A.W. Frey, 1965, Ronald Press Company. A comprehensive reference book for persons concerned with marketing goods and services.

6. *Office Management Handbook,* ed. Harry L. Wylie, Ronald Press Company. Gives standard principles and practices for running an efficient office, large or small.

7. *Production Handbook,* 3rd ed., ed. Gordon B. Carson, 1972, Ronald Press Company. Gives information about plant layout and location, production planning and control, quality control, and manufacturing processes.

8. *Purchasing Handbook,* ed. George W. Aljian, 1973, McGraw-Hill Book Company, Inc. Gives thorough treatment of purchasing department organization, management, and operating procedures.

9. *Tax Guide for Small Business,* Internal Revenue Service, U.S. Department of the Treasury, revised annually. Available at district offices of Internal Revenue Service. Designed to assist businesspeople in the preparation of their federal tax returns. Discusses tax problems incident to conducting a trade, business, profession, or acquiring or selling a business.

Directories

Business firms often need information concerning products, potential buyers, or trade associations. Directories of various types are available. The most obvious are telephone books and their classified sections. Many libraries keep some out-of-town telephone directories for business reference. For further listings of directories, consult the following, available at most libraries:

1. *Guide to American Directories,* 9th ed., 1975, B. Klein Publications, Inc. Gives information on directories classified by industry, by profession, and by function. Useful for identifying specific directories to aid in locating new markets or sources of supply.

2. *Federal Government,* rev. ed., U.S. Library of Congress, Washington, DC, GPO. A directory of information resources in the United States with a supplement of government-sponsored information analysis centers.

3. *Encyclopedia of Government Advisory Organizations,* quarterly, Gale Research Company. A reference guide to federal agency, interagency, and government-related boards, committees, councils, conferences, and other similar units serving in an advisory, consultative, or investigative capacity.

Directories Serving the Business Community

Associations

1. *Directory of National and International Labor Unions in the United States,* 1973. U.S. Department of Labor, biennial, GPO. Gives facts about the structure and membership of national and international labor unions.

2. *Encyclopedia of Associations,* vol. I, National Organizations of the United States, biennial. Gale Research Company. Lists trade, business, professional, labor, scientific, educational, fraternal, and social organizations of the United States, includes historical data.

3. *National Trade and Professional Associations of the United States and Canada and Labor Unions,* annual, 1975, Columbia Books Publisher. Lists the names, telephone number, address, chief executive officer, size of staff and membership, and year formed of more than 4,000 national business and professional associations.

Financial

1. *Dunn & Bradstreet Reference Book,* 6/year. Contains the names and ratings of nearly 3 million businesses of all types located throughout the United States and Canada. (Dunn & Bradstreet also publish other specialized reference books and directories—for example, *Apparel Trades Book* and *Metalworking Marketing Directory.*)

2. *Moody's Banks and Finance,* annual with twice-weekly supplements, Moody's Investor Service. Indexes more than 9,700 American banks and financial institutions, listing their officers, directors, and other top-level personnel.

4. *Rand-McNally International Banker's Directory,* semi-annual, Rand-McNally & Company. Lists over 37,000 banks and branches, giving their officials, and statement figures. It also includes the American Bank Association's check routing numbers for all U.S. banks, and a digest of U.S. banking laws.

Government

The following references include directories of municipal, state, and federal agencies, their personnel, and functions.

1. *Municipal Year Book,* annual, International City Management Association.

2. *Book of the States,* biennial, Council of State Government.

3. *State Bluebooks and Reference Publications,* Council of State Governments. A selected bibliography of bluebooks, reports, directories, and other reference publications produced by various departments of each state.

4. *Congressional Directory,* annual, Joint Committee on Printing, GPO, 1975. Biographical data on members of Congress, membership and staff of congressional committees; directory of the executive and

judiciary, diplomatic corps; and other useful information on federal and state agencies.

5. *Directory of Post Offices,* annual, U.S. Post Office Department, GPO, 1974. List of post offices by state, alphabetical list, and post office addresses for Army and Air Force installations.

6. *Sources of State Information and State Industrial Directories,* triennial, Chamber of Commerce of the United States. Contains names and addresses of private and public agencies which furnish information about their states. Also listed under each state are industrial directories and directories of manufacturers published by state and private organizations. Some regional directories are included.

7. *United States Government Organization Manual,* annual, National Archives and Records Service, GPO, 1974–75. The official organization handbook of the federal government containing descriptive information on the agencies in the legislative, judicial, and executive branches. Abolished or transferred agencies are listed in an appendix.

Individuals

The following lists only the most general works. *Who's Who* directories are also available for specific occupations and locations.

1. *Current Biography,* monthly, H.W. Wilson Company. Extensive biographical data on prominent contemporary personalities.

2. *Standard & Poor's Register of Corporations, Directors, and Executives,* annual, 3 vol., Standard & Poor's Corporation.

3. *Who's Who in America,* biennial, Marquis—Who's Who, Inc.

4. *Who's Who of American Women,* biennial, Marquis—Who's Who, Inc.

5. *World's Who's Who in Finance and Industry,* Marquis—Who's Who, Inc.

Manufacturers

In addition to the directories listed, there are available many state manufacturers' and industrial directories. These are too numerous to list here. Ask your librarian if such a directory is published for the state in which you are interested.

1. *U.S. Industrial Directory,* annual, 3 vols., Cahners Publishing Company. Alphabetical listing of manufacturers showing product lines, code for number of employees, addresses, and telephone numbers. Classified section lists products with names and addresses of manufacturers.

Special chemical and mechanical sections, and trademark and trade name identification.

2. *MacRae's Blue Book,* annual, 5 vols., MacRae's Blue Book Company. Lists sources of industrial equipment, products, and materials; alphabetical listing of company names and trade names.

3. *Thomas' Register of American Manufacturers,* annual, 11 vols., Thomas Publishing Company. Purchasing guide listing names of manufacturers, producers, and similar sources of supply in all lines.

World Trade

International Yellow Pages, The Reuben H. Donnelly Corporation. Lists business and professional firms and individuals from 150 countries under headings descriptive of the products and services they have to offer in worldwide trade.

Economic and Marketing Information

The nation's economy and, in turn, its marketing trends, are changing constantly. Businesspeople can keep abreast by using the current books, booklets, and periodicals as issued by commercial firms and government agencies. Much of the basic statistical information in the economic and marketing area is collected by the federal government. Commercial organizations use these data and supplement it with surveys of their own. Listed below are some basic reference publications which present statistical and marketing information; many are issued on a continuing basis.

Books/Booklets

1. *Bibliography of 1973 Publications of University Bureaus of Business and Economic Research.* Association for University Business and Economic Research, University of Colorado, Boulder, Colorado.

2. *Business Statistics,* biennial, U.S. Department of Commerce, 1973, GPO. Supplementary and historical data for the economic statistics published in the *Survey of Current Business.*

3. *County and City Data Books,* 1972, Bureau of the Census, U.S. Department of Commerce, GPO. Presents statistical information on business, manufacturers, governments, agriculture, population, housing, vital statistics, bank deposits, and other subjects. Issued every several years.

4. *Data Sources for Business and Market Analysis,* 1978, N.D. Frank, Scarecrow Press. Provides market research information, its origins and retrieval. Gives basic sources and specific references for the study of business trends.

5. *Directory of Business and Financial Services,* Mary M. Grant and Norma Cote, 1974, Special Libraries Association. An annotated listing of several hundred business, economic, and financial services.

6. *Editor & Publisher Market Guide,* annual, 1975, Editor and Publisher Company. Tabulates current estimates of population, households, retail sales for nine major sales classifications, income for states, counties, metropolitan areas, and 1,500 daily newspaper markets. For each area, gives information on transportation and utilities, local newspapers, climate, and employment. Includes state maps.

7. *McGraw-Hill Dictionary of Modern Economics,* 2nd ed., 1973, McGraw-Hill Book Company, Inc. Defines more than 1,300 terms currently used in economics, marketing, and finance. Also describes approximately 200 government and private agencies, and nonprofit associations concerned with the fields of economics and marketing.

8. *Rand McNally Commercial Atlas and Marketing Guide,* annual, 1975 (leased on an annual basis), Rand McNally & Company. An extensive U.S. Atlas presenting marketing data in the form of maps and area statistics.

9. *SM's Survey of Buying Power,* 1974, Sales Management. Gives population, income, and retail sales estimates for state, county, and metropolitan area (as defined by *Sales Management Magazine*).

10. *Sources of Business Information,* ed. F.T. Coman, 1964, University of California Press. Guide to general sources with coverage for specific fields of business and industry.

11. *The Statesman's Year Book,* rev. annually, ed. S.H. Steinberg and John Paxton, 1973–74, St. Martin's Press, Inc. This book is a storehouse of information on the United Nations, all countries of the world, and each of the 50 states of the United States.

12. *Statistical Abstract of the United States,* 1974, Bureau of the Census, U.S. Department of Commerce, GPO. The standard summary of national statistics, includes information on the labor force, population, business enterprises, and national income.

13. *Statistical Services of the United States Government,* annual, Bureau of the Budget, GPO. Serves as a basic reference document on U.S. government statistical programs.

14. *Statistics Sources,* 4th ed., Paul Wasserman, Gale Research Company. Arranged in dictionary style, cites periodicals, yearbooks, directories,

and other compilations issued by state, federal, and foreign agencies, associations, companies, universities, and other organizations.

Periodicals—U.S. Government

The following are some of the basic federal government periodicals which contain business and general economic reports and are widely used by businesspeople for keeping abreast of developments in their specific areas of interest.

1. *Construction Review,* monthly, U.S. Department of Commerce, GPO. Brings together virtually all the government's current statistics pertaining to construction, plus some nongovernment statistical information.

2. *Current Industrial Reports,* Bureau of the Census, U.S. Department of Commerce. Lists of titles and prices available from the Bureau of the Census. These reports give information at the factory level for different industries on inventory, production, shipments, and other business activities.

3. *Current Business Reports,* Bureau of the Census, U.S. Department of Commerce, GPO. Includes a series of four reports: *Weekly Retail Sales Report; Advance Monthly Retail Sales Report; Monthly Retail Trade;* and *Retail Annual Report.* Estimated sales of retail stores by kinds of business and some data for regions and metropolitan areas.

4. *Economic Indicators,* prepared for the Joint Economic Committee by the Council of Economic Advisers, monthly, GPO. Presents tables and charts dealing with prices, employment and wages, production and business activity, purchasing power, credit, and federal finance.

5. *Federal Reserve Bulletin,* Board of Governors of the Federal Reserve System, monthly. Has monthly tables of financial and business statistics. Interest rates, money supply, consumer credit, and industrial production are some of the subjects included. Special articles cover the state of economy, financial institutions, statistical methodology.

6. *Monthly Labor Review,* U.S. Department of Labor, monthly, GPO. The medium through which the Labor Department publishes its regular monthly reports on such subjects as trends of employment and payrolls, hourly and weekly earnings, working hours, collective agreements, industrial accidents and disputes, as well as special features covering such topics as automation, and profit sharing.

7. *Monthly Wholesale Trade Reports: Sales and Inventories,* Bureau of the

Census, U.S. Department of Commerce, GPO. Reports trends in sales and inventories. Also gives some geographic data.

8. *Survey of Current Business,* U.S. Department of Commerce, monthly, GPO. Includes statistics and articles on significant economic developments. Presents statistics on national income, business population, manufacturers sales, inventories, and orders. Carries special articles on personal income, foreign trade, and other aspects of the economy.

General Reference Sources

Some of the sources for general information are almanacs, encyclopedias and their yearbooks, and specialized encyclopedias.

Almanacs

For short factual information, consult the yearly almanacs. These are available for reference at any library or may be purchased from local bookstores. Examples are:

Information Please Almanac, Simon & Schuster.
World Almanac, Doubleday & Company, Inc.

Encyclopedias

For information on almost any topic, encyclopedias are readily available. Many contain general information, others are specialized. Often included are illustrations and maps, as well as bibliographies listing standard works on the topic under consideration. They are kept up to date by yearbooks.

Among the encyclopedias available are: *Colliers Encyclopedia, Encyclopedia Americana, Encyclopedia Britannica,* and the *World Book Encyclopedia.*

Specialized Encyclopedias

The more specialized encyclopedias include: *Van Nostrand's Scientific Encyclopedia, McGraw-Hill Encyclopedia of Science and Technology, Encyclopedia of Banking and Finance, Encyclopedia of Chemistry, Encyclopedia Dictionary of Business Finance,* and *Accountant's Encyclopedia.*

Information Services

When the information being sought is too recent for inclusion in almanacs and encyclopedias, consult the following services, available at most reference libraries.

1. *Facts on File,* a weekly digest of world events, Facts on File, Inc. This useful and time-saving weekly index digests significant news of the day from a number of metropolitan dailies. The indexes are cumulated quarterly, then annually.

2. *Public Affairs Information Service Bulletin,* weekly, Public Affairs Information Service, Inc. Cumulated five times a year, bound annual volume. This is a selective subject list of the latest books, government publications, reports, and periodical articles, relating to economic conditions, public administration and international relations. An especially useful feature is the extensive listing of many types of directories.

Where to Find Publications

For the convenience of the user, publication listings are divided into three sections: Commercial Publications; Federal Government Publications; and State Publications.

Commercial Publications

Most libraries have the following reference sources for identifying books, periodicals, and periodical articles.

Books: For additional listings of books, consult:

1. *Cumulative Book Index,* monthly, H.W. Wilson Company. A subject, title, author index to books in the English language. Gives price, publisher, number of pages, and date of publication for each book.

2. *Books in Print,* annual, 4 vol.: Vol. I—Author index, A–J; Vol. II—Author index, K–Z; Vol. III—Titles and Publishers, A–J; Vol. IV—Titles and Publishers, K–Z. R.R. Bowker Company. An author and title index to books currently available from major publishers.

3. *Forthcoming Books,* bimonthly, R.R. Bowker Company. This service provides a regular updating of *Books in Print.*

4. *Subject Guide to Books in Print,* 2 vols., alphabetized, R.R. Bowker Company. Useful reference for identifying books currently available on a specific topic.

Newspapers and periodicals: can be identified through use of the following index listing.

1. *Ayer Directory of Newspapers and Periodicals,* annual, Ayer Press. Provides a geographical listing of magazines and newspapers printed in the United States and its possessions. Listings are also given for Canada, Bermuda, Panama, and the Philippines. Has an alphabetical index and a classified section which increase its usefulness.

2. *Business Publication Rates and Data,* monthly, Standard Rate and Data Service, Inc. Contains a descriptive listing of business magazines and latest advertising rates. Indexed by name of magazine and business fields covered.

3. *National Directory of Newsletters and Reporting Services,* Gale Research Company. Provides basic facts concerning the type of periodical publication not covered in the bibliographic tools concerned with the conventional types of periodicals, such as national, international, and selected foreign newsletters, association bulletins, information, and financial services.

4. *Standard Periodical Directory,* 1973–74, Oxbridge Publishing Company, Inc. Gives comprehensive coverage to periodicals in the United States and Canada. Lists over 70,000 entries, including magazines, journals, newsletters, house organs, government publications, advisory services, directories, transactions and proceedings of professional societies, yearbooks, and major city dailies (weekly and daily newspapers are excluded).

5. *Ulrich's International Periodicals Directory,* 15th ed., ed. Merle Robinsky, 1973, 2 vols. R.R. Bowker Company. Vol. I covers scientific, technical, and medical periodicals; Vol. II covers arts, humanities, business and social sciences. Classified by subject.

Articles in business and professional magazines: specific subject indexes to periodical articles, such as those listed below, are available at libraries for reference.

1. *Applied Sciences and Technology Index,* monthly, H.W. Wilson Company. Subject index covering periodicals in the fields of engineering, applied science, and industry.

2. *Business Periodicals Index,* monthly, H.W. Wilson Company. Subject index covering periodicals in the fields of business, finance, labor relations, insurance, advertising, office management, marketing, and related subjects.

3. *Readers' Guide to Periodical Literature,* semimonthly, except monthly in

July and August, H.W. Wilson Company. A general index to periodicals such as the *New York Times Magazine*.

Federal Government Publications

Libraries usually maintain listings of both state and federal government publications. A few examples are given of such listings that serve as guides to government publications.

Most of the U.S. government publications are the result of research and activities of various federal agencies. Some are free from the issuing agency, while others cost a nominal fee. Since most of these publications are relatively inexpensive and are usually some of the most recent and authoritative writings in a particular field, this reference material proves most helpful to the public.

By law, the established system of government depository libraries makes federal publications available for public reference. Libraries designated within this system can elect to receive from the Superintendent of Documents, Government Printing Office, those classes of federal publications which are appropriate to their type of library reference service.

Superintendents of Documents (GPO) also issues a number of price lists (single copy, free) on selected federal (for sale) publications related to specific subjects. For a complete list of price list subjects, request *How to Keep in Touch with U.S. Government Publications,* free from GPO. Examples of titles that may be of interest to readers of this bibliography are: *Finance PL 28, Commerce PL 62,* and *Census PL 70.* These price lists of U.S. government publications on selected subjects give prices and title of publications and may be consulted in depository libraries.

Most libraries have some federal publication listings to identify currently available materials of most of the federal agencies and they keep some of these publications for ready reference. Some of the guides to federal publications are:

1. *Monthly Catalog of United States Government Publications,* Superintendent of Documents, GPO. The most comprehensive catalog of government publications. It lists by agency both printed and processed publications issued each month, including congressional hearings, documents, and reports.

2. *SBA 115A–Free Management Assistance Publications,* and SBA 115B— *For Sale Booklets,* Small Business Administration. Complete listings of

currently available management assistance publications issued by SBA. Both lists are free from the nearest SBA field office or SBA, Washington, DC, 20416.

3. *Publications Lists of Other U.S. Government Departments and Agencies.* Most federal agencies issue, periodically or intermittently, lists (titles of the lists vary) of their current publications. If not available at local libraries, these lists are free from the issuing agency—check with the nearest field office of the government agency. (For local office addresses, look for the agency under U.S. government in the telephone directory.)

State Publications

Most reference libraries keep current and historical materials of local civic interest, including newspapers, magazines, and books. An example of a guide to state publications is listed below.

Monthly Checklist of State Publications, Library of Congress, GPO. List by state and agency of the state documents received by the Library of Congress.

The services offered by United States Trademark Association (USTA) concern all aspects of the trademark field; federal, state, and foreign legislation; education, promotion advertising and merchandising; publicity and use by the press; proper handling of trademarks by corporate personnel, sales staff, dealers; and more. An important caveat: the services of USTA do not purport to substitute for or duplicate in any way the advice of legal counsel.

To obtain information about ordering any publications, write:

The United States Trademark Association
6 East 45th Street
New York, NY 10017

19

Directory of Operating Small Business Investment Companies

This is a list of all Small Business Investment Companies, including their branch offices, whose licenses, issued by SBA, remain outstanding except those companies that are in process of surrendering their licenses or are subject to legal proceedings, which may have the effect of terminating their activity as Small Business Investment Companies. This list does not purport to characterize the relative merits, as investment companies or otherwise, of these licensees. Inclusion on this list may in no way be construed as approval of a company's operations or as a recommendation by the Small Business Administration.

PART I: Small Business Investment Companies
Alphabetically by State
Part II: 301(d) Licensees Alphabetically by State
(Limited to Assisting Small Business Concerns
Owned by Socially or Economically Disadvantaged
Persons.)

KEY FOR CODE NUMBER OF EACH TYPE OF OWNERSHIP

CODE NUMBER	TYPE OF OWNERSHIP
1	BANK DOMINATED (50% OR MORE OWNED BY BANK OR BANK HOLDING COMPANY)
2	BANK ASSOCIATED (10% TO 49% OWNED BY BANK OR BANK HOLDING COMPANY)
3	FINANCIAL ORGANIZATION OTHER THAN BANK OR BANK HOLDING COMPANY (PUBLIC OR NON-PUBLIC)
4	NON-FINANCIAL ORGANIZATION (PUBLIC OR NON-PUBLIC)
5	INDIVIDUALLY OWNED (PRIVATELY HELD)
6	40 ACT COMPANY

NOTE: Ownership Code followed by "P" signifies Partnership.

PART I - SBICs

LICENSEE	LICENSE NUMBER	PRIVATE CAPITAL	OBLIGATION TO SBA	INVESTMENT POLICY	OWNER CODE
ALABAMA					
BENSON INVESTMENT COMPANY, INC. WILLIAM T. BENSON, PRESIDENT 406 SOUTH COMMERCE ST. GENEVA, ALABAMA 36340 (205) 684-2824	04/04-0147	505,000	0	DIVERSIFIED	5
CHRISTOPHER SBIC (THE) DAVID DELANEY, PRESIDENT 3202 DAUPHIN ST., SUITE B MOBILE, ALABAMA 36606 (205) 476-0700	04/04-0143	500,000	1,000,000	DIVERSIFIED	5
COASTAL CAPITAL COMPANY CHRIS C. DELANEY, PRESIDENT 3201 DAUPHIN ST., SUITE B MOBILE, ALABAMA 36606 (205) 432-0064	04/04-0117	500,000	1,000,000	BUILDERS	3
H&T CAPITAL CORP. JOHN R. BLOOM, PRESIDENT 4750 SELMA HIGHWAY P.O. DRAWER Q MONTGOMERY, ALABAMA 36105 (205) 288-6250	04/04-0116	305,000	600,000	DIVERSIFIED	5
ARIZONA					
AMERICAN BUSINESS CAPITAL CORP. LEONARD A. FRANKEL, PRESIDENT 3550 NORTH CENTRAL AVE. SUITE 520 PHOENIX, ARIZONA 85012 (602) 277-6259	09/09-0204	500,000	0	DIVERSIFIED	5
ARKANSAS					
FIRST SBIC OF ARKANSAS, INC. FRED BURNS, PRESIDENT WORTHEN BANK BUILDING SUITE 702 LITTLE ROCK, ARKANSAS 72201 (501) 378-1876	06/06-0182	500,000	0	DIVERSIFIED	1

LICENSEE	LICENSE NUMBER	PRIVATE CAPITAL	OBLIGATION TO SBA	INVESTMENT POLICY	OWNER CODE
ARKANSAS(CONT)					
SMALL BUSINESS INV. CAP. INC. CHARLES E. TOLAND, PRESIDENT 10003 NEW BENTON HWY. MAIL TO: P.O. BOX 3627 LITTLE ROCK, ARKANSAS 72203 (501) 562-3590	06/06-0175	750,000	2,250,000	RETAIL GROCERS	4
CALIFORNIA					
ASSET MANAGEMENT CAPITAL CO. FRANKLIN JOHNSON, JR., PRESIDENT 1417 EDGEWOOD DR. PALO ALTO, CALIFORNIA 94301 (415) 321-3131	09/09-0170	420,000	600,000	DIVERSIFIED	5
BRANTMAN CAPITAL CORP. WILLIAM T. BRANTMAN, PRESIDENT 2476 MAR EAST MAIL TO: P.O. BOX 877 TIBURON, CALIFORNIA 94920 (415) 435-4747	09/09-0163	350,100	400,000	DIVERSIFIED	5
BRENTWOOD ASSOC., INC. TIMOTHY PENNINGTON 3RD, PRESIDENT 11661 SAN VINCENTE BLVD. LOS ANGELES, CALIFORNIA 90049 (213) 826-6581	09/09-0162	2,000,000	6,000,000	DIVERSIFIED	3
BRENTWOOD CAPITAL CORPORATION T.M. PENNINGTON, CHAIRMAN OF BOARD 11661 SAN VINCENTE BLVD. LOS ANGELES, CALIFORNIA 90049 (213) 826-6581	09/09-0239	5,000,000	0	DIVERSIFIED	3
BRYAN CAPITAL CORP. JOHN M. BRYAN, PRESIDENT 235 MONTGOMERY ST. SUITE 2220 SAN FRANCISCO, CALIFORNIA 94104 (415) 421-9990	09/12-0079	1,028,720	3,217,079	50% MAJOR GROUP 36	5
BUILDERS CAPITAL CORP. VICTOR H. INDIEK, PRESIDENT 2716 OCEAN PARK BOULEVARD SANTA MONICA, CALIFORNIA 90404 (213) 450-0779	09/09-0209	1,000,000	2,000,000	100% MAJOR GROUP 15	5

LICENSEE	LICENSE NUMBER	PRIVATE CAPITAL	OBLIGATION TO SBA	INVESTMENT POLICY	OWNER CODE
CALIFORNIA(CONT)					
CALIFORNIA NORTHWEST FUND, INC. KIRK L. KNIGHT, PRESIDENT 3000 SAND HILL RD. MENLO PARK, CALIFORNIA 94025 (415) 854-2940	09/13-0007	5,409,582	750,000	DIVERSIFIED	2
CITY CAPITAL CORP. MORTON HELLER, PRESIDENT 9300 WILSHIRE BLVD., #328 BEVERLY HILLS, CALIFORNIA 90212 (212) 273-4080	09/14-0060	400,000	250,000	DIVERSIFIED	5
CONTINENTAL CAPITAL CORPORATION FRANK G. CHAMBERS, PRESIDENT 555 CALIFORNIA ST. SAN FRANCISCO, CALIFORNIA 94104 (415) 989-2020	09/12-0002	4,619,962	6,550,086	100% MAJOR GROUPS 35 & 36	6
CROCKER CAPITAL CORP. CHARLES CROCKER, PRESIDENT 111 SUTTER ST., SUITE 600 SAN FRANCISCO, CALIFORNIA 94104 (415) 983-2156	09/12-0150	895,500	2,205,834	66-2/3% MAJOR GROUP 36	2
CROCKER VENTURES INCORPORATED JOHN M. BOYLE, GENERAL MANAGER ONE MONTGOMERY STREET SAN FRANCISCO, CALIFORNIA 94104 (415) 983-7024	09/09-0227	1,000,000	0	DIVERSIFIED	1
DEVELOPERS EQUITY CAPITAL CORP. LARRY SADE, CHAIRMAN OF BOARD 9201 WILSHIRE BLVD. SUITE 204 BEVERLY HILLS, CALIFORNIA 90210 (213) 278-3611	09/14-0079	355,000	485,107	100% REAL ESTATE	5
EDVESTCO, INC. WILLIAM C. EDWARDS, PRESIDENT 150 ISABELLA AVE. ATHERTON, CALIFORNIA 94025 (415) 421-9990	09/12-0075	1,028,802	3,199,956	50% MAJOR GROUP 36	5

LICENSEE	LICENSE NUMBER	PRIVATE CAPITAL	OBLIGATION TO SBA	INVESTMENT POLICY	OWNER CODE
CALIFORNIA(CONT)					
EQUILEASE CAPITAL CORP (MAIN OFFICE: NEW YORK, N.Y.) 315 SO. BEVERLY DRIVE BEVERLY HILLS, CALIFORNIA 90212					
FIRST SBIC OF CALIFORNIA TIM HAY, PRESIDENT 333 SOUTH HOPE ST. LOS ANGELES, CALIFORNIA 90017 (213) 613-5215	09/14-0009	5,500,000	0	DIVERSIFIED	1
FLORISTS CAPITAL CORPORATION CHRISTOPHER M. CONROY, CHAIRMAN 10524 WEST PICO BLVD. LOS ANGELES, CALIFORNIA 90064 (213) 836-6169	09/09-0211	500,000	500,000	DIVERSIFIED	5
GROCERS CAPITAL CO. ELLIOT GOLDSTONE, MANAGER 2601 S. EASTERN AVE. LOS ANGELES, CALIFORNIA 90040 (213) 728-3322	09/09-0184	500,000	500,000	GROCERY STORES	4
H & R INVESTMENT CAPITAL CO. HERMAN CHRISTENSEN, PRESIDENT 801 AMERICAN ST. SAN CARLOS, CALIFORNIA 94070 (415) 365-4691	09/12-0083	483,000	185,036	66-2/3% REAL ESTATE	5
IMPERIAL VENTURES INCORPORATED GEORGE M. ELTINGE, CHAIRMAN 9920 SOUTH LACIENEGA BLVD. MAIL TO:P.O. BOX 92991, LOS ANGELES INGLEWOOD, CALIFORNIA 90301 (213) 649-4444	09/09-0203	500,000	0	DIVERSIFIED	1
JERMYN VENTURE CAPITAL CORPORATION 190 NORTH CANON DRIVE SUITE 400 BEVERLY HILLS, CALIFORNIA 90210 (213) 550-8819	09/09-0210	11,500,000	0	MOVIE SPECIALIST	5

LICENSEE	LICENSE NUMBER	PRIVATE CAPITAL	OBLIGATION TO SBA	INVESTMENT POLICY	OWNER CODE
CALIFORNIA(CONT)					
KRASNE FUND FOR SMALL BUSINESS, INC. CLYDE A. KRASNE, PRESIDENT 9350 WILSHIRE BLVD., SUITE 219 BEVERLY HILLS, CALIFORNIA 90212 (213) 274-7007	09/14-0074	300,000	366,667	90% REAL ESTATE	5
LANDERS CAPITAL CORP. HAROLD A. LANDERS, PRESIDENT 9255 SUNSET BLVD. LOS ANGELES, CALIFORNIA 90069 (213) 550-8819	09/09-0220	500,000	0	DIVERSIFIED	5
MARWIT CAPITAL CORP. MARTIN W. WITTE, PRESIDENT 610 NEWPORT CENTER DR. SUITE 480 NEWPORT BEACH, CALIFORNIA 92660 (714) 640-6234	09/02-0175	780,537	821,800	DIVERSIFIED	5
MONTGOMERY STREET PARTNERS INC. ROSLYN BRAEMAN PAYNE, PRESIDENT 44 MONTGOMERY STREET SAN FRANCISCO, CALIFORNIA 94104 (415) 433-6191	09/09-0223	300,000	0	DIVERSIFIED	5
OCEANIC CAPITAL CORP. ROBERT H. CHAPPELL, PRESIDENT 350 CALIFORNIA ST., SUITE 2090 SAN FRANCISCO, CALIFORNIA 94104 (415) 398-7677	09/14-0085	1,339,000	4,331,175	DIVERSIFIED	4
PRODUCERS INVESTMENT CORPORATION GRAHAM LOVING, PRESIDENT 9300 WILSHIRE BLVD., SUITE 470 BEVERLY HILLS, CALIFORNIA 90212 (213) 550-1358	09/09-0207	500,000	0	DIVERSIFIED	5
PROFESSIONAL SBIC DAVID M. ZERNER, PRESIDENT 5979 WEST 3RD ST., SUITE 200 LOS ANGELES, CALIFORNIA 90036 (213) 936-5243	09/14-0020	897,115	901,097	66-2/3% REAL ESTATE	5
ROE FINANCIAL CORP. MARTIN J. ROE PRESIDENT 449 S. BEVERLY DR., SUITE 208 BEVERLY HILLS, CALIFORNIA 90212 (213) 553-4723	09/12-0122	335,000	580,000	66-2/3% RENTAL AND LEASING	5

LICENSEE	LICENSE NUMBER	PRIVATE CAPITAL	OBLIGATION TO SBA	INVESTMENT POLICY	OWNER CODE
CALIFORNIA(CONT)					
SAN JOAQUIN CAPITAL CORPORATION RICHARD ROBINS, PRESIDENT 200 NEW STINE RD., SUITE 228 MAIL TO: P.O. BOX 9596 BAKERSFIELD, CALIFORNIA 93309 (805) 834-6616	09/14-0037	837,330	1,921,311	DIVERSIFIED	5
SAN JOSE CAPITAL CORP. H. BRUCE FURCHTENICHT, PRESIDENT 100 PARK CENTER PLAZA SAN JOSE, CALIFORNIA 95113 (408) 293-7708	09/09-0195	420,530	0	DIVERSIFIED	5
SMALL BUSINESS ENTERPRISES CO STEVEN L. MERRILL, PRESIDENT 555 CALIFORNIA ST. SAN FRANCISCO, CALIFORNIA 94104 (415) 622-2582	09/12-0007	12,500,000	0	45% MAJOR GROUPS 26 & 38	1
UNION VENTURE CORP. BRENT T. RIDER, PRESIDENT 445 S. FIGUEROA ST. LOS ANGELES, CALIFORNIA 90017 (213) 687-5797	09/12-0145	2,000,000	3,000,000	DIVERSIFIED	1
WALDEN CAPITAL CORP. ARTHUR S. BERLINER, PRESIDENT 303 SACRAMENTO STREET SAN FRANCISCO, CALIFORNIA 94109 (415) 391-7225	09/09-0175	1,205,000	600,000	DIVERSIFIED	2
WARDE CAPITAL CORP. (MAIN OFFICE: BEVERLY HILLS, CA) 3440 WILSHIRE BLVD. LOS ANGELES, CALIFORNIA 90005					
WARDE CAPITAL CORP. THOMAS R. WARDE, PRESIDENT 8929 WILSHIRE BLVD., SUITE 500 BEVERLY HILLS, CALIFORNIA 90211 (213) 657-0500	09/14-0057	470,000	394,497	66-2/3% REAL ESTATE	5
WELLS FARGO INVESTMENT COMPANY ROBERT G. PERRING, PRESIDENT 475 SANSOME ST. SAN FRANCISCO, CALIFORNIA 94111 (415) 396-3293	09/12-0147	4,020,000	12,000,000	DIVERSIFIED	1

LICENSEE	LICENSE NUMBER	PRIVATE CAPITAL	OBLIGATION TO SBA	INVESTMENT POLICY	OWNER CODE
CALIFORNIA(CONT)					
WESTAMCO INVESTMENT COMPANY LEONARD G. MUSKIN, PRESIDENT 8929 WILSHIRE BLVD., SUITE 400 BEVERLY HILLS, CALIFORNIA 90211 (213) 652-8288	09/14-0024	500,000	808,000	66-2/3% REAL ESTATE	4
WESTERN BANCORP VENTURE CAP CO RICHARD G. SHAFFER, PRESIDENT 707 WILSHIRE BLVD. LOS ANGELES, CALIFORNIA 90017 (213) 614-3040	09/09-0224	2,500,000	0	DIVERSIFIED	1
COLORADO					
ASSOCIATED CAPITAL CORPORATION RODNEY J. LOVE, PRESIDENT 5151 BANNOCK STREET DENVER, COLORADO 80216 (303) 534-1155	08/08-0039	500,000	0	GROCERY STORES	4
CENTRAL INVESTMENT CORP. OF DENVER (M.O.: NORTHWEST GROWTH FUND, INC. MINNEAPOLIS, MINN.) 811 CENTRAL BANK BLDG. DENVER, COLORADO 80202 (303) 825-3351					
COLORADO SBIC MELVIN J. ROBERTS, PRESIDENT 918 SEVENTEENTH ST. P.O. BOX 5168 DENVER, COLORADO 80217 (303) 222-0465	08/11-0023	699,800	0	DIVERSIFIED	1
ENERVEST, INC. MARK KIMMEL, PRESIDENT 5500 SOUTH SYRACUSE CIRCLE, SUITE 269 ENGLEWOOD, COLORADO 80110 (303) 771-9650	08/08-0043	757,961	0	DIVERSIFIED	5
EQUILEASE CAPITAL CORP (MAIN OFFICE: NEW YORK, N.Y.) 120 BRYANT STREET DENVER, COLORADO 80219					

LICENSEE	LICENSE NUMBER	PRIVATE CAPITAL	OBLIGATION TO SBA	INVESTMENT POLICY	OWNER CODE
CONNECTICUT					
A B SBIC, INC. ADAM J. BOZZUTO, PRESIDENT SCHOOL HOUSE ROAD CHESHIRE, CONNECTICUT 06410 (203) 272-0203	01/01-0280	500,000	1,000,000	RETAIL GROCERY STORES	4
ACTIVEST CAPITAL CORP. (MAIN OFFICE: OKLAHOMA CITY,OKLA.) P.O. BOX 76 CORNWALL BRIDGE, CONNECTICUT 06754 (203) 672-6651					
ALL STATE VENTURE CAPITAL CORP. THOMAS H. BROWN, JR., PRESIDENT 830 POST ROAD EAST P.O. BOX 442 WESTPORT, CONNECTICUT 06880 (203) 226-9376	01/02-0215	338,230	462,493	DIVERSIFIED	6
APCO CAPITAL CORP. S. DAVID LEIBOWITT, PRESIDENT 63 BROAD STREET MILFORD, CONNECTICUT 06460 (203) 877-5101	01/05-0069	853,998	2,015,303	DIVERSIFIED	5
CAPITAL ASSISTANCE CORP. OF CONN. ROBERT A. FOISIE, PRESIDENT 33 BROOK STREET WEST HARTFORD, CONNECTICUT 06110 (203) 232-6118	01/01-0289	500,000	0	DIVERSIFIED	5
CAPITAL RESOURCE CO. OF CONNECTICUT I. MARTIN FIERBERG, PRESIDENT 345 NORTH MAIN STREET SUITE 304 WEST HARTFORD, CONNECTICUT 06117 (203) 232-1769	01/01-0285	525,000	1,000,000	DIVERSIFIED	5
CONNECTICUT CAPITAL CORPORATION ALBERT CARBONARI, PRESIDENT 419 WHALLEY AVENUE NEW HAVEN, CONNECTICUT 06511 (203) 777-8802	01/02-0029	249,650	452,889	DIVERSIFIED	5

LICENSEE	LICENSE NUMBER	PRIVATE CAPITAL	OBLIGATION TO SBA	INVESTMENT POLICY	OWNER CODE
CONNECTICUT(CONT)					
DEWEY INVESTMENT CORP. GEORGE E. MROSEK, PRESIDENT 101 MIDDLE TURNPIKE WEST MANCHESTER, CONNECTICUT 06040 (203) 649-0654	01/02-0145	489,468	1,118,366	DIVERSIFIED	6
EQUI-TRONICS CAPITAL CORPORATION FRANK J. PITASSI, PRESIDENT 724 NORTH STREET GREENWICH, CONNECTICUT 06830 (203) 661-7478	01/02-0118	505,998	1,503,000	DIVERSIFIED	5
FIRST CONNECTICUT SBIC DAVID ENGELSON, PRESIDENT 177 STATE STREET BRIDGEPORT, CONNECTICUT 06604 (203) 366-4726	01/02-0013	7,304,250	18,594,282	50% REAL ESTATE	6
FIRST MIAMI SBIC (MAIN OFFICE: MIAMI BEACH, FLA.) 293 POST ROAD ORANGE, CONNECTICUT 06477 (203) 227-6824					
J. H. FOSTER & CO. JOHN H. FOSTER, PRESIDENT 1010 SUMMER STREET STAMFORD, CONNECTICUT 06905 (203) 348-4385	01/02-0305	1,890,894	2,000,000	DIVERSIFIED	5
MANUFACTURERS SBIC, INCORPORATED LOUIS W. RUGGIERO, PRESIDENT 310 MAIN STREET EAST HAVEN, CONNECTICUT 06512 (203) 469-7901	01/02-0062	408,326	1,194,720	DIVERSIFIED	6
MARCON CAPITAL CORP. MARTIN A. COHEN, PRESIDENT 49 RIVERSIDE AVENUE WESTPORT, CONNECTICUT 06880 (203) 226-7751	01/01-0277	305,000	600,000	DIVERSIFIED	4
NATIONWIDE FUNDING CORPORATION NEIL H. ELLIS, PRESIDENT 306 PROGRESS DRIVE P.O. BOX 209 MANCHESTER, CONNECTICUT 06040 (203) 646-6555	01/02-0029	156,000	235,149	DIVERSIFIED	5

LICENSEE	LICENSE NUMBER	PRIVATE CAPITAL	OBLIGATION TO SBA	INVESTMENT POLICY	OWNER CODE
CONNECTICUT(CONT)					
NORTHERN BUSINESS CAPITAL CORP. JOSEPH W. KAVANEWSKY, PRESIDENT 7-9 ISSAC STREET NORWALK, CONNECTICUT 06850 (203) 866-1651	01/02-0227	173,570	125,198	DIVERSIFIED	5
NUTMEG CAPITAL CORP. LEIGH B. RAYMOND, V. PRESIDENT 35 ELM STREET NEW HAVEN, CONNECTICUT 06510 (203) 776-0643	01/02-0218	333,300	295,274	DIVERSIFIED	5
SBIC OF CONNECTICUT INC., THE KENNETH F. ZARRILLI, PRESIDENT 1115 MAIN STREET BRIDGEPORT, CONNECTICUT 06603 (203) 367-3282	01/02-0052	617,160	865,216	DIVERSIFIED	6
D.C.					
ALLIED INVESTMENT CORPORATION GEORGE C. WILLIAMS, PRESIDENT 1625 EYE STREET, N.W. SUITE 603 WASHINGTON, D.C. 20006 (202) 331-1112	03/04-0003	3,375,330	8,304,003	100% IN ANY ONE INDUSTRY	6
CAPITAL INVESTMENT CO. OF WASHINGTON EDWARD S. FLEMING, PRESIDENT 1010 WISCONSIN AVE., N.W. WASHINGTON, D.C. 20007 (202) 337-5600	03/04-0081	502,197	558,080	DIVERSIFIED	5
DESTAN CAPITAL CORPORATION FRANK J. DEFRANCIS, CHAIRMAN 4340 CONNECTICUT AVE., N.W. WASHINGTON, D.C. 20008 (202) 362-1896	03/03-0132	500,000	0	DIVERSIFIED	5
GREATER WASHINGTON INVESTORS, INC. DON A. CHRISTENSEN, PRESIDENT 1015 - 18TH ST., N.W. WASHINGTON, D.C. 20036 (202) 466-2210	03/04-0011	1,109,589	3,823,990	DIVERSIFIED	6

LICENSEE	LICENSE NUMBER	PRIVATE CAPITAL	OBLIGATION TO SBA	INVESTMENT POLICY	OWNER CODE
D.C.(CONT)					
HOUSING CAPITAL CORP. GEORGE W. DEFRANCEAUX, CHAIRMAN 1133 FIFTEENTH ST., N.W. SUITE 700 WASHINGTON, D.C. 20005 (202) 857-5757	03/03-0119	2,000,000	6,000,000	OPERATIVE BUILDERS	4
FLORIDA					
ALLIED CAPITAL CORP. (MAIN OFFICE: WASHINGTON, D.C.) ONE FINANCIAL PLAZA SUITE 1614 FORT LAUDERDALE, FLORIDA 33301					
CORPORATE CAPITAL, INC JERRY THOMAS, PRESIDENT 2001 BROADWAY RIVIERA BEACH, FLORIDA 33404 (305) 844-6070	04/04-0150	1,266,000	0	DIVERSIFIED	1
DADELAND CAPITAL INVESTMENT CORP. I. ROBERT EISENMANN, PRESIDENT 7545 NORTH KENDALL DRIVE MIAMI, FLORIDA 33156 (305) 667-1213	04/04-0140	500,000	0	DIVERSIFIED	1
FIRST MIAMI SBIC IRVE L. LIBBY PRESIDENT 420 LINCOLN RD., RM. 235 MIAMI BEACH, FLORIDA 33139 (305) 531-0891	04/05-0008	515,520	515,000	50% REAL ESTATE	5
FIRST NORTH FLORIDA J. B. HIGDON, PRESIDENT 107 NORTH MADISON ST. P.O. BOX 386 QUINCY, FLORIDA 32351 (904) 627-7188	04/05-0022	300,000	87,500	GROCERY STORES	5
GOLD COAST CAPITAL CORPORATION WILLIAM I. GOLD, PRESIDENT 3550 BISCAYNE BLVD., ROOM 601 MIAMI, FLORIDA 33137 (305) 371-5456	04/05-0010	839,050	1,653,333	DIVERSIFIED	5

LICENSEE	LICENSE NUMBER	PRIVATE CAPITAL	OBLIGATION TO SBA	INVESTMENT POLICY	OWNER CODE
FLORIDA(CONT)					
MARKET CAPITAL CORP. E. E. EADS, PRESIDENT 1102 NORTH 28TH ST. P.O. BOX 22667 TAMPA, FLORIDA 33622 (813) 247-1357	04/05-0086	515,400	959,200	GROCERY STORES	4
SBAC OF PANAMA CITY FLORIDA J. R. ARNOLD, PRESIDENT 2612 WEST FIFTEENTH ST PANAMA CITY, FLORIDA 32401 (904) 785-9577	04/05-0082	3,600,000	11,194,380	80% IN LODGING PLACES, AMUSEMENT, AND RECREATION	1
SOUTHEAST SBIC, INC. CLEMENT L. HOFMANN, PRESIDENT 100 S. BISCAYNE BLVD. MIAMI, FLORIDA 33131 (305) 577-3174	04/05-0095	2,001,169	4,000,000	DIVERSIFIED	1
SUWANNEE CAPITAL CORP. WILLIAM LOVETT, CHAIRMAN OF BOARD 1010 EAST ADAMS ST. JACKSONVILLE, FLORIDA 32202 (904) 355-8315	04/04-0136	1,005,000	500,000	RETAIL GROCERY STORES	5
GEORGIA					
AFFILIATED INVESTMENT FUND, INC. SAMUEL WEISSMAN, PRESIDENT 2225 SHURFINE DRIVE COLLEGE PARK, GEORGIA 30337 (404) 766-0221	04/04-0118	512,000	500,000	RETAIL GROCER	4
CSRA CAPITAL CORP. (MAIN OFFICE: AUGUSTA, GA.) 1401 WEST PACES FERRY RD., N.W. SUITE E116 ATLANTA, GEORGIA 30327 (404) 231-1313					
CSRA CAPITAL CORP. ALLEN F. CALDWELL, JR., PRESIDENT 1058 CLAUSSEN ROAD AUGUSTA, GEORGIA 30907 (404) 736-2236	04/05-0057	2,353,831	9,083,500	DIVERSIFIED	2

LICENSEE	LICENSE NUMBER	PRIVATE CAPITAL	OBLIGATION TO SBA	INVESTMENT POLICY	OWNER CODE
GEORGIA(CONT)					
EQUILEASE CAPITAL CORP (MAIN OFFICE: NEW YORK, N.Y.) 22-61 PENIMETER PK., SUITE 12 ATLANTA, GEORGIA 30309					
FIDELITY CAPITAL CORP. ALFRED F. SKIBA, VICE PRES. & TRES 380 INTERSTATE NORTH SUITE 150 ATLANTA, GEORGIA 30339 (404) 955-3880	04/05-0028	3,531,631	9,630,000	100% REAL ESTATE	3
FIRST AMERICAN INV. CORPORATION CLIFTON HOFMAN, PRESIDENT 300 INTERSTATE NORTH ATLANTA, GEORGIA 30339 (404) 955-0000	04/05-0023	3,710,132	10,526,700	100% REAL ESTATE	4
INVESTOR'S EQUITY, INCORPORATED I. WALTER FISHER, PRESIDENT 2902 FIRST NATIONAL BANK TOWER ATLANTA, GEORGIA 30303 (404) 658-1002	04/05-0018	315,500	200,000	DIVERSIFIED	5
MOME CAPITAL CORP. JAMES A. HUTCHINSON, PRESIDENT 234 MAIN STREET THOMSON, GEORGIA 30824 (404) 595-1507	04/05-0084	600,000	1,110,000	MOBILE HOMES	5
RIO INVESTMENT CORP. JOHN MALLORY, GENERAL MANAGER 1415 INDUSTRY AVENUE ALBANY, GEORGIA 31702 (912) 435-3575	04/04-0115	300,000	0	RETAIL GROCERY STORES	5
SOUTHEASTERN CAPITAL SBI CORP. J. RAY EFIRD, PRESIDENT SUITE 505, NORTHCREEK 3715 NORTHSIDE PARKWAY, N.W. ATLANTA, GEORGIA 30327 (404) 237-1567	04/05-0003	1,500,000	0	DIVERSIFIED	6

LICENSEE	LICENSE NUMBER	PRIVATE CAPITAL	OBLIGATION TO SBA	INVESTMENT POLICY	OWNER CODE
HAWAII					
SBIC OF HAWAII JAMES WONG, CHAIRMAN OF BOARD 1575 SOUTH BERETANIA ST. HONOLULU, HAWAII 96814 (808) 949-3677	09/12-0099	317,100	450,000	66-2/3% REAL ESTATE	3
IDAHO					
FIRST IDAHO VENTURE CAP. CORP. DICK MILLER, VICE PRESIDENT SUITE 1102, ONE CAPITAL CENTER 999 MAIN STREET, DRAWER Y BOISE, IDAHO 83702 (208) 345-3460	10/10-0161	500,000	500,000	DIVERSIFIED	3
ILLINOIS					
ABBOTT CAPITAL CORP. RICHARD E. LASSAR, PRESIDENT 120 SOUTH LASALLE ST. CHICAGO, ILLINOIS 60603 (312) 726-3803	05/07-0082	525,500	1,750,000	DIVERSIFIED	5
ADAMS STREET CAPITAL, INCORPORATED MARVIN A. MARDER, PRESIDENT 1866 SHERIDAN RD., SUITE 217 HIGHLAND PARK, ILLINOIS 60035 (312) 368-0077	05/07-0029	153,000	250,000	DIVERSIFIED	5
ADVANCE GROWTH CAPITAL CORPORATION CHARLES F. SEBASTIAN, PRESIDENT RADIO CENTER 9355 WEST JOLIET ROAD LAGRANGE, ILLINOIS 60526 (312) 352-2650	05/07-0031	3,901,186	319,999	DIVERSIFIED	6
ANDROCK CAPITAL CORP. JOHN R. ANDERSON, PRESIDENT 1307 SAMUELSON RD. ROCKFORD, ILLINOIS 61101 (615) 397-5000	05/05-0090	703,000	0	DIVERSIFIED	4
CERTIFIED GROCERS INV. CORPORATION ROBERT A. KORINK, PRESIDENT 4800 SOUTH CENTRAL AVENUE CHICAGO, ILLINOIS 60638 (312) 585-7000	05/05-0107	500,000	0	RETAIL GROCERY STORES	4

LICENSEE	LICENSE NUMBER	PRIVATE CAPITAL	OBLIGATION TO SBA	INVESTMENT POLICY	OWNER CODE
ILLINOIS(CONT)					
CHICAGO EQUITY CORP. MORRIS WEISER, PRESIDENT ONE IBM PLAZA, SUITE 3625 CHICAGO, ILLINOIS 60611 (312) 321-9662	05/07-0057	231,220	130,000	DIVERSIFIED	5
CONTINENTAL ILLINOIS VENTURE CORP. JOHN L. HINES, PRESIDENT 231 SOUTH LASALLE ST. CHICAGO, ILLINOIS 60604 (312) 828-8023	05/07-0078	3,111,800	2,500,000	DIVERSIFIED	1
EQUILEASE CAPITAL CORP (MAIN OFFICE: NEW YORK, N. Y.) 2400 EAST DEVON DES PLAINES, ILLINOIS 60018					
FIRST CAPITAL CORP. OF CHICAGO STANLEY C. GOLDER, PRESIDENT ONE FIRST NATIONAL PLAZA CHICAGO, ILLINOIS 60670 (312) 732-8068	05/07-0042	10,000,000	2,500,000	DIVERSIFIED	1
FRONTENAC CAPITAL CORP MARTIN J. KOLDYKE, PRESIDENT 208 SOUTH LASALLE STREET CHICAGO, ILLINOIS 60604 (312) 368-0047	05/05-0114	3,000,000	0	DIVERSIFIED	2
HEIZER CAPITAL CORP. E. F. HEIZER, PRESIDENT SUITE 4100, 20 NORTH WACKER DR. CHICAGO, ILLINOIS 60606 (312) 641-2200	05/05-0096	12,000,000	0	DIVERISFIED	3
SB MANAGEMENT INVESTORS, INC. KENNETH EATON, PRESIDENT 17 EAST CHESTNUT CHICAGO, ILLINOIS 60611 (312) 943-0750	05/07-0016	150,650	237,500	DIVERSIFIED	5
UNITED CAP. CORP. OF ILLINOIS WILLARD C. MILLS, PRESIDENT UNITED CENTER, STATE & WYMAN STS. P.O. BOX 998 ROCKFORD, ILLINOIS 61105 (815) 987-2179	05/07-0079	3,100,000	1,400,000	DIVERSIFIED	4

LICENSEE	LICENSE NUMBER	PRIVATE CAPITAL	OBLIGATION TO SBA	INVESTMENT POLICY	OWNER CODE
IOWA					
MORAMERICA CAPITAL CORPORATION ROBERT ALLSOP, PRESIDENT SUITE 200, AMERICAN BLDG. CEDAR RAPIDS, IOWA 52401 (319) 363-0263	07/07-0006	3,700,000	11,416,986	DIVERSIFIED	1
KANSAS					
KANSAS VENTURE CAPITAL, INC. GEORGE L. DOAK, PRESIDENT 1030 FIRST NATIONAL BANK TOWER ONE TOWNSITE PLAZA TOPEKA, KANSAS 66603 (913) 235-3437	07/07-0077	1,075,240	0	DIVERSIFIED	3
KENTUCKY					
FINANCIAL OPPORT- UNITIES, INC. ANTHONY W. FOELLGER, PRESIDENT 981 SOUTH THIRD ST. LOUISVILLE, KENTUCKY 40203 (502) 584-1281	04/04-0113	500,000	2,000,000	DIVERSIFIED	4
MOUNTAIN VENTURES, INCORPORATED FREDERICK J. BESTE II, PRESIDENT 911 NORTH MAIN STREET MAIL:P.O. BOX 628 LONDON, KY 40741 LONDON, KENTUCKY 40741 (606) 864-5175	04/04-0145	1,300,000	0	DIVERSIFIED	5
LOUISIANA					
AFFILIATED SBIC INCORPORATED CHARLES J. SIMMONS, PRESIDENT AFFILIATED RD. & KENNEDY ST. BROUSSARD, LOUISIANA 70518 (318) 837-6636	06/06-0198	502,500	0	GROCERY STORES	4
CAPITAL FOR TERREBONNE, INC. HARTWELL A. LEWIS, PRESIDENT 1613 BARROW STREET HOUMA, LOUISIANA 70360 (504) 868-3930	06/06-0195	500,000	200,000	DIVERSIFIED	5

LICENSEE	LICENSE NUMBER	PRIVATE CAPITAL	OBLIGATION TO SBA	INVESTMENT POLICY	OWNER CODE

LOUISIANA(CONT)

COMMERCIAL CAPITAL,
  INCORPORATED
(MAIN OFFICE: COVINGTON, LA.)
1809 WEST THOMAS ST.
HAMMOND, LOUISIANA 70404
(504) 748-7157

COMMERCIAL CAPITAL,
  INCORPORATED
(MAIN OFFICE: COVINGTON, LA.)
HIGHWAY 190 BY PASS
BOGUE FALAYA PLAZA SHOPPING CENTER
COVINGTON, LOUISIANA 70433

LICENSEE	LICENSE NUMBER	PRIVATE CAPITAL	OBLIGATION TO SBA	INVESTMENT POLICY	OWNER CODE
COMMERCIAL CAPITAL, INCORPORATED FREDERICK W. PIERCE, PRESIDENT P.O. BOX 939 COVINGTON, LOUISIANA 70433 (504) 892-4291	06/10-0124	630,000	1,879,100	DIVERSIFIED	3
DIXIE BUSINESS INVESTMENT CO. STEVE K. CHEEK, PRESIDENT 406 LAKE ST. LAKE PROVIDENCE, LOUISIANA 71254 (318) 559-1558	06/06-0173	432,100	900,000	DIVERSIFIED	2
FIRST BUSINESS INVESTMENT CORP. ALBERT J. PREVOT, PRESIDENT P.O. BOX 1299 115 NORTH COURT STREET OPELOUSAS, LOUISIANA 70570 (318) 948-3115	06/10-0015	542,000	838,333	DIVERSIFIED	
FIRST SBIC OF LOUISIANA, INC. MRS. N. HOOPER, EXEC. V.P. 133 SOUTH DORGENOIS ST. NEW ORLEANS, LOUISIANA 70119 (504) 522-3534	06/10-0016	161,801	225,000	WATER TRANS-PORTATION	5
FIRST SOUTHERN CAPITAL CORPORATION DENNIS CROSS, PRESIDENT COMMERCE BLDG., SUITE 1214 821 GRAVIER ST. NEW ORLEANS, LOUISIANA 70112 (504) 561-1337	06/12-0023	1,029,224	2,950,000	DIVERSIFIED	6

LICENSEE	LICENSE NUMBER	PRIVATE CAPITAL	OBLIGATION TO SBA	INVESTMENT POLICY	OWNER CODE
LOUISIANA(CONT)					
LOUISIANA EQUITY CAPITAL CORP. (MAIN OFFICE: BATON ROUGE, LA) C/O MR. RALPH FRANCE BANK OF NEW ORLEANS BOX 52499 NEW ORLEANS, LOUISIANA 70152					
LOUISIANA EQUITY CAPITAL CORP. (MAIN OFFICE: BATON ROUGE, LA.) C/O MR. ED MATHEWS OUACHITA NATIONAL BANK, BOX 1412 MONROE, LOUISIANA 71201					
LOUISIANA EQUITY CAPITAL CORP. THOMAS NICHOLSON, PRESIDENT 451 FLORIDA ST. BATON ROUGE, LOUISIANA 70801 (504) 389-4421	06/06-0169	900,000	1,000,000	DIVERSIFIED	1
ROYAL STREET INV. CORPORATION WILLIAM D. HUMPHRIES, PRESIDENT SUITE 4646, ONE SHELL SQUARE NEW ORLEANS, LOUISIANA 70139 (504) 588-9271	06/10-0096	1,323,500	1,794,998	DIVERSIFIED	4
SAVINGS VENTURE CAP. CORPORATION DALE ANDERSON, PRESIDENT 6001 FINANCIAL PLAZA SHREVEPORT, LOUISIANA 71130 (318) 686-9200	06/06-0200	1,000,000	0	DIVERSIFIED	4
VENTURTECH CAPITAL, INCORPORATED W. A. BRUCE, EXEC. V.P. SUITE 706, REPUBLIC TOWER 5700 FLORIDA BLVD. BATON ROUGE, LOUISIANA 70806 (504) 926-5482	06/06-0163	1,115,200	2,230,000	TECHNOLOGY FIELD	4
MARYLAND					
REAL ESTATE CAPITAL CORPORATION (MAIN OFFICE: BALA CYNWYD, PA.) 9823 CENTRAL AVENUE LARGO, MARYLAND 20870 (301) 336-2345					

LICENSEE	LICENSE NUMBER	PRIVATE CAPITAL	OBLIGATION TO SBA	INVESTMENT POLICY	OWNER CODE
MASSACHUSETTS					
ADVENT CAPITAL CORP. WILLIAM P. EGAN, PRESIDENT 111 DEVONSHIRE ST. BOSTON, MASSACHUSETTS 02109 (617) 725-2301	01/01-0291	2,991,574	0	DIVERSIFIED	5
ATLAS CAPITAL CORP. HERBERT CARVER, PRESIDENT 55 COURT STREET BOSTON, MASSACHUSETTS 02108 (617) 482-1218	01/01-0030	1,254,156	2,372,768	50% REAL ESTATE	3
BEACON CAPITAL CORP. GEORGE S. CHALETZKY, TREASURER 587 BEACON STREET BOSTON, MASSACHUSETTS 02215 (617) 566-6000	01/01-0035	212,950	203,269	50% REAL ESTATE	5
BUSINESS ACHIEVEMENT CORPORATION JULIAN H. KATZEFF, PRESIDENT 93 UNION STREET NEWTON CENTER, MASSACHUSETTS 02159 (617) 965-0550	01/01-0055	271,402	455,120	DIVERSIFIED	5
CHARLES RIVER RESOURCES, INC. RICHARD M. BURNES, JR., PRESIDENT 133 FEDERAL STREET BOSTON, MASSACHUSETTS 02110 (617) 482-9370	01/01-0283	2,500,000	4,000,000	DIVERSIFIED	4
DEVONSHIRE CAPITAL CORPORATION C. KELVIN LANDRY, PRESIDENT 111 DEVONSHIRE STREET BOSTON, MASSACHUSETTS 02109 (617) 725-2306	01/01-0278	2,196,750	4,000,000	DIVERSIFIED	5
EQUILEASE CAPITAL CORP (MAIN OFFICE: NEW YORK, N.Y.) 393 TOTTEN POND RD., SUITE 651 WALTHEM, MASSACHUSETTS 02154					
FEDERAL STREET CAPITAL CORPORATION JOHN H. LAMOTHE, PRESIDENT 75 FEDERAL STREET BOSTON, MASSACHUSETTS 02110 (617) 542-1380	01/01-0002	3,579,244	2,500,000	DIVERSIFIED	1

LICENSEE	LICENSE NUMBER	PRIVATE CAPITAL	OBLIGATION TO SBA	INVESTMENT POLICY	OWNER CODE
MASSACHUSETTS(CONT)					
FIRST CAPITAL CORP. OF BOSTON RICHARD A. FARRELL, PRESIDENT 100 FEDERAL STREET BOSTON, MASSACHUSETTS 02110 (617) 434-2441	01/01-0001	2,500,000	7,500,000	DIVERSIFIED	1
FIRST UNITED SBIC, INCORPORATED ALFRED W. FERRARA, V. PRESIDENT 135 WILL DRIVE CANTON, MASSACHUSETTS 02021 (617) 828-6150	01/01-0284	300,000	300,000	DIVERSIFIED	4
MASSACHUSETTS CAPITAL CORPORATION DAVID HARKINS, PRESIDENT 100 FEDERAL STREET BOSTON, MASSACHUSETTS 02110 (617) 426-2488	01/01-0018	650,438	865,000	DIVERSIFIED	5
NEW ENGLAND ENTERPRISE CAPITAL CORP. Z. DAVID PATTERSON, ASST. V.P. 28 STATE ST. BOSTON, MASSACHUSETTS 02106 (617) 742-0285	01/01-0023	1,945,000	2,027,063	DIVERSIFIED	1
NORTHEAST SMALL BUS. INV. CORP. JOSEPH MINDICK, TREASURER 16 CUMBERLAND ST. BOSTON, MASSACHUSETTS 02115 (617) 267-3983	01/01-0275	378,802	1,130,000	DIVERSIFIED	5
PRIME CAPITAL CORP. JASON ROSENBERG, PRESIDENT 10 COMMERCIAL WHARF SOUTH SUITE 502 BOSTON, MASSACHUSETTS 02210 (617) 723-2103	01/01-0276	325,000	200,000	DIVERSIFIED	5
SCHOONER CAPITAL CORP. VINCENT RYAN, JR., PRESIDENT 141 MILK STREET BOSTON, MASSACHUSETTS 02109 (617) 357-9031	01/01-0011	1,783,159	1,991,574	DIVERSIFIED	5

LICENSEE	LICENSE NUMBER	PRIVATE CAPITAL	OBLIGATION TO SBA	INVESTMENT POLICY	OWNER CODE
MASSACHUSETTS(CONT)					
UST CAPITAL CORP. STEPHEN R. LEWINSTEIN, PRESIDENT 40 COURT ST. BOSTON, MASSACHUSETTS 02108 (617) 726-7265	01/01-0027	482,800	655,645	DIVERSIFIED	1
WORCESTER CAPITAL CORPORATION W. KENNETH KIDD, MANAGER 446 MAIN STREET WORCESTER, MASSACHUSETTS 01608 (617) 853-7585	01/01-0068	650,000	500,000	DIVERSIFIED	1
YANKEE CAPITAL CORP. RICHARD F. POLLARD, PRESIDENT 175 FEDERAL STREET BOSTON, MASSACHUSETTS 02110 (617) 482-1041	01/01-0041	750,000	0	DIVERSIFIED	1
MICHIGAN					
DOAN RESOURCES CORP. HERBERT D. DOAN, PRESIDENT 110 EAST GROVE STREET MIDLAND, MICHIGAN 48640 (517) 631-2623	05/05-0098	1,987,500	4,225,000	DIVERSIFIED	3
FEDERATED CAPITAL CORPORATION LOUIS P. FERRIS, JR., PRESIDENT 20000 WEST TWELVE MILE ROAD SOUTHFIELD, MICHIGAN 48076 (313) 557-9100	05/05-0130	300,000	0	DIVERSIFIED	3
MICHIGAN CAPITAL & SERVICE, INC. JOSEPH CONWAY, MANAGER 580 CITY CENTER BUILDING ANN ARBOR, MICHIGAN 48104 (313) 663-0702	05/15-0021	592,200	1,200,000	DIVERSIFIED	2
MINNESOTA					
CONSUMER GROWTH CAPITAL, INC. JOHN T. GERLACH, PRESIDENT 430 OAK GROVE, SUITE 404 MINNEAPOLIS, MINNESOTA 55403 (612) 874-0694	05/05-0123	700,617	0	DIVERSIFIED	5

LICENSEE	LICENSE NUMBER	PRIVATE CAPITAL	OBLIGATION TO SBA	INVESTMENT POLICY	OWNER CODE
MINNESOTA(CONT)					
CONTROL DATA CAPITAL CORPORATION EDWARD E. STRICKLAND, PRESIDENT 8100 - 34TH AVENUE SOUTH BLOOMINGTON, MINNESOTA 55420 (612) 853-8100	05/05-0117	1,000,000	0	DIVERSIFIED	4
EAGLE VENTURES, INC. LAWRENCE L. HORSCH, PRESIDENT SUITE 700, SOO LINE BUILDING MINNEAPOLIS, MINNESOTA 55402 (612) 339-9694	05/10-0104	808,349	1,495,000	DIVERSIFIED	4
FIRST MIDWEST CAPITAL CORPORATION ALAN K. RUVELSON, PRESIDENT 15 SOUTH FIFTH ST., SUITE 700 MINNEAPOLIS, MINNESOTA 55402 (612) 339-9391	05/08-0002	1,025,000	2,885,000	DIVERSIFIED	3
NORTH STAR VENTURES, INCORPORATED GERALD A. RAUENHORST, PRESIDENT SUITE 1845 NORTHWESTERN FINANCIAL 7900 XERXES AVE. SOUTH MINNEAPOLIS, MINNESOTA 55431 (612) 830-4550	05/05-0099	1,081,627	1,750,000	DIVERSIFIED	5
NORTHLAND CAPITAL CORPORATION GEORGE G. BARNUM, JR., PRESIDENT 613 MISSABE BUILDING DULUTH, MINNESOTA 55802 (218) 722-0545	05/08-0018	321,500	400,000	DIVERSIFIED	5
NORTHWEST GROWTH FUND, INCORPORATED ROBERT F. ZICARELLI, PRESIDENT 960 NORTHWESTERN BANK BUILDING MINNEAPOLIS, MINNESOTA 55402 (612) 372-8770	05/08-0006	3,088,491	14,668,731	DIVERSIFIED	1
P.R. PETERSON VENTURE CAPITAL CORP. P.R. PETERSON, PRESIDENT 3726 OREGON AVENUE, SOUTH ST. LOUIS PARK, MINNESOTA 55426 (612) 935-3130	05/05-0129	300,000	0	DIVERSIFIED	5

LICENSEE	LICENSE NUMBER	PRIVATE CAPITAL	OBLIGATION TO SBA	INVESTMENT POLICY	OWNER CODE
MINNESOTA(CONT)					
RETAILERS GROWTH FUND, INCORPORATED E. O. WACK, PRESIDENT 5100 GAMBLE DR. MINNEAPOLIS, MINNESOTA 55416 (612) 374-6250	05/08-0015	700,000	1,150,000	FRANCHISED RETAILERS	4
WESTLAND CAPITAL CORP. ROBERT S. DUNBAR, PRESIDENT SUITE 115 HENNEPIN SQ. 2021 EAST HENNEPIN AVE. MINNEAPOLIS, MINNESOTA 55413 (612) 331-9210	05/14-0039	1,000,000	1,728,000	DIVERSIFIED	6
MISSISSIPPI					
DE SOTO CAPITAL CORP. WILLIAM B. RUDNER, PRESIDENT PINE CREEK COMMERCIAL PLAZA, 9991 OLD CREEK HIGHWAY 7, SUITE 10 OLIVE BRANCH, MISSISSIPPI 38654 (601) 895-4145	04/04-0125	500,000	400,000	DIVERSIFIED	5
INVESAT CORPORATION J. THOMAS NOOJIN, PRESIDENT 1414 DEPOSIT GUARANTY PLAZA JACKSON, MISSISSIPPI 39201 (601) 969-3242	04/04-0110	2,892,180	1,100,000	DIVERSIFIED	6
VICKSBURG SBIC EDWARD H. RUSSELL, PRESIDENT 302 FIRST NATIONAL BANK BUILDING VICKSBURG, MISSISSIPPI 39180 (601) 636-4762	04/05-0011	365,000	627,322	DIVERSIFIED	5
MISSOURI					
ATLAS SMALL BUSINESS INVESTMENT CORP. RONALD JARVIS, JR., PRESIDENT 1808 MAIN ST. KANSAS CITY, MISSOURI 64108 (816) 471-1750	07/09-0004	152,750	180,000	DIVERSIFIED	4
BANKERS CAPITAL CORP. RAYMOND E. GLASNAPP, PRESIDENT 4049 PENNSYLVANIA, SUITE 304 KANSAS CITY, MISSOURI 64111 (816) 531-1600	07/07-0075	302,000	900,000	DIVERSIFIED	5

LICENSEE	LICENSE NUMBER	PRIVATE CAPITAL	OBLIGATION TO SBA	INVESTMENT POLICY	OWNER CODE
MISSOURI(CONT)					
CAPITAL FOR BUSINESS, INCORPORATED JAMES LINN, PRESIDENT P.O. BOX 13686 KANSAS CITY, MISSOURI 64199 (816) 234-2344	07/09-0002	1,400,000	0	DIVERSIFIED	1
EQUILEASE CAPITAL CORP (MAIN OFFICE: NEW YORK, N.Y.) 7700 CLAYTON ROAD ST. LOUIS, MISSOURI 63117					
INTERCAPCO WEST, INC. THOMAS E. PHELPS, PRESIDENT 7800 BONHOMME AVENUE ST. LOUIS, MISSOURI 63105 (314) 863-0600	07/07-0076	525,000	500,000	DIVERSIFIED	4
MORAMERICA CAPITAL CORPORATION (MAIN OFFICE: CEDAR RAPIDS, IOWA) 911 MAIN ST., SUITE 2710 COMMERCE TOWER BLDG. KANSAS CITY, MISSOURI 64152					
MORAMERICA CAPITAL CORPORATION (MAIN OFFICE: CEDAR RAPIDS, IOWA) SUITE 600, 111 WEST PORT PLAZA ST. LOUIS, MISSOURI 63141					
NEBRASKA					
MORAMERICA CAPITAL CORPORATION (MAIN OFFICE: CEDAR RAPIDS, IOWA) SUITE 376, EMBASSY PLAZA 9110 WEST DODGE ROAD OMAHA, NEBRASKA 68114					
NEW JERSEY					
CAPITAL SBIC, INC. ISADORE COHEN, PRESIDENT 143 EAST STATE STREET TRENTON, NEW JERSEY 08608 (609) 394-5221	02/03-0051	480,316	398,866	85% REAL ESTATE	5

LICENSEE	LICENSE NUMBER	PRIVATE CAPITAL	OBLIGATION TO SBA	INVESTMENT POLICY	OWNER CODE
NEW JERSEY(CONT)					
DELAWARE VALLEY SBIC (MAIN OFFICE: PHILA., PA.) PLAZA APTS. ATLANTIC CITY, NEW JERSEY 08201					
ENGLE INVESTMENT CO. MURRAY HENDEL, PRESIDENT 35 ESSEX STREET HACKENSACK, NEW JERSEY 07601 (201) 489-3583	02/02-0216	425,657	665,036	DIVERSIFIED	5
LLOYD CAPITAL CORP. SOLOMON SCHARF, PRESIDENT 77 STATE HIGHWAY 5 P.O. BOX 180 EDGEWATER, NEW JERSEY 07020 (201) 947-1717	02/02-0314	2,000,000	5,000,000	DIVERSIFIED	6
MAIN CAPITAL INV. CORPORATION SAM KLOTZ, PRESIDENT 818 MAIN STREET HACKENSACK, NEW JERSEY 07601 (201) 489-2080	02/03-0056	160,000	244,333	DIVERSIFIED	5
MONMOUTH CAPITAL CORP. EUGENE W. LANDY, PRESIDENT 125 WYCKOFF ROAD 1ST MERCHANTS BANK BLDG-P.O.BOX 335 EATONTOWN, NEW JERSEY 07724 (201) 542-4927	02/02-0088	2,453,931	6,218,644	DIVERSIFIED	6
QUIDNET CAPITAL CORP. STEPHEN W. FILLO, PRESIDENT 32 NASSAU STREET PRINCETON, NEW JERSEY 08540 (609) 924-7665	02/02-0350	1,500,000	0	DIVERSIFIED	3
VENTURTECH CAPITAL, INCORPORATED (MAIN OFFICE: BATON ROUGE, LA.) 12 BANK STREET SUMMIT, NEW JERSEY 07901					
NEW MEXICO					
ALBUQUERQUE SBIC ALBERT T. USSERY, PRESIDENT 501 TIJERAS AVENUE, N.W. P.O. BOX 487 ALBUQUERQUE, NEW MEXICO 87103 (505) 247-0145	06/06-0191	302,000	0	DIVERSIFIED	5

LICENSEE	LICENSE NUMBER	PRIVATE CAPITAL	OBLIGATION TO SBA	INVESTMENT POLICY	OWNER CODE
NEW MEXICO(CONT)					
FIRST CAPITAL CORP. OF NEW MEXICO MELVIN I. HERTZ, PRESIDENT 8425 OSUNA ROAD, N.E. ALBUQUERQUE, NEW MEXICO 87111 (505) 293-5057	06/06-0202	504,000	0	DIVERSIFIED	5
FRANKLIN CORP. (THE) (MAIN OFFICE: NEW YORK, N.Y.) AMERICAN BANK OF COMMERCE COMPLEX 200 LOMAS BLVD., SUITE 818 ALBUQUERQUE, NEW MEXICO 87102					
NEW MEXICO CAPITAL CORPORATION WILLIAM R. CHRISTY, EXEC. V.P. 2900 LOUISIANA BLVD., N.E. SUITE 201 ALBUQUERQUE, NEW MEXICO 87110 (505) 293-7600	06/11-0024	2,985,001	11,915,000	DIVERSIFIED	5
SOUTHWEST CAPITAL INV., INC. ROGER L. FORD, PRESIDENT 8000 PENNSYLVANIA CIRCLE, N.E. ALBUQUERQUE, NEW MEXICO 87110 (505) 265-9564	06/06-0179	500,000	1,000,000	DIVERSIFIED	3
VENTURE CAPITAL CORP. OF NEW MEXICO BENIRWIN BRONSTEIN, PRESIDENT 5301 CENTRAL AVENUE, N.E SUITE 1600 ALBUQUERQUE, NEW MEXICO 87108 (505) 266-0066	06/06-0172	719,937	2,860,000	DIVERSIFIED	5
NEW YORK					
BASIC CAPITAL CORP. PAUL KATES, PRESIDENT 40 WEST 37TH STREET NEW YORK, NEW YORK 10018 (212) 868-9645	02/02-0034	450,000	147,165	DIVERSIFIED	4
BENEFICIAL CAPITAL CORPORATION JOHN HOEY, PRESIDENT 645 FIFTH AVENUE NEW YORK, NEW YORK 10022 (212) 752-1291	02/02-0076	363,886	1,087,500	DIVERSIFIED	5

LICENSEE	LICENSE NUMBER	PRIVATE CAPITAL	OBLIGATION TO SBA	INVESTMENT POLICY	OWNER CODE
NEW YORK(CONT)					
BOHLEN CAPITAL CORP. HARVEY J. WERTHEIM, PRESIDENT SUITE 1260 - 230 PARK AVENUE NEW YORK, NEW YORK 10017 (212) 867-9435	02/02-0317	1,000,000	1,500,000	DIVERSIFIED	5
BT CAPITAL CORP. WILLIAM M. EATON, PRESIDENT 600 THIRD AVENUE NEW YORK, NEW YORK 10016 (212) 867-0606	02/02-0295	600,000	600,000	DIVERSIFIED	1
CANAVERAL CAPITAL CORPORATION MICHAEL PRATTER, PRESIDENT 26 COURT STREET, SUITE 902 BROOKLYN, NEW YORK 11201 (212) 375-5216	02/05-0068	431,604	692,410	DIVERSIFIED	5
CAPITAL FOR FUTURE, INC. (SBIC) JAY SCHWAMM, PRESIDENT 635 MADISON AVENUE NEW YORK, NEW YORK 10022 (212) 759-8060	02/02-0082	301,000	235,000	50% REAL ESTATE	3
CENTRAL NEW YORK SBIC (THE) ROBERT E. ROMIG, PRESIDENT 351 SO. WARREN STREET SYRACUSE, NEW YORK 13202 (315) 469-7711	02/02-0044	150,000	195,000	VENDING MACHINE	4
CHASE MANHATTAN CAPITAL CORP. ROBERT HUBBARD, PRESIDENT 1411 BROADWAY, 4TH FLOOR NEW YORK, NEW YORK 10018 (212) 223-6170	02/02-0228	24,785,000	17,000,000	DIVERSIFIED	1
CLARION CAPITAL CORP. (MAIN OFFICE: CLEVELAND, OHIO) TWO PENN. PLAZA NEW YORK, NEW YORK 10001					
CMNY CAPITAL COMPANY, INCORPORATED ROBERT DAVIDOFF, VICE PRESIDENT 77 WATER STREET NEW YORK, NEW YORK 10005 (212) 437-7078	02/02-0180	1,776,480	5,197,500	DIVERSIFIED	3

LICENSEE	LICENSE NUMBER	PRIVATE CAPITAL	OBLIGATION TO SBA	INVESTMENT POLICY	OWNER CODE
NEW YORK(CONT)					
COMMUNICATIONS FUNDS, INCORPORATED BLAIR WALLISER, PRESIDENT 1271 AVENUE OF AMERICAS NEW YORK, NEW YORK 10020 (212) 245-2870	02/02-0073	171,250	282,500	RADIO & T.V.	5
ENGLE INVESTMENT COMPANY (MAIN OFFICE: HACKENSACK, N.J.) 135 WEST 50 STREET NEW YORK, NEW YORK 10020 (212) 757-9580					
EQUILEASE CAPITAL CORPORATION NORBERT WEISSBERG, PRESIDENT 750 THIRD AVENUE NEW YORK, NEW YORK 10017 (212) 557-6800	02/02-0269	500,000	1,000,000	DIVERSIFIED	3
EQUITABLE SBI CORP. DAVID GOLDBERG, PRESIDENT 350 FIFTH AVE., SUITE 5820 NEW YORK, NEW YORK 10001 (212) 564-5420	02/02-0016	250,200	180,000	66-2/3% HEALTH AND RELATED	5
ESIC CAPITAL, INC. GEORGE BOOKBINDER, PRESIDENT 110 EAST 59TH STREET SUITE 1008 NEW YORK, NEW YORK 10022 (212) 421-1605	02/04-0048	1,853,673	7,206,400	DIVERSIFIED	5
FAIRFIELD EQUITY CORP. MATTHEW A. BERDON, PRESIDENT 200 EAST 42 STREET NEW YORK, NEW YORK 10017 (212) 867-0150	02/02-0151	1,035,942	2,466,669	DIVERSIFIED	5
FIFTY-THIRD STREET VENTURES ALAN J. PATRICOF, CHAIRMAN ONE EAST 53RD STREET NEW YORK, NEW YORK 10022 (212) 753-6797	02/02-0315	2,600,000	1,000,000	DIVERSIFIED	5

LICENSEE	LICENSE NUMBER	PRIVATE CAPITAL	OBLIGATION TO SBA	INVESTMENT POLICY	OWNER CODE
NEW YORK(CONT)					
FIRST CONNECTICUT SBIC (MAIN OFFICE: BRIDGEPORT, CONN.) 68 FIFTH AVENUE NEW YORK, NEW YORK 10003					
FIRST WALL STREET SBIC, INC. JOHN W. CHAPPELL, PRESIDENT ONE WALL STREET NEW YORK, NEW YORK 10005 (212) 943-0987	02/02-0330	504,380	0	DIVERSIFIED	5
FIRST WOMEN'S SBI CORPORATION DR. SANDRA BROWN, PRESIDENT 134 EAST 38TH STREET NEW YORK, NEW YORK 10016 (212) 754-0606	02/02-0331	1,300,000	3,400,000	DIVERSIFIED	5
FNCB CAPITAL CORP. THOMAS HIGGS, ASST. V.P. 399 PARK AVENUE NEW YORK, NEW YORK 10022 (212) 559-1000	02/02-0266	37,000,000	2,500,000	DIVERSIFIED	1
FRANKLIN CORP. (THE) HERMAN GOODMAN, PRESIDENT ONE ROCKEFELLER PLAZA SUITE 2614 NEW YORK, NEW YORK 10022 (212) 581-4900	02/02-0005	9,183,027	11,930,000	DIVERSIFIED	6
FUNDEX CAPITAL CORP HOWARD SOMMER, PRESIDENT 525 NORTHERN BLVD. GREAT NECK, NEW YORK 11021 (516) 466-8551	02/02-0340	496,398	1,000,000	DIVERSIFIED	5
HAMILTON CAPITAL FUND, INC. (THE) ADOLPH GROSS, PRESIDENT 555 MADISON AVE. NEW YORK, NEW YORK 10022 (212) 838-8382	02/02-0100	240,280	250,000	DIVERSIFIED	5
HANOVER CAPITAL CORP. (THE) DANIEL J. SULLIVAN, PRESIDENT 223 EAST 62ND ST. NEW YORK, NEW YORK 10021 (212) 532-6670	02/02-0102	501,000	1,880,000	DIVERSIFIED	5

LICENSEE	LICENSE NUMBER	PRIVATE CAPITAL	OBLIGATION TO SBA	INVESTMENT POLICY	OWNER CODE
NEW YORK(CONT)					
INTERCOASTAL CAPITAL CORPORATION HERBERT KRASNOW, PRESIDENT 380 MADISON AVENUE NEW YORK, NEW YORK 10017 (212) 758-0209	02/02-0194	608,800	1,057,568	66% REAL ESTATE	6
INTERGROUP VENTURE CAPITAL CORP. BEN HAUBEN, PRESIDENT 551 FIFTH AVENUE NEW YORK, NEW YORK 10017 (212) 661-5333	02/02-0345	502,500	0	DIVERSIFIED	5
INTERNATIONAL FILM INVESTORS, L.P. JOSIAH H. CHILD, JR. PRESIDENT-CORPORATE GENERAL PARTNER 595 MADISON AVE., 11TH FLOOR NEW YORK, NEW YORK 10022 (212) 843-1920	02/02-0354	7,670,000	0	100% MOVIE SPECIALIST	4-P
IRVING CAPITAL CORP. ANDREW MCWETHY, V.P. & GEN. MGR. ONE WALL STREET NEW YORK, NEW YORK 10015 (212) 487-3474	02/02-0321	4,150,000	0	DIVERSIFIED	1
LAKE SUCCESS CAPITAL CORPORATION HERMAN SCHNEIDER, PRESIDENT 5000 BRUSH HOLLOW RD. WESTBURY, NEW YORK 11590 (516) 997-4300	02/02-0140	700,000	1,909,999	DIVERSIFIED	5
M & T CAPITAL CORPORATION HAROLD M. SMALL, PRESIDENT ONE M & T PLAZA BUFFALO, NEW YORK 14240 (716) 842-3786	02/02-0268	2,200,000	4,500,000	DIVERSIFIED	1
MARWIT CAPITAL (MAIN OFFICE: NEWPORT BEACH, CAL.) 6 EAST 43RD STREET NEW YORK, NEW YORK 10017 (212) 867-3906					

LICENSEE	LICENSE NUMBER	PRIVATE CAPITAL	OBLIGATION TO SBA	INVESTMENT POLICY	OWNER CODE
NEW YORK(CONT)					
MID ATLANTIC FUND, INCORPORATED WILLIAM MORRIS, PRESIDENT 9 WEST 57TH STREET NEW YORK, NEW YORK 10019 (212) 421-3940	02/02-0163	861,037	1,980,000	DIVERSIFIED	5
MIDLAND CAPITAL CORP. DONALD PRICE, VICE PRESIDENT 110 WILLIAM ST. NEW YORK, NEW YORK 10038 (212) 577-0750	02/02-0040	16,775,806	6,895,000	DIVERSIFIED	6
MULTI-PURPOSE CAPITAL CORPORATION ELI B. FINE, PRESIDENT 31 SOUTH BROADWAY YONKERS, NEW YORK 10701 (914) 963-2733	02/02-0232	190,300	318,000	DIVERSIFIED	5
NELSON CAPITAL CORP. IRWIN NELSON, PRESIDENT 591 STEWART AVE. GARDEN CITY, L.I, NEW YORK 11530 (516) 294-9595	02/02-0297	390,000	1,170,000	DIVERSIFIED	5
NEW COURT VENTURES, INCORPORATED CHARLES LEA, JR., PRESIDENT ONE ROCKEFELLER PLAZA SUITE 2814 NEW YORK, NEW YORK 10020 (212) 757-6000	02/02-0349	500,000	0	DIVERSIFIED	3
NEW HORIZONS CAPITAL CORPORATION JAY INGLIS, PRESIDENT 90 BROAD STREET NEW YORK, NEW YORK 10004 (212) 422-2595	02/02-0344	1,500,000	0	DIVERSIFIED	4
NIS CAPITAL CORP. HOWARD BLANK, PRESIDENT 34 S. BROADWAY WHITE PLAINS, NEW YORK 10601 (914) 428-8600	02/02-0310	500,000	1,000,000	DIVERSIFIED	4

LICENSEE	LICENSE NUMBER	PRIVATE CAPITAL	OBLIGATION TO SBA	INVESTMENT POLICY	OWNER CODE
NEW YORK(CONT)					
NYBDC CAPITAL CORP. MARSHALL R. LUSTIG, PRESIDENT 41 STATE STREET ALBANY, NEW YORK 12207 (518) 463-2268	02/02-0303	300,000	0	DIVERSIFIED	4
PERCIVAL CAPITAL CORPORATION GEORGE A. SIMPSON, PRESIDENT 2 WEST 46TH STREET NEW YORK, NEW YORK 10036 (212) 689-4040	02/02-0352	505,000	0	DIVERSIFIED	5
PETER J. SCHMITT SBIC, INCORPORATED WILLIAM WANNSTEDT, PRESIDENT 678 BAILEY AVENUE BUFFALO, NEW YORK 14206 (716) 825-1111	02/02-0346	500,000	0	RETAIL GROCERS	4
PIONEER INVESTORS CORPORATION JAMES G. NIVEN, PRESIDENT ONE BATTERY PARK PLAZA NEW YORK, NEW YORK 10004 (212) 344-4490	02/02-0324	2,510,000	3,000,000	DIVERSIFIED	5
PRINTERS CAPITAL CORP. HERBERT BRANDON, PRESIDENT 1 WORLD TRADE CENTER SUITE 3169 NEW YORK, NEW YORK 10048 (212) 432-0750	02/02-0248	154,720	190,000	PRINTING & DUPLICATING FIRMS	5
R&R FINANCIAL CORP. IMRE ROSENTHAL, PRESIDENT 1451 BROADWAY NEW YORK, NEW YORK 10036 (212) 564-4500	02/02-0135	305,000	525,000	DIVERSIFIED	3
RAND SBIC, INC. DONALD ROSS, PRESIDENT 2205 MAIN PLACE BUFFALO, NEW YORK 14202. (716) 853-0802	02/02-0311	505,000	200,000	DIVERSIFIED	6
REALTY GROWTH CAPITAL CORPORATION LAWRENCE BENENSON, PRESIDENT 575 LEXINGTON AVENUE NEW YORK, NEW YORK 10022 (212) 755-9043	02/02-0097	399,000	830,000	100% REAL ESTATE SPECIALIST	5

LICENSEE	LICENSE NUMBER	PRIVATE CAPITAL	OBLIGATION TO SBA	INVESTMENT POLICY	OWNER CODE
NEW YORK(CONT)					
ROYAL BUSINESS FUNDS CORPORATION DAVID MELMAN, PRESIDENT 60 EAST 42ND STREET NEW YORK, NEW YORK 10017 (212) 986-8463	02/02-0012	6,370,481	18,947,397	100% REAL ESTATE	6
ROYAL BUSINESS FUNDS CORPORATION (MAIN OFFICE: NEW YORK, N.Y.) 600 OLD COUNTRY RD., SUITE 441 GARDEN CITY L.I., NEW YORK 11530					
SB ELECTRONICS INVESTMENT CO. STANLEY MEISELS, PRESIDENT 60 BROAD STREET NEW YORK, NEW YORK 10004 (212) 952-7531	02/02-0026	362,125	887,836	DIVERSIFIED	5
SOUTHERN TIER CAPITAL CORPORATION HAROLD GOLD, SECRETARY-TREASURER 55 SOUTH STREET LIBERTY, NEW YORK 12754 (914) 292-3030	02/02-0095	350,111	568,500	MAJOR GROUP 70 (HOTELS & ROOMING HOUSES)	5
SPROUT CAPITAL CORP. ROBERT B. GOERGEN, PRESIDENT 140 BROADWAY NEW YORK, NEW YORK 10005 (212) 344-7169	02/02-0339	1,500,000	0	DIVERSIFIED	3
TAPPAN ZEE CAPITAL CORPORATION KARL KIRCHNER, PRESIDENT 120 NORTH MAIN STREET NEW CITY, NEW YORK 10956 (914) 359-0550	02/02-0209	500,000	1,097,000	66% REAL ESTATE	5
TELESCIENCES CAPITAL CORPORATION GEORGE E. CARMODY, PRESIDENT 135 EAST 54TH STREET NEW YORK, NEW YORK 10022 (212) 935-2550	02/02-0341	1,250,000	0	DIVERSIFIED	4

LICENSEE	LICENSE NUMBER	PRIVATE CAPITAL	OBLIGATION TO SBA	INVESTMENT POLICY	OWNER CODE
NEW YORK(CONT)					
VAN RIETSCHOTEN CAPITAL CORP. HARVEY J. WERTHEIM, PRESIDENT SUITE 1260 - 230 PARK AVENUE NEW YORK, NEW YORK 10017 (212) 867-9435	02/02-0313	1,000,000	2,000,000	DIVERSIFIED	5
VEGA CAPITAL CORP. VICTOR HARZ, PRESIDENT 10 EAST 40TH STREET NEW YORK, NEW YORK 10016 (212) 685-8222	02/02-0270	2,405,760	6,300,002	DIVERSIFIED	6
VENTURE SBIC, INC. ARNOLD FELDMAN, PRESIDENT 249-12 JERICHO TURNPIKE BELLEROSE, NEW YORK 11426 (212) 343-8188	02/02-0334	510,000	1,500,000	DIVERSIFIED	5
WINFIELD CAPITAL CORP. STANLEY M. PECHMAN, PRESIDENT 237 MAMARONECK AVENUE WHITE PLAINS, NEW YORK 10605 (914) 949-2600	02/02-0292	600,000	1,800,000	DIVERSIFIED	5
NORTH CAROLINA					
DELTA CAPITAL, INC. ALEX B. WILKINS, JR., PRESIDENT 202 LATTA ARCADE 320 SOUTH TRYON STREET CHARLOTTE, NORTH CAROLINA 28202 (704) 372-1410	04/10-0082	1,250,000	3,275,000	50% REAL ESTATE	3
HERITAGE CAPITAL CORP. J. RANDOLPH GREGORY, PRESIDENT 2290 JEFFERSON FIRST UNION PLAZA CHARLOTTE, NORTH CAROLINA 28282 (704) 334-2867	04/04-0047	1,250,265	2,227,403	50% REAL ESTATE	3
LOWCOUNTRY INVESTMENT CORPORATION (MAIN OFF: CHARLESTON HGHTS, S.C.) VERNON AVENUE KINSTON, NORTH CAROLINA 28659					

LICENSEE	LICENSE NUMBER	PRIVATE CAPITAL	OBLIGATION TO SBA	INVESTMENT POLICY	OWNER CODE
NORTH CAROLINA(CONT)					
NORTHWESTERN CAPITAL CORPORATION CLYDE R. BROWN, PRESIDENT 924 B STREET MAIL: P.O. BOX 310 NORTH WILKESBORO, NORTH CAROLINA 286 (919) 667-2111	04/04-0075	1,363,000	2,885,000	DIVERSIFIED	6
NORTH DAKOTA					
FIRST DAKOTA CAPITAL CORPORATION JAMES S. LINDSAY, PRESIDENT 317 SOUTH UNIVERSITY DR. FARGO, NORTH DAKOTA 58102 (701) 237-0450	08/08-0034	365,000	600,000	DIVERSIFIED	5
OHIO					
CAPITAL FUNDS CORP. GARY PEASE, CHIEF INV. OFFICER 127 PUBLIC SQUARE CLEVELAND, OHIO 44114 (216) 861-4000	05/06-0011	1,000,000	0	COMMUNICATIONS	1
CLARION CAPITAL CORP. PETER VAN OOSTERHOUT, PRESIDENT UNION COMMERCE BANK BLDG. SUITE 2011 CLEVELAND, OHIO 44115 (216) 687-1096	05/07-0023	7,903,628	15,400,000	DIVERSIFIED	6
COLUMBUS CAPITAL CORP. JAMES E. KOLLS, VICE PRESIDENT 100 EAST BROAD ST. COLUMBUS, OHIO 43215 (614) 461-5832	05/06-0020	340,000	0	DIVERSIFIED	1
COMMUNITY VENTURE CORPORATION RICHARD H. STOWELL, PRESIDENT 88 EAST BROAD STREET SUITE 1520 COLUMBUS, OHIO 43215 (614) 228-2800	05/06-0007	150,000	28,990	DIVERSIFIED	1
DYCAP, INC. A. G. IMHOFF, PRESIDENT 88 EAST BROAD STREET SUITE 1980 COLUMBUS, OHIO 43215 (614) 228-6641	05/06-0017	450,000	712,475	DIVERSIFIED	5

LICENSEE	LICENSE NUMBER	PRIVATE CAPITAL	OBLIGATION TO SBA	INVESTMENT POLICY	OWNER CODE
OHIO(CONT)					
FOURTH STREET CAPITAL CORPORATION ROBERT H. LESHNER, PRESIDENT 508 DIXIE TERMINAL BLDG. CINCINNATI, OHIO 45202 (513) 579-0414	05/05-0113	520,000	800,000	DIVERSIFIED	5
GRIES INVESTMENT CORP. ROBERT D. GRIES, PRESIDENT 2310 TERMINAL TOWER BLDG. CLEVELAND, OHIO 44113 (216) 861-1146	05/06-0031	688,446	1,495,500	DIVERSIFIED	5
INTERCAPCO, INC. RONALD E. WEINBERG, PRESIDENT ONE ERIEVIEW PLAZA, 10TH FLOOR CLEVELAND, OHIO 44114 (216) 241-7170	05/05-0112	1,510,000	500,000	DIVERSIFIED	5
NATIONAL CITY CAPITAL CORPORATION MICHAEL SHERWIN, PRESIDENT 623 EUCLID AVENUE CLEVELAND, OHIO 44114 (216) 861-4900	05/05-0137	2,500,000	0	DIVERSIFIED	1
TAMCO INVESTORS (SBIC), INC. NATHAN H. MONUS, PRESIDENT 375 VICTORIA ROAD YOUNGSTOWN, OHIO 44515 (216) 792-3811	05/05-0116	300,000	300,000	RETAIL GROCERS	4
TOMLINSON CAPITAL CORPORATION JOHN A. CHERNAK, VICE PRESIDENT 13700 BROADWAY CLEVELAND, OHIO 44125 (216) 663-3363	05/05-0105	400,000	1,350,000	MINATURE SUPERMARKET	4
OKLAHOMA					
ACTIVEST CAPITAL CORP. GEORGE J. RECORDS, CHAIRMAN 1501 CLASSEN BLVD., SUITE 101 OKLAHOMA CITY, OKLAHOMA 73106 (405) 525-7479	06/10-0088	500,000	706,500	100% REAL ESTATE	4

LICENSEE	LICENSE NUMBER	PRIVATE CAPITAL	OBLIGATION TO SBA	INVESTMENT POLICY	OWNER CODE
OKLAHOMA(CONT)					
ALLIANCE BUSINESS INVESTMENT CO. BARRY DAVIS, VICE PRESIDENT 500 MCFARLIN BLDG. TULSA, OKLAHOMA 74103 (918) 584-3581	06/10-0012	1,753,018	3,351,501	DIVERSIFIED	5
BARTLESVILLE INV. CORPORATION JAMES L. DIAMOND, PRESIDENT P.O. BOX 548 BARTLESVILLE, OKLAHOMA 74003 (918) 333-3022	06/10-0139	645,000	1,895,150	DIVERSIFIED	5
FIRST OKLAHOMA VENTURE CORPORATION JON R.K. TINKLE, PRESIDENT VENTURE BUILDING, THE QUARTERS BARTLESVILLE, OKLAHOMA 74003 (918) 333-8820	06/06-0171	1,459,033	3,000,000	DIVERSIFIED	1
HENDERSON FUNDING CORPORATION C. A. HENDERSON PRESIDENT 2629 N.W. 39TH EXPRESSWAY OKLAHOMA CITY, OKLAHOMA 73112 (405) 947-5746	06/10-0117	500,703	825,000	DIVERSIFIED	5
INVESTMENT CAPITAL, INCORPORATED LLOYD O. PACE, PRESIDENT 1301 MAIN STREET DUNCAN, OKLAHOMA 73533 (405) 255-3140	06/10-0133	374,981	505,000	DIVERSIFIED	5
OKLAHOMA CAPITAL CORP. BILL DANIEL, SR., PRESIDENT SUITE 550, 2200 CLASSEN BLVD. OKLAHOMA CITY, OKLAHOMA 73106 (405) 525-5544	06/06-0178	411,300	1,200,000	DIVERSIFIED	5
SOUTHWEST VENTURE CAPITAL, INC. DONALD J. RUBOTTOM, PRESIDENT 1920 FIRST PLACE TULSA, OKLAHOMA 74103 (918) 584-4201	06/06-0186	500,000	500,000	DIVERSIFIED	5

LICENSEE	LICENSE NUMBER	PRIVATE CAPITAL	OBLIGATION TO SBA	INVESTMENT POLICY	OWNER CODE
OKLAHOMA(CONT)					
UNITED BUSINESS CAPITAL, INC. PAUL ROEBER, VICE PRESIDENT ONE EAST MAIN P.O. BOX 322 IDABEL, OKLAHOMA 74745 (405) 286-7652	06/10-0098	392,799	960,000	DIVERSIFIED	5
OREGON					
CASCADE CAPITAL CORPORATION (M.O.: NORTHWEST GROWTH FUND, INC. MINNEAPOLIS, MINN.) 1300 S.W. 5TH ST., SUITE 3018 PORTLAND, OREGON 97201 (503) 223-6622					
FIRST FARWEST CAPITAL FUND, INC. C. M. ARMSTRONG, PRESIDENT 400 SW SIXTH AVE., 2ND FL. P.O. BOX 4162 PORTLAND, OREGON 97208 (503) 224-7740	10/13-0018	1,210,000	2,202,014	DIVERSIFIED	3
NORTHERN PACIFIC CAPITAL CORP. JOHN J. TENNANT, JR., PRESIDENT 2611 S.W. 3RD AVE., SUITE 315 P.O. BOX 1530 PORTLAND, OREGON 97207 (503) 224-4600	10/13-0014	306,000	542,500	DIVERSIFIED	5
PENNSYLVANIA					
AMERICAN VENTURE CAPITAL CO. CLAIR A. SNYDER, PRESIDENT AXE WOOD WEST, SUITE 200 SHIPPACK PIKE & BUTLER PIKE AMBLER, PENNSYLVANIA 19002 (215) 643-5956	03/03-0127	1,000,000	0	DIVERSIFIED	5
CAPITAL CORPORATION OF AMERICA MARTIN M. NEWMAN, PRESIDENT 1521 WALNUT STREET PHILADELPHIA, PENNSYLVANIA 19102 (215) 563-7423	03/03-0040	796,938	1,247,500	DIVERSIFIED	6

LICENSEE	LICENSE NUMBER	PRIVATE CAPITAL	OBLIGATION TO SBA	INVESTMENT POLICY	OWNER CODE
PENNSYLVANIA(CONT)					
EQUILEASE CAPITAL CORPORATION (MAIN OFFICE: NEW YORK, N.Y.) ONE PARKWAY CENTER, RM. 213 PITTSBURGH, PENNSYLVANIA 19102					
FIDELITY AMERICA SBIC HOWARD I. GREEN, PRESIDENT 1520 LOCUST ST. PHILADELPHIA, PENNSYLVANIA 19102 (215) 732-0707	03/03-0050	560,359	1,612,770	DIVERSIFIED	6
OSHER CAPITAL CORP. LEONARD CANTOR, PRESIDENT WYNCOTE HOUSE TOWNSHIP LINE RD. & WASHINGTON LANE WYNCOTE, PENNSYLVANIA 19095 (215) 624-4800	03/03-0062	300,000	600,000	DIVERSIFIED	5
PENNSYLVANIA GROWTH INV. CORPORATION WILLIAM L. MOSENSON, PRESIDENT TWO GATEWAY CENTER, SUITE 277 PITTSBURGH, PENNSYLVANIA 15222 (412) 281-1403	03/03-0036	627,375	543,250	DIVERSIFIED	3
REAL ESTATE CAPITAL CORPORATION WILLIAM J. LEVITT, JR., PRESIDENT 111 PRESIDENTIAL BLVD. BALA CYNWYD, PENNSYLVANIA 19004 (215) 569-4400	03/03-0124	1,260,444	1,427,500	100% REAL ESTATE SPECIALISTS	5
SHARON SMALL BUSINESS INVESTMENT CO. H. DAVID ROSENBLUM, PRESIDENT 385 SHENANGO AVE. SHARON, PENNSYLVANIA 16146 (412) 981-1500	03/03-0022	255,000	500,000	GROCERY STORE	4
TDH CAPITAL CORP. J. MAHLON BUCK, JR., PRESIDENT 2 RADNOR CORPORATE CENTER RADNOR, PENNSYLVANIA 19087 (215) 293-9787	03/03-0138	4,000,000	0	DIVERSIFIED	5

LICENSEE	LICENSE NUMBER	PRIVATE CAPITAL	OBLIGATION TO SBA	INVESTMENT POLICY	OWNER CODE
PUERTO RICO					
CREDITO INVESTMENT COMPANY, INC. JESUS MONLLOR, VICE PRESIDENT BANCO CREDITO & AHORRO PONCENO INTERNATIONAL AIRPORT BRANCH CAROLINA, PUERTO RICO 00936 (106) O/S OPER	02/02-0265	838,100	0	DIVERSIFIED	1
RHODE ISLAND					
INDUSTRIAL CAPITAL CORPORATION ALBERT A.T. WICKERSHAM, PRESIDENT 111 WESTMINSTER ST. PROVIDENCE, RHODE ISLAND 02903 (401) 278-6770	01/01-0067	3,000,000	0	DIVERSIFIED	1
NARRAGANSETT CAPITAL CORPORATION ARTHUR LITTLE, PRESIDENT 40 WESTMINSTER ST. PROVIDENCE, RHODE ISLAND 02903 (401) 751-1000	01/01-0003	13,697,921	29,720,000	DIVERSIFIED	6
SOUTH CAROLINA					
CHARLESTON CAPITAL CORPORATION HENRY YASCHIK, PRESIDENT P.O. BOX 696, 134 MEETING ST. CHARLESTON, SOUTH CAROLINA 29402 (803) 723-6464	04/04-0042	637,000	1,266,000	DIVERSIFIED	5
FALCON CAPITAL CORP. MONA G. SOKOL, PRESIDENT 100 BROAD STREET CHARLESTON, SOUTH CAROLINA 29401 (803) 723-8624	04/04-0091	152,237	130,000	DIVERSIFIED	5
FLOCO INVESTMENT CO. INC. (THE) WILLIAM H. JOHNSON, SR., PRESIDENT P.O. BOX 919 LAKE CITY, SOUTH CAROLINA 29560 (803) 389-2731	04/04-0032	365,464	100,000	FOOD RETAILERS	5
LOWCOUNTRY INVESTMENT CORPORATION JOSEPH T. NEWTON, JR., PRESIDENT 4444 DALEY ST., P.O. BOX 10447 CHARLESTON, SOUTH CAROLINA 29411 (803) 554-9880	04/04-0021	1,908,950	5,537,500	GROCERY STORE	4

LICENSEE	LICENSE NUMBER	PRIVATE CAPITAL	OBLIGATION TO SBA	INVESTMENT POLICY	OWNER CODE
TENNESSEE					
C&C CAPITAL CORPORATION DONALD L. JONES, PRESIDENT CITY AND COUNTY BANK BUILDING ONE REGENCY SQUARE KNOXVILLE, TENNESSEE 37909 (615) 637-9220	04/04-0105	1,000,000	600,000	DIVERSIFIED	1
FINANCIAL RESOURCES, INCORPORATED MILTON PICARD, CHAIRMAN OF BOARD 2211 STERICK BLDG. MEMPHIS, TENNESSEE 38103 (901) 527-9411	04/05-0064	405,320	699,750	DIVERSIFIED	5
THIRD'S SBIC, THE K. D. STACH, PRESIDENT UPTOWN STATION BOX 2874 NASHVILLE, TENNESSEE 37219 (615) 748-4274	04/05-0002	1,001,878	500,000	DIVERSIFIED	1
TEXAS					
ALLIANCE BUSINESS INVESTMENT CO. (MAIN OFFICE: TULSA, OKLAHOMA) 2660 SOUTH TOWER HOUSTON, TEXAS 77002					
BRITTANY CAPITAL CORP. ROBERT E. CLEMENTS, PRESIDENT 5153 FIRST INTERNATIONAL BUILDING DALLAS, TEXAS 75270 (214) 742-5810	06/10-0152	325,000	805,000	DIVERSIFIED	2
CAMERON FINANCIAL CORPORATION A. BAKER DUNCAN, PRESIDENT 1410 FROST BANK TOWER SAN ANTONIO, TEXAS 78205 (512) 223-9768	06/06-0204	500,000	0	DIVERSIFIED	5
CAPITAL MARKETING CORPORATION NATHANIEL GIBBS, PRESIDENT P.O. BOX 225293 DALLAS, TEXAS 75222 (214) 638-1913	06/10-0150	4,293,030	12,880,000	RETAIL GROCERS	4

LICENSEE	LICENSE NUMBER	PRIVATE CAPITAL	OBLIGATION TO SBA	INVESTMENT POLICY	OWNER CODE
TEXAS(CONT)					
CENTRAL TEXAS SBI CORPORATION WALTER G. LACY, JR., PRESIDENT P.O. BOX 829 WACO, TEXAS 76703 (817) 753-6461	06/10-0076	300,000	240,000	DIVERSIFIED	1
CSC CAPITAL CORP. CLIFFORD J. OSBORN, PRESIDENT SUITE 700, 12900 PRESTON ROAD DALLAS, TEXAS 75230 (214) 233-8242	06/10-0065	2,901,319	3,900,000	DIVERSIFIED	6
DALLAS BUSINESS CAPITAL CORP. EDGAR S. MEREDITH, SR. V.P. SUITE 333, MEADOWS BLDG. 5646 MILTON STREET DALLAS, TEXAS 75206 (214) 691-0711	06/07-0024	4,012,473	4,125,000	DIVERSIFIED	6
DIMAN FINANCIAL CORP. DON R. DIXON, PRESIDENT 13601 PRESTON RD., SUITE 717E DALLAS, TEXAS 75240 (214) 233-7610	06/06-0181	404,000	1,200,000	DIVERSIFIED	4
ENTERPRISE CAPITAL CORPORATION PAUL Z. BROCHSTEIN, PRESIDENT SUITE 465 W. EXECUTIVE PLAZA 4635 SOUTHWEST FREEWAY HOUSTON, TEXAS 77027 (713) 626-7171	06/10-0154	750,000	2,828,750	DIVERSIFIED	5
FIRST BANCORP CAPITAL, INC. OLIVER ALBRITTION, JR., PRESIDENT 100 NORTH MAIN STREET P.O. BOX 613 CORSICANA, TEXAS 75110 (214) 874-4711	06/06-0193	505,000	0	DIVERSIFIED	1
FIRST CAPITAL CORP. JOHN R. PAYNE, PRESIDENT 4925 DAVIS BLVD. FORT WORTH, TEXAS 76118 (817) 281-1667	06/10-0021	875,310	1,725,000	DIVERSIFIED	5

LICENSEE	LICENSE NUMBER	PRIVATE CAPITAL	OBLIGATION TO SBA	INVESTMENT POLICY	OWNER CODE
TEXAS(CONT)					
FIRST DALLAS CAPITAL CORPORATION ERIC C. NEUMAN, PRESIDENT SUITE 245, FIRST NATIONAL BANK BLDG P.O. BOX 83385 DALLAS, TEXAS 75283 (512) 223-9768	06/10-0056	5,000,000	2,851,000	DIVERSIFIED	1
FIRST TEXAS INVESTMENT COMPANY LYNN D. ROWNTREE, PRESIDENT 2700 S. POST OAK, SUITE 250 TRANSCO TOWER HOUSTON, TEXAS 77056 (713) 629-5512	06/10-0013	795,000	3,102,350	DIVERSIFIED	5
GREAT AMERICAN CAPITAL INVESTORS, INC. ALBERT S. DILLARD, PRESIDENT 1006 HOLLIDAY STREET WICHITA FALLS, TEXAS 76301 (817) 322-4448	06/06-0203	510,000	0	DIVERSIFIED	1
GROCERS SBI CORP. MILTON E. LEVIT, PRESIDENT 3131 EAST HOLCOMBE BLVD. SUITE 101 HOUSTON, TEXAS 77021 (713) 747-7913	06/06-0187	1,000,000	0	RETAIL GROCERS	4
MERCANTILE TEXAS CAPITAL CORP. JAMES B. GARDNER, PRESIDENT 1704 MAIN STREET DALLAS, TEXAS 75201 (214) 741-4181	06/06-0188	6,600,000	19,800,000	DIVERSIFIED	1
PERMIAN BASIN CAPITAL CORPORATION DOUGLAS B. HENSON, PRESIDENT P.O. BOX 1599 MIDLAND, TEXAS 79701 (915) 683-4231	06/06-0161	500,000	0	DIVERSIFIED	1
RED RIVER VENTURES, INCORPORATED THOMAS H. SCHNITZIUS, PRESIDENT 535 HOUSTON NATURAL GAS BLDG. HOUSTON, TEXAS 77002 (713) 658-9806	06/06-0170	751,000	1,300,000	DIVERSIFIED	3

LICENSEE	LICENSE NUMBER	PRIVATE CAPITAL	OBLIGATION TO SBA	INVESTMENT POLICY	OWNER CODE
TEXAS(CONT)					
REPUBLIC VENTURE GROUP, INC. WILLIAM R. CAIN, PRESIDENT P.O. BOX 225961 DALLAS, TEXAS 75222 (214) 653-5942	06/10-0059	2,756,220	0	DIVERSIFIED	1
RICE COUNTRY CAPITAL, INCORPORATED WILLIAM H. HARRISON, JR., PRES. P.O. BOX 215 EAGLE LAKE, TEXAS 77434 (713) 234-2506	06/06-0205	405,000	0	DIVERSIFIED	1
RICE INVESTMENT COMPANY ALVIN DIAMOND, SECRETARY 3200 PRODUCE ROW HOUSTON, TEXAS 77023 (713) 652-2015	06/10-0057	1,180,770	3,328,500	RETAIL GROCERS	5
SAN ANTONIO VENTURE GROUP, INC. WILLIAM A. FAGAN, PRESIDENT 2300 WEST COMMERCE ST. SAN ANTONIO, TEXAS 78207 (512) 225-4241	06/06-0190	1,050,000	0	DIVERSIFIED	4
SBIC OF HOUSTON (THE) WILLIAM E. LADIN, PRESIDENT 1510 NEILS ESPERSON BLDG. HOUSTON, TEXAS 77002 (713) 223-5337	06/10-0022	270,000	792,500	DIVERSIFIED	5
SOUTH TEXAS SBIC ARTHUR E. BUCKERT, TREASURER 120 SOUTH MAIN ST. P.O. BOX 1698 VICTORIA, TEXAS 77901 (512) 573-5151	06/10-0019	400,000	45,000	DIVERSIFIED	1
TEXAS CAPITAL CORP. JOHN GATTI, PRESIDENT 2424 HOUSTON NATURAL GAS BLDG. 1200 TRAVIS STREET HOUSTON, TEXAS 77002 (713) 658-9961	06/10-0004	2,550,068	5,585,833	DIVERSIFIED	4

LICENSEE	LICENSE NUMBER	PRIVATE CAPITAL	OBLIGATION TO SBA	INVESTMENT POLICY	OWNER CODE
TEXAS(CONT)					
TRAMMELL CROW INVESTMENT CO. ROBERT KOLBA, PRESIDENT 2001 BRYAN TOWER SUITE 3200 DALLAS, TEXAS 75201 (214) 742-2000	06/10-0044	529,000	283,334	100% REAL ESTATE	5
TSM CORPORATION JOE JUSTICE, GENERAL MANAGER 4171 NORTH MESA, SUITE A-203 EL PASO, TEXAS 79912 (915) 533-6375	06/06-0184	430,142	900,000	DIVERSIFIED	5
WEST CENTRAL CAPITAL CORPORATION HOWARD W. JACOB, PRESIDENT SUITE 206 440 NORTHLAKE CENTER DALLAS, TEXAS 75238 (214) 348-3969	06/10-0118	152,853	172,500	DIVERSIFIED	5
VERMONT					
MANSFIELD CAPITAL CORPORATION STEPHEN H. FARRINGTON, PRESIDENT MOUNTAIN ROAD STOWE, VERMONT 05672 (802) 253-9400	01/01-0295	350,000	0	DIVERSIFIED	5
SBIC OF VERMONT, INC. ROBERT B. MANNING, PRESIDENT 121 WEST STREET RUTLAND, VERMONT 05701 (802) 775-3393	01/01-0287	1,127,000	0	DIVERSIFIED	1
VERMONT INVESTMENT CAPITAL, INC. PHILLIP KRATKY, PRESIDENT ROUTE 14, BOX 84 SOUTH ROYALTON, VERMONT 05068 (802) 763-8835	01/01-0072	221,000	550,000	DIVERSIFIED	5
VIRGINIA					
INVERNESS CAPITAL CORPORATION HARRY S. FLEMMING, PRESIDENT 424 N. WASHINGTON ST. ALEXANDRIA, VIRGINIA 22314 (703) 549-3900	03/02-0273	2,333,845	6,248,500	DIVERSIFIED	5

LICENSEE	LICENSE NUMBER	PRIVATE CAPITAL	OBLIGATION TO SBA	INVESTMENT POLICY	OWNER CODE
VIRGINIA(CONT)					
METROPOLITAN CAPITAL CORPORATION F. W. SCOVILLE, PRESIDENT 2550 HUNTINGTON AVE. ALEXANDRIA, VIRGINIA 22303 (703) 960-4698	03/04-0107	470,000	1,260,000	DIVERSIFIED	4
SBI CORPORATION OF NORFOLK D. H. BURLAGE, PRESIDENT 1216 GRANBY ST., SUITE 3 NORFOLK, VIRGINIA 23510 (804) 625-0534	03/04-0056	300,606	384,543	DIVERSIFIED	4
TIDEWATER INDUSTRIAL CAPITAL CORP. ARMAND CAPLAN, PRESIDENT SUITE 1424 UNITED VIRGINIA BANK BLDG. NORFOLK, VIRGINIA 23510 (804) 622-1501	03/04-0065	758,200	1,339,000	DIVERSIFIED	4
TIDEWATER SBI CORP. CHARLES M. ETHERIDGE, PRESIDENT 740 DUKE STREET DUKE GRACE BLDG., SUITE 520 NORFOLK, VIRGINIA 23510 (804) 627-2315	03/04-0100	1,000,000	1,940,000	DIVERSIFIED	4
VIRGINIA CAPITAL CORP. ROBERT H. PRATT, PRESIDENT 515 ROSS BLDG. P.O. BOX 1493 RICHMOND, VIRGINIA 23212 (804) 644-5496	03/04-0008	1,250,197	4,058,334	DIVERSIFIED	6
WASHINGTON					
FIRST SBIC OF CALIF. ALAN BRADLEY, VICE PRESIDENT (MAIN OFFICE: LOS ANGELES, CALIF) 1101 DEXTER-HORTON BLDG. SEATTLE, WASHINGTON 98104 (206) 622-2193					
NORTHWEST BUSINESS INV. CORPORATION C. PAUL SANDIFUR, PRESIDENT 929 WEST SPRAGUE AVE. SPOKANE, WASHINGTON 99204 (509) 838-3111	10/13-0005	194,400	559,750	DIVERSIFIED	5

LICENSEE	LICENSE NUMBER	PRIVATE CAPITAL	OBLIGATION TO SBA	INVESTMENT POLICY	OWNER CODE
WASHINGTON(CONT)					
NORTHWEST CAPITAL INV. CORPORATION FRED L. BURROWS, PRESIDENT 321 EAST A STREET YAKIMA, WASHINGTON 98901 (509) 248-7440	10/10-0159	656,000	1,660,000	DIVERSIFIED	5
SBIC OF AMERICA HAROLD T. WOSEPKA, PRESIDENT 3211 N.E. 78TH STREET VANCOUVER, WASHINGTON 98665 (206) 694-8452	10/13-0011	327,695	55,000	100% REAL ESTATE	5
WASHINGTON CAPITAL CORPORATION G.A. SCHERZINGER, MGR & ASST V.P. 1417 FOURTH AVE. P.O. BOX 1770 SEATTLE, WASHINGTON 98111 (206) 682-5400	10/13-0008	4,591,500	13,577,475	50% READ ESTATE	3
WESTERN VENTURE RESORUCES, INC. DAVID E. KRATTER, PRESIDENT 3734 SEATTLE FIRST NATL BK BLDG. 1001 FOURTH AVE. SEATTLE, WASHINGTON 98154 (206) 622-9300	10/08-0037	1,000,000	2,174,049	DIVERSIFIED	4
WISCONSIN					
77 CAPITAL CORP. SHELDON B. LUBAR, PRESIDENT 777 EAST WISCONSIN AVE. SUITE 3060 MILWAUKEE, WISCONSIN 53202 (414) 291-9004	05/05-0122	2,520,000	0	DIVERSIFIED	5
BANKIT FINANCIAL CORP. ROY D. TERRACINA, EXEC. V.P. 733 NORTH VANBUREN ST. MILWAUKEE, WISCONSIN 53202 (414) 271-5050	05/05-0097	350,000	300,000	GROCERY STORES	4
CAPITAL INVESTMENTS, INCORPORATED ROBERT L. BANNER, VICE PRESIDENT 515 WEST WELLS ST. MILWAUKEE, WISCONSIN 53203 (414) 273-6560	05/07-0003	2,993,845	7,602,175	DIVERSIFIED	6

LICENSEE	LICENSE NUMBER	PRIVATE CAPITAL	OBLIGATION TO SBA	INVESTMENT POLICY	OWNER CODE
WISCONSIN(CONT)					
CERTCO CAPITAL CORP. HOWARD E. HILL, PRESIDENT 6150 MCKEE ROAD MADISON, WISCONSIN 53707 (608) 271-4500	05/05-0119	405,000	0	RETAIL GROCERS	4
MORAMERICA CAPITAL CORPORATION (MAIN OFFICE: CEDAR RAPIDS, IOWA) 710 N. PLANKINTON AVE. SUITE 333 WILWAUKEE, WISCONSIN 53203 (414) 276-3839					
SUPER MARKET INVESTORS INCORPORATED JOHN W. ANDORFER, PRESIDENT 1300 BURLEIGH STREET WAUWATOSE, WISCONSIN 53222 (414) 453-6211	05/05-0136	500,000	0	RETAIL GROCERS	4
WISCONSIN CAPITAL CORPORATION LAWRENCE J. KUJAWSKI, GEN. MANAGER 312 EAST WISCONSIN AVE, SUITE 308 MILWAUKEE, WISCONSIN 53202 (414) 289-9893	05/07-0012	525,000	714,000	DIVERSIFIED	5

SBIC
TOTALS BY STATES

STATE	SIZE 1	SIZE 2	SIZE 3	SIZE 4	TOTAL	TOTAL PRIVATE CAP	TOTAL OBLIGATIONS TO SBA
ALABAMA	0	4	0	0	4	1,910,000	2,600,000
ALASKA	0	0	0	0	0	0	0
ARIZONA	0	1	0	0	1	500,000	0
ARKANSAS	0	2	0	0	2	1,250,000	2,250,000
CALIFORNIA	2	20	10	4	36	71,895,178	52,567,645
COLORADO	0	3	0	0	3	1,957,761	0
CONNECTICUT	3	11	1	1	16	15,150,844	31,461,892
DELAWARE	0	0	0	0	0	0	0
D.C.	0	2	3	0	5	7,487,116	18,686,073
FLORIDA	1	4	4	0	9	10,542,139	18,909,413
GEORGIA	1	3	4	0	8	12,823,094	31,050,200
HAWAII	0	1	0	0	1	317,100	450,000
IDAHO	0	1	0	0	1	500,000	500,000
ILLINOIS	3	3	4	2	12	37,376,356	9,087,499
INDIANA	0	0	0	0	0	0	0
IOWA	0	0	1	0	1	3,700,000	11,416,986
KANSAS	0	0	1	0	1	1,075,240	0
KENTUCKY	0	1	1	0	2	1,800,000	2,000,000
LOUISIANA	1	7	3	0	11	8,135,325	12,017,431
MAINE	0	0	0	0	0	0	0
MARYLAND	0	0	0	0	0	0	0
MASSACHUSETTS	3	6	8	0	17	22,771,275	28,700,439
MICHIGAN	1	1	1	0	3	2,879,700	5,425,000
MINNESOTA	1	6	3	0	10	10,025,613	24,076,731
MISSISSIPPI	0	2	1	0	3	3,757,180	2,127,322
MISSOURI	1	2	1	0	4	2,379,750	1,580,000
MONTANA	0	0	0	0	0	0	0
NEBRASKA	0	0	0	0	0	0	0
NEVADA	0	0	0	0	0	0	0
NEW HAMPSHIRE	0	0	0	0	0	0	0
NEW JERSEY	1	2	3	0	6	7,019,904	12,526,879
NEW MEXICO	0	4	1	0	5	5,010,938	15,775,000
NEW YORK	7	28	12	6	53	142,069,760	116,426,446
NORTH CAROLINA	0	0	3	0	3	3,863,265	8,387,403
NORTH DAKOTA	0	1	0	0	1	365,000	600,000
OHIO	2	6	2	1	11	15,762,074	20,586,965
OKLAHOMA	0	7	2	0	9	6,536,834	12,943,151
OREGON	0	1	1	0	2	1,516,000	2,744,514
PENNSYLVANIA	2	4	2	0	8	8,800,116	5,931,020
PUERTO RICO	0	1	0	0	1	838,100	0
RHODE ISLAND	0	0	1	1	2	16,697,921	29,720,000
SOUTH CAROLINA	1	2	1	0	4	3,063,651	7,033,500
SOUTH DAKOTA	0	0	0	0	0	0	0
TENNESSEE	0	2	1	0	3	2,407,198	1,799,750
TEXAS	3	15	8	1	27	39,746,185	65,854,767
UTAH	0	0	0	0	0	0	0
VERMONT	1	1	1	0	3	1,698,000	550,000
VIRGINIA	0	4	2	0	6	6,112,848	15,230,377
WASHINGTON	1	3	1	0	5	6,769,595	18,026,274
WEST VIRGINIA	0	0	0	0	0	0	0
WISCONSIN	0	4	2	0	6	7,293,845	8,616,175
WYOMING	0	0	0	0	0	0	0
TOTAL	35	165	89	16	305	493,704,905	597,658,852

SBIC
TOTALS BY PRIVATE CAPITAL SIZE CLASS

TOTAL PRIVATE CAPITAL SIZE CLASS	TOTAL NUMBER OF SBICS	TOTAL PRIVATE CAP	TOTAL OBLIGATIONS TO SBA
SIZE 1 - BELOW $300,000	35	7,925,233	8,771,865
SIZE 2 - $300001 TO $1.MM	165	91,567,444	123,990,370
SIZE 3 - $1.MM TO $5.MM	89	200,012,533	320,859,938
SIZE 4 - OVER $5.MM	16	194,199,695	144,036,679
TOTAL	305	493,704,905	597,658,852

SBIC
TOTALS BY TYPE OF OWNERSHIP

TYPE OF OWNERSHIP	TOTAL NUMBER OF SBICS	TOTAL PRIVATE CAP	TOTAL OBLIGATIONS TO SBA
BANK DOMINATED	49	166,821,535	127,127,795
BANK ASSOCIATED	8	14,213,213	15,544,334
FINANCIAL ORGANIZATION	27	46,683,247	60,024,510
NON-FINANCIAL ORG.	52	55,626,684	79,324,663
INDIVIDUALLY OWNED	139	105,993,836	141,527,005
40 ACT COMPANY	30	104,366,390	174,110,545
TOTAL	305	493,704,905	597,658,852

SBIC
PRIVATE CAPITAL BY TYPE OF OWNERSHIP

PRIVATE CAPITAL SIZE CLASS

TYPE OF OWNERSHIP	SIZE 1		SIZE 2		SIZE 3		SIZE 4	
	NUM	DOLLARS	NUM	DOLLARS	NUM	DOLLARS	NUM	DOLLARS
BANK DOMINATED	2	450000	19	12080700	22	57905835	6	96385000
BANK ASSOCIATED	0	0	4	2244800	3	6558831	1	5409582
FINANCIAL ORG.	1	300000	11	5431475	14	28951772	1	12000000
NON-FINANCIAL ORG.	6	1457750	32	18859054	13	27639880	1	7670000
INDIVIDUALLY OWNED	26	5717483	90	47627134	22	41149219	1	11500000
40 ACT COMPANY	0	0	9	5324281	15	37806996	6	61235113

PART II - 301(d) LICENSEES

LICENSEE	LICENSE NUMBER	PRIVATE CAPITAL	OBLIGATION TO SBA	INVESTMENT POLICY	OWNER CODE
ALASKA					
ALYESKA INVESTMENT COMPANY W. J. DARCH, PRESIDENT 1835 SOUTH BRAGAW ST. ANCHORAGE, ALASKA 99512 (907) 279-9584	10/13-5027	1,000,000	0	DIVERSIFIED	4
ARIZONA					
ASSOCIATED SOUTHWEST INVESTORS, INC. F. BRENT STEWART, GEN'L MGR. 114 WEST ADAMS, SUITE 719 PHOENIX, ARIZONA 85003 (602) 252-3973	09/14-5086	707,000	1,700,000	DIVERSIFIED	4
ARKANSAS					
CAPITAL MANAGEMENT SERVICES, INC. LOUISE LINGO, PRESIDENT 4801 NORTH HILLS BOULEVARD N. LITTLE ROCK, ARKANSAS 72116 (501) 758-4553	06/06-5207	152,500	0	DIVERSIFIED	5
KAR-MAL VENTURE CAPITAL, INC. THOMAS KARAM, PRESIDENT UNIVERSITY TOWER BLDG. SUITE 917 LITTLE ROCK, ARKANSAS 72204 (501) 664-6667	06/06-5185	500,000	500,000	DIVERSIFIED	4
CALIFORNIA					
ASSOCIATES VENTURE CAPITAL CORP. WALTER P. STRYCKER, PRESIDENT 632 KEARNY ST. SAN FRANCISCO, CALIFORNIA 94108 (415) 397-0351	09/09-5222	525,000	500,000	DIVERSIFIED	5
BEAUHAN MINORITY INV. CORP. GERALD E. WEBB, PRESIDENT 2 COMMERCIAL BLVD. NOVATO, CALIFORNIA 94947 (415) 479-4310	09/09-5193	300,000	300,000	INSURANCE AGENCIES	5

LICENSEE	LICENSE NUMBER	PRIVATE CAPITAL	OBLIGATION TO SBA	INVESTMENT POLICY	OWNER CODE
CALIFORNIA(CONT)					
BUSINESS EQUITY & DEV. CORP. RICHARDO J. OLIVAREZ, GEN'L MGR. 1411 WEST OLYMPIC BLVD. SUITE 200 LOS ANGELES, CALIFORNIA 90015 (213) 385-0351	09/12-5151	1,756,933	1,400,000	DIVERSIFIED	4
EQUITABLE CAPITAL CORPORATION JOHN C. LEE, PRESIDENT 419 COLUMBUS AVENUE SAN FRANCISCO, CALIFORNIA 94133 (415) 982-4026	09/09-5231	500,000	0	DIVERSIFIED	5
HUB ENTERPRISES, LTD. JOHN B. LACOSTE, PRESIDENT 5874 DOYLE STREET EMERYVILLE, CALIFORNIA 94608 (415) 521-2946	09/09-5218	318,500	300,000	DIVERSIFIED	5
MCA NEW VENTURES, INC. NORBERT A. SIMMONS, PRESIDENT 100 UNIVERSAL CITY PLAZA UNIVERSAL CITY, CALIFORNIA 91608 (213) 985-4321	09/09-5194	3,000,000	3,000,000	ENTERTAINMENT FIELD	4
MINORITY ENTERPRISE FUNDING, INC. HOWARD D. BALSHAN, PRESIDENT 4061 EAST WHITTIER BOULEVARD LOS ANGELES, CALIFORNIA 90023 (213) 269-7335	09/09-5230	500,000	0	DIVERSIFIED	5
OPPORTUNITY CAPITAL CORP. OF CALIF. CHARLES E. STANLEY, PRESIDENT 100 CALIFORNIA ST., SUITE 714 SAN FRANCISCO, CALIFORNIA 94111 (415) 421-5935	09/12-5155	1,225,535	2,350,535	DIVERSIFIED	2
SPACE VENTURES, INC. WILLIAM J. SMOLLEN, PRESIDENT 2230 EAST IMPERIAL HIGHWAY EL SEGUNDO, CALIFORNIA 90245 (213) 532-5510	09/09-5176	1,010,070	1,000,000	DIVERSIFIED	4

LICENSEE	LICENSE NUMBER	PRIVATE CAPITAL	OBLIGATION TO SBA	INVESTMENT POLICY	OWNER CODE
CONNECTICUT					
COMINVEST OF HARTFORD, INCORPORATED ROBERT W. BEGGS, JR., PRESIDENT 18 ASYLUM ST. HARTFORD, CONNECTICUT 06103 (203) 246-7259	01/01-5269	500,119	1,500,000	DIVERSIFIED	1
HARTFORD COMMUNITY CAPITAL CORP. MS. JAN-GEE W. MCCOLLAM, PRESIDENT 777 MAIN STREET - 7TH FLOOR ATTN: JAN-GEE MCCOLLAM HARTFORD, CONNECTICUT 06115 (203) 728-2840	01/02-5265	300,100	150,000	DIVERSIFIED	2
D.C.					
DISTRICT OF COLUMBIA INV. CO. JOSEPH D. JACKSON, PRESIDENT 1120 CONN. AVE., N.W. SUITE 340 WASHINGTON, D.C. 20036 (202) 452-1030	03/03-5114	1,750,000	2,350,000	DIVERSIFIED	4
FULCRUM VENTURE CAPITAL CORP. STEPHEN L. LILLY, PRESIDENT 2021 K ST., N.W. SUITE 701 WASHINGTON, D.C. 20006 (202) 833-9580	03/03-5135	2,000,000	2,000,000	DIVERSIFIED	3
SCI MEDIA VENTURES, INCORPORATED HERBERT P. WILKINS, PRESIDENT 1625 I STREET, N.W., SUITE 304 WASHINGTON, D.C. 20006 (202) 293-9428	03/03-5137	1,000,000	1,000,000	COMMUNICATIONS MEDIA	4
FLORIDA					
ALLIED INVESTMENT DEVELOPERS, INC. ROBERT V. MILBERG, PRESIDENT 1200 BISCAYNE BLVD. SUITE 202 MIAMI, FLORIDA 33132 (305) 358-8010	04/04-5114	275,000	550,000	FAST FOOD FRANCHISES	5

LICENSEE	LICENSE NUMBER	PRIVATE CAPITAL	OBLIGATION TO SBA	INVESTMENT POLICY	OWNER CODE
FLORIDA(CONT)					
BURGER KING MESBIC, INCORPORATED DON CHRISTOPHERSON, PRESIDENT P.O. BOX 520783 BISCAYNE ANNEX MIAMI, FLORIDA 33152 (305) 274-7011	04/04-5106	250,000	500,000	BURGER KING FRANCHISES	4
JETS VENTURE CAPITAL CORPORATION LARRY D. BARNETTE, PRESIDENT 2721 PARK STREET JACKSONVILLE, FLORIDA 32205 (904) 384-3471	04/04-5164	520,000	0	DIVERSIFIED	5
M VENTURE CAPITAL CORPORATION RAUL F. MASVIDAL, PRESIDENT 1309 BRICKELL AVENUE MIAMI, FLORIDA 33130 (305) 374-7667	04/04-5139	500,000	0	DIVERSIFIED	5
MIAMI CAPITAL CORP. ROBERT M. ENTIN, PRESIDENT 265 SEVILLA AVE. MAIL TO: P.O. BOX 2037, MIAMI BEACH CORAL GABLES, FLORIDA 33134 (305) 448-8205	04/04-5149	500,000	500,000	DIVERSIFIED	5
THE MESBIC, INC. DR. DANIEL H. HARRIS, PRESIDENT 3830 WEST FLAGLER ST. CORAL GABLES, FLORIDA 33134 (305) 573-9770	04/04-5135	600,000	2,100,000	DIVERSIFIED	4
UNIVERSAL FINANCIAL SERVICES, INC. MRS. GERTRUDE ZIPKIN, PRESIDENT 225 N.E. 35TH STREET MIAMI, FLORIDA 33137 (305) 573-7496	04/04-5153	500,000	500,000	DIVERSIFIED	5
VENTURE OPPORTUNITIES CORPORATION A. FRED MARCH, PRESIDENT 1438 BRICKELL AVENUE MIAMI, FLORIDA 33131 (305) 358-0359	04/04-5151	500,000	500,000	DIVERSIFIED	5

LICENSEE	LICENSE NUMBER	PRIVATE CAPITAL	OBLIGATION TO SBA	INVESTMENT POLICY	OWNER CODE
FLORIDA(CONT)					
VERDE CAPITAL CORP. STEVEN J. GREEN, CHAIRMAN OF BOARD 255 ALHAMBRA CIRCLE, SUITE 720 CORAL GABLES, FLORIDA 33134 (305) 448-6300	04/04-5156	505,000	500,000	DIVERSIFIED	5
GEORGIA					
COTTON BELT INVESTMENT CORPORATION LYNWOOD A. MADDOX, PRESIDENT 4542 MEMORIAL DRIVE DECATUR, GEORGIA 30032 (404) 292-2626	04/04-5144	500,000	0	DIVERSIFIED	5
ENTERPRISES NOW, INC. JOSEPH E. LOWERY, PRESIDENT 898 BECKWITH ST., S.W. ATLANTA, GEORGIA 30314 (404) 753-1163	04/05-5102	329,222	200,000	DIVERSIFIED	4
SOUTHERN INVESTMENT & FUNDING CORP INC GEORGE ENG, PRESIDENT 300 W. PEACHTREE ST., N.W ATLANTA, GEORGIA 30308 (404) 522-9151	04/04-5133	500,000	1,000,000	DIVERSIFIED	5
HAWAII					
PACIFIC VENTURE CAPITAL, LTD. MICHAEL J. COY, PRESIDENT 1505 DILLINGHAM BLVD. HONOLULU, HAWAII 96817 (808) 847-6502	09/09-5182	700,000	700,000	DIVERSIFIED	4
ILLINOIS					
AMERICAN INDIAN INV. OPPORT., INC. JOHN F. GODFREY, PRESIDENT 201 NORTH WELLS ST., SUITE 1208 CHICAGO, ILLINOIS 60606 (312) 726-3652	06/10-5156	443,476	290,957	DIVERSIFIED	4

LICENSEE	LICENSE NUMBER	PRIVATE CAPITAL	OBLIGATION TO SBA	INVESTMENT POLICY	OWNER CODE
ILLINOIS(CONT)					
AMOCO VENTURE CAPITAL COMPANY LYLE E. SCHAFFER, PRESIDENT 200 E. RANDOLPH DR. CHICAGO, ILLINOIS 60601 (312) 856-6523	05/07-5083	726,750	1,625,000	DIVERSIFIED	4
CEDCO CAPITAL CORP. FRANK B. BROOKS, PRESIDENT 180 NORTH MICHIGAN AVENUE CHICAGO, ILLINOIS 60601 (312) 984-5950	05/07-5086	668,800	500,000	DIVERSIFIED	4
CHICAGO COMMUNITY VENTURES, INC. BENJAMIN C. DUSTER, PRESIDENT 19 SOUTH LASALLE ST., RM.1114 CHICAGO, ILLINOIS 60603 (312) 726-6084	05/05-5089	1,005,000	1,005,000	DIVERSIFIED	4
COMBINED OPPORTUNITIES INCORPORATED WALLACE BUYA, PRESIDENT 300 NORTH STATE STREET CHICAGO, ILLINOIS 60610 (312) 266-3050	05/07-5084	500,000	500,000	DIVERSIFIED	4
NEIGHBORHOOD FUND, INC. (THE) RONALD A. GRZYWINSKI, PRESIDENT 7058 SOUTH CHAPPEL AVENUE CHICAGO, ILLINOIS 60649 (312) 648-8074	05/05-5124	150,000	0	DIVERSIFIED	1
NIA CORPORATION CHRIS H. HOWARD, V. PRESIDENT 2400 SOUTH MICHIGAN AVE. CHICAGO, ILLINOIS 60616 (312) 842-5125	05/05-5110	196,709	0	INSURANCE COMPANIES	4
NORTHERN CAPITAL CORPORATION JOSEPH DUCHARME, PRESIDENT 1017 WALNUT STREET BATAVIA, ILLINOIS 60510 (312) 879-7317	05/05-5133	300,000	0	DIVERSIFIED	5

LICENSEE	LICENSE NUMBER	PRIVATE CAPITAL	OBLIGATION TO SBA	INVESTMENT POLICY	OWNER CODE
ILLINOIS(CONT)					
TOWER VENTURES, INC. STANLEY C. PIKET, GENERAL MANAGER SEARS TOWER, BSC 9-29 CHICAGO, ILLINOIS 60684 (312) 875-9628	05/05-5104	1,000,000	1,000,000	DIVERSIFIED	4
URBAN FUND OF ILLINOIS INC., THE PETER H. ROSS, PRESIDENT 300 N. STATE STREET CHICAGO, ILLINOIS 60610 (312) 266-3050	05/07-5080	650,000	650,000	DIVERSIFIED	1
INDIANA					
MINORITY VENTURE COMPANY, INC. FREDERICK L. HOWARD, GEN'L MGR. KNUTE ROCKNE MEMORIAL BLDG. P.O. BOX 382 SOUTH BEND, INDIANA 46624 (219) 283-1115	05/05-5095	150,000	150,000	DIVERSIFIED	4
TYLER REFRIGERATION CAPITAL CORP. WILLIAM P. LINNEN, PRESIDENT 2222 EAST MICHIGAN BLVD. MICHIGAN CITY, INDIANA 46360 (616) 683-2000	05/05-5125	303,000	0	DIVERSIFIED	4
KENTUCKY					
EQUAL OPPORTUNITY FINANCE, INC. FRANKLIN JUSTICE, JR., V.P. & MGR. 224 EAST BROADWAY LOUISVILLE, KENTUCKY 40202 (502) 583-0601	04/05-5096	578,898	500,000	DIVERSIFIED	4
LOUISIANA					
BUSINESS CAPITAL CORP. DAVID R. BURRUS, PRESIDENT 1732 CANAL STREET NEW ORLEANS, LOUISIANA 70112 (504) 581-4002	06/06-5177	500,000	4,100,000	DIVERSIFIED	5

LICENSEE	LICENSE NUMBER	PRIVATE CAPITAL	OBLIGATION TO SBA	INVESTMENT POLICY	OWNER CODE
LOUISIANA(CONT)					
EDICT INVESTMENT CORP. REV. ROBER P. MORIN, PRESIDENT 2908 S. CARROLLTON AVE. NEW ORLEANS, LOUISIANA 70118 (504) 861-9521	06/06-5176	192,500	150,000	DIVERSIFIED	4
LOUISIANA VENTURE CAPITAL CORP. BEN D. JOHNSON, PRESIDENT 315 NORTH STREET NATCHITOCHES, LOUISIANA 71457 (318) 352-9138	06/06-5174	500,000	500,000	DIVERSIFIED	4
SCDF INVESTMENT CORP. REV. ALBERT J. MCKNIGHT, PRESIDENT 1006 SURREY STREET LAFAYETTE, LOUISIANA 70501 (318) 232-3767	06/10-5157	1,000,010	1,000,000	DIVERSIFIED	4
MARYLAND					
BALTIMORE COMMUNITY INV. CO. JAMES CROCKETT, PRESIDENT SUITE 110, METRO PLAZA BALTIMORE, MARYLAND 21215 (301) 669-2863	03/04-5106	152,300	300,000	DIVERSIFIED	5
MINORITY INVESTMENTS, INCORPORATED FREDERICK L. SIMS, PRESIDENT 8121 GEORGIA AVE., SUITE 800 SILVER SPRING, MARYLAND 20901 (301) 585-3444	03/04-5111	199,335	567,500	DIVERSIFIED	6
MASSACHUSETTS					
GREATER SPRINGFIELD INV. CORP. FRANK P. FITZGERALD, PRESIDENT 145 STATE ST., SUITE 611 SPRINGFIELD, MASSACHUSETTS 01103 (413) 781-7130	01/01-5073	211,000	380,000	DIVERSIFIED	2
MASSACHUSETTS VENTURE CAPITAL CORP. CHARLES T. GRIGSBY, PRESIDENT 141 MILK ST., ROOM 1115 BOSTON, MASSACHUSETTS 02109 (617) 426-0208	01/01-5273	710,000	700,000	DIVERSIFIED	2

LICENSEE	LICENSE NUMBER	PRIVATE CAPITAL	OBLIGATION TO SBA	INVESTMENT POLICY	OWNER CODE
PENNSYLVANIA					
ALLIANCE ENTERPRISE CORPORATION SHALLIE M. BEY, JR., PRESIDENT 1616 WALNUT ST., SUITE 802 PHILADELPHIA, PENNSYLVANIA 19103 (215) 972-4230	03/03-5066	2,709,100	1,000,000	DIVERSIFIED	4
COTTMAN CAPITAL CORP. RICHARD O. SILVA, PRESIDENT 575 VIRGINIA DRIVE FORT WASHINGTON, PENNSYLVANIA 19034 (215) 628-9540	03/03-5122	300,000	900,000	COTTMAN TRANS. CTRS. FRANCHISES	4
GREATER PHILA. VENTURE CAP. CORP. INC. J. WALTON ST. CLAIR, JR. PRESIDENT 920 LEWIS TOWER BLDG. 225 SOUTH FIFTEENTH ST. PHILADELPHIA, PENNSYLVANIA 19102 (215) 732-3415	03/03-5112	524,083	505,000	DIVERSIFIED	2
PUERTO RICO					
NORTH AMERICA INV. CORP. CARLOS J. POU, PRESIDENT BANCO DE PONCE BLDG. 19TH FLOOR HATO REY, PUERTO RICO 00918 (809) 751-6161	02/02-5308	750,000	1,500,000	DIVERSIFIED	5
TENNESSEE					
CHICKASAW CAPITAL CORPORATION WAYNE J. HASKINS, PRESIDENT UNION PLANTERS BANK BLDG. 67 MADISON AVE., 4TH FL. MEMPHIS, TENNESSEE 38103 (901) 523-6851	04/04-5128	500,000	500,000	DIVERSIFIED	1
R.P.B. INVESTMENT ENTERPRISES, INC M. HALL OAKLEY, PRESIDENT FALLS BUILDING 22 NORTH FRONT STREET MEMPHIS, TENNESSEE 38103 (901) 526-0063	04/04-5131	500,000	500,000	DIVERSIFIED	5

LICENSEE	LICENSE NUMBER	PRIVATE CAPITAL	OBLIGATION TO SBA	INVESTMENT POLICY	OWNER CODE
NEW YORK(CONT)					
PIONEER CAPITAL CORP. JAMES G. NIVEN, PRESIDENT ONE BATTERY PARK PLAZA 28TH FLOOR NEW YORK, NEW YORK 10004 (212) 483-9127	02/02-5274	701,261	1,400,000	DIVERSIFIED	5
SITUATION VENTURES CORPORATION SAM HOLLANDER, PRESIDENT 4522 FORT HAMILTON PKWY. BROOKLYN, NEW YORK 11219 (212) 438-4909	02/02-5323	500,000	900,000	DIVERSIFIED	5
TAROCO CAPITAL CORP. DAVID R. C. CHANG, PRESIDENT 120 BROADWAY NEW YORK, NEW YORK 10005 (212) 964-6877	02/02-5318	505,000	1,010,000	CHINESE AMERICANS	5
NORTH CAROLINA					
VANGUARD INVESTMENT COMPANY, INC. JAMES F. HANSLEY, PRESIDENT SUITE 309, PEPPER BLDG. FOURTH AND LIBERTY ST. WINSTON-SALEM, NORTH CAROLINA 27101 (919) 724-3676	04/04-5092	500,053	1,270,000	DIVERSIFIED	4
OHIO					
DAYTON MESBIC, INC. LEO A. LUCAS, PRESIDENT MIAMI VALLEY TOWER, SUITE 1820 40 WEST FOURTH ST. DAYTON, OHIO 45402 (513) 223-9405	05/05-5092	500,000	1,500,000	DIVERSIFIED	4
GLENCO ENTERPRISES, INCORPORATED DR. LEWIS F. WRIGHT, V.P. 1464 E. 105 ST., SUITE 101 CLEVELAND, OHIO 44106 (216) 721-1200	05/05-5091	500,000	500,000	DIVERSIFIED	5
OKLAHOMA					
AMERICAN INDIAN INV. OPPORT., INC. (MAIN OFFICE: CHICAGO, ILL.) 205 EAST MAIN STREET NORMAN, OKLAHOMA 73069					

LICENSEE	LICENSE NUMBER	PRIVATE CAPITAL	OBLIGATION TO SBA	INVESTMENT POLICY	OWNER CODE
NEW YORK(CONT)					
CVC CAPITAL CORP. JOERG G. KLEBE, PRESIDENT 666 FIFTH AVENUE NEW YORK, NEW YORK 10019 (212) 246-1980	02/02-5338	2,000,000	2,000,000	TELEVISION INDUSTRY	5
EQUICO CAPITAL CORP. CLARENCE C. LOFTIN III, EXEC. V.P. 1285 AVENUE OF THE AMERICAS NEW YORK, NEW YORK 10019 (212) 489-7033	02/02-5286	4,650,000	4,650,000	DIVERSIFIED	4
EXIM CAPITAL CORP. VICTOR K. CHUN, PRESIDENT 489 FIFTH AVENUE NEW YORK, NEW YORK 10017 (212) 490-0250	02/02-5351	510,000	0	DIVERSIFIED	5
KING SBI CORP. NEIL RITZ, PRESIDENT 902 ELLICOTT SQUARE BUILDING BUFFALO, NEW YORK 14202 (716) 856-4413	02/02-5332	500,183	1,000,000	DIVERSIFIED	4
MERIT FUNDING, INC. ROGER L. COHEN, PRESIDENT 60 EAST 42ND STREET NEW YORK, NEW YORK 10017 (212) 697-9660	04/04-5138	500,000	500,000	DIVERSIFIED	5
MINORITY EQUITY CAP. CO., INC. PATRICK O. BURNS, GEN'L MGR. 470 PARK AVE. SOUTH, SUITE 300 NEW YORK, NEW YORK 10016 (212) 889-0880	02/02-5288	2,204,047	1,707,000	DIVERSIFIED	4
NORTH STREET CAPITAL CORPORATION LEE A. ARCHER, JR., PRESIDENT 250 NORTH STREET WHITE PLAINS, NEW YORK 10625 (914) 631-3000	02/02-5285	500,000	1,000,000	DIVERSIFIED	4
ODA CAPITAL CORP. PHILIP KLEIN, EXECUTIVE DIRECTOR 82 LEE AVENUE BROOKLYN, NEW YORK 11211 (212) 963-9260	02/02-5307	301,500	600,000	DIVERSIFIED	5

LICENSEE	LICENSE NUMBER	PRIVATE CAPITAL	OBLIGATION TO SBA	INVESTMENT POLICY	OWNER CODE
NEW MEXICO					
ASSOCIATED SOUTHWEST INVESTORS, INC. (MAIN OFFICE: PHOENIX, ARIZONA) 2403 SAN MATEO BLVD., N.E. SUITE 514 ALBUQUERQUE, NEW MEXICO 87110 (505) 268-2421					
NEW YORK					
AMERICAN ASIAN CAPITAL CORPORATION HOWARD H. LIN, PRESIDENT 79 WALL ST., ROOM 907 NEW YORK, NEW YORK 10005 (212) 422-6880	02/02-5316	503,000	500,000	DIVERSIFIED	5
AMISTAD DOT VENTURE CAPITAL, INC. PERCY E. SUTTON, PRESIDENT 801 SECOND AVENUE NEW YORK, NEW YORK 10017 (212) 725-4500	02/02-5358	500,000	0	COMMUNICATIONS &TRANSPORTATION	5
BANCAP CORPORATION WILLIAM L. WHITELY, PRESIDENT 420 LEXINGTON AVE., RM. 2352 NEW YORK, NEW YORK 10017 (212) 687-6470	02/02-5287	1,000,000	2,000,000	DIVERSIFIED	1
CEDC MESBIC, INC. JOHN L. KEARSE, PRESIDENT 106 MAIN STREET HEMPSTEAD, NEW YORK 11550 (516) 292-9710	02/02-5296	500,000	500,000	DIVERSIFIED	4
COALITION SBIC, CORP. REGINALD F. LEWIS, PRESIDENT 30 BROAD STREET NEW YORK, NEW YORK 10004 (212) 399-0229	02/02-5289	173,350	336,700	DIVERSIFIED	4
COHEN CAPITAL CORP. EDWARD H. COHEN, PRESIDENT 8 EAST 36TH STREET NEW YORK, NEW YORK 10016 (212) 689-9030	02/02-5335	500,000	500,000	DIVERSIFIED	5

LICENSEE	LICENSE NUMBER	PRIVATE CAPITAL	OBLIGATION TO SBA	INVESTMENT POLICY	OWNER CODE
MINNESOTA					
CONTROL DATA COMMUNITY VENTURES FUND PHILIP J. BIFULK, PRESIDENT 8100 - 34TH AVENUE SOUTH BLOOMINGTON, MINNESOTA 55420 (612) 853-8100	05/05-5134	502,500	0	DIVERSIFIED	4
SAGERA VENTURE CORP., INCORPORATED GERALD A. STONE, PRESIDENT 2850 METRO DRIVE BLOOMINGTON, MINNESOTA 55426 (612) 854-2258	05/05-5121	500,000	1,000,000	DIVERSIFIED	4
MISSISSIPPI					
INVESAT CAPITAL CORP. J. THOMAS NOOJIN, PRESIDENT 162 EAST AMITE STREET, SUITE 204 JACKSON, MISSISSIPPI 39201 (601) 969-3242	04/04-5112	150,000	450,000	DIVERSIFIED	6
NEBRASKA					
COMMUNITY EQUITY CORP. OF NEBRASKA WILLIAM C. MOORE, PRESIDENT 5620 AMES AVE., ROOM 103 OMAHA, NEBRASKA 68104 (402) 455-1500	07/07-5078	300,000	300,000	DIVERSIFIED	4
NEW JERSEY					
BROAD ARROW INVESTMENT CORPORATION CHARLES N. BELLM, PRESIDENT 33 SOUTH STREET P.O. BOX 2231R MORRISTOWN, NEW JERSEY 07960 (201) 540-8018	02/02-5278	156,700	150,000	DIVERSIFIED	5
RUTGERS MINORITY INV. CO. LOUIS T. GERMAN, PRESIDENT 92 NEW STREET NEWARK, NEW JERSEY 07102 (201) 648-5287	02/02-5283	905,000	1,155,000	DIVERSIFIED	4

LICENSEE	LICENSE NUMBER	PRIVATE CAPITAL	OBLIGATION TO SBA	INVESTMENT POLICY	OWNER CODE
MASSACHUSETTS(CONT)					
W.C.C.I. CAPITAL CORP. MICHAEL W. TIERNEY, PRESIDENT 791 MAIN STREET WORCESTER, MASSACHUSETTS 01610 (617) 791-3259	01/01-5268	252,500	0	DIVERSIFIED	4
MICHIGAN					
DEARBORN CAPITAL CORP. ROBERT C. CHAMBERS, PRESIDENT THE AMERICAN ROAD DEARBORN, MICHIGAN 48121 (313) 337-8577	05/05-5135	500,000	0	DIVERSIFIED	4
INDEPENDENCE CAPITAL FORMATION, INC. WALTER MCMURTRY, JR., PRESIDENT 3049 E. GRAND BLVD. DETROIT, MICHIGAN 48202 (313) 875-7669	05/05-5094	1,033,293	3,099,786	DIVERSIFIED	4
METRO-DETROIT INV. CO. WILLIAM J. FOWLER, PRESIDENT 18481 WEST TEN MILE ROAD, SUITE 202 SOUTHFIELD, MICHIGAN 48075 (313) 557-3818	05/05-5126	1,000,000	1,500,000	FOOD STORES	4
MOTOR ENTERPRISES, INCORPORATED JAMES KOBUS, MANAGER 3044 WEST GRAND BLVD. DETROIT, MICHIGAN 48202 (313) 556-4273	05/15-5024	1,250,000	1,700,000	DIVERSIFIED	4
PRIME, INC. JAMES THOMAS, PRESIDENT 1845 DAVID WHITNEY BLDG. DETROIT, MICHIGAN 48226 (313) 964-3380	05/15-5025	1,007,500	2,380,000	DIVERSIFIED	4
TYLER REFRIGERATION CAPITAL CORP. (MAIN OFFICE: MICHIGAN CITY, IND.) 1329 LAKE STREET NILES, MICHIGAN 49120					

LICENSEE	LICENSE NUMBER	PRIVATE CAPITAL	OBLIGATION TO SBA	INVESTMENT POLICY	OWNER CODE
LOUISIANA(CONT)					
EDICT INVESTMENT CORP. REV. ROBER P. MORIN, PRESIDENT 2908 S. CARROLLTON AVE. NEW ORLEANS, LOUISIANA 70118 (504) 861-9521	06/06-5176	192,500	150,000	DIVERSIFIED	4
LOUISIANA VENTURE CAPITAL CORP. BEN D. JOHNSON, PRESIDENT 315 NORTH STREET NATCHITOCHES, LOUISIANA 71457 (318) 352-9138	06/06-5174	500,000	500,000	DIVERSIFIED	4
SCDF INVESTMENT CORP. REV. ALBERT J. MCKNIGHT, PRESIDENT 1006 SURREY STREET LAFAYETTE, LOUISIANA 70501 (318) 232-3767	06/10-5157	1,000,010	1,000,000	DIVERSIFIED	4
MARYLAND					
BALTIMORE COMMUNITY INV. CO. JAMES CROCKETT, PRESIDENT SUITE 110, METRO PLAZA BALTIMORE, MARYLAND 21215 (301) 669-2863	03/04-5106	152,300	300,000	DIVERSIFIED	5
MINORITY INVESTMENTS, INCORPORATED FREDERICK L. SIMS, PRESIDENT 8121 GEORGIA AVE., SUITE 800 SILVER SPRING, MARYLAND 20901 (301) 585-3444	03/04-5111	199,335	567,500	DIVERSIFIED	6
MASSACHUSETTS					
GREATER SPRINGIFELD INV. CORP. FRANK P. FITZGERALD, PRESIDENT 145 STATE ST., SUITE 611 SPRINGFIELD, MASSACHUSETTS 01103 (413) 781-7130	01/01-5073	211,000	380,000	DIVERSIFIED	2
MASSACHUSETTS VENTURE CAPITAL CORP. CHARLES T. GRIGSBY, PRESIDENT 141 MILK ST., ROOM 1115 BOSTON, MASSACHUSETTS 02109 (617) 426-0208	01/01-5273	710,000	700,000	DIVERSIFIED	2

LICENSEE	LICENSE NUMBER	PRIVATE CAPITAL	OBLIGATION TO SBA	INVESTMENT POLICY	OWNER CODE
ILLINOIS(CONT)					
TOWER VENTURES, INC. STANLEY C. PIKET, GENERAL MANAGER SEARS TOWER, BSC 9-29 CHICAGO, ILLINOIS 60684 (312) 875-9628	05/05-5104	1,000,000	1,000,000	DIVERSIFIED	4
URBAN FUND OF ILLINOIS INC., THE PETER H. ROSS, PRESIDENT 300 N. STATE STREET CHICAGO, ILLINOIS 60610 (312) 266-3050	05/07-5080	650,000	650,000	DIVERSIFIED	1
INDIANA					
MINORITY VENTURE COMPANY, INC. FREDERICK L. HOWARD, GEN'L MGR. KNUTE ROCKNE MEMORIAL BLDG. P.O. BOX 382 SOUTH BEND, INDIANA 46624 (219) 283-1115	05/05-5095	150,000	150,000	DIVERSIFIED	4
TYLER REFRIGERATION CAPITAL CORP. WILLIAM P. LINNEN, PRESIDENT 2222 EAST MICHIGAN BLVD. MICHIGAN CITY, INDIANA 46360 (616) 683-2000	05/05-5125	303,000	0	DIVERSIFIED	4
KENTUCKY					
EQUAL OPPORTUNITY FINANCE, INC. FRANKLIN JUSTICE, JR., V.P. & MGR. 224 EAST BROADWAY LOUISVILLE, KENTUCKY 40202 (502) 583-0601	04/05-5096	578,898	500,000	DIVERSIFIED	4
LOUISIANA					
BUSINESS CAPITAL CORP. DAVID R. BURRUS, PRESIDENT 1732 CANAL STREET NEW ORLEANS, LOUISIANA 70112 (504) 581-4002	06/06-5177	500,000	4,100,000	DIVERSIFIED	5

LICENSEE	LICENSE NUMBER	PRIVATE CAPITAL	OBLIGATION TO SBA	INVESTMENT POLICY	OWNER CODE
TENNESSEE(CONT)					
TENNESSEE EQUITY CAPITAL CORP. RICHARD KANTOR, PRESIDENT 711 UNION STREET NASHVILLE, TENNESSEE 37219 (615) 256-1331	04/04-5157	502,000	0	DIVERSIFIED	5
TEXAS					
MESBIC FINANCIAL CORP. OF HOUSTON PETER D. STERLING, PRESIDENT 2903 RICHMOND AVENUE SUITE 201 HOUSTON, TEXAS 77056 (713) 528-2061	06/06-5180	840,350	854,000	DIVERSIFIED	2
MESBIC FINANCIAL CORP. OF DALLAS WALTER W. DURHAM, PRESIDENT 7701 N. STEMMONS FREEWAY SUITE 850 DALLAS, TEXAS 75247 (214) 637-0445	06/10-5153	1,539,317	1,350,000	DIVERSIFIED	2
VIRGINIA					
EAST WEST UNITED INV. CO. BUI TRAC, CHAIRMAN 6723 WHITTIER AVE., SUITE 205B MCLEAN, VIRGINIA 22101 (703) 821-6616	03/03-5125	500,000	1,000,000	DIVERSIFIED	5
FIRST COLONIAL INV. CORP. MARION G. ROBERTSON, PRESIDENT PEMBROKE FOUR VIRGINIA BEACH, VIRGINIA 23463 (804) 499-8201	03/03-5130	500,000	500,000	DIVERSIFIED	5
NORFOLK INVESTMENT COMPANY, INC. KIRK W. SAUNDERS, GEN'L MGR. SUITE 515, GRANBY MALL BLDG. 201 GRANBY STREET NORFOLK, VIRGINIA 23510 (804) 623-1042	03/03-5116	700,000	1,400,000	DIVERSIFIED	4

LICENSEE	LICENSE NUMBER	PRIVATE CAPITAL	OBLIGATION TO SBA	INVESTMENT POLICY	OWNER CODE
<u>WASHINGTON</u>					
MODEL CAPITAL CORP. JEROME W. PAGE, PRESIDENT C/O SEATTLE URBAN LEAGUE 105 - 14TH AVENUE SEATTLE, WASHINGTON 98122 (206) 447-3799	10/13-5029	150,000	0	DIVERSIFIED	4
<u>WEST VIRGINIA</u>					
LICO MESBIC INVESTMENT COMPANY EDWARD T. LIU, PRESIDENT 350 RAGLAND ROAD BECKLEY, WEST VIRGINIA 25801 (304) 252-5942	03/03-5128	500,000	500,000	DIVERSIFIED	5
<u>WISCONSIN</u>					
SC OPPORTUNITIES, INC. ROBERT L. ABLEMAN, SECRETARY 1112 SEVENTH AVENUE MONROE, WISCONSIN 53566 (608) 328-8400	05/05-5109	300,000	600,000	SWISS COLONY FRANCHISES	5

301(D)SBIC
TOTALS BY STATES

STATE	SIZE 1	SIZE 2	SIZE 3	SIZE 4	TOTAL	TOTAL PRIVATE CAP	TOTAL OBLIGATIONS TO SBA
ALABAMA	0	0	0	0	0	0	0
ALASKA	0	1	0	0	1	1,000,000	0
ARIZONA	0	1	0	0	1	707,000	1,700,000
ARKANSAS	1	1	0	0	2	652,500	500,000
CALIFORNIA	1	4	4	0	9	9,136,038	8,850,535
COLORADO	0	0	0	0	0	0	0
CONNECTICUT	0	2	0	0	2	800,219	1,650,000
DELAWARE	0	0	0	0	0	0	0
D.C.	0	1	2	0	3	4,750,000	5,350,000
FLORIDA	2	7	0	0	9	4,150,000	5,150,000
GEORGIA	0	3	0	0	3	1,329,222	1,200,000
HAWAII	0	1	0	0	1	700,000	700,000
IDAHO	0	0	0	0	0	0	0
ILLINOIS	3	6	1	0	10	5,640,735	5,570,957
INDIANA	1	1	0	0	2	453,000	150,000
IOWA	0	0	0	0	0	0	0
KANSAS	0	0	0	0	0	0	0
KENTUCKY	0	1	0	0	1	578,898	500,000
LOUISIANA	1	2	1	0	4	2,192,510	5,750,000
MAINE	0	0	0	0	0	0	0
MARYLAND	2	0	0	0	2	351,635	867,500
MASSACHUSETTS	2	1	0	0	3	1,173,500	1,080,000
MICHIGAN	0	2	3	0	5	4,790,793	8,679,786
MINNESOTA	0	2	0	0	2	1,002,500	1,000,000
MISSISSIPPI	1	0	0	0	1	150,000	450,000
MISSOURI	0	0	0	0	0	0	0
MONTANA	0	0	0	0	0	0	0
NEBRASKA	1	0	0	0	1	300,000	300,000
NEVADA	0	0	0	0	0	0	0
NEW HAMPSHIRE	0	0	0	0	0	0	0
NEW JERSEY	1	1	0	0	2	1,061,700	1,305,000
NEW MEXICO	0	0	0	0	0	0	0
NEW YORK	1	13	3	0	17	16,048,341	18,603,700
NORTH CAROLINA	0	1	0	0	1	500,053	1,270,000
NORTH DAKOTA	0	0	0	0	0	0	0
OHIO	0	2	0	0	2	1,000,000	2,000,000
OKLAHOMA	0	0	0	0	0	0	0
OREGON	0	0	0	0	0	0	0
PENNSYLVANIA	1	1	1	0	3	3,533,183	2,405,000
PUERTO RICO	0	1	0	0	1	750,000	1,500,000
RHODE ISLAND	0	0	0	0	0	0	0
SOUTH CAROLINA	0	0	0	0	0	0	0
SOUTH DAKOTA	0	0	0	0	0	0	0
TENNESSEE	0	3	0	0	3	1,502,000	1,000,000
TEXAS	0	1	1	0	2	2,379,667	2,204,000
UTAH	0	0	0	0	0	0	0
VERMONT	0	0	0	0	0	0	0
VIRGINIA	0	3	0	0	3	1,700,000	2,900,000
WASHINGTON	1	0	0	0	1	150,000	0
WEST VIRGINIA	0	1	0	0	1	500,000	500,000
WISCONSIN	1	0	0	0	1	300,000	600,000
WYOMING	0	0	0	0	0	0	0
TOTAL	20	63	16	0	99	69,283,494	83,736,478*

301(D)SBIC
TOTALS BY PRIVATE CAPITAL SIZE CLASS

TOTAL PRIVATE CAPITAL SIZE CLASS	TOTAL NUMBER OF SBICS	TOTAL PRIVATE CAP	TOTAL OBLIGATIONS TO SBA
SIZE 1 — BELOW $300,000	20	4,311,894	35,334,200
SIZE 2 — $300001 TO $1.MM	63	35,830,795	16,409,957
SIZE 3 — $1.MM TO $5.MM	16	29,140,805	31,992,321
SIZE 4 — OVER $5.MM	0	0	0
TOTAL	99	69,283,494	83,736,478*

301(D)SBIC
TOTALS BY TYPE OF OWNERSHIP

TYPE OF OWNERSHIP	TOTAL NUMBER OF SBICS	TOTAL PRIVATE CAP	TOTAL OBLIGATIONS TO SBA
BANK DOMINATED	5	2,800,119	4,650,000
BANK ASSOCIATED	7	5,350,385	6,289,535
FINANCIAL ORGANIZATION	1	2,000,000	2,000,000
NON-FINANCIAL ORG.	47	40,505,894	48,069,443
INDIVIDUALLY OWNED	37	18,277,761	21,710,000
40 ACT COMPANY	2	349,335	1,017,500
TOTAL	99	69,283,494	83,736,478*

301(D)SBIC
PRIVATE CAPITAL BY TYPE OF OWNERSHIP

PRIVATE CAPITAL SIZE CLASS

TYPE OF OWNERSHIP	SIZE 1 NUM	SIZE 1 DOLLARS	SIZE 2 NUM	SIZE 2 DOLLARS	SIZE 3 NUM	SIZE 3 DOLLARS	SIZE 4 NUM	SIZE 4 DOLLARS
BANK DOMINATED	1	150000	4	2650119	0	0	0	0
BANK ASSOCIATED	1	211000	4	2374533	2	2764852	0	0
FINANCIAL ORG.	0	0	0	0	1	2000000	0	0
NON-FINANCIAL ORG.	9	1965059	26	16164882	12	22375953	0	0
INDIVIDUALLY OWNED	7	1636500	29	14641261	1	2000000	0	0
40 ACT COMPANY	2	349,335	0	0	0	0	0	0

*DATA ON TOTAL OBLIGATIONS FOR 301(d) SBIC'S IS NOT COMPARABLE WITH PREVIOUSLY PUBLISHED DATA DUE TO THE ADDITION OF PREFERRED STOCK PURCHASED BY SBA.

Sources of Help

This is probably the most valuable section of the book. Within this chapter are fundamental organizations designed to help small businesses; here also are all the difficult-to-classify pieces of information. When a source could reasonably be listed under this category or another, we opted to place it under this general broad category because it is the most comprehensive category.

This section is actually more than a reference—it's worth reading independently because each of the sources listed may be of value to your business. If you can't see the source for an immediate problem, an awareness of its existence could actually prevent some of your future problems.

COMPANIES AND SERVICES

1. Advanced Management Research is a leader in executive education and management development for both large and small business. It conducts numerous seminars on a host of topics. The organization does extensive mailing and if you have an interest in a short, effective seminar on a specific topic, write:

Advanced Management Research
1370 Avenue of the Americas
New York, NY 10019
(212)765-6400

2. The AMACOM division of the American Management Association offers numerous books and seminars on small business. The Amacom program also features newsletters. Write:

AMACOM
American Management Association
135 West 50th Street
New York, NY 10020
(212)586-8100

3. The International Entrepreneur's Association is one of the finest organizations dedicated to promoting entrepreneurship in the country. It offers a monthly magazine entitled *Entrepreneur,* and it is full of good ideas for succeeding in a business of your own. The magazine has over 100 special reports available on specific business opportunities. It specializes in hot new retail-related opportunities like gift shops, skateboard parks, dry cleaning, etc. There are about 40,000 members. Write:

International Entrepreneurs' Association
631 Wilshire Boulevard
Santa Monica, CA 90401

4. Besides the low-cost pamphlets offered by the Small Business Administration, numerous services and seminars are also offered. Inquire about Service Corporation of Retired Executives (SCORE) and the student team of the Small Business Institute (SBI). Each may be of value to you and are available from your local SBA office, which can be found in the yellow pages of your telephone directory.

5. *Common Sense* is a source of help for the very small, one or two person business. This monthly newsletter provides unique moral support and assistance to this type of business. The editor/entrepreneur has a down-to-earth way of making everything understandable. Write:

Stephen White, Pub.
David "Andy" Bangs, Ed.
Upstart Publishing Co. Inc.
366 Islington St.
Portsmouth, NH 03801
(603)436-0219

6. The Support Services Alliance, Inc., is a fascinating non-profit organization that acts as a general purchasing agent for

small-business owners. It was launched in 1977 with an $800,000 grant from the Rockefeller Foundation. Designed to offer four basic services to start with, it will undoubtedly be expanding to offer other services. Here is what it offers:

1. Blue Cross and major insurance coverage (even disability insurance) at discount rates
2. Legal referral service, and brief legal pamphlets answering small business-type questions
3. A discount from Hertz rent-a-car
4. A discount for Xerox machines
5. A discount on Prentice-Hall looseleaf publications
6. An arrangement to guarantee bank loans for college tuition of members' children

For information, write:

Support Services Alliance, Inc.
Crossroads Building
Two Times Square
New York, NY 10036
(212)398-7800

7. Ever wonder where lawyers go to discover, in simple language, the law concerning securities regulations? One of the better sources of low-price, high-quality information is also the publisher of numerous booklets on legal issues. This source has information on Rule 144, 146, 140, and 257. It can also help in registration information on S-1, Reg A's, blue-sky laws, and other SEC rules. Write for the brochure to:

Bowne & Company, Inc.
345 Hudson Street
New York, NY 10014
(212)924-5500

8. *International Endeavor* is an outgrowth of the International Symposium on Entrepreneurship and Enterprise Development, which took place in Cincinnati, Ohio in June 1975. It was given life at the East-West Center Technology and Development Institute in Honolulu, Hawaii in 1972. This is an international association of entrepreneurs, and a small contribution entitles you to membership. Write:

Endeavor International
IMPAC Sdn Bhd
105 F Jalan Ampang
Kuala, Lumpur
MALAYSIA

PUBLICATIONS

1. The fundamental objective of the *American Journal of Small Business* is to contribute to the growth of the broad area of small business from an academic, scholastic point of view by publishing quality manuscripts of both a theoretical and practical nature which are related to any aspect of small-business management. The *Journal* attempts to promote the interests of those interested in this field; namely, practitioners, academicians, consultants, policymakers, and students. The *AJSB,* a referred quarterly publication, has board members all over the U.S. and in Canada and France. Write:

American Journal of Small Business
University of Baltimore
1420 No. Charles Street
Baltimore, MD 21201
(301)727-6350, ext. 223

2. *Boardroom Reports* is management's source of practical, useful business information. It is a digest of useful information from all business magazines and newsletters plus original practical advice from America's experts in over 30 vital areas. Write:

Boardroom Reports
500 Fifth Avenue
New York, NY 10036
Circulation: 100,000

3. *Business Conditions Digest,* successor to Business Cycle Developments, is published monthly by the Bureau of Census. It presents almost 500 economic indicators in a form convenient for analysts with different approaches to the study of current business conditions and prospects (e.g., the national income model, the leading indicators, and anticipations and intentions), as well as for analysts who use combinations of these approaches. The subscrip-

tion service includes a separate summary table which is mailed in advance of the monthly report. Write:

Business Conditions Digest
U.S. Government Printing Office
Superintendent of Documents
Washington, DC 20402

4. General Electric offers manufacturing ideas and cost improvement techniques for your use through its *Tips* abstract service. Abstracted articles are conveniently catalogued from over 60 classifications. Every month this service reviews pertinent manufacturing advances and techniques to increase productivity and it allows a 48-hour reprint service for any requested article.

Business Growth Services
General Electric Company
120 Erie Boulevard
Schenectady, NY 12305
(518)385-2128

5. *Business Monthly* is eight pages of articles written by experts to help business managers run their businesses successfully. Subjects: overall business management topics, including accounting, tax questions, personnel, marketing, financial planning, new laws, government regulations, production, fringe benefits, etc. This is one of the better management newsletters. Write:

Business Monthly
United Media International, Inc.
306 Dartmouth Street
Boston, MA 02116
(617)267-7100
Circulation: 25,000

6. *Business Opportunities Journal* is a national investment newspaper which is published monthly by Business Service Corporation. Write:

Business Opportunities Journal
Business Service Corporation
1449 Garnet Avenue
San Diego, CA 92109

7. *Business Owner* is a new journal that aims to keep the small and medium-sized business owner abreast of new developments in

taxation, accounting, insurance, estate planning, and corporate law and to monitor available government financing programs. Examples of regular features are "Washington Watch," "Business Briefs," "Tax Thoughts," and "Small Business Speaks Out." This may be the best single source of help for entrepreneurs yet. Write:

> The Business Owner
> 50 Jericho Turnpike
> Jericho, NY 11753
> (516)997-7010

8. Commerce Clearing House, Inc. publishes more than 150 series of reports on specific tax or business law subjects. This organization publishes the topical law reports and is an excellent source of current rulings on income tax. It is a source of help used primarily by lawyers and accountants. Write:

> Commerce Clearing House, Inc.
> Publishers of Topical Law Reports
> 4025 West Peterson Avenue
> Chicago, IL 60404

9. *Consultant News* is an interesting newsletter featuring current information about the management consulting profession and other consulting professions. Often, entrepreneurs seek consulting assistance and this newsletter may prove helpful in identifying sources of such assistance. The monthly newsletter is very well prepared and informative. Write:

> Consultants News
> Box 84
> Fitzwilliam, NH 03447

10. The Department of Labor has published two new "answer" booklets concerning the Employee Retirement Income Security Act. *Reporting and Disclosure, ERISA* and *Often-Asked Questions about ERISA* can be obtained free of charge by writing to:

> Department of Labor
> Labor Management Administration
> Room N-5432
> Washington, DC 20216

11. The Enterprise Publishing Company is a unique source of self-help books and audio cassettes for the small-business owner. Write:

Enterprise Publishing Company
1300 Market Street
Wilmington, DE 19810

for the following material:

101 How and Where to Raise Venture Capital to Finance a Business
102 How to Set Up Your Own Medical Reimbursement Plan
103 Income Portfolio
201 Don't Be Afraid—Start Your Own Business
202 A.M.—How to Teach Yourself Meditation
401 How to Form Your Own Corporation
402 Where the Money Is and How to Get It
405 How to Self-Publish Your Own Book and Make It a Best Seller
406 How to Do Business Tax Free
407 How to Form Your Own Professional Corporation
409 How to Get Out If You're in Over Your Head

12. The Executive Reports Corporation is an excellent source of data for small-company presidents. *The President's Guide,* which they publish, is a one-volume encyclopedia that offers many valuable pieces of information. Write also for a newsletter known as the *Prentice-Hall Management Letter.*

Prentice-Hall, Inc.
Executive Reports Corporation
Englewood Cliffs, NJ 07632

13. One source, the Financial Management Association, offers unusual, entertaining, and interesting books for small-business owners:

Why S.O.B.'s Succeed and Nice Guys Fail in a Small Business

Small Business Loans (2 vols.) (Heavy or small business loans including blank SBA loan applications)

How to Form Your Own Corporation (a book on avoiding unnecessary expenses, legal fees, and unlimited personal liabilities)

To find out about the above three books write:
Financial Management Association
3824 East Indian School Road
Phoenix, AZ 85018
(800)528-3606

14. "The magazine that makes you money" is known as *Free Enterprise Magazine*. This magazine was formerly known as the *Capitalist Reporter*. The magazine is published bimonthly and the circulation is about 30,000 per issue. The magazine is capturing a unique place in the area of small business. It is clearly one of the better sources of help for entrepreneurs. Write:

Main Editorial Office
Free Enterprise
The Capitalist Reporter
1212 Avenue of the Americas
New York, NY 10036
(212)354-4100

15. The Institute for Business Planning, Inc., a subsidiary of Prentice-Hall, has some excellent material available for entrepreneurs. The booklets and monthly notes on tax planning and on the closely held corporation are very good. It offers information tax planning, tax-tested forms of business agreements, closely held businesses, corporate formation operation and management, pay planning programs, estate planning, life insurance planning, real estate investment planning, corporate regulations of securities, financial planning, tax-sheltered investments, and estate practices and procedures. Write:

Institute for Business Planning, Inc.
IBP Plaza
Englewood Cliffs, NJ 07632

16. The Institute for New Enterprise Development offers many aids to venture development. To obtain information about any of the following publications, write:

Institute for New Enterprise Development
385 Concord Avenue
Belmont, MA 02178
(617)489-3950

First Stage Venture Analysis contains (1) "Approach to Developing a First Stage Venture Analysis" and (2) "First Stage Analysis—Product or Service Venture."

Item (1) provides some guidance for making a preliminary assessment of the feasibility of a venture. Item (2) is designed to identify any fatal flaws in a venture, and help an investor and entrepreneur(s) determine whether or not to pursue it further.

The Entrepreneurial Team: Formation and Development describes the venture creation process and the critical elements involved in success-

fully developing a team that can manage the venture. The benefits and typical setbacks involved in forming a venture are discussed, as are ways of avoiding common mistakes.

Business Plan contains (1) "Approach to Developing a Business Plan" and (2) "How to Prepare a Business Plan—Guidelines for Entrepreneurs." Item (1) is a discussion of the most important sections of a business plan, and how to approach the task of developing one. Item (2) is a detailed guideline for preparing a business plan—the document which describes a potential investment in enough detail for an investor to determine whether or not to invest. A business plan, when done thoroughly, can also be used as a guideline for running a business.

Equity and Other Compensation describes several methods of compensating venture management (stock splits, salaries, fringes), and discusses the benefits and drawbacks of each. To assist investors in identifying what percent of a venture an outside investor can expect, a commonly used method of valuing investments is explained.

Introduction to Investment Agreements details the various items covered in an investment agreement. It explains and gives examples of the most frequently used protections and warranties, and many of the covenants typically sought by both investors and entrepreneurs.

17. *In Touch* focuses on the small-business owner and provides resources, business-building tips, and stories about a wide variety of creative enterprises. The emphasis is on entrepreneuring as a means of greater personal growth and self-discovery. The approach is unique and of special interest to those who have tried functioning in a traditional, corporate setting and found something missing. Most of the material comes from within the subscriber network, and the newsletter serve a double purpose as a public relations tool for the beginning entrepreneur who is working on a limited budget. Write:

In Touch, The Newsletter of Personal Possibilities
P.O. Box 3471
Santa Barbara, CA 93105
Circulation: 2,000

18. The *Journal of Small Business Management* is the official publication of the International Council of Small Business, a nonprofit organization devoted to continuing management education for small-business owners and managers. For over a decade, this journal has fostered progress in all phases of management development for small business, and is read by businesspeople, educators, consultants, government representatives, students, and others interested in this important subject. Now internationally circulated, each edi-

tion contains some eight to ten articles, regular features on the Washington scene, and "Resources" (abstracts of books and articles), plus book reviews. It is published quarterly to just under 2,000 subscribers. Write:

Journal of Small Business Management
General Secretary, ICSB
UW-Extension
929 North Sixth Street
Milwaukee, WI 53203

19. *Management Contents* is a biweekly publication which compiles the tables of contents from 220 business and management journals, transactions and proceedings. Full text of articles appearing in publication are available through a document retrieval service. Write:

Management Contents
Management Information Services
Box 1054
Skokie, IL 60076
(312)982-7381
Circulation: 2,500

20. One of the finest sources of information on small business is Merrill, Lynch, especially on financial and securities data. Of particular value are the following booklets:

Investments in Small Business Administration and Farmers Home Administration (August 1977) is about "full faith and credit" guaranteed loan participations.

Small Business Administration Loan Participation (August 1977) is a question-and-answer booklet about SBA loans.

How to Read a Financial Report, 5th ed. (1977) is a superb presentation of a balance sheet, cash flow, and income statement.

All of these publications and more are available free from:

Merrill Lynch, Pierce, Fenner & Smith
One Liberty Plaza
165 Broadway
New York, NY 10006

21. Without a doubt the highest quality publication in terms of editorial format is *Money Magazine,* a monthly publication of *Time,*

Inc. While the editorial material is not directed toward small businesses as a rule, the articles and staff reports often deal with issues of vital concern to entrepreneurs. Consequently, it serves this need at a higher level than any of the other publications.

It is widely circulated and an index to back issues is provided every January and July. Back issues are available and offered for sale. Write:

Money Magazine
Time and Life Building
Rockefeller Center
New York, NY 10020
(212)586-1212

22. Understanding new federal warranty regulations is made easier for both manufacturers and retailers by *Summary of Magnuson-Moss Warranty Act and Federal Trade Commission Rules,* a publication that covers compliance with the new rules as well as methods of informing consumers about their rights. Write:

National Retail Merchants Association
100 West 31st Street
New York, NY 10001

23. The Senate Select Committee on Small Business offers a free newsletter describing its activities. It is very informative and useful. Write:

Chairman, Senate Select Committee on Small Business
Room 221
Russell Senate Office Building
Washington, DC 20510

24. The *Small Business Newsletter* offers items of interest to all small-business owners. It is especially relevant to small business and the government. Write:

Newsletter, Small Business
1225 19th Street, N.W.
Washington, DC 20036

25. The 1977 OSHA *Handbook for Small Management* is a 41-page brief designed to help the small-business owner create and operate his or her own safety program. It demonstrates ways of avoiding costly penalties, provides checklists for inspections, and presents a seven-point safety plan. It's free from:

OSHA
U.S. Department of Labor
Room N-3641
Third and Constitution Avenue
Washington, DC 20210

26. *The Professional Report* is a monthly tax and management magazine that provides information and advice for the owners of small businesses specifically. It covers insurance, business legal matters, techniques for better advertising, bill collecting, office procedures, record keeping, business tax deductions, etc. Write:

The Professional Report
321 Harwood Building
Scarsdale, NY 10583
(914)472-0366
Circulation: 30,000

27. Dun & Bradstreet produces an excellent 50-page booklet which identifies many of the good articles and books on small business. This is especially valuable for specific industries, because the reports on special opportunities are numerous. It is organized around the same format as *The Small Business Reporter* (Bank of America) and the industry-by-industry orientation almost uniformly assures everyone of some specific information. It also lists SBA publications. In addition, D&B publishes: *Key Business Ratios in 125 Lines, The Pitfalls of Managing a Small Business,* and *How to Control Accounts Receivable for Greater Profits.* Write:

Public Relations Department
Dun & Bradstreet
99 Church Street
New York, NY 10007

28. One of the few original sources of new ideas for small businesses and not a repackaging of other people's ideas is the Research Institute of America. It is the world's largest private business advisory service, supported by industry through its membership. It has the following general categories of information: tax opportunities and pitfalls, labor and personnel, RIA membership surveys, European and political developments, and business and finance. Beside some special reports on "a new kind of found money for the executive," and "the way executives cut taxes," this is an excellent source of continuing information, especially concerning taxes. The

Research Institute's Recommendations is about business and taxes, and several other publications and newsletters are also available at a wide range of prices. Write:

The Research Institute of America
Research Institute Building
589 Fifth Avenue
New York, NY 10017

29. The *Retail Management Letter* is a monthly report which brings busy retailers information they need to keep up to date, and the perspective they need to look ahead. This letter covers a broad range of publications and industry sources for retail owners and executives with expanding responsibilities. Write:

The Retail Management Letter
311 Hamilton Street
Plymouth, MI 48170

30. The Select Information Exchange offers a directory of investment advisory publications for investors. The organization acts as a packager of subscriptions to journals and magazines of interest to businesspeople and investors. For a specific fee, you can receive trial subscriptions for one to five months for several dozen publications in a number of broad categories. This is a very useful way to get acquainted with the wide variety of publications within specific fields. Select Information Exchange also offers a *Guide to Business and Investment Books*. Write:

Select Information Exchange
2095 Broadway
New York, NY 10023

31. *Small Business Clinic* is a business newsletter of Austin M. Elliott and its strength and weakness is that he is the only contributor and it's hard to write something new every month. But he tries. I especially enjoy his choice of quotations. Write:

Austin M. Elliott
113 Vista Del Lago
Scotts Valley, CA 95066

32. *Small Business Newsletter* offers information to owners and managers of small businesses in all management areas, especially taxes, advertising and promotion, and money management. Write:

Small Business Newsletter
7514 North 53rd Street
Milwaukee, WI 53223
(414)354-4260

33. *The Small Business Report* is a monthly publication containing vital information for small-business owners/managers. Write:

Small Business Report
Box 1138
Paso Robles, CA 93446

34. There are more than 40 titles in the *Small Business Reporter* series. The series has two sections: *Business Profiles* are reports that deal with specific businesses, discussing investment requirements and operational formats; and *Business Operations* explain general aspects of business management and operation. There is a postage and handling charge for these reports, but a *Publication Index* is available without charge. Approximate circulation is 300,000. Write:

Small Business Reporter
Bank of America
Department 3120
P.O. Box 37000
San Francisco, CA 94137
(415)622-2491, 2492, 2493

35. A gem of a small upbeat magazine, *Success Unlimited,* is published by W. Clement Stone, of insurance fame. The "magazine of the positive mental attitude" is a totally unique publication. Circulation is about 150,000 per issue. It offers an interesting collection of books in each issue through the Success Unlimited Book Club, and also conducts seminars. Write:

Success Unlimited
6355 Broadway
Chicago, IL 60660
(312)973-7650

36. *Publications for Business* is a free 20-page booklet published by the U.S. Department of Commerce. Also available is a list of publishers and committee memberships of the Select Committee on Small Business of the House of Representatives (Pamphlet 87-842). Write:

Superintendent of Documents
Government Printing Office
Washington, DC 20401

37. The *Morgan Guaranty* is a monthly review of business and economic conditions. Additionally, it includes articles on a broad spectrum of economic-financial subjects. This is a free publication sent to 50,000 subscribers. Write:

Morgan Guaranty Survey
23 Wall Street
New York, NY 10015
(212)483-2361

38. The *U.S. Newsletter* is a weekly newsletter published for business and professional readers by U.S. News and World Report, Inc. The publication forecasts legislation, regulation, administration policy, trends in finance, taxation, labor, and other fields. It has four pages weekly with occasional supplements. Write:

The U.S. Newsletter, U.S. News and World Report
2300 N Street, N.W.
Washington, DC 20037
(202)333-7400
Circulation: 60,000

39. The Federal Reserve Bank of Boston offers two free publications of value to entrepreneurs. The first is the *Business Planning Guide* (1976), a booklet on how to write a business plan. This handbook helps you design, write, and use a business plan tailored to your specific business needs; it includes worksheets for financial data. It has about 100 well-organized pages and it's free.

Second is *Business Resource Directory* (1975), a source of assistance groups for the New England entrepreneur. While this booklet is especially helpful for Northeasterners, it may offer ideas of likely local sources to people in other parts of the country. It is available at no charge. For both publications write:

Federal Reserve Bank of Boston
30 Pearl Street
Boston, MA 02106

40. Small Business Magazines. A huge market gap opened recently in the area of small business magazines. Six or seven new magazines appeared on the market within a relatively short period

of time. Too many magazines, in our opinion, with each seeking to carve its own special niche. Now, according to Bernie Goldhirsh, the colorful enterpreneur/publisher of *Inc.* magazine, there is one less competitor. *Inc.*, in an upcoming announcement, has bought the assets of one of its major competitors, *Successful Business.* While Goldhirsh will discontinue publishing this quarterly magazine for independent businesses, he will utilize its subscriptions and personnel. In fact, some of the editorial staff will give *Inc.* a needed boost in editorial depth. During the initial adjustment period, *Inc.* has had editorial turmoil, but this trouble has not prevented it from becoming the front runner in this blossoming market. The 13-30 Corporation of Knoxville, Tennessee, which started *Successful Business,* with the help of Control Data Corporation, will now concentrate its efforts on its most recent acquisition, *Esquire* magazine. The following are the current contenders in the small business magazine race and they are all jockeying for position. The list will change again, in our opinion, so why not read a few and vote for your favorite to stay the whole race? The contenders are:

Frequency	Magazine	Advertising Accepted	Hero
Monthly	*The Business Owner* 50 Jericho Tpke. Jericho, NY 11753	No	Thomas J. Martin

The Business Owner is getting better editorially since the recent sale of the magazine by Tom Martin to the Transamerican Media Corporation in Riverton, Connecticut. Although Martin and his co-founder, Mark Gustafson still write it, they are now investing more editorial time to be producing quality work. But we feel it is still a little too arithmetically-oriented. Circulation is confidential, but probably under 10,000.

Monthly	*Venture Magazine* 35 W. 45th Street New York, NY 10037	Yes	Joe Giarraputo

Venture is the number two magazine in the field. The premier issue arrived in March, 1979 and its editorial content is superior. It is fighting to be number one and Joe Giarraputo, its founder, is a good competitor—don't count it out. Circulation is just under 100,000, but very few readers have converted to paid as yet. It focuses on venture capital and deal-making.

Monthly	*Inc. Magazine* 38 Commercial Wharf Boston, MA 02110	Yes	Bernard Goldhirsh

Inc. is the number one small business magazine. Goldhirsh is going after *Business Week* and *Fortune* magazines and he is doing it well. He followed a similar course in competing with *Yachting* (an older, more prestigious publication), with his two previous magazines, *Sail* and *Motor Boating.* Circulation is growing toward a paid 400,000. He instantly added 250,000 with the purchase of *Successful Business.*

Monthly	*Entrepreneur* 631 Wilshire Blvd. Santa Monica, CA 90401	Yes	Chase Revel

Entrepreneur is an excellent magazine, achieving what it claims to be, an opportunity magazine. It is superior for retailing and retail trades. To receive it, you must be a member of the International Entrepreneurial Association (IEA). Paid circulation is claimed to be about 70,000.

Monthly	*Small Business Report* 550 Hartnell Street Monterey, CA 93940	No	Gene E. Mattauch

Small Business Report is a pleasant, helpful and non-controversial magazine that competes more directly with *The Business Owner* magazine. Circulation is probably less than 5,000.

Monthly	*The Professional Report* 118 Brook Street Scarsdale, NY 10583	No	John L. Springer

The Professional Report is basically a tax and management newsletter of well-established quality. It has been around much longer than any of the newsletters and it is an excellent value. Circulation is unpublished, but it is probably around 75,000.

Bimonthly	*In Business* 18 So. 7th Street Emmaus, PA 18049	Yes	Jerome Goldstein

In Business is a new magazine that combines nature and small business, somewhat of an entrepreneur's "mother earth catalog." It is given free to members of the Support Service Alliance of New York. Circulation is under 10,000.

Bimonthly	*Journal of Applied Management* 1200 Mt. Diablo Blvd. Walnut Creek, CA 94596	Yes	John Stickler

Journal of Applied Management was originally founded by Bob Roth and is now owned by John Stickler. It is making a transition from being geared toward consultants to being geared toward the entrepreneur. Many of the readers are from the American Institute for Management in Boston. Circulation is about 5,000.

41. *New Venture* Magazine is aimed at successful business people who want to branch out into a wider range of business endeavors. It gives you names and addresses to contact for further information on promising ventures and helpful, practical advice on ways to plan for the future.

When you subscribe, a step-by-step report on how to get started in the mini-warehouse business will be sent to you free. The newsletter is published on alternate Mondays and they devote each issue to a description and an analysis of new ventures. They cover topics like golf shops, licensing, franchising, real estate, and in their dozen pages they show the economics of the venture plus they list sources of help for that business opportunity.

If you are about to move into a new venture, this newsletter could be the best around. It's a little overpriced at $97.00 per year, but it is well researched and presented. Write:

George Spencer
Observer Publishing Company
Canal Square
Washington, DC, 20007

42. *Ca$h Newsletter* gives you ways to make, save, invest, and keep money. It also offers businesses you can start with little or no capital for big income, and tells you ways to save on purchases, taxes, etc. Subscribers can send questions for individual answers. The same company also publishes and distributes *The Road Map to Easy Riches* and the following books by Maxwell Sackheim: *Seven Deadly Mail Order Mistakes, Seven Deadly Advertising Mistakes,* and *Seven Deadly Direct Mail Mistakes.* The company will also accept a limited number of copywriting assignments and is available for consultation on problems of running small businesses. Write:

Ca$h Newsletter
P.O. Box 1999
Brooksville, FL 33512
(904)796-3050

43. Looking for a director for your business? The use of outside professional directors has been increasing within the larger

companies. Like so many other trends, it is now becoming a more common practice in smaller companies. In fact, it is making better sense every day to consider expanding your board to use outside directors. They can provide a valuable new resource for the creative entrepreneur. Further, their votes can help alleviate IRS charges of excessive compensation for entrepreneurial owners of successful ventures.

In practice, boards of directors of small companies fall into three categories, with varying degrees of usefulness. Most entrepreneurs don't consider their boards very important; they only appoint them because the laws say there must be at least three directors.

The most common type of board can mislead you about the whole purpose of boards. It usually meets quarterly, and although it appears to be establishing company policy, it's really a social event in disguise. If one member begins to take his/her role too seriously and actually tries to affect the operation, he is considered something of a "party-pooper." Since he or she is always spoiling all the fun, he or she is usually asked to resign.

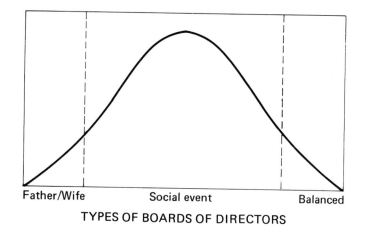

Father/Wife   Social event   Balanced

TYPES OF BOARDS OF DIRECTORS

On one extreme is the second kind of board, consisting of the entrepreneur and his wife and father. This is the most honest kind of board because it doesn't pretend to be anything more than what it is. After all, most entrepreneurs wouldn't heed the advice of a real board, and if any issue ever had to be decided by a vote of stockholders, the entrepreneur is usually the majority stockholder anyhow. So who's kidding whom?

But some entrepreneurs go to the opposite extreme and actually appoint a balanced board of seasoned professionals who vote,

have conflicts, and determine company policy. This kind of board might decide that the entrepreneur is what's wrong with the company. Of course, if you are the majority stockholder that's not much of a problem, so don't worry.

A balanced board of experienced businessmen can help maintain a sensible and profitable business plan. They can make valuable contacts for the company and add to its stature in the eyes of the financial community. Pick this kind of board only if you want your company to succeed.

One final word about boards of directors: Good boards have conflicts; bad boards always say "yes."

If you decide to search for outside directors, I can generally recommend most executive search firms as a source of contacts. The management consulting firms of Korn/Ferry and Heidrick and Struggles also offer this service. I'm told that Booz Allen has one full-time person whose only responsibility is searching for directors. There's a small firm located in New Hampshire called Director's Search, which specializes in finding women directors.

You can contact Frank E. Conant or William H. Chisholm of Boardroom Consultants, Inc., 230 Park Avenue, New York, NY 10017 ([212]697-4757) because searching for outside members of boards of directors in their primary business.

21

Taxes

Information regarding taxes is very difficult to provide. These are the fundamental publishers of tax information. I recommend that you examine their literature, and seek each source out independently. This area of help is extremely important because the tax laws are changing all the time. Moreover, included is some unique information on tax shelters.

HOW TO INCREASE THE PROFITS IN YOUR PENSION FUND

Are you interested in having your retirement funds grow at above 60% annually on an after tax basis? Conventional wisdom says the single greatest value of owning a small independent business is due to the tax shelters allowed by the IRS for: Keogh, IRA or corporate pension plans. Essentially, a Keogh or HR-10 plan allows a self-employed person to shield up to 15% (with a ceiling of $7,500) of his annual income. An IRA is for individuals with no other pension plan (Keogh is for self-employed persons who may or may not have an additional pension plan) and these IRA individuals can shield up to $1500 annually ($1750 if your spouse doesn't work, $7500 if your employer contributes).

1) IRA—If you have no other pension plan ($1750 annual ceiling)
2) Keogh-HR-10—Self-employed persons ($7,500 annual ceiling)
3) Corporate pension—25% of annual income (no effective ceiling).

Insurance companies (especially the life insurance salesmen), banks, and financial institutions are heavily promoting IRA and Keogh Plans. And all for a good reason, they want to have you place your plan with them so they can invest your retirement funds. This is what most people do and this is precisely the course of action I followed in the late 1960's. I initially installed a Keogh Plan because a life insurance agent convinced me of the merits of this tax shelter.

After a few years, a friend explained that I should transfer these retirement monies out of insurance into a bank managed plan, as I actually didn't need the insurance. I did and I noticed that my retirement pool finally began to grow. I was annoyed by the bank's annual service charge to manage my Keogh retirement funds but I didn't resent the custodial fees when the investment performed well. When the bank's investments (my Keogh fund) dropped in value by 24% and the bank still wanted its annual "management fee," I squawked but I eventually paid. I was told my choice was to suffer the horrendous tax consequences of breaking the tax shelter.

A few years later I discovered a bank which would allow me to specify the composition of stocks and bonds in my retirement plan. I always felt I could out perform the trust officers (I probably can't) and I reasoned if I lost my retirement money it would be better than if someone else who also received a management fee lost it. So, I switched my Keogh to this bank in Brockton, MA.

I still wasn't fully satisfied so I asked the bank if I could form a limited real estate partnership and buy shares in the partnership with my Keogh funds. They said, "Yes," as they had done for several other partnerships. Now, comes the heretofore unpublished information.

Myself, along with a dozen others, switched plans to this bank and formed a limited partnership whose business it was to loan money in real estate. The details are not crucial but I'll just say that during the first year, we managed a return of 33% and during the second year, 30%. During the past two years the return has been sheltered and consequently it is equivalent to a 66% and a 60% gain for a 50% bracket taxpayer.

The new data is that certain financial institutions will allow a self-directed Keogh, IRA, or corporate pension plan. In other

words, they will allow the trustee responsible for the plan to decide on how to invest the pension funds for the pension plan. While this is not a panacea and it has some inherent risks, with a prudent program the return on investment can be increased at a much faster rate than the corresponding risk. But, that's for you to decide. My job is to tell you which banks allow self-directed Keogh, IRA, and corporate pension plans. Only a handful allow this self-directing feature, and some allow you to go so far as invest in gold coins, in partnerships, or in your own business, under certain circumstances.

To the best of our research, below is a partial current list of banks:

1) Plymouth Home National Bank
   (617)583-7400
   34 School Street
   Brockton, MA 02403

They offer Keogh, IRA and corporate pension plans and are the most flexible and least costly of all the sources.

2) National Bank of Georgia
   (404)586-8101
   34 Peachtree Street, N.W.
   Atlanta, GA 30303

They offer IRA, Keogh and corporate pension plans. This has been known in Washington DC as Bert Lance's bank.

3) Farmers Bank of the State of
   Delaware
   (302)421-2281
   Wilmington, DE 19899

They only offer Keogh and IRA programs, no corporate programs.

4) Security National Bank
   (303)534-4000
   425 16th Street
   Denver, CO 80202

They offer IRA, Keogh, and corporate pension plans.

5) Mercantile National Bank at Dallas
   1704 Main Street
   Dallas, TX 75201 (214)741-4181

They offer Keogh and have some IRA and corporate programs but they are more restrictive.

6) A.D.P Pension Service
   (714)644-4360
   (Formerly Certified Pension
   Plans, Inc.—CPI)
   180 Newport Center Drive
   Box 2090
   Newport Beach, CA 92663

They offer IRA, Keogh and corporate plans and they are not a bank.

NEW DOMICILE CAN CUT TAXES

Many individuals have wondered about the best state to claim your home base from a tax point of view. Given the wide range of state taxes, this issue is of growing concern. Many of my former neighbors have moved to southern New Hampshire from Massachusetts just to escape these taxes. For instance, New Hamsphire has no sales or income or capital gains taxes, while Massachusetts has all three. Florida is another tax haven for the retired as it has no income or capital gains taxes. The same holds for Connecticut.

If you are considering changing your domicile, how can it be done? There are examples of individuals selling a business who established residence in another state six months prior to selling the business just to avoid the capital gains tax. It can be worth a good deal of money.

How does one go about changing his or her domicile? Is permission of the state required? Is it necessary to file certain forms? What exactly is a domicile?

Black's Law Dictionary defines "domicile" as "that place where a man has his true, fixed and permanent home and principal establishment, and to which, whenever he is absent, he has the intention of returning. Not for a special or temporary purpose but with the present intention of making a permanent home for an unlimited or indefinite period. It is his legal residence as distinguished from his

Tax Laws

State by State Comparison — State	No personal income tax	No corporate income tax	No inventory tax	No real property (plant, machinery, land) tax	No corporate franchise tax	No sales and use tax on manufacturing	Unemployment Insurance Tax % 1979	Present Minimum	New Minimum	Effective Date
Alabama			X			X	1.0 4.0			
Alaska			X		X	X	2.6 5.1	$3.15	$3.40	1/79
Arizona			X		X		0.15 3.75			
Arkansas						X	0.5 4.4	2.0	2.30	1/79
California							1.3 4.9	2.65	2.90	1/79
Colorado						X	0.2 4.0			
Connecticut	X		X		X	X	1.5 6.0	2.66	2.91	1/79
Delaware			X	X		X	1.6 4.5			
District of Columbia							1.0 5.4			
Florida	X					X	Not Avail			
Georgia			X			X	0.07 5.71			
Guam										
Hawaii			X				3.4 4.5	2.65	2.90	7/79
Idaho			X		X	X	0.9 4.0			
Illinois			X		X	X	1.0 4.3			
Indiana			X			X	0.3 3.3	1.75	2.00	1/79
Iowa			X		X	X	0.6 6.0			
Kansas					X	X	0.0 3.5			
Kentucky						X	0.5 5.0	2.00	2.15	7/79
Louisiana							1.6 4.5			
Maine			X		X		2.4 5.0	2.65	2.90	1/79
Maryland			X		X		2.1 5.0	2.65	2.90	1/79
Massachusetts			X	X	X	X	2.6 6.4	2.65	2.90	1/79
Michigan			X		X	X	1.0 8.0	2.65	2.90	1/79
Minnesota			X		X	X	1.0 7.5			
Mississippi			X				1.7 2.7			
Missouri							0.5 4.1			
Montana					X	X	3.1			
Nebraska			X			X	0.1 3.7			
Nevada	X	X	X			X	1.1 3.5			
New Hampshire	X		X		X	X	0.01 6.5	2.65	2.90	1/79
New Jersey			X			X	1.2 6.2			
New Mexico							0.9 4.5			
New York			X		X	X	1.5 5.2	2.65	2.90	1/79
North Carolina						X	0.1 5.7			
North Dakota			X			X	Not Avail			
Ohio						X	0.9 4.6			
Oklahoma						X	0.4 4.7			
Oregon			X		X		2.6 4.0			
Pennsylvania			X	X		X	1.0 4.0	2.65	2.90	1/79
Puerto Rico			X		X	X				
Rhode Island			X			X	Not Avail			
South Carolina			X			X	1.3 4.1			
South Dakota	X	X	X			X	0.0 5.0			
Tennessee	X					X	0.4 4.0			
Texas	X	X				X	Not Avail			
Utah			X		X	X	1.3 2.8			
Vermont			X	X	X		1.7 6.0	2.65	2.90	1/79
Virginia			X			X	0.07 4.48	2.20	2.35	1/79
Virgin Islands										
Washington	X	X	X				3.3			
West Virginia						X	2.7 3.3			
Wisconsin			X			X	0.5 6.5			
Wyoming	X	X	X			X	0.37 3.07			

temporary place of abode; his home as distinguished from a place to which business or pleasure may temporarily call him."

But how is such intent proved to the satisfaction of the taxing authorities of a state looking for their share of income or capital gain or estate taxes?

Obviously, it takes more than a self-serving affidavit by the taxpayer declaring his intent to make the change. In fact, the most effective way to "prove" a change in domicile is to show that the acts and activities of the taxpayer in his new state of domicile were those reasonably expected of one who truly changed his domicile.

Recommendation: The following list, although not exhaustive, would help prove the intent of the taxpayer to be permanently domiciled in his new state:

1. Register to vote.
2. Open savings and checking accounts, and safe deposit box.
3. Register automobile in new state.
4. Obtain driver's license in new state.
5. Open local charge accounts or establish local credit.
6. Join local organizations.
7. Purchase real estate or sign long-term lease for residence.
8. Notify Social Security office of new address.
9. Notify all business and other contacts of new address.
10. Notify Internal Revenue Service of new address and file tax returns (when due) showing new address; (don't forget to file "non-resident" returns to old state).
11. Close all bank accounts in old state.
12. Sell, rent or give away real estate in old state. (If rented or gifted, it may still be used periodically by arrangement with the lessee or donee.) Remember, however, that if ownership is retained, as it would be in the case of a rental, the property will be subject to any estate taxes in the state in which it is situated on the death of the owner.
13. Move all other tangible property out of old state.
14. Have new will (or codicil) prepared in new state.
15. Borrow books from the local library.

In short, do everything that a person who changed his domicile would normally do. Although not foolproof, if all these items were present, it would be extremely difficult for the taxing authorities to support a position that you are still domiciled in your old state.

All that it takes then, from a purely legal standpoint, is that the

person INTEND to change his domicile; when this happens, the change occurs.

SOURCES OF TAX HELP

1. Matthew Bender & Company publishes *Current Legal Forms with Tax Analysis,* by Rabkin and Johnson. To assist tax accountants, Matthew Bender also offers the following:

Taxation of Securities Transactions

Tax Techniques for Foundations and Other Exempt Organizations (7 vols.)

Federal Income Taxation of Corporations Filing Consolidated Returns (2 vols.)

Income Taxation of Foreign Related Transactions (2 vols.)

Federal Taxation of Life Insurance Companies (2 vols.)

Family Tax Planning (2 vols.)

Trust Administration and Taxation (4 vols.)

Tax Return Manual for 1978

U.S. Tax Week contains cases and rulings, as well as current events.

Federal Income, Gift, and Estate Taxation (Desk ed.), by Prigal, emphasizes convenience and practicality and includes 47 pages of indexing.

Federal Income, Gift, and Estate Taxation (13 vols.), by Rabkin and Johnson, is a reference work which combines tax scholarship with a practical approach to tax problems arising from personal, business, and family transactions. A monthly newsletter is included in the cost of the service.

This company is an excellent source of continuing tax information. For further information, write:

Matthew Bender & Company, Inc.
235 East 45th Street
New York, NY 10017

2. Among the publications offered by Commerce Clearing House of Chicago, Illinois, are the following:

Federal Tax Articles (1 vol.)

Private Foundations Reporter (2 vols.)

Income Taxes Worldwide (5 vols.)

Pension Plan Guide (5 vols.)

Payroll Management Guide (2 vols.)

Federal Excise Tax Reports (1 vol.)

CCH State Tax Reports; Tax Treaties (2 vols.)

Standard Federal Tax Reports (14 vols.) is a compilation of official texts or source material, editorial explanations, and digests of rulings and decisions, arranged topically to follow the order of the code.

Taxes on Parade is an 8-page publication issued weekly; it discusses current events involving news items, recent decisions, IRS rulings, etc.

Federal Tax Guide Reports (4 vols.) breaks down the law according to the order of the code and offers editorial explanations and citations to official texts. The complete edition includes the code, regulations, and several explanatory divisions.

In addition, CCH publishes two single-volume non-supplemented texts on taxes:

Federal Tax Return Manual
Master Tax Guide

For all of the above, write:

Commerce Clearing House, Inc.
4025 W. Peterson Avenue
Chicago, IL 60646
(312)CO7-9010

3. *Inflation Survival Letter* is published 24 times a year every second Wednesday, with a couple of exceptions. The information contained in this newsletter has been carefully compiled from sources believed to be reliable. Write:

Inflation Survival Letter
6737 Annapolis Road
P.O. Box 2599
Landover Hills, MD 20784

4. A newsletter which arrives every other Monday morning is known as the *Kiplinger Tax Letter*. It has been around since 1925 and it is one of the good sources of help. It is a source of personal help on taxes as well as business assistance. Write:

The Kiplinger Tax Letter
1729 H Street, N.W.
Washington, DC 20006
(202)298-6400

5. An excellent semimonthly source of tax and financial information is the *J.K. Lasser Tax Report*. The same company also of-

fers many books focused on financial issues for tax planning. Below is a list of these books offered by this single source. Write:

J.K. Lasser Tax Report
Business Reports, Inc.
One West Avenue
Larchmont, NY 10538

J.K. Lasser's Stock Record Book (and refills)

J.K. Lasser's Tax Diary

Successful Tax Planning in Real Estate

Three Point Reversal Method of Point and Figure Trading

Profits in Volume: Equivolume Charting

The Profitability of Stock Options

Using Leverage in Warrants and Calls for Successful Investment

Your Estate and Gift Taxes

Profile of a Growth Stock

A New Technical Approach to Stock Market Timing

Commodity Options

Encyclopedia of Stock Market Techniques

Ticker Tape Trading

Technical Indicator Analysis by P&F Technique

It Can Be Done—Buy Low, Sell High

Preplanning a Profitable Call Writing Program

Saving Tax Money with Trusts

Life Insurance Protection at Lowest Cost

The Power of Leverage

What Makes a Winner or Loser in Stock and Commodity Markets

Relative Strength Concept of Common Stock Price Forecasting

Managing Your Family Finances

J.K. Lasser's Check Record Book

P&F Commodity Trading Techniques

Borrowed Money and Stock Market Trends

Tax Basis Guide for Fair Market Value of Securities

Guide to Successful Fund Raising

6. You'll find the answers to any federal income tax problem in *Mertens Law of Federal Income Taxation* (47 vols.), by Jacob Mertens. The volumes are comprehensive, cited and quoted by the courts, easy to use, up-to-date, authoritative, time-saving.

Mertens Law of Federal Income Taxation, by James J. Doheny, is also published by Callaghan & Company. This service is offered on a continuing basis on federal income tax consisting of two basic elements which are sold as a unit. One is a 17-volume treatise which contains analysis and explanation of the federal income tax law. The second item offered is the code analysis service, 8 volumes of code and code commentary, 12 volumes of regulations, and 10 volumes of IRS rulings. For information, write:

Mertens Tax Service
Callaghan & Company
3201 Old Glenview Road
Wilmette, IL 60091
(312)256-7000

7. The Moneytree Club includes a monthly newsletter called *Moneytree* containing the "inside track" to money. The club also offers a booklet called *Tax Tricks.* Write:

Moneytree Club
Executive Offices
Kerrville, TX 78028

8. Irving Schreiber, J.D., CPA, is a professor of Taxation in the graduate division of the School of Professional Accounting, C.W. Post College, Long Island University in New York. He offers:

How to Handle Tax Audits, requests for rulings, fraud cases, and other procedures before the IRS

Partnerships and Taxes: A Practical Guide

How to Set Up and Run a Qualified Pension or Profit Sharing Plan, for small or medium-sized business

How to Take Money Out of a Closely Held Corporation

Estate Planners' Complete Guide and Workbook

This single source is useful for lawyers and accountants to gain the information and pass it along to their respective small-business clients. The information is generally excellent. Write:

Panel Publishers
14 Plaza Road
Greenvale, NY 11548
A division of Canton, Fitzgerald Group, Ltd.

9. Prentice-Hall, Inc. publishes the following services. For information, write:

Prentice-Hall
Englewood Cliffs, NJ 07632

Tax Ideas

Pension and Profit Sharing (3 vols.)

Oil and Gas/Natural Resources (2 vols.)

U.S. Taxation of International Operations (1 vol.)

Property Tax Service, State Inheritance Taxes, State Income Tax Service, State and Local Taxes, and *All States Tax Guide*

Successful Estate Planning Ideas (2 vols.)

The following nonsupplemented texts on taxes are offered by Prentice-Hall:

Federal Tax Course

Federal Tax Handbook

Federal Tax Guide (5 vols.) contains explanation, an optional code and regulations and an operational federal estate and gift volume.

P-H Federal Taxes (14 vols.) is a code-arranged service; Seven volumes deal with analysis and case annotations, one volume consists of a multifaceted index. The basic set has a two volume estate and gift tax service. The service is kept up-to-date with weekly report bulletins consisting of replacement sheets.

Accountant's Weekly Report is a 6-page newsletter written especially for accountants.

10. Research Institute of America publishes many helpful books, such as the *Tax Preparer's Liability Service,* which is updated monthly and includes official source material, and analyses of federal regulations on tax returns, as well as of liabilities and state regulations. The Institute also offers the *Master Federal Tax Manual* and *Weekly Alert,* which is a weekly 8-page newsletter that analyzes the latest decisions and rulings affecting federal income, estate, gift, and excise taxes.

Federal Tax Coordinator (2nd ed.) is a 28-volume service which provides source material in addition to analytical commentary. *Tax Guide* is a 1-volume looseleaf analytical service covering income, estate, and gift excise taxes, administration and procedure. For information on any of these publications write:

Research Institute of America, Inc.
589 Fifth Avenue
New York, NY 10017

11. *Small Business Tax Control,* published in a double-sized, 3-ring binder, contains over 250 tax briefs written in simple, easy-to-understand language. Every month the reader receives revised and supplemental briefs, along with a 6-page *Tax Prompter.* The *Prompter* and the briefs emphasize tax-savings ideas, and both are written specifically for the small-business owner. Write:

Small Business Tax Control
P.O. Box 3158
Richmond, VA 23235
(804)272-1006
Circulation: 9,500

12. *Tax Angles* is a monthly newsletter offering tax-savings ideas, strategies, and techniques. It is especially appealing to entrepreneurs, self-employed professionals, and investors. Written by Vernon K. Jacobs, it is easy to read quickly. Write:

Tax Angles
5809 Annapolis Road
Box 2311
Bladensburg, MD 20710

13. *Tax Management—Primary Sources Series II,* offered by the Bureau of National Affairs, includes information on current developments as well as legislative history of the code from the 1976 Tax Reform Act forward. The Bureau also offers a newsletter and is a primary publisher of original tax information. Books on tax management include *U.S. Income* and *Foreign Income.* For information, write:

Bureau of National Affairs
Tax Management, Inc.
1231 25th Street, N.W.
Washington, DC 20037

14. *Tax Savings Advantages for Everyone* explains many deductions used by corporations and the wealthy that are available to everyone, if they know what they are and know how to get them. It is dedicated to those in the $10,000 to $25,000 income bracket, but still applicable to anyone who would prefer to pay less in taxes than they do now. Write:

Mariner Publishing
P.O. Box 272
Arlington, MA 02174

15. For information on a monthly tax newsletter called IRS Practices and Procedures, write:

Tax Report Clearinghouse, Inc.
P.O. Box 213
Janesville, WI 53545

16. *Taxsaver's Newsletter* contains personalized tax-saving ideas, and is guaranteed to save your tax dollars. It comes three times a month. Write:

Taxsavers' Incorporated
6715 Sunfish Lake, N.E.
Rockford, MI 49341

17. The Department of the Treasury recently released a report entitled *How the IRS Selects Individual Income Tax Returns for Audit.* This 142-page report covers such items as "Why Your Return Might Be Selected for Audit." Write:

U.S. General Accounting Office
Room 4522
441 G Street, N.W.
Washington, DC 20548
(202)275-6241

18. The following updated tax services are published by Warren, Gorham & Lamont:

Taxation of the Closely Held Corporation

Federal Income Tax Law

Federal Income Taxation of Corporations and Shareholders

Federal Taxation of Partnerships and Partners

Taxation of Patents, by Bischel

Federal Income Taxation of Real Estate, by Robinson

Index to Federal Tax Articles (3 vols.) by Goldstein

Tax Fraud and Evasion, by Balter

The Tax Practice Desk Book, by Freeman and Freeman

Tax Court Practice, by Garbis and Schwait

The Consolidated Tax Return, by Crestol, Hennessey, and Rua

Federal Estate and Gift Taxation (1 vol.) by Stephens, Maxfield, and Lind

For all these publications, write:

Warren, Gorham & Lamont, Inc.
210 South Street
Boston, MA 02111

19. Following are magazines available to tax accountants and offering from 6 to 12 issues per year. They average between 60 and 70 pages each:

Estate Planning
Institute for Business Planning, Inc.
IBP Plaza
Englewood Cliffs, NJ 07132

Journal of Taxation
Taxation for Accountants
Journal of Taxation, Ltd.
Box 158
Titusville, FL 32780

The Practical Accountant
Institute for Continuing and Professional Development
964 Third Avenue
New York, NY 10022

The Tax Magazine
Community Clearing House
4025 W. Peterson Avenue
Chicago, IL 60646

The Tax Adviser
American Institute of Certified Public Accountants
1211 Avenue of the Americas
New York, NY 10036

United States Department of Commerce

The United States Department of Commerce is the Federal agency charged with promoting commerce within the United States and overseas. Its field officers offer a wide variety of services. A visit to your local department of commerce should acquaint you with the department's many programs. A listing of regional offices is also offered.

The United States Department of Commerce compiles the latest data on domestic and international markets and develops programs to assist American business from its 43 district offices. Each district office maintains a staff of trade specialists and an extensive library of business publications. They are especially effective in selling U.S. products overseas.

GOVERNMENT PROCUREMENT

The federal government spends over $50 billion annually on purchases from American business firms. Its purchases cover the entire spectrum of business products and services. Some contracts are better suited for large firms; others for small firms.

Any company interested in government business will want to receive the *Commerce Business Daily*. Issued daily from Monday through Friday, this informative publication lists U.S. government

Requests for bids and proposals

Procurement reserved for small business

Prime contracts awarded

Contractors seeking subcontract assistance

Upcoming sales of surplus government property (including real estate, machinery, equipment, and supplies)

Commerce Business Daily also lists U.S. research and development proposals, proposed foreign government procurements, and foreign trade leads.

BUSINESS PERSPECTIVE

To help every businessperson become better informed, the Commerce Department publishes *Commerce America,* a biweekly magazine packed with information and policy guidance useful to the whole spectrum of American business. It is illustrated, concisely written, and organized to fit the businessman's needs.

Commerce America offers an analysis of the economy, an energy management digest, a domestic business report, a worldwide business outlook, and in-depth feature articles of interest and value to businesspeople.

Check your local district office for further information on this or any other business publication of the Department of Commerce.

INDUSTRY AND TRADE ADMINISTRATION

Alabama

Birmingham

Suite 200-201
908 South 20th Street
Birmingham 35205
(205)254-1331, FTS 229-1331

Alaska

Anchorage

412 Hill Building
632 Sixth Avenue
Anchorage, Alaska 99501
(907)265-5307, FTS Dial
8-339-0150, ask for 265-5307

Arizona

Phoenix

Suite 2950
Valley Bank Center
201 North Central Avenue
Phoenix, AZ 85073
(602)261-3285, FTS 261-3285

Arkansas

Little Rock
(Dallas, Texas District)

1100 North University
Suite 109
Little Rock, ARK 72207
(501)378-5157, FTS 740-5157

California

Los Angeles

Room 800
11777 San Vicente Boulevard
Los Angeles, CA 90049
(213)824-7591, FTS 799-7591

San Diego

233 A Street
Suite 310
San Diego, CA 92101
(714)293-5395, FTS 895-5395

San Francisco

Federal Building
Box 36013
450 Golden Gate Avenue
San Francisco, CA 94102
(415)556-5860, FTS 556-5868

Colorado

Denver

Room 165
Customhouse
19th and Stout Street
Denver, CO 80202
(303)837-3246, FTS 327-3246

Connecticut

Hartford

Room 610-B
Federal Office Building
450 Main Street
Hartford CT 06103
(203)244-3530, FTS 244-3530

Florida

Miami

Room 821
City National Bank Building
25 West Flagler Street
Miami, FL 33130
(305)350-5267, FTS 350-5267

Clearwater

128 North Osceola Avenue
Clearwater, FL 33515
(813)446-4081

Jacksonville

815 S. Main Street
Suite 100
Jacksonville, FL 32207
(904)791-2796, FTS 946-2796

Tallahassee

Collins Building
Room G-20
Tallahassee, FL 32304
(904)488-6469, FTS 946-4320

Georgia

Atlanta

Suite 600
1365 Peachtree Street, N.E.
Atlanta, GA 30309
(404)881-7000, FTS 257-7000

Savannah

222 U.S. Courthouse and P.O.
Box 9746
125–29 Bull Street
Savannah, GA 31402
(912)232-4321, ext. 204, FTS
248-4204

Hawaii

Honolulu

4106 Federal Building
P.O. Box 50026
300 Ala Moana Boulevard
Honolulu, HI 96850
(808)546-8694, FTS Dial 8,
556-0220, ask for 546-8694

Illinois

Chicago

1406 Mid Continental Plaza
Building
55 East Monroe Street
Chicago, IL 60603
(312)353-4450, FTS 353-4450

Indiana

Indianapolis

357 U.S. Courthouse and Federal Office Building
46 East Ohio Street
Indianapolis, IN 46204
(317)269-6214, FTS 331-6214

Iowa

Des Moines

817 Federal Building
210 Walnut Street
Des Moines, IA 50309
(515)284-4222, FTS 862-4222

Kentucky

Frankfort
(Memphis, Tennessee District)

Capitol Plaza Office Tower
Room 2425
Frankfort, KY 40601
(502)875-4421

Louisiana

New Orleans

432 International Trade Mart
No. 2 Canal Street
New Orleans, LA 70130
(504)589-6546, FTS 682-6546

Maine

Portland
(Boston, Massachusetts District)

Maine State Pier
40 Commercial Street
Portland, ME 04111
(207)773-5608, FTS 833-3407

Maryland

Baltimore

415 U.S. Customhouse
Gay and Lombard Streets
Baltimore, MD 21202
(301)962-3560, FTS 922-3560

Massachusetts

Boston

10th Floor
441 Stuart Street
Boston, MA 02116
(617)223-2312, FTS 223-2312

Michigan

Detroit

445 Federal Building
231 West Lafayette
Detroit, MI 48226
(313)226-3650, FTS 226-3650

Grand Rapids

350 Ottawa Street, N.W.
Grand Rapids, MI 49503
(616)456-2411/33, FTS 372-2411

Minnesota

Minneapolis

218 Federal Building
110 South Fourth Street
Minneapolis, MN 55401
(612)725-2133, FTS 725-2133

314

Mississippi

Jackson
(Birmingham, Alabama District)

P.O. Box 849
1202 Walter Sillers Building
Jackson, MS 39205
(601)969-4388, FTS 490-4388

Missouri

St. Louis

120 South Central Avenue
St. Louis, MO 63105
(314)425-3302-4, FTS 279-3302

Kansas City

Room 1840
601 East 12th Street
Kansas City, MO 64106
(816)374-3142, FTS 758-3142

Montana

Butte
(Cheyenne, Wyoming District)

225 S. Idaho Street
Room 101
P.O. Box 3809
Butte, MT 59701
(406)723-6561, ext. 2317, FTS
585-2317

Nebraska

Omaha

Capitol Plaza
Suite 703A
1815 Capitol Avenue
Omaha, NE 68102
(402)221-3665, FTS 864-3665

Nevada

Reno

777 W. 2nd Street
Room 120
Reno, NE 89503
(702)784-5203, FTS 470-5203

New Jersey

Newark

4th Floor
Gateway Building
Market Street and Penn Plaza
Newark, NJ 07102
(201)645-6214, FTS 341-6214

New Mexico

Albuquerque

505 Marquette Avenue, N.W.
Suite 1015
Albuquerque, NM 87102
(505)766-2386, FTS 474-2386

New York

Buffalo

1312 Federal Building
111 West Huron Street
Buffalo, NY 14202
(716)846-4191, FTS 437-4191

New York

Room 3718
Federal Office Building
26 Federal Plaza
Foley Square
New York, NY 10007
(212)264-0634, FTS 264-0600

North Carolina

Greensboro

203 Federal Building
West Market Street
P.O. Box 1950
Greensboro, NC 27402
(919)378-5345, FTS 699-5345

Asheville

151 Haywood Street
Asheville, NC 28802
(704)254-1981, FTS 672-0342

Ohio

Cincinnati

10504 Federal Office Building
550 Main Street
Cincinnati, OH 45202
(513)684-2944, FTS 684-2944

Cleveland

Room 600
666 Euclid Avenue
Cleveland, OH 44114
(216)522-4750, FTS 293-4750

Oklahoma

Oklahoma City
(Dallas, Texas District)

4020 Lincoln Boulevard
Oklahoma City, OK 73105
(405)231-5302, FTS 736-5302

Oregon

Portland

Room 618
1220 S.W. 3rd Avenue
Portland, OR 97204
(503)221-3001, FTS 423-3001

Pennsylvania

Philadelphia

9448 Federal Building
600 Arch Street
Philadelphia, PA 19106
(215)597-2850, FTS 597-2866

Pittsburgh

2002 Federal Building
1000 Liberty Avenue
Pittsburgh, PA 15222
(412)644- 2850, FTS 722-2850

Puerto Rico

San Juan (Hato Rey)

Room 659
Federal Building
San Juan, PR 00918
(809)753-4555, ext. 555,
FTS, Dial 9, 472-6620,
ask for 753-4555

Rhode Island

Providence
(Boston, Massachusetts District)

1 Weybossett Hill
Providence, RI 02903
(401)277-2605, ext. 22, FTS
838-4482

South Carolina

Columbia

2611 Forest Drive
Forest Center
Columbia, SC 29204
(803)765-5345, FTS 677-5345

Charleston

Suite 631
Federal Building
334 Meeting Street
Charleston, SC 29403
(803)577-4361, FTS 677-4361

Tennessee

Memphis

Room 710
147 Jefferson Avenue
Memphis, TN 38103
(901)521-3213, FTS 222-3213

Nashville

4014 Aberdeen Road
Nashville, TN 37216
(615)297-5233, FTS 852-5161

Texas

Dallas

Room 7A5
1100 Commerce Street
Dallas, TX 75242
(214)749-1515, FTS 749-1513

Houston

2625 Federal Building
Courthouse
515 Rusk Street
Houston, TX 77002
(713)226-4231, FTS 527-4231

San Antonio	University of Texas at San Antonio Division of Continuing Education San Antonio, TX 78285 (512)229-5875, FTS 229-5875

Utah

Salt Lake City	1203 Federal Building 125 South State Street Salt Lake City, UT 84138 (801)524-5116, FTS 588-5116

Virginia

Richmond	8010 Federal Building 400 North 8th Street Richmond, VA 23240 (804)782-2246, FTS 925-2246
Fairfax	8550 Arlington Boulevard Fairfax, VA 22031 (703)560-6460, FTS 235-1519

Washington

Seattle	Room 706 Lake Union Building 1700 Westlake Avenue, North Seattle, WA 98109 (206)442-5615, FTS 399-5615

West Virginia

Charleston	3000 New Federal Building 500 Quarrier Street Charleston, WV 25301 (304)343-6181, ext. 375, FTS 924-1375

Wisconsin

Milwaukee

Federal Building/U.S. Courthouse
517 East Wisconsin Avenue
Milwaukee, WI 53202
(414)291-3473, FTS 362-3473

Wyoming

Cheyenne

6022 O'Mahoney Federal Center
2120 Capitol Avenue
Cheyenne, WY 82001
(307)778-2220, ext. 2151, FTS
328-2151

DOMESTIC AND INTERNATIONAL BUSINESS ADMINISTRATION

American business today is presented with a challenging opportunity in world trade. U.S. manufacturers are increasingly aware
that every market is a world market, whether it is in the neighboring
state or on the opposite side of the globe. Instant communications,
rapid transportation, lower foreign tariffs, narrowing wage dif-
ferentials, and higher standards of living have created rising demands everywhere for more products from other countries.

Headed by the Assistant Secretary of Commerce for Domestic
and International Business, DIBA has as its primary mission the
conduct of the department's activities aimed at promoting progressive American business policies, economic growth, and strengthening the international commercial position of the United States. Its
mission is carried out by five bureaus and 43 district offices strategi-
cally located throughout the United States and Puerto Rico, and by
numerous overseas trade promotion facilities. The five bureaus are
the Bureau of International Commerce, Bureau of Domestic Commerce, Bureau of Resources and Trade Assistance, Bureau of International Economic Policy and Research, and the Bureau of
East-West Trade.

Through its bureaus and supporting staffs at home and
abroad, DIBA conducts programs involving:

Expansion of exports

Expansion of East–West trade and other commercial relations with state trading economies

Expansion of trade in the Near East and North Africa

Support in U.S. negotiations to improve the nation's international trade and financial situation

Promotion of business-consumer relations

Competitive assessment of U.S. industry in domestic and world markets

Foreign investment in the United States

Import program administration

Export control administration

Collection, analysis, and dissemination of selected information on various industries, commodities, and markets·

Preparation and execution of plans for industrial mobilization readiness

Federal recognition and participation in international expositions and trade fairs held in the United States

Where to Order

CAGNE/BIC, Commerce Action Group for the Near East
Bureau of International Commerce
Room 3203
U.S. Department of Commerce
Washington, DC 20230

CSDIV, Consumer Goods and Services Division
Bureau of Domestic Commerce
Room 1104
U.S. Department of Commerce
Washington, DC 20203

EID/BIC, Export Information Division
Office of Export Development
Bureau of International Commerce
Room 1033
U.S. Department of Commerce
Washington, DC 20230

MADVI, Materials Division, Bureau of Domestic Commerce
Room 2008
U.S. Department of Commerce
Washington, DC 20230

OED/BIC, Office of Export Development
Bureau of International Commerce
Room 3056
U.S. Department of Commerce
Washington, DC 20230

OER, Office of Economic Research
International Economic Policy and Research
Room 4824
U.S. Department of Commerce
Washington, DC 20230

OIM/BIC, Office of International Marketing
Bureau of International Commerce
Room 4015-B
U.S. Department of Commerce
Washington, DC 20230

OOB, Office of Ombudsman for Business
Bureau of Domestic Commerce
Room 3800
U.S. Department of Commerce
Washington, DC 20230

NTIS, National Technical Information Service
U.S. Department of Commerce
Springfield, VA 22151

PSB, Publications Sales Branch
Room 1617
U.S. Department of Commerce
Washington, DC 20230

SD, Superintendent of Documents
U.S. Government Printing Office
Washington, DC 20402

SEDIV, Science and Electronics Division
Bureau of Domestic Commerce
Room 1001
U.S. Department of Commerce
Washington, DC 20230

TCDIV, Transportation and Capital Equipment Division
Bureau of Domestic Commerce
Room 2130
U.S. Department of Commerce
Washington, DC 20230

DOMESTIC COMMERCE

Periodicals

Construction Review (monthly), SD

Containers and Packaging (quarterly) SD

Copper (quarterly) SD

Printing and Publishing (quarterly) SD

Pulp, Paper, and Board (quarterly) SD

Studies, Reports, and Brochures

Air Conditioning and Refrigeration Equipment Trade Data (March 1974, free), TCDIV

Aluminum Metal Supply and Shipments to Consumers (semiannual, free), MADIV

Annual Report of the President to the Congress on the Operation of the Automotive Products Trade Act of 1965 (annual, November 1975), SD

Anti-Friction Bearings Production, Shipments, Unfilled Orders (October 1975, free), TCDIV

Business Equipment and Systems Outlook: The Netherlands (1974, free), SEDIV

Business Machines Industry Outlook: West Germany (1974, free), SEDIV

Business Machine Market Information Sources (1971), PSB

Business Machines Outlook: Japan (1975, free), SEDIV

Business Machines Outlook: Sweden (1975, free), SEDIV

Computer Industry Outlook: Australia (1975, free), SEDIV

Computers and Other Information, Processing Equipment Outlook: United Kingdom (1975, free), SEDIV

Confectionery Manufacturers' Sales and Distribution (annual, May 1975, free), CSDIV

The Cost of Crimes Against Business (1974), SD

Crime in Retailing (August 1975), SD

Current Fertilizer Production and Trade Data (monthly; news release, U.S. Department of Commerce News Room, Washington, DC 20230)

323

Data Communications Market Information Sources (1972), SD

Department Store Retailing in an Era of Change (June 1975), SD

The Effects of Electrical Power Variations Upon Computers: An Overview (1974), SD

Electric Current Abroad (May 1975), SD

The Electrical Measuring and Test Instruments Industry: A Review and Analysis (1974), SD

Electronic Calculator Industry Outlook: France (1975, free), SEDIV

Electronic Calculator Industry Outlook: Peru (1975, free), SEDIV

Electronic Calculators Outlook: West Germany (1974, free), SEDIV

Electronic Products and Telecommunications Equipment Outlook: Brazil (1975, free), SEDIV

Engineers Overseas Handbook (1971), SD

Federal Government Sources on Crimes Against Business (November 1974), SD

A Study of Ferrous Scrap Futures (June 1974, free), MADIV

Financial Study of the US Steel Industry (2 vols., October 1975), NTIS

Food Industries Data Sources (March 1975, free), CSDIV

The Foundry Industry (March 1975, free), MADIV

Franchising in the Economy 1974–76 (annual, January 1976), SD

Franchise Opportunities Handbook (annual, 1975), SD

The German Photographic Equipment and Sensitized Materials Industry (1975, free), SEDIV

Household Furniture and Appliances: Basic Information Sources (June 1975, free), CSDIV

The Japanese Photographic Equipment and Sensitized Materials Industry (1975, free), SEDIV

Industrial Growth and International Trade Balance for Selected Electronic Industries, 1967–1972 (1974), SD

Mayonnaise, Salad Dressings, and Related Products (September 1974, free), CSDIV

Measuring Markets: A Guide to the Use of Federal and State Statistical Data (1974), SD

Notification of Aluminum Set-Aside (quarterly, free), MADIV

Productivity and Technological Innovation: Selected Information Sources (March 1975, free), CSDIV

Retail Data Sources for Market Analysis (November 1974, free), CSDIV

Sales Potential of Computers and Business Machines in Lebanon, 1969 (1975 free), SEDIV

Sales Potential of Health Care Industries Equipment in Lebanon, 1969–72 (1975, free), SEDIV

Service Industries: Trends and Prospects (1975), SD

Situation Reports (free), OOB

Home Canning Lids (Bulletin 3, July 1975).

Legislation Affects New Product Warranties (September 1975)

New Federal Pension Law Now in Effect, Employment Benefit Security Act of 1974 (H.R. 2) Signed by President Ford on August 23, 1974 (October 1974)

Partial Listing of Proposed Legislation by 94th Congress of Significance to Business (as of April 29, 1975) (May 1975)

Productivity Series Bulletins

Bulletins 1, 2, 3, *Tips on Productivity Improvement: Capital Formation; A Measurement Technique; and Importance of Measurement* (June 1975)

Bulletins 4, 5, 6, 7, *Pittsburgh Productivity Measurement Seminar: Improving Human Productivity—Making Effective Use of People; Productivity Monitoring and Measurements; On Company Productivity Measurement: Why, What, How; and Summary of Panel Discussion Pittsburgh Productivity Measurement Seminar* (August 1975)

Bulletin 8, *How to Obtain Copies of Productivity References Cited in Previous Productivity Bulletins* (August 1975)

Bulletins 9, 10, 11, *Dayton Productivity Enhancement Seminar: Job Enrichment and Quality of Work Life; Key Elements of Productivity Enhancement Programs; and Measurement as an Instrument of Management* (August 1975)

Bulletin 12, *Tips on Productivity–Labor Management Relations* (September 1975)

Responsibilities of Business and Industry Under the Consumer Product Safety Act (October 1974, free)

Workers' Compensation (October 1974, free)

Telecommunications Equipment Outlook: Sweden (free, 1975), SEDIV

Textile Machinery Trade Data (biannual, 1974, free), TCDIV

U.S. Aluminum Exports (July 1975), MADIV

U.S. Aluminum Imports (May 1975, free), MADIV

U.S. Aluminum Imports and Exports (Monthly, free), MADIV

The US Consumer Electronics Industry (September 1975), SD

U.S. Exports of Non-Rubber Footwear (April 1975, free), CSDIV

U.S. Imports of Footwear Other Than Rubber (April 1975, free), CSDIV

U.S. Industrial Outlook 1976, with Projections Through 1985, (annual, January 1976), SD

U.S. International Trade of Communication and Selected Electronic Products for Calendar Years 1967–72: Consolidated Tabulation (1973), PSB

World Motor Vehicle Production and Registration, (annual, March 1975), PSB

Wholesale Data Sources for Market Analysis (November 1974, free), CSDIV

EAST—WEST TRADE

Periodicals

Denial and Probation Orders Currently Affecting Export Privileges (1979 ed., semiannual, free), Compliance Division, Office of Export Administration, Room 2635, U.S. Department of Commerce, Washington, DC, 20220

East-West Trade Information Bulletin (monthly, free), United States Trade Development Office, Vienna, Austria

Export Administration Regulations (June 1, 1975 ed., annual), SD

Export Administration Report on U.S. Export Controls to the President and the Congress (semi-annual, free), Operations Division, Office of Export Administration, Room 1617M, U.S. Department of Commerce, Washington, DC, 20230

Foreign Economic Trends and Their Implications for the United States (irregular),

Overseas Business Reports (irregular), current year, SD; other years, PSB

U.S. Trade Status with Socialist Countries (monthly, free), Bureau of East-West Trade, Room 4813, U.S. Department of Commerce, Washington, DC 20230

Studies, Reports, and Brochures

Advanced Business Equipment: A Market Assessment for Hungary (1975, free)

Advanced Business Equipment: A Market Assessment for the U.S.S.R. (1975, free)

American-Polish Trade Accords, 1972–73 (1974), SD

American-Romanian Economic Accords, 1973–74 (1975), SD

Chemical Industry Products and Equipment: A Market Assessment for Hungary (1975, free)

Chemical Industry Projects and Equipment: A Market Assessment for Poland (1975, free)

Chemical Industry Projects and Equipment: A Market Assessment for Romania (1975, free)

EDP Equipment: A Market Assessment for Czechoslovakia (1974, free)

Environmental Monitoring and Analysis Instrumentation: A Market Assessment for the U.S.S.R (1975, free)

Foreign Economic Trends and Their Implications for the United States, PSB

Bulgaria, FET 75-035 (1975)

Czechoslovakia, FET 75-053 (1975)

Hungary, FET 73-103 (1975)

Poland, FET 74-017 (1974)

Romania, FET 74-093 (1974)

Foreign Trade Organizations in the U.S.S.R.: Product Index and Directory (1974, free), Trade Development Assistance Division

Industrial Instrumentation: A Market Assessment for the German Democratic Republic (1975, free)

Overseas Business Reports, SD

Basic Data on the Economy of China, OBR 74-21 (June 1974)

Basic Data on the Economy of East Germany, OBR 73-17 (1973)

Basic Data on the Economy of Hungary, OBR 70-91 (1970)

Basic Data on the Economy of Romania, OBR 71-057 (1970)

Basic Data on the Economy of the U.S.S. R., OBR 74-25 (1974)

China's Foreign Trade Policy: A Current Appraisal, OBR 74-60 (1974)

Doing Business with China, OBR 74-49 (1974)

---

*Can be obtained from Bureau of East-West Trade, Room 4813, U.S. Department of Commerce, Washington, DC 20230.

Doing Business with Czechoslovakia, OBR 74-15 (1974)

Financial Practices in U.S.–China Trade, OBR 74-64 (1974)

Five Year Plan Summary: East Germany, OBR 74-08 (1974)

Five Year Plan Summary: Hungary, OBR 73-29A (1973)

Five Year Plan Summary: Poland, OBR 73-29B (1973)

Five Year Plan Summary: Romania, OBR 73-29C (1973)

Summary of the Fifth Czechoslovakia Five-Year Plan (1971–1975) OBR 74-03 (1974)

Summary of the Sixth Bulgarian Five-Year Plan (1971–1975), OBR 74-14 (1974)

Summary of the U.S.S.R. Annual Plan for 1975, OBR 75-33 (1975)

Trade of the United States with Socialist Countries in Eastern Europe and Asia, OBR 75-35 (1975)

Trading and Investing in Romania, OBR 73-36 (1973)

Trading in Hungary, OBR 74-32 (1974)

Trade in Poland, OBR 73-50 (1973)

Trading with East Europe, OBR 70-52 (rev. 1972)

Trading with the U.S.S.R., OBR 74-01 (1974)

World Trade Outlook for Eastern Europe, U.S.S.R., and People's Republic of China, OBR 75-19 (1975)

Overview of the Export Control Program. Export control policies and procedures (irregular, free, single copies), Exporters' Service and Procedures Branch, Office of Export Administration, U.S. Department of Commerce, Washington, DC, 20230

*Polymerization Processes and Related Production Equipment: A Market Assessment for the U.S.S.R. (1974, free)

*Pumps, Valves and Compressors: A Market Assessment for the U.S.S.R. (1974, free)

*Selected Trade and Economic Data of the Centrally Planned Economies (May 1975 ed. annual, free)

Soviet Information Distribution System May Help U.S. Firms (reprint from *Commerce Today*) (1973, free), Bureau of East-West Trade, Room 4323, U.S. Department of Commerce, Washington, DC, 20230

A Summary of U.S. Export Administration Regulations. When and how to apply for an export license (irregular), SD

U.S.S.R.—'75 Turnover to Grow; Longer Term Clouded (reprint from *Commerce Today*) (1975, free). Bureau of East-West Trade, Room 4323, U.S. Department of Commerce, Washington, DC, 20230

---

*Can be obtained from Bureau of East-West Trade, Room 4813, U.S. Department of Commerce, Washington, DC 20230.

The United States Role in East-West Trade—Problems and Prospects (1975)

United States Commercial Relations with Cuba: A Survey (1975), SD

U.S.–Soviet Commercial Agreements, 1972: Texts, Summaries, and Supporting Papers (1973), SD

FIELD OPERATIONS

Periodicals

Commerce Business Daily (daily except Sat. and Sun.), SD

Studies, Reports, and Brochures

Let Our District Serve Your Business, Brochure 2 (free), PSB

INTERNATIONAL COMMERCE

Periodicals

Foreign Economic Trends and Their Implications for the United States (also see *Studies, Reports, and Brochures, Foreign Economic Trends*) (145–155 issues/annum), SD

Index to Foreign Market Reports (monthly), PSB

Overseas Business Reports (also see *Studies, Reports, and Brochures, Overseas Business Reports*) (60–70 reports/annum), current year SD, other years PSB

Overseas Export Promotion Calendar (quarterly, free), OED/BIC

Studies, Reports, and Brochures

Agent/Distributor Service (1975, free), OED/BIC

Arabian Peninsula Market Survey: Materials Handling Equipment (1973, free), CAGNE/BIC

A Basic Guide to Exporting (1975), SD

Brazil: Survey of U.S. Export Opportunities (August 1974), SD

A Businessman's Introduction to Oman (1973, free), CAGNE/BIC

A Directory of U.S. Export Management Companies (1975), SD

Do You Know Your Export Customer?—World Traders Data Reports (1975, free), OED/BIC

Doing Business with NATO (1975, free), OED/BIC

Eastern Arab Demand for Building Materials and Construction Technology (1974, free), CAGNE/BIC

Eastern Arab Demand for Computers (1974, free), CAGNE/BIC

Eastern Arab Railways (1974, free), CAGNE/BIC

The EMC—Your Export Department (1973, free), OED/BIC

Export Information Services for U.S. Business Firms (1975, free), OED/BIC

Export Services of the Bureau of International Commerce (1975, free), OED/BIC

Foreign Economic Trends (individual country reports; most are issued semiannually), PSB

Afghanistan, FET 75-018 (1975)

Algeria, FET 73-074 (1973)

Angola, FET 73-069 (1973)

Argentina, FET 75-005 (1975)

Australia, FET 75-056 (1975)

Austria, FET 75-080 (1975)

Bahamas, FET 74-128 (1974)

Bahrain, FET 75-009 (1975)

Bangladesh, FET 74-040 (1974)

Barbados, FET 74-101 (1974)

Belgium, FET 75-046 (1975)

Belize (British Honduras), *FET* 75-038 (1975)

Bermuda, FET 74-109 (1974)

Bolivia, FET 74-107 (1974)

Botswana, FET 73-039 (1973)

Brazil, FET 75-054 (1975)

Bulgaria, FET 75-035 (1975)

Burma, FET 75-016 (1975)

Burundi, FET 75-042 (1975)

Cameroon, FET 75-027 (1975)

Canada, FET 75-045 (1975)

Central African Republic, FET 75-043 (1975)

Chad, FET 74-132 (1974)

Chile, FET 75-094 (1975)

China (Taiwan), *FET* 75-034 (1975)

Colombia, FET 75-014 (1975)

Costa Rica, FET 75-019A (1975)

Cyprus, FET 75-092 (1975)

Czechoslovakia, FET 75-053 (1975)

Dahomey, FET 74-010 (1974)

Denmark, FET 75-099 (1975)

Dominican Republic, FET 75-101 (1975)

Ecuador, FET 75-061 (1975)

El Salvador, FET 74-141 (1974)

Ethiopia, FET 75-057 (1975)

Fiji, FET 75-030 (1975)

Finland, FET 75-058 (1975)

France, FET 75-083 (1975)

French West Indies/Guyane, FET 75-088 (1975)

Gabon, FET 74-118 (1974)

German Democratic Republic, FET 74-043 (1974)

Germany, Federal Republic of, FET 75-068 (1975)

Ghana, FET 74-087 (1974)

Greece, FET 75-047 (1975)

Grenada, FET 75-033 (1975)

Guatemala, FET 74-121 (1974)

Guinea, FET 75-032 (1975)

Guyana, FET 74-102 (1974)

Haiti, FET 74-104 (1974)

Honduras, FET 75-023 (1975)

Hong Kong, FET 75-072 (1975)

Hungary, FET 75-103 (1975)

Iceland, FET 74-124 (1974)

India, FET 75-060 (1975)

Indonesia, FET 75-036 (1975)

Iran, FET 75-079 (1975)

Ireland, FET 75-062 (1975)

Israel, FET 75-039 (1975)

Italy, FET 75-063 (1975)

Ivory Coast, FET 75-067 (1975)

Jamaica, FET 74-127 (1974)

Japan, FET 75-090 (1975)

Jordan, FET 75-091 (1975)

Kenya, FET 75-095 (1975)

Korea, FET 75-044 (1975)

Kuwait, FET 75-037 (1975)

Laos, FET 75-049 (1975)

Lebanon, FET 75-012 (1975)

Liberia, FET 75-040 (1975)

Libya, FET 73-028 (1973)

Luxembourg, FET 75-098 (1975)

Malagasy Republic, FET 75-074 (1975)

Malawi, FET 75-085 (1975)

Malaysia, FET 75-089 (1975)

Mali, FET 75-081 (1975)

Mexico, FET 75-052 (1975)

Morocco, FET 75-102 (1975)

Mozambique, FET 74-089 (1974)

Nepal, FET 74-105 (1974)

Netherlands, FET 75-075 (1975)

Netherlands Antilles, FET 74-138 (1974)

New Zealand, FET 75-029 (1975)

Nicaragua, FET 75-013 (1975)

Niger, FET 74-032 (1974)

Nigeria, FET 75-100 (1975)

Norway, FET 75-082 (1975)

Oman, FET 75-008 (1975)

Pakistan, FET 75-041 (1975)

Panama, FET 75-084 (1975)

Paraguay, FET 75-073 (1975)

Peru, FET 75-086 (1975)

Philippines, FET 75-064 (1975)

Poland, FET 74-017 (1974)

Portugal, FET 75-093 (1975)

Romania, FET 74-093 (1974)

Rwanda, FET 74-103 (1974)

Saudi Arabia, FET 75-069 (1975)

Senegal, FET 74-099 (1974)

Sierra Leone, FET 75-097 (1975)

Singapore, FET 75-087 (1975)

Somalia, FET 75-020 (1975)

South Africa, FET 75-078 (1975)

Spain, FET 75-048 (1975)

Sri Lanka, FET 75-006 (1975)

Sudan, FET 75-055 (1975)

Surinam, FET 74-097 (1974)

Swaziland, FET 75-076 (1975)

Sweden, FET 75-077 (1975)

Switzerland, FET 75-050 (1975)

Tanzania, FET 74-094 (1974)

Thailand, FET 75-051 (1975)

Togo, FET 75-096 (1975)

Trinidad/Tobago, FET 75-059 (1975)

Tunisia, FET 75-010 (1975)

Turkey, FET 75-065 (1975)

Turks/Cacios Islands, FET 73-098 (1973)

Uganda, FET 73-129 (1973)

United Kingdom, FET 75-066 (1975)

Upper Volta, FET 75-025 (1975)

Uruguay, FET 75-070 (1975)

U.S.S.R., FET 75-026 (1975)

Venezuela, FET 75-071 (1975)

Yugoslavia, FET 75-028 (1975)

Zaire, FET 74-068 (1974)

Zambia, FET 74-065 (1974)

Foreign Direct Investors in the United States (October 1973, free), OED/BIC

Foreign Direct Investors in the U.S.—Addendum (January 1975, free), OED/BIC

Foreign Investment Organizations Assist U.S. Firms (1974, free), OED/ BIC

Foreign Investment and Licensing Checklist (1972, free), OED/BIC

Foreign Products Available for Licensed Manufacture in the U.S. (1975, free), OED/BIC

14 Ways the U.S. Department of Commerce Can Help Make Your Business More Profitable (1975, free), OED/BIC

Global Market Surveys

Agricultural Machinery and Refrigeration Equipment (January 1973), SD

Avionics and Aviation Support Equipment (May 1975), SD

Biomedical Equipment (June 1973), SD

Computers and Related Equipment (October 1973), SD

Electronic Components (October 1974), SD

Electronic Industry Production and Test Equipment (April 1974), SD

Food Processing and Packaging Equipment (August 1975), SD

Materials Handling Equipment (January 1974), SD

Metalworking and Finishing Equipment (January 1975), SD

Micrographic Equipment and Suppliers (April 1973), SD

Printing and Graphic Arts Equipment (June 1974), SD

Process Control Instrumentation (July 1975), SD

A Guide to Financing Exports (1975, free), OED/BIC

How to Get the Most from Overseas Exhibitions (1972, free), OIM/BIC

Index to International Business Publications (June 1975, free), PSB

Joint Export Establishing Promotion (1974, free), OED/BIC

Miscellaneous Economic Data, by States and Regions—Tables (1974, free), OED/BIC

The Near East and North Africa: A Report to US Business (December 1974), SD

Overseas Business Reports (individual series and country reports), current year SD, other years PSD

Basic Data on the Economy of (countries series)

Algeria, OBR 71-006 (1971)

Australia, OBR 70-34 (1970)

Austria, OBR 73-13 (1973)

Bahamas, OBR 71-032 (1971)

Bahrain, OBR 72-013 (1972)

Belgium, OBR 71-071 (1971)

Belize (British Honduras), *OBR* 70-88 (1970)

Brazil, OBR 73-71 (1973)

British Leeward Islands, OBR 60-86 (1970)

Canada, OBR 70-47 (1970)

Central American Common Market, OBR 70-43 (1970)

Chad, OBR 73-15 (1973)

China, P.R., OBR 74-21 (1974)

Colombia, OBR 71-048 (1971)

Cyprus, OBR 72-034 (1972)

East Africa, OBR 72-020 (1970)

Ecuador, OBR 71-056 (1971)

Egypt, OBR 72-073 (1972)

Finland, OBR 70-84 (1970)

France, OBR 73-43 (1973)

German Democratic Republic, OBR 73-17 (1973)

Germany, F.R., OBR 70-95 (1970)

Ghana, OBR 72-056 (1972)

Guyana, OBR 73-19 (1973)

Haiti, OBR 70-13 (1973)

Hungary, OBR 70-91 (1970)

Indonesia, OBR 71-023 (1971)

Iran, OBR 71-070 (1971)

Italy, OBR 70-59 (1970)

Ivory Coast, OBR 71-060 (1971)

Japan, OBR 71-072 (1971)

Jordan, OBR 70-93 (1970)

Kuwait, OBR 71-017 (1971)

Laos, OBR 72-035 (1972)

Lebanon, OBR 71-040 (1971)

Libya Arab Republic, OBR 70-25 (1973)

Malaysia, OBR 70-94 (1970)

Morocco, OBR 72-055 (1972)

Netherlands, OBR 70-12 (1970)

Norway, OBR 70-5 (1970)

Panama, OBR 72-53 (1972)

Portugal, OBR 71-036 (1971)

Romania, OBR 71-057 (1971)

Saudi Arabia, OBR 71-025 (1971)

Southern Africa, OBR 72-030 (1972)

Surinam, OBR 71-005 (1971)

Trinidad and Tobago, OBR 70-87 (1970)

Turkey, OBR 71-047 (1971)

U.S.S.R., OBR 74-25 (1974)

United Arab Emirates, OBR 73-06 (1973)

United Kingdom, OBR 71-028 (1971)

Venezuela, OBR 71-058 (1971)

Yugoslavia, OBR 70-60 (1970)

Establishing A Business in *(country series)*

Australia, OBR 70-89 (1970)

Belgium, OBR 70-49 (1970)

Canada, OBR 70-4 (1970)

Denmark, OBR 70-11 (1970)

Dominican Republic, OBR 70-92 (1970)

France, OBR 71-012 (1971)

Germany, F.R., OBR 70-44 (1970)

Hong Kong, OBR 72-018 (1972)

India, OBR 72-009 (1972)

Indonesia, OBR 73-02 (1973)

Iran, OBR 73-14 (1973)

Italy, OBR 71-034 (1971)

Kenya, OBR 72-008 (1972)

Kuwait, OBR 72-033 (1972)

Malaysia, OBR 70-7 (1970)

Mexico, OBR 72-027 (1972)

Morocco, OBR 70-51 (1970)

Pakistan, OBR 73-65 (1973)

Philippines, OBR 72-017 (1972)

Saudi Arabia, OBR 70-38 (1970)

Singapore, OBR 71-68 (1971)

Southern Africa, OBR 70-50 (1970)

Spain, OBR 72-052 (1972)

Sweden, OBR 71-042 (1971)

Thailand, OBR 72-038 (1972)

Turkey, OBR 73-63 (1973)

Zambia, OBR 73-09 (1973)

Foreign Trade Regulations of *(country series)*

Afghanistan, OBR 71-002 (1971)

Algeria, OBR 71-054 (1971)

Australia, OBR 71-065 (1971)

Bahamas, OBR 72-042 (1972)

Bangladesh, OBR 73-25 (1973)

Belgium and Luxembourg, OBR 73-26 (1973)

Brazil, OBR 72-050 (1972)

Burma, OBR 71-043 (1971)

Burundi, OBR 71-007 (1971)

Central African Customs and Economic Union and Chad, OBR 70-65 (1970)

Canada, OBR 72-069 (1972)

Central American Common Market OBR 70-66 (1970)

Cyprus, OBR 70-17 (1970)

Denmark, OBR 71-051 (1971)

Dominican Republic, OBR 72-022 (1972)

Egypt, OBR 73-67 (1973)

Ethiopia, OBR 72-023 (1972)

Finland, OBR 71-064 (1971)

France, OBR 70-40 (1970)

Germany, F.R., OBR 71-029 (1971)

Ghana, OBR 72-068 (1972)

Guyana, OBR 70-70 (1970)

Haiti, OBR 70-24 (1970)

Hong Kong, OBR 73-68 (1973)

Iceland, OBR 71-008 (1971)

India, OBR 72-051 (1972)

Indonesia, OBR 71-067 (1971)

Iran, OBR 71-052 (1971)

Israel, OBR 71-031 (1971)

Italy, OBR 72-032 (1972)

Japan, OBR 73-72 (1973)

Korea, OBR 73-66 (1973)

Lebanon, OBR 70-64 (1970)

Libyan Arab Republic, OBR 73-08 (1973)

Malaysia, OBR 73-34 (1973)

Malta, OBR 71-003 (1971)

Mauritius, OBR 70-68 (1971)

Mexico, OBR 72-072 (1972)

Morocco, OBR 73-07 (1973)

Netherlands, OBR 73-58 (1973)

Netherlands Antilles, OBR 70-2 (1970)

Nigeria, OBR 72-049 (1972)

Pakistan, OBR 73-24 (1973)

Panama, OBR 71-066 (1971)

Peru, OBR 73-20 (1973)

Philippines, OBR 71-019 (1971)

Portugal, OBR 70-54 (1970)

Rwanda, OBR 70-77 (1970)

Singapore, OBR 72-001 (1972)

Southern Africa, OBR 71-061 (1971)

Spain, OBR 72-024 (1972)

Surinam, OBR 70-39 (1970)

Sweden, OBR 73-35, (1973)

Switzerland, OBR 72-070 (1972)

Taiwan, OBR 71-013 (1971)

Thailand, OBR 73-37 (1973)

Trinidad and Tobago, OBR 70-15 (1970)

Tunisia, OBR 70-67 (1970)

Turkey, OBR 73-63 (1973)

United Kingdom, OBR 72-066 (1972)

Urguay, OBR 71-015 (1971)

West Africa Customs Union and Togo, OBR 70-16 (1970)

Yugoslavia, OBR 72-063, (1972)

Zambia, OBR 73-32 (1973)

Market Factors in (country series)

Afghanistan, OBR 75-34 (1975)

Burma, OBR 75-27 (1975)

Belgium, OBR 72-062 (1972)

Denmark, OBR 72-076, (1972)

Germany, F.R., OBR 70-75 (1970)

Iran, OBR 72-015 (1972)

Israel, OBR 73-10 (1973)

Netherlands, OBR 72-006 (1972)

South Africa, Republic of, OBR 74-57 (1974)

Switzerland, OBR 70-69 (1970)

Turkey, OBR 70-037 (1972)

United Kingdom, OBR 73-40 (1973)

Yugoslavia, OBR 72-061 (1972)

Marketing in (country series)

Algeria, OBR 74-30 (1974)

Argentina, OBR 75-12 (1975)

Australia, OBR 74-67 (1974)

Austria, OBR 74-61 (1974)

Belgium and Luxembourg, OBR 74-33 (1974)

Brazil, OBR 75-07 (1975)

Cameroon, OBR 75-20 (1975)

Canada, OBR 75-06 (1975)

Central American Common Market, OBR 75-29 (1975)

China (Taiwan), OBR 75-11 (1975)

Denmark, OBR 75-31 (1975)

Dominican Republic, OBR 75-28 (1975)

Ecuador, OBR 75-25 (1975)

Finland, OBR 75-04 (1975)

France, OBR 75-05 (1975)

Germany, F.R., OBR 74-55 (1974)

Ghana, OBR 75-30 (1975)

Greece, OBR 74-11 (1974)

Hong Kong, OBR 75-21 (1975)

Iceland, OBR 75-10 (1975)

Indonesia, OBR 75-02 (1975)

Iran, OBR 74-36 (1974)

Ireland, OBR 74-56 (1974)

Israel, OBR 75-23 (1975)

Italy, OBR 74-31 (1974)

Ivory Coast, OBR 74-51 (1974)

Japan, OBR 74-68 (1974)

Kenya, OBR 74-53 (1974)

Korea, OBR 74-45 (1974)

Kuwait, OBR 74-27 (1974)

Malaysia, OBR 74-60 (1974)

Mexico, OBR 74-58 (1974)

Morocco, OBR 74-47 (1974)

Netherlands, OBR 74-65 (1974)

New Zealand, OBR 74-29 (1974)

Nigeria, OBR 74-66 (1974)

Norway, OBR 74-54 (1974)

Pakistan, OBR 74-10 (1974)

Panama, OBR 75-13 (1975)

Philippines, OBR 74-46 (1974)

Portugal, OBR 74-52 (1974)

Senegal, OBR 75-26 (1975)

Singapore, OBR 75-08 (1975)

Spain, OBR 74-05 (1974)

Sweden, OBR 74-28 (1974)

Switzerland, OBR 74-62 (1974)

Thailand, OBR 74-37 (1974)

Turkey, OBR 75-36 (1975)

United Kingdom, OBR 75-03 (1975)

Yugoslavia, OBR 74-07 (1974)

Zaire, OBR 74-23 (1974)

Zambia, OBR 75-32 (1975)

Selling in (country series)

Algeria, OBR 73-11 (1973)

Australia, OBR 74-43 (1973)

Austria, OBR 72-029 (1972)

Belgium, OBR 72-048 (1972)

Brazil, OBR 73-51 (1973)

Denmark, OBR 70-35 (1970)

Finland, OBR 71-069 (1971)

France, OBR 72-007 (1972)

Germany, F.R., OBR 71-055 (1971)

Greece, OBR 73-30 (1973)

India: Dealing with the Private Sector, OBR 73-74 (1973)

India: Government Procurement Practices, OBR 73-69 (1973)

Indonesia, OBR 73-64 (1973)

Iran, OBR 70-55 (1970)

Ireland, OBR 70-6 (1970)

Israel, OBR 70-71 (1970)

Italy, OBR 73-31 (1973)

Ivory Coast, OBR 71-018 (1973)

Japan, OBR 72-046 (1972)

Lebanon, OBR 72-057 (1972)

Liberia, OBR 72-036 (1972)

Morocco, OBR 71-016 (1971)

Netherlands, OBR 72-060 (1972)

Nigeria, OBR 73-41 (1973)

Norway, OBR 72-043 (1972)

Peru, OBR 73-42 (1973)

Singapore, OBR 73-52 (1973)

Spain, OBR 73-28 (1973)

Sweden, OBR 71-035 (1971)

Switzerland, OBR 72-028 (1972)

Turkey, OBR 72-016 (1972)

United Kingdom, OBR 72-064 (1972)

Yugoslavia, OBR 73-27 (1973)

World Trade Outlook for (region series)

Africa, OBR 75-16 (1975)

Eastern Europe, U.S.S.R. and P.R. of China, OBR 75-19 (1975)

Far East and South Asia, OBR 75-17 (1975)

Latin America, OBR 75-14 (1975)

Near East and South Asia, OBR 75-15 (1975)

Western Europe and Canada, OBR 75-18 (1975)

Miscellaneous Overseas Business Reports

The Andean Common Market: Implications for U.S. Business, OBR 73-49 (1973)

The Caribbean Community and Common Market: The Implications for U.S. Business, OBR 75-24 (1975)

The Caribbean Free Trade Association, OBR 72-058 (1972)

China's Foreign Trade Policy: A Current Appraisal, OBR 74-60 (1974)

Digest of Economic Development Plans for Selected Countries in Africa, OBR 73-21 (1973)

EEC and EFTA Rules of Origin Governing Preferential Trade, OBR 74-04 (1974)

Financial Practices in U.S.–China Trade, OBR 74-64 (1974)

Government Procurement Practices in Selected Countries of Africa, OBR 72-021 (1972)

Investing in Yugoslavia, OBR 73-23 (1973)

Investment Laws of Selected Countries in Africa, OBR 73-32 (1973)

Market Surveys of African Countries (Supplement 2), *OBR* 70-36 (1970)

Patents, Trademarks, and Licensing in Japan, OBR 73-04 (1973)

Pharmaceutical Regulations of Selected Countries of Africa, OBR 71-046 (1971)

Special Requirements on Imports Into Canada, OBR 72-065 (1972)

President's/Regional/District Export Councils: Membership Director (March 1975, free), OED/BIC

Recognizing Export Effort with the President's "E" and "E Star" Awards (1974, free), OED/BIC

Seven Surprising Facts about Exporting (1973, free), OED/BIC

Sources of Information on American Firms for International Businessmen (1974, free), OED/BIC

State Tax Table (August 1975, free), OED/BIC

States Providing Incentives and Special Services to Industry—Tables (1973, free), OED/BIC

Trade Lists

Business Firms Trade Lists, EID/BIC

Bahamas (1975)	Iceland (1973)
Bahrain (1975)	Iran (1975)
Belize (1975)	Ireland (1973)
Bolivia (1973)	Ivory Coast (1975)
Cameroon (1975)	Jamaica (1975)
Egypt (1975)	Kenya (1975)
El Salvador (1973)	Kuwait (1973)
Ethiopia (1975)	Malagasy Republic (1975)
Guyana (1975)	Malawi (1975)

Morocco (1975)   Sierra Leone (1975)

Mozambique (1975)   Sudan (1975)

Nepal (1975)   Trinidad and Tobago (1975)

Nigeria (1975)   United Arab Emirates (1973)

Oman (1975)   Yugoslavia (1975)

Qatar (1973)   Zaire (Congo-Kinshasa) (1975)

Saudi Arabia (1975)   Zambia (1973)

Senegal (1975)

East-West Trading Firms, Series, EID/BIC

Austria (1974)

Switzerland (1973)

State Trading Organizations Series, EID/BIC

Algeria (1975)   Hungary (1973)

Bulgaria (1974)   Poland (1973)

Czechoslovakia (1974)   U.S.S.R. (1975)

Germany, East (1972)

Target Market Trade Lists

Agricultural Machinery (all 1973) EID/BIC (Brazil, Colombia, Costa Rica, Dominican Republic, Ecuador, El Salvador, Guatemala, Honduras, Kenya, Malaysia, Mexico, Nicaragua, Panama, Philippines, Thailand, Venezuela, Yugoslavia)

Biomedical Equipment (all 1973), EID/BIC (Australia, Austria, Belgium, Brazil, Denmark, Finland, France, Germany, F.R., Israel, Italy, Japan, Mexico, Netherlands, Norway, Spain, Sweden, Switzerland, United Kingdom, Venezuela, Yugoslavia)

Computers and Related Equipment (all 1973), EID/BIC (Argentina, Australia, Austria, Belgium, Brazil, Finland, France, Germany, F.R., Hong Kong, Israel, Italy, Japan, Mexico, Netherlands, Norway, Spain, Sweden, Switzerland, Venezuela, Yugoslavia)

Electronic Components, (all 1974), EID/BIC (Hong Kong, India, Japan, Korea, Mexico, Netherlands, Spain, Switzerland)

Electronics Production Equipment (1973, 1974), EID/BIC (Australia, Brazil, Germany, Hong Kong, Israel, Italy, Switzerland, Taiwan)

Food Processing and Packaging Equipment (1974, 1975), EID/BIC (Australia, Belgium, Denmark, Finland, France, Hong Kong, Iran, Ireland, Israel, Italy, Japan, Malaysia, Mexico, Netherlands, Norway, Spain, Thailand, U.S.S.R.)

Materials Handling Equipment (1973, 1974), EID/BIC (Australia, Belgium, Brazil, Colombia, France, Germany, Mexico, Netherlands, Peru, Singapore, Spain, Turkey, Venezuela)

Metalworking and Finishing Equipment (1974, 1975) EID/BIC (Australia, Austria, France, Germany, F.R., Israel, Italy, Japan, Mexico, Philippines, Poland, Spain)

Micrographics (1973), EID/BIC (Australia, Belgium, Canada, Denmark, France, Germany, Italy, Japan, Netherlands, Spain, Sweden, Switzerland, United Kingdom)

Printing and Graphic Arts Equipment (all 1974), EID/BIC (Belgium, Denmark, France, Hong Kong, Israel, Italy, Japan, Mexico, Netherlands, Norway, Philippines, Switzerland, United Kingdom, Venezuela, U.S.S.R.)

Process Control Instrumentation (1974, 1975), EID/BIC (Belgium, Brazil, Germany, F.R., Iran, Italy, Japan, Philippines, Spain, Taiwan, Venezuela)

Trade Missions, A Handbook for Trade Mission Members (all 1974, free), OIM/BIC

Trade Opportunities Program (1973, free), OED/BIC

U.S. Trade Promotion Facilities Abroad (1974, free), OED/BIC

INTERNATIONAL ECONOMIC POLICY AND RESEARCH

Periodicals

International Economic Indicators and Competitive Trends (quarterly), SD

Multilateral Trade Negotiation News (monthly, free), Office of International Trade Policy, Room 3027, U.S. Department of Commerce, Washington, DC, 20230

Studies, Reports, and Brochures

The Automotive Industry in 1974: An International Survey, ER-8 (1975, free), OER

Capital Goods: The $20 Billion Trade Surplus, ER-10 (1975, free), OER

Changes in U.S. Foreign Trade: The Post–1971 Experience in Perspective, ER-4 (1974, free), OER

The Effect of Price Controls in U.S. Exports of Selected Industrial Supplies and Materials (1975, free), International Trade Analysis Staff, Room 5618, U.S. Department of Commerce, Washington, DC, 20230

Free Trade Zones and Related Facilities Abroad (1970) SD

The Impact of the Proposed Energy Conservation Program on U.S. Foreign Trade in Manufactures, with an Emphasis on Petrochemicals, ER-7 (1975, free), OER

Market Penetration: Measuring and Evaluating U.S. Export Competitiveness of the Office Machine Industry in a Six Country Market (1975, free), Office of Competitive Assessment, Room 3024, U.S. Department of Commerce, Washington, DC, 20230

Market Share Reports—country series

Separate reports on 82 import markets comparing U.S. performance in 880 manufactured products with that of 8 other principal suppliers, 1969–73. Order number: add the common prefix COM-74-1090 to the four-digit number following the individual country title. See also *Market Share Reports Catalog* (annual, 1975), NTIS.

Algeria, 5001

Argentina, 5002

Australia, 5003

Austria, 5004

Belgium-Luxembourg, 5005

Bolivia, 5006

Brazil (1968-72), 5007

Bulgaria, 5077

Cameroon, 5008

Canada, 5009

Chile, 5010

People's Republic of China, 5076

Colombia, 5011

Costa Rica, 5013

Czechoslovakia, 5078

Denmark, 5014

Dominican Republic, 5015

Ecuador, 5016

Egypt (1968-72), 5068

El Salvador, 5017

Ethiopia, 5018

Finland, 5019

France, 5020

Federal Republic of Germany, 5021

Democratic Republic of Germany, 5079

Ghana, 5022

Greece, 5023

Guatemala, 5024

Honduras, 5025

Hong Kong (1968-72), 5026

Hungary, 5080

India, 5027

Indonesia, 5028

Iran, 5029

Ireland, 5030

Israel (1968-72), 5031

Italy, 5032

Ivory Coast, 5033

Jamaica, 5034

Japan, 5035

Kenya, 5036

Republic of Korea (1968–72), 5037

Kuwait, 5038

Lebanon, 5039

Liberia, 5040

Libya (1968–72), 5041

Malaysia (1970–73 data only), 5042

Mexico (1968–72), 5043

Morocco, 5044

Netherlands, 5045

New Zealand (1968–72), 5046

Nicaragua, 5047

Nigeria, 5048

Norway, 5049

Pakistan, (1968–72), 5050

Panama, 5051

Peru, 5052

Philippines, 5053

Poland, 5074

Portugal, 5054

Romania, 5081

Saudi Arabia, 5055

Singapore, 5056

South Africa, 5057

Spain, 5058

Sweden, 5059

Switzerland, 5060

Taiwan, 5061

Tanzania, 5062

Thailand (1968–72), 5063

Trinidad and Tobago, 5064

Tunisia, 5065

Turkey (1968–72), 5066

Uganda, 5067

United Arab Emirates (1972–73 data only), 5082

United Kingdom, 5069

U.S.S.R., 5075

Venezuela, 5070

Republic of Vietnam, 5071

Yugoslavia, 5072

Zaire, 5012

Zambia, 5073

Market Share Reports—commodity series

Separate reports on 880 manufactured products comparing U.S. export performance in the world market and in 92 designated markets with that of 13 other major exporting countries, 1969–73. For example, 512-Organic Chemicals, COM-74-10900-0075. See *Market Share Reports Catalog* (annual, 1975), NTIS.

Market Share Reports Catalog, COM-75-10212 (free), NTIS

The Multinational Corporation: Studies on U.S. Foreign Investment, Vol. 1 (1972), Vol. 2 (1973), SD

Ocean Freight Rate Guidelines for Shippers (1974), SD

Overseas Business Reports

Trade of the United States with Socialist Countries in Eastern Europe and Asia, 1972–74, OBR 75-35 (annual, 1975), SD

U.S. Foreign Trade by Quarters, July–September 1972—July–September 1974, OBR 75-01 (quarterly, 1975), SD

United States Foreign Trade, 1968–74, OBR 75-22 (annual, 1975), SD

United States Trade with Major Trading Partners, 1968–74, OBR 75-43 (annual, 1975), SD

United States Trade with Major World Areas, 1969–74, OBR 75-38 (annual, 1975), SD

An Overview of Investment: The U.S. and Major Foreign Economies, ER-3 (1974, free), OER

Reinsurance Transactions Abroad (1974, free), Office of International Finance and Investment, Room 2031, U.S. Department of Commerce, Washington, DC, 20230

Selling Prices and Taxes on Motor Gasoline, Diesel Fuel, and Heating Oil in Selected Countries as of October 1974, ER-6 (1975, free), OER

Survey of Current International Economic Research, ER-11 (an annotated bibliography) (1975, free), OER

U.S. Trade and Developing Economies: The Growing Importance of Manufactured Goods, ER-9 (1975, free), OER

RESOURCES AND TRADE ASSISTANCE

Studies, Reports, and Brochures

Annual Report of the Foreign-Trade Zones Board to the Congress of the United States (1974), SD

Correlation: Textiles and Apparel Categories with Tariff Schedules of the United States, Annotated (1975, free), Office of Textiles, U.S. Department of Commerce, Room 2815, Washington, DC, 20230

Sources of Statistical Data, Textiles, and Apparel (1974), SD

Venture Capital

Since the launching of Small Business Investment Companies (SBIC's) by the Small Business Administration (SBA), its very nature has changed. How to raise capital for a growing enterprise is a fundamental question. The listing in this chapter is one of the broadest original sources of information on venture capital ever compiled.

How Are SBIC's Doing?

A Small Business Investment Company (SBIC) is a licensee of the federal government charged with making investments in small entrepreneurial ventures. A MESBIC is a Minority Enterprise SBIC which does the same thing for businesses with strong minority group interests. The way it works is simple. A pool of money is established (currently a minimum of five hundred thousand dollars for an SBIC, three hundred thousand for a MESBIC) and then the manager of the pool of money applies to the SBIC division of the Small Business Administration (SBA) for an SBIC license. Once the pool of money qualifies for an SBIC license, you can accomplish the following:

1. A loan of between 3:1 and 4:1 times the amount in the pool of equity funds; you can leverage the equity by 3 or 4 times with an SBA loan.
2. The loan will be subordinated to bank debt. Consequently, with the

344

total capital you should be able to borrow several million dollars on a short term basis from the banks.

3. The loan will be unsecured and all investors will have limited liabilities.
4. The loan will be a balloon payment loan with interest only payable.
5. The interest rate is currently three points under prime rate.

The above features are a few of the incentives to reach the minimum targets of paid investment capital. There are some disadvantages to an SBIC and it is not a panacea, but the advantages often outweigh the disadvantages. One disadvantage is that any investment is limited to 20 percent of the paid-in capital ($500,000) hence you could only invest up to one hundred thousand dollars on any single deal. A second disadvantage is the paperwork which the SBA creates to prevent fraud in distribution of their funds.

For the months of April-June of 1979, the number of SBIC's making investments was 161 as compared to MESBIC's making 39. The number of financing made by SBIC's was 558 and 113 for MESBIC's. The total amount financed was $7.14 M for SBIC's and $10 M for MESBIC's.

Approximately 60 percent of the SBIC financing by number (and a little higher by dollars) were first or initial financings. This has been a fairly constant pattern for SBIC's over the years. About half of the SBIC dollar financing was in the form of straight debt versus straight equity. The average interest on the debt was just under 13 percent annually. The SBIC's have an interest ceiling of 15 percent and rather than charge excessive interest, they are motivated to opt for equity in the form of warrants along with a debt financing.

How Have SBIC's Done In 1978?

The Small Business Administration reports Small Business Investment Companies and Minority Enterprise SBIC's were more active in 1978 than ever before—the highest level in the twenty-year history of the program. Loans and investments in smaller firms last year totaled $223,000,000. Of this amount, 40 percent was allocated to firms which were one year old or less, while 54.5 percent went to those firms three years old or less.

Typically, manufacturing firms received more in loans (36 percent) than any other classification. SBIC's interest rates increased

only slightly over previous years with the average rate on straight loans charged at 12.46 percent.

While three states (Alaska, Maine, and Wyoming) received no SBIC monies, Texas firms were awarded the most dollars: $34.2 million. Following Texas was New York with $33.5 million—an encouraging year for SBIC loan recipients. Ten SBIC's made more than thirty investments last year. The total number of businesses receiving SBIC investments in 1978 was 1,515.

To receive information about SBIC financing, we recommend that you write to:

SBIC Division
SBA
1411 L Street N.W.
Washington, DC 20005

Entrepreneurial Bank Borrowing

I've noticed a small but developing trend which may be of interest to entrepreneurs currently searching for a new banking relationship. My philosophy on this subject has never changed, as I suggest picking a banker not a bank. Then I usually go on to tell you the qualities of the young loan officer, who makes the ideal banker. It's good wisdom.

But, of late, two major changes have occurred in the overall U.S. banking structure which have created some measurable differences between banks. The first of these changes are in foreign banks doing business in the U.S. In 1972, when the Federal Reserve started keeping statistics on such issues, there were 52 foreign banks with 100 offices in the U.S. By mid 1978, the number of foreign banks had more than doubled to 123 and they operated 268 offices. The assets of these foreign-owned U.S. based banks have grown by more than four times during the five year period and today their assets are over $100 billion. The second is the two-tier prime rate structure now being charged to small business. But more about that in a minute.

Why are these foreign banks expanding in the U.S.? There are two basic answers; the relative devaluation of the U.S. dollar and the ability of these banks to avoid U.S. banking regulations. Because of these factors, these banks have generally been taking a more aggressive posture toward loans to entrepreneurial ventures. This is not

true for every banker at every bank, but it is true in general. So, if you're considering a banking relationship why not consider Britain's Barclay Bank, or the Bank of Montreal, or the host of Japanese, Swiss or French banks.

These foreign-owned banks are allowed to open branches outside their counties (U.S. banks are not) and they often have offices in the major cities of the country. They are seldom located in small towns, much preferring the New York or Los Angeles type of city. This ability to operate across counties can also be a feature for your company if they operate in the same cities where branches of your business are located. Beside this benefit, these banks are not required to tie up a portion of their assets with the Federal Reserve System because they most often choose to operate under state banking regulations. These two fundamental reasons allow these banks the slight tendency to be more aggressive in securing new business. Hence, it may prove to be to your advantage to do business with them.

Further, with this expansion continuing, I would predict a major overhaul in the U.S. banking restrictions to allow U.S. banks to compete on more favorable terms with these foreign banks. Hence, if this happens, this opportunity for more aggressive banking will prove to be available only for a moment in time. When the windows open, the entrepreneurial manager at least pokes his or her head in.

For the foreign bank nearest you, consult the yellow pages of the largest city nearest you. And, please remember, I haven't mentioned the obvious advantage of doing business with a foreign based bank, if your entrepreneurial venture happens to sell or buy from the host country.

The second major change was triggered by the heroes of small business at The Mellon National Bank in Pittsburgh, PA. They began offering small businesses a borrowing rate below the prime rate. They did this in times of money shortages (now) to help entrepreneurs, and they deserve pioneering recognition! For an up-to-date list of banks who offer a two-tier lending rate which is revised monthly write to:

Chief Counsel for Advocacy
SBA
1441 "L" St. N.W.
Washington, DC 20416
(202)653-6998

The Two-Tier Small Business Prime Rate: How to Pick A Banker

The small business interest rate structure has caused a great deal of interest ever since the champion of small business, the Mellon Bank in Pittsburgh, Pennsylvania, instituted a two-tier prime rate.

I sent letters and questionnaires to the 100 or so banks rated in the SBA's list of two-tier prime rate banks. This source list was compiled by Milton Stuart's SBA Office of Advocacy in Washington, D.C. As of March 5, 1979, 90 banks have claimed to follow the two-tier prime rate system. During this time of high money costs, these banks are offering to small businesses which qualify, a lower interest rate than even the financially more stable larger companies could obtain from the bank. We sent letters to these "helpful" banks (we had a hard time believing that banks were lending to small businesses at cheaper rates because it went against previous experiences with banks and money), to probe below the surface. Here is what our investigation discovered:

1. Limitations generally in effect to qualify:
   a. assets will not exceed $1.5 million
   b. total borrowing from all sources will not exceed $400,000.*
   c. there is usually a floor rate never to drop below (presently it is about 9½%)
   d. investment for speculative loans do not qualify
2. The small business prime rate is generally about 1 to 1½% below the published prime rate.

These loans are also available to individuals to be used for business (not speculative) purposes. Therefore, the concept is a positive step forward to help small business during tight money.

We received responses from about two dozen banks and we followed up with a second round of telephone calls and questionnaires. We were disappointed with our findings. We concluded that the selection of the bank should not be soley based upon the so-called list of the "good guys." Most small business loans are based on prime rate plus one percent, two percent, three percent, and in some cases, four percent above the prime lending rate. The amount above prime charged by the bank varies depending upon the bank's assessment of the quality of the loan. Our investigation found, generally, that if you begin 1 to 1½% below prime with a "good guy"

*Some banks allow $500,000 of borrowing, not including real estate.

348

bank (the small business prime), the resultant difference contrasted to so-called "non-good guy" banks is usually only ½%. Here is the example:

"Good" Bank with Two-Tier Prime Rate		"Bad" Bank with One-Tier Prime Rate
10½%	—Prime—	11¾%
3	—Add-on Interest—	2
13½%	Actual Interest Rate	13¾%

So the difference in practice is usually not sufficient to warrant picking the bank on the "good" and "bad" criteria.

Don't select a bank solely because it belongs to the so-called list of "good guy" two-tier banks. Rather, our old advice still holds. Pick a banker, not a bank. If he is with a large bank, or a bank with a captive small business investment company (SBIC), so much the better. Many bankers are really venture capitalists in disguise and can be sources of valuable financial assistance.

Here again, forget the big titles and pick a young-thinking loan officer or assistant vice-president, then gain his confidence. Supply him with detailed pro forma cash flow projections to show what your cash needs will be. Then meet or exceed your projections. Getting financial aid will be easy from then on.

In working with your friendly banker, you'll soon learn that he expects you to personally countersign your company's bank debt. Don't let it throw you. It's the only way he has to certify your numbers and your confidence in what you're doing. But don't take this responsibility lightly either.

Unusual Sources of Capital

Lending institutions prefer to loan money against collateral because they maintain the option of liquidating the collateral to repay the loan. Below is the rule of thumb for what can be loaned against different forms of collateral from the balance sheet of an entrepreneurial venture.

In practice, the actual ratios are even more pronounced. In other words, banks prefer not to lend against inventory as contrasted to lending against receivables.

In turn, easily liquidated fixed assets are the most attractive type of collateral (automobiles) and they usually command both a

high percentage of their lendable market value as well as a subsequently lower interest rate.

A lender is basically unsure of an inventory's value until it is converted to cash by being sold. That's the underlying reason that lenders shy away from accepting inventory or certain types of fixed assets as collateral for a loan. Thus, the role of T.H.E. Insurance Company is to write an insurance policy to protect a lender against bankruptcy. They essentially appraise the collateral asset and insure to repossess it from a lender at the assessed rates.

Rather than paying off the insurance policy on a death, the policy is paid upon default in the loan. Here's how it works:

	PERCENTAGE TO BE LOANED AGAINST
Accounts Receivable	75%–80%, under 90 days
Inventory	10%–20%
Fixed Assets	70%–80% market value

1. T.H.E. appraises the assets to be pledged, including both inventory and fixed assets.
2. T.H.E. will then issue an insurance policy for the amount of their appraisal.
3. The company hands this policy over to the lender and then borrows 100 percent of the value of the policy in a loan.
4. If the company defaults, T.H.E. takes title to the collateral and sells it. The lender is paid in full using T.H.E.'s credit and capital to be reimbursed.

What does all this insurance protection cost?

1. Appraisal fee: minimum amount: $1,000. This is for the appraisal and it is 1 percent of the appraised value of the collateral plus out-of-pocket (travel) expenses.
2. A 2 percent add-on interest rate on the outstanding loan balance, not on the full appraisal of the collateral. The premium interest rate of 2 percent is charged only on what's borrowed or what is at risk.

The value of T.H.E. policy allows more capital to be secured from existing lenders. On the one hand, a lender will typically allow only 10 percent of inventory value to be used as loan collateral, with a policy the inventory allowed as collateral might be above 50 percent of its value, depending upon T.H.E.'s assessment. This often

allows a two or three times greater amount to be loaned against an asset.

Often times, an asset or inventory can be borrowed against when it was given zero valuation by a bank because of the T.H.E. formula. On a theoretical basis, the lending interest rate can be reduced if you can convince the lender of the merits and security of the guarantee. In effect, given the policy, the lender should advance funds on T.H.E.'s credit, not the credit of your entrepreneurial venture.

In practice, you are seldom ever able to negotiate the bank interest rate lower by securing a T.H.E. guarantee and, in total, you are paying 5-6% above prime rate for this type of lending. If your entrepreneurial venture can service debt, write:

> Mr. Ed Shifman, Vice President
> T.H.E. Insurance Company
> 52 Church Street
> Boston, MA 02116
> (617)367-5225

Farmers Home Loan

The SBA is supposedly the government agency charged with helping the entrepreneur, but, in practice, other federal agencies also provide a great deal of help. The FmHa is the loan program of the Farmers Home Administration which offers guaranteed loans to growing businesses. Unlike the SBA's program with a $500,000 ceiling, the FmHa loan program has no ceiling. In fact, loans have ranged from $7,000 to $33 million, with an average of about $900,000.

The FmHa loan gives preference to distressed areas, and rural communities of less than 25,000 inhabitants. It will loan money for any worthwhile business purpose. The minimum equity requirement is 10 percent and, if your venture can be shown to be job creating, your loan has a greater chance of approval. Unlike the SBA, you do not have to prove to be an unbankable company to secure a FmHa loan. The loans are for fairly long terms, thirty years for construction, fifteen years for equipment, and seven years for working capital. The interest rate is about the same as can be negotiated with a bank, but the FmHa has a one-time fee that is calculated by multiplying one percent of the principal loan amount by the percentage of the guarantee. Even given the one-time fee, the

good standing of the U.S. government stands behind the guaranteed portions of the loan and the interest rate eventually negotiated often effects these favorable considerations.

Why not write the FmHa in care of the (USDA) United States Dept. of Agriculture, Washington, DC 20250, or you could look in your nearest largest city yellow pages for one of the 1,800 county offices. Look under US Government—Agriculture.

EDA Funds

If your company needs funds to expand or strengthen an existing business, you may be eligible for federal funds without knowing it.

The federal government has designated two-thirds of all counties in the U.S. as "economically depressed." If you're located in one of these areas, you may apply for a loan under the special program of the Economic Development Administration.

To qualify for such a loan, a company must show that it has been unable to borrow under similar terms and conditions from other sources.

There is no limit on the amount that may be requested. Most of the loans are under $1 million, or $10,000 per job created or saved.

On direct loans for fixed assets, or where there is mortgagable collateral, the interest rate is currently under 10 percent. EDA would provide up to 65 percent of the total funds, but the applicant has to put at least 15 percent of his own and get 5 percent from his state or a non-governmental community organization, such as a Community Development Corporation. The repayment time is usually the useful life of the fixed assets.

The interest rate on a direct loan for working capital or for less mortgagable assets is usually only a ¼ percent higher than fixed assets.

A list of economically depressed areas, the loan application form, and other details of the loan program can be obtained from any of EDA's six regional offices. For the address of the office nearest you, write or call:

Office of Business Development
Economic Development Administration
Room 7876 14th & Constitution Avenue, N.W.
Washington, DC 20230
(202)377-2000

An Excellent Investment Opportunity

A continuing problem is an opportunity when it is viewed in a positive manner. This is the case in the phenomenon of the currency devaluation of the United States dollar. It's not surprising that most experts judge that the U.S. dollar will continue to fall in relation to other currencies because of the ineffectual U.S. economic policies. The Swiss franc's performance has made it the best foreign currency due to the outstanding performance of the Swiss economy. Just look at the chart below:

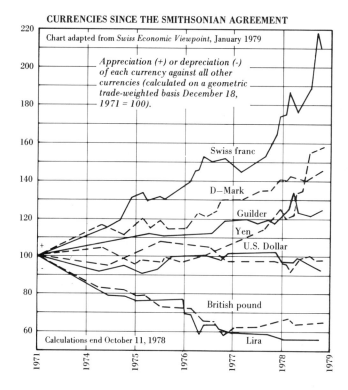

CURRENCIES SINCE THE SMITHSONIAN AGREEMENT

Chart adapted from *Swiss Economic Viewpoint*, January 1979

Appreciation (+) or depreciation (-) of each currency against all other currencies (calculated on a geometric trade-weighted basis December 18, 1971 = 100).

Swiss franc

D–Mark

Guilder

Yen

U.S. Dollar

British pound

Calculations end October 11, 1978

Lira

The reason for the Swiss franc's outstanding performance to date has to do with how well the Swiss government manages their economy. The Swiss have an inflation rate of less than 1% and they have virtually no unemployment. The United States has too much of both and experts predict that the dollar will continue to underperform as our government works on symptoms rather than attacking these decreases. In my opinion, this is a creeping crisis for individuals who hold fixed annuities payable in U.S. dollars and an opportu-

nity for those holding fixed annuities in currencies which are stable or rising.

I'd suggest you consider holding a life insurance policy in Swiss companies rather than in United States companies because your income can be paid in Swiss francs. Not only will you receive a guaranteed benefit, the actual value of your policy can climb, as the Swiss franc has dramatically risen in relation to the U.S. dollar. The difference is that the policy will be payable in a stable or rising currency. An individual is not easily allowed to speculate or accumulate foreign currencies and this method of buying fixed annuities is one of the so-called loopholes available to profit from the decline of our government's dollar.

A Swiss franc annuity is a life income guaranteed by a Swiss life insurance company in which you receive your life income in Swiss francs. As long as you are not a resident of Switzerland, you will not be liable for any Swiss taxes. Also, the annuity is covered by the same desirable banking laws which cover bank privacy in Switzerland. How do you obtain information about one of these programs?

Assurex S.A. is an international insurance consulting firm, specializing in the placement of annuity, endowment, and life insurance contracts for non-residents of Switzerland. Write:

> Assurex S.A.
> Volkmarstrasse 10
> 8033 Zurich, Switzerland
> Telephone: 01-602510
> Telex: 53177

Further, they sell a booklet entitled *The Autumn Annuities Life Income in Swiss Francs.*

BUSINESS DEVELOPMENT CORPORATIONS

The purpose of business development corporations is to attract and retain business in their respective states, and thus increase employment. Although they sound like government agencies, they are not. BDCs are private organizations that operate within a state. Their shareholders are normally other private financial institutions

located within the state, mainly savings banks and insurance companies, although industrial companies are sometimes investors.

Interest rates on BDC loans normally are a function of the prime rate and range from 2 to 4 percent above the prevailing rate. In addition, some BDCs charge application fees and commitment fees. These fees generally do not total more than 1½ percent of the loan.

A prime advantage of BDC loans is the longer maturities available. While a bank will rarely go beyond five years for a term loan, BDC loans have averaged maturities of between four and ten years.

While most BDCs require collateral, many accept second liens. However, the owners should be prepared to assign key-man life insurance and to personally guarantee the loan if the business is a closely held one.

BDCs are lenders, not investors, and are normally not interested in equity positions in the business. However, some—such as the New York Business Development Corporation—have formed small business investment company subsidiaries. The SBIC will take equity positions generally via subordinated debt with warrants (or a convertible feature) to round out a financing package.

Business development corporations are specifically designed to provide long-term capital to small businesses. With capital tough to get today, it is a good idea to become familiar with your state BDC.

For further information, contact your local chamber of commerce or write to:

National Association of Business Development Associations
Industrial Development Corp. of Florida
801 North Magnolia Avenue, Suite 218
Orlando, FL 32803
(305)841-2640

The National Association of Business Development Corporations are at the following locations:

First Arkansas Development Finance Corporation
910 Pyramid Life Building
Little Rock, AR 72201
(501)374-9247

Alaska State Development Corporation
Pouch D
Juneau, AK 99811
(907)586-2775

Statewide California Business & Industrial Development Corporation
717 Lido Park Drive
Newport Beach, CA 92663
(714)675-8030

Connecticut Development Credit Corporation
99 Colony Street, P.O. Box 714
Meriden, CT 06450
(203)235-3327

Industrial Development Corporation of Florida
Suite 218, 801 North Magnolia Avenue
Orlando, FL 32802
(305)841-2640

Business Development Corporation of Georgia, Inc.
822 Healey Building
Atlanta, GA 30303
(404)577-5715

Iowa Business Development Credit Corporation
247 Jewett Building
Des Moines, IA 50309
(515)282-9546

Kansas Development Credit Corporation
First National Bank Tower, Suite 620
One Townsite Plaza
Topeka, KS 66603
(913)235-3437

Business Development Corporation of Kentucky
1940 Commonwealth Building
Louisville, KY 40202
(502)584-3519

Development Credit Corporation of Maine
P.O. Box 262
Manchester, ME 04351
(207)724-3507

Development Credit Corporation of Maryland
1301 First National Bank Building
Baltimore, MD 21202
(301)685-6454

Massachusetts Business Development Corporation
One Boston Place, Suite 3607
Boston, MA 02108
(617)723-7515

First Missouri Development Finance Corporation
302 Adams Street, P.O. Box 252
Jefferson City, MO 65101
(314)635-0138

Development Credit Corporation of Montana
P.O. Box 916
Helena, MT 59601
(406)442-3850

Business Development Corporation of Nebraska
Suite 1044, Stuart Building
Lincoln, NE 68508
(402)474-3855

New Hampshire Business Development Corporation
10 Fort Eddy Road
Concord, NH 03301
(603)224-1432

New York Business Development Corporation
41 State Street
Albany, NY 12207
(518)463-2268

Business Development Corporation of North Carolina
505 Oberlin Road, P.O. Box 10665
Raleigh, NC 27605
(919)828-2331

North Dakota State Development Credit Corporation
Box 1212
Bismark, ND 58501
(701)223-2288

Oklahoma Business Development Corporation
1018 United Founders Life Tower
Oklahoma, City, OK 73112
(405)840-1674

RIDC Industrial Development Fund
Union Trust Building
Pittsburgh, PA 15219
(412)288-9206

Pennsylvania Development Credit Corporation
232 North Second Street
Harrisburg, PA 17101
(717)234-3241

Southeastern Pennsylvania Development Fund
3 Penn Center Plaza
Philadelphia, PA 19102
(215)568-4677

Business Development Company of Rhode Island
40 Westminster Street
Providence, RI 02903
(401)751-1000

Business Development Corporation of South Carolina
Palmetto State Life Building, P.O. Box 11606
Columbia, SC 29211
(803)252-3759

Virginia Industrial Development Corporation
201 Mutual Building, P.O. Box 474
Richmond, VA 23204
(804)643-1289

Business Development Corporation of Eastern Washington
417 Hyde Building
Spokane, WA 99201
(509)838-2731

West Virginia Business Development Corporation
P.O. Box 289
Charleston, WV 25301
(304)346-8545

Wyoming Industrial Development Corporation
P.O. Box 612
Casper, WY 82601
(307)234-5351

PUBLICATIONS

1. The United States Small Business Administration publishes on a quarterly basis a complete listing of SBICs (Small Business Investment Companies) as well as MESBICs (Minority Enterprise Small Business Investment Companies), listing name, address, and size category. The *AAMESBIC Newsletter* is sent monthly to about 1,000 subscribers. Write:

SBA Investments Division
1441 1 Street, N.W.
Washington, DC 20416

and/or

American Association of MESBICs
1413 K Street, N.W., 13th floor
Washington, DC 20005
(202)347-8600

2. The Capital Publishing Corporation has been the single clearinghouse for most industrywide venture capital information. It offers the following publications:

A monthly newsletter entitled *Venture Capital,* which highlights a number of useful areas of what's happening within the industry. The newsletter is widely read but its paid circulation is less than 1,000.

The Guide to Venture Capital Sources (4th ed.), by Stanley Rubel (1977), is the most valuable single source on venture capital ever published. Besides providing a nicely indexed listing of venture capital sources by state and by product-group interest, the front half of this guide has several valuable articles. About $550 million is invested annually by about 450 professional venture capital firms with assets of about $3 billion. The directory lists 600 sources.

Source Guide for Borrowing Capital, by Leonard Smollen, Stanley Rubel, and Mark Rollinson (1977), tells how to raise capital without having to give up any equity. There are 50 federal programs for financing small business handled by nine different government agencies. This includes the Small Business Administration, the Farmers' Home Administration, and others. The directory also lists state agencies, commercial banks, insurance companies, commercial finance companies, leasing companies, and investors in industrial revenue bonds. It's a valuable directory.

Guide to Selling a Business, by Stanley Rubel (1977), lists about 1,500 acquisition-oriented corporations. In addition, about 100 companies that are seeking leveraged buyouts as well as about 500 professional merger intermediaries are listed. This is a unique and valuable book.

For information on these publications, write:

Capital Publishing Corporation
10 South LaSalle Street
Chicago, IL 60603
(312)641-0922

or

Capital Publishing Company
2 Laurel Avenue, Box 348
Wellesley Hills, MA 02181
(617)235-5405

3. The Center for Community and Economic Development (CCED), along with the Institute for New Enterprise Development (INED), has authored *Sources of Capital for Community and Economic Development,* an excellent source book on capital. In addition, the CCED offers a free bimonthly newsletter for interested parties. This nonprofit group works to promote the concept of community-based economic development. It also publishes 55 other books and booklets on this topic. Write:

Center for Community and Economic Development
639 Massachusetts Avenue
Suite 316
Cambridge, MA 02139
(617)547-9695

or

Institute for New Enterprise Development
385 Concord Avenue
Belmont, MA 02178

4. *The Directory of State and Federal Funds* is a single source for basic data on the financial assistance programs of the 50 states and 12 federal agencies. This concise directory is the starting point for any business, large or small, which seeks to relocate or expand. The book helps management to "shop," compare, select, and discard a wide range of aid programs without having to go through mountains of promotional literature. Write:

Directory of State and Federal Funds
   for Business Development
Pilot Books
347 Fifth Avenue
New York, NY 10016

5. *How and Where to Raise Venture Capital,* by Ted Nicholas (1978), is an excellent 68-page pamphlet on venture capital. Another booklet by Nicholas is *Where the Money Is and How to Get It.* Write:

Enterprise Publishing Company
1300 Market Street
Wilmington, DE 19801
(302)656-3174

6. *How to Finance a Growing Business,* by Royce Diener (1965), is a book on capital security, written from the viewpoint of the businessperson-borrower. It not only describes what is available in the field of finance but also provides insight into what goes on in the lender's mind and by what standards the funding source operates. This is an exceedingly readable and understandable basic work on the serious business of raising capital to start a company, keeping a growing concern solvent, financing the purchase of other companies, issuing securities and international finance, from the point of view of the businessman. Write:

Frederick Fell Publishers, Inc.
386 Park Avenue, South
New York, NY 10016
(212)685-9017

7. The Business Research and Service Institute of the College of Business at Western Michigan University publishes a spiral-bound book entitled *Johnson's Directory of Risk Capital for Small Business* (1976), edited by James M. Johnson, PhD. a member of the finance faculty. This several hundred-page listing and categorizing of venture capital lists 373 venture firms. Write:

Professor James Johnson
Faculty of Finance
Western Michigan University
Kalamazoo, MI 49008

8. *Venture Capital,* by John R. Dominquez (1974), includes a list of venture capital firms by investment limits. Write:

D.C. Heath Company
125 Spring Street
Lexington, MA 02173
(617)862-6650

9. Howard and Company publishes an excellent guide for borrowing capital. It also publishes a twice-monthly newsletter "The Borrower," which is a complete guide to capital sources and techniques. Another helpful source is Howard's *1978 Market for Risk*

Capital Directory and the *Program for Successful Bank Borrowing.* A quarterly newsletter entitled *Going Public* provides information on initial public stock offerings. A special 74-page issue of this profiles all companies that conducted initial public stock offerings in 1978 and 1979. This is not a well-known source of venture capital information—but it is a good source. Write:

> Howard and Company
> 1529 Walnut Street, 5th Floor
> Philadelphia, PA 19102
> (215)603-8030

10. *How to Raise Money to Make Money (The Executive's Guide to Financing a Business)* (1978) is an excellent book that is easy to read and extremely comprehensive. The Institute for Business Planning, a subsidiary of Prentice-Hall, has some excellent material available for entrepreneurs, including a monthly newsletter called *Closely Held Business,* which contains almost every known way to boost profits and generate personal wealth from a closely held business. Business, financial, and tax implications of buying, operating, expanding, selling, or terminating a business are discussed in this newsletter. Write:

> Institute for Business Planning, Inc.
> IBP Plaza
> Englewood Cliffs, NJ 07632
> (201)592-2040

11. A source of international venture capital offers a newsletter, *Finance International,* and several directories on venture capital. One of the directories is called *Guide to Corporate Borrowing: Sources and Rates.* Write:

> Institute for International Research
> 95 Madison Avenue
> New York, NY 10016

12. If you've ever tried to raise capital for a business venture, consider this book, *A Guide to Money Sources and How to Approach Them Successfully,* (1978). The book covers such topics as various sources of loans, preparation of loan requests, government financing, and financial data and analysis as it relates to loans. The book is available from:

> Kephart Communications, Inc.
> 901 Washington Street, Suite 200
> Alexandria, VA 22314

13. The following three books are available from B. Klein Publishing Company:

Business Capital Sources (1977) lists hundreds of firms, banks, mortgage lenders, etc., having capital available for business loans. It also gives many hints on running a business successfully.

How and Where to Get Capital (1977) gives information on over 4,500 organizations and foundations that make capital loans, with requirements for borrowing. It also supplies information on raising capital through venture and risk capital sources.

Small Business Investment Company Directory and Handbook (1977) lists more than 400 small-business investment companies interested in helping various businesses; it also gives the recommended procedures for running a profitable business. Write:

B. Klein Publishing, Inc.
P.O. Box 8503
Coral Springs, FL 33065
(305)752-1708

14. The *Money Market Directory* lists the 4,600 largest institutional funds, their addresses, telephone numbers, amounts of money managed, and the money managers and investment counselors for each. These investors own securities with a market value of $1 trillion, with annual investment purchases and sales of $200 billion. Write:

Money Market Directory
Money Market Directories, Inc.
370 Lexington Avenue
New York, NY 10017

15. The National Association of Small Business Investment Companies (SBICs) offers a free twice-monthly newsletter, The *NASBIC News*, from Washington, DC. This is an excellent source of what is happening within the venture capital industry. The NASBIC Membership Directory is also free. The directory lists names, addresses, telephone numbers, key executives, and a code to distinguish; preferred limit for loans or investments, investment policy, and industry preference.

About 5,000 directories are given away annually. Approximate circulation of the newsletter is 500; it is extremely helpful for keeping up with legislation affecting the venture capital industry. Write:

NASBIC News
512 Washington Building
Washington, DC 20005
(202)638-3411

16. *New England Venture Capital Directory*, by John McKiernan (1978), lists about 100 of the most popular sources of venture capital around the country. Its real strength lies in its commentaries about the venture groups in the northeast. The other half of the book discusses entrepreneurs, business plans, and venture capitalists. Write:

Management Associates
Box 230
Chestnut Hill, MA 02167

17. A 134-page study by the Management Department at Boston College entitled *Venture Capital—A Guidebook for New Enterprise* (1972) is especially good for northeastern USA businesses. Write:

Superintendent of Documents
U.S. Government Printing Office
Re: Committee Print No. 75-292
Washington, DC 20416

18. *Venture Capital in the United States: An Analysis* (1972) is an excellent guide on risk capital and venture management as practiced by large corporations. Write:

Venture Development Corporation
One Washington Street
Wellesley, MA 02181
(617)237-5080

19. Western Association of Venture Capitalists provides a list of members and periodic bulletins on west coast ventures. Write:

Directory of Members
244 California Street
Room 700
San Francisco, CA 94111
(415)781-6897

20. *A Handbook of Business Finance and Capital Sources.* This hard-cover handbook is 460 pages and an excellent reference book on more than 1,000 capital sources. It contains information on financing techniques and instruments for both private and govern-

ment sources of capital. It is a very detailed, well-presented reference book. It would be useful for anyone trying to raise capital.

The author/editor is Dileep Rao, Ph.D., who was also India's number one ranked junior table tennis player. Not only is the author an academician, but also an entrepreneur by way of his self-published book. Write:

Dileep Rao
InterFinance Corporation
305 Foshay Tower
Minneapolis, MN 55402
(612)338-8185

Women
Entrepreneurs

One of the great changes since the 1970s has been the emergence of the woman entrepreneur. The Women's Liberation Movement has liberated many women out of the home and into the work force. Now women understand the value and the importance of the start-your-own-business process, and they are becoming entrepreneurs at a faster and faster rate. In 1978, about 4 percent of all businesses were owned by women. However, more than half of the U.S. wealth is in the hands of females. Consequently, we can anticipate an upward shift in these two numbers as more women become entrepreneurs. Sources geared especially to women are listed in this chapter; but don't disregard the other sources of information throughout the book; they are equally valuable.

COURSES

California

"The Entrepreneurial Woman'
Women's Program/UCLA
Los Angeles, CA 90024
(213)825-3301

Colorado

"How to Manage Your Own Business"
Colorado Economic Development Association
Denver, CO 80204
(303)537-3919

Illinois

"Women Going into Business"
"Building Self-Employment"
YWCA, 37 South Wabash
Chicago, IL 60603
(312)372-6600

ORGANIZATIONS

1. For information about becoming an entrepreneur, contact:

American Women's Economic Development
  Corporation
250 Broadway
New York, NY 10007

2. National Association for Female Executives, Inc., seeks out opportunities, provides information, arranges special offers, and gives information on extending your money power. Write:

NAFE Executive Office
32 East 39th Street
New York, NY 10016

or

NAFE Administrative Office
31 Jeremys Way
Annapolis, MD 21403
(301)267-0630

3. Another helpful organization is:

National Association of
   Women Business Owners
200 P Street, N.W., Suite 511
Washington, DC 20036
(202)338-8966

4. More and more women are becoming entrepreneurs. A special source of help is:

New England Women Business Owners
c/o SBANE
69 Hickory Drive
Waltham, MA 02154
(617)890-9070

5. Another good source of help, which offers a monthly newsletter, *The Enterprising Women,* to 8,000 subscribers is Artemis Enterprises. Write:

New York Association of Women Business
   Owners/Enterprising Women
525 West End Avenue
New York, NY 10024

PUBLICATIONS

1. *Small Business Ideas for Women and How to Get Started,* by Terri Hilton (1978), is a worthwhile book. Write:

Pilot Books
347 Fifth Avenue
New York, NY 10016

2. *The Woman's Guide to Starting a Business,* by Claudia Jessup and Genie Chipps (1978), is a two-part guide concerned with the special problems that women face when establishing a business. Part I consists of basic information on getting started; Part II is a collection of interviews with successful women entrepreneurs. Write:

Holt, Rinehart & Winston
383 Madison Avenue
New York, NY 10017

3. A monthly, 12-page digest of affirmative action news, *Womanpower* is a newsletter designed to keep employers up to date with the laws, government regulations, suits, and court decisions which affect the employment of women of all races, ages, religions, and ethnic origins. Write:

Betsy Hogan Association
222 Rawson Road
Brookline, MA 02146
(617)232-0066

4. *Women Entrepreneurs*

Women Entrepreneurs
P.O. Box 26738
San Francisco, CA 94126
Contact: Sue Easton, (415)474-3000

5. *Women-Owned Businesses,* (1972, 1976) provides basic economic data on businesses owned by all women and on minority firms owned by women. Data include number of firms, gross receipts, and number of paid employees, listed geographically by industry, size of firm, and legal form of organization of firm. Order from:

Superintendent of Documents
U.S. Government Printing Office
Washington, DC 20402

6. A good source of current information is:

The Businesswoman's Letter
P.O. Box 337
Wall Street Station
New York, NY 10005

7. The Entrepreneurial Woman. Without a doubt, the fastest changing pattern in the entrepreneurial movement in the United States is the emergence of the entrepreneurial woman. In the nineteen eighties this will cause a fascinating change in society. The movement will continue to bloom and could eventually erode the last bastion of male dominance. Here are two current sources of information on the female of the species.

Sandra Winston has just authored a new book entitled *The Entrepreneurial Woman,* (Newsweek Books). It's a 740 page easy reader. Sandra is both a marriage counselor and a business consultant. Her book focuses on the people side of the issue with a great understand-

ing of women but with less insight into the process of launching entrepreneurial ventures. One of the chapter titles is "How to be Assertive." It leads the reader to believe she's talking to would-be-entrepreneurs who are now housewives. On the other hand, her writing style is excellent and she does have a good bibliography.

Speaking of bibliographies, I've come across a great one on the subject. The title is *Women in the Economy* and it is an $8\frac{1}{2} \times 11$-inch, forty page bibliography compiled in 1979. It is a source of information on careers and education in business for women. It was prepared as a project by the Empire State College for Business and Economic Information with the assistance of Hauppauge unit of Empire State College.

Empire State College
Long Island Regional Center
Old Westbury State University
   of New York
Box 130
Old Westbury, NY 11568
(516)997-4700

Miscellaneous
Publications

The following publications contain valuable information for the entrepreneur. They cover important facts, from how to manage your business to changes and/or new ideas in the business field.

AACSB Bulletin
760 Office Parkway, Suite 50
St. Louis, MO 63141
(314)872-8481

The *AACSB Bulletin* is a scholarly journal of limited general interest. Topics covered range from enrollment studies and curriculum changes to developing trends in higher education for business administration. Articles address issues of current concern to deans and others interested in the management and administration of collegiate schools of business. Published four times a year; circulation approximately 2,500.

Abacus
Sydney University Press
University of Sydney
New South Wales, Australia 2006
(02)660-4997

The *Abacus* is of very limited general interest. It is, however, well done and well-researched. Somewhat innovative in its publication of exploratory constructive and critical articles on all aspects of accounting. Also covers those phases of the theory and administration of organi-

zations and of economic behavior generally which are related to accounting and finance. Published biannually; circulation about 1,200.

Academy of Management Journal
P.O. Box K3
Mississippi State
MS 39762
(601)325-4944

A thought-provoking journal that publishes original empirical research. Gets into theoretical, conceptual review as well as book review materials. Worth a try for those involved in this field. Published quarterly; circulation about 4,500.

Accountancy
56/66 Goswell Road
London, England EC1 M7AB
01-628-7060

The monthly journal of the Institute of Chartered Accountants in England and Wales. Covers the interests of accountants in practice, commerce, and public service. Encompasses such subjects as accounting, costing, mathematics, statistics, economics, and fiscal policy. A valuable tool for those involved in overseas business. Circulation: about 47,000.

The Accountant's Digest
Germain Publishing Company
P.O. Box 6549
Syracuse, NY 13217
(315)424-1145

A reprint journal, *The Accountant's Digest* presents the substance of articles selected from the leading accounting journals of the English-speaking world in compact form. A useful tool to keep abreast of current changes and/or new ideas in this field. Published quarterly; circulation approximately 1,400.

The Accountant's Magazine
27 Queen Street
Edinburgh, Scotland EH2 1LA
031-225-3687

Official journal of the Institute of Chartered Accountants of Scotland. Articles on management, computers, economics, and related fields are regularly included. Features include the reports of tax cases, book

reviews, and reports on the investment scene. Published monthly; approximate circulation 12,800.

Accounting and Business Research
56/66 Goswell Road
London, England EC1
01-628-7060

This quarterly journal covers a wide range of accounting and business-related topics and has published the works of many of the world's leading academics in these areas. *Accounting and Business Research* attempts to bridge the gap between academic thinking and common practice in industry and commerce and is the journal of the Institute of Chartered Accountants in England and Wales. Circulation: approximately 2,400.

The Accounting Forum
17 Lexington Avenue
New York, NY 10306

The objective of *Accounting Forum* is to gather and bring new and untested accounting concepts to the attention of students, academicians, and practitioners in the field of accounting. A limited-interest journal. Published semiannually; circulation about 1,000.

ACIL Bulletin
1725 K Street, N.W.
Room 301
Washington, DC 20006
(202)659-3766

Reports on developments of interest to members of the American Council of Independent Laboratories and their clients. Published quarterly; circulation about 3,000.

Administration and Society
Sage Publications, Inc.
275 South Beverly Drive
Beverly Hills, CA 90212

This quarterly journal publishes empirically oriented research reports as well as theoretically specific articles the editors believe might contribute to the advancement of understanding in the fields of human service. Of interest are studies that analyze the effects of the introduction of administrative strategies.

Administrative Management
51 Madison Avenue
New York, NY 10010
(212)689-4411

An informative, well-done systems magazine of value and interest to administrative executives. Published monthly; circulation approximately 53,000.

Administrative Science Quarterly
Cornell University
Graduate School of Business & Public Administration
Ithaca, NY 14853
(607)256-5117

This quarterly publication is a multidisciplinary journal designed to be accessible to students of social science at all levels. Overly technical language is explained and emphasis is placed on integrating theory and data. New books in all aspects of organizational behavior are reviewed and an index of each volume year appears in the December issue. Circulation: about 5,000.

AIIE Transactions
25 Technology Park/Atlanta
Norcross, GA 30092
(404)449-0460

An industrial engineering research and development publication. The journal attempts to foster an exchange of new developments and to keep the industrial and systems engineers up to date. Published quarterly by the American Institute of Industrial Engineers. Circulation: approximately, 4,100.

Akron Business and Economic Review
University of Akron
302 East Buchtel Avenue
Akron, OH 44325
(216)375-7045

An excellent professional journal combining academic inquiry and informed practice. Commentary on contemporary problems, applied research, and the results of research in all areas of business and economics. Circulation: approximately 2,400.

American Legion Magazine
P.O. Box 1954
Indianapolis, IN 46206
(317)635-8411

A monthly magazine published by the well-known veterans' organization, the American Legion. Widely circulated and mainly of value to those interested in U.S. military history. Circulation: approximately 2,500,000.

The Appraisal Journal
430 North Michigan Avenue
Chicago, IL 60611
(312)440-8174

A highly technical journal on appraising and real estate economics. Published quarterly by the American Institute of Real Estate Appraisers, this is a good magazine of limited interest. Circulation: about 15,000.

Arizona Business Industry
2823 North 48th Street
Phoenix, AZ 85008
(602)955-3411

A monthly magazine of interest to those residing or doing business in the state of Arizona—or to those contemplating either in the future. Presents feature articles, business news, new products, plus other regular monthly features. Circulation: approximately 5,000.

Armed Forces Comptroller
American Society of Military Comptrollers
P.O. Box 91
Mt. Vernon, VA 22121
(703)780-6164

A special-interest magazine of value primarily to those in the military and civilian employ associated with resource management at the governmental level. Published quarterly; circulation about 5,000.

Atlanta Economic Review
College of Business Administration
Georgia State University
Atlanta, GA 30303
(404)658-4253

A special-interest bimonthly review providing coverage of new trends and applications-oriented research in many aspects of business, economics, and associated sciences. Articles are generally well researched and clearly presented. Contributors range from small-business owners and scholars to top-level executives and other professionals. Circulation: approximately 10,000.

Atlanta Magazine
1104 Commerce Building
Atlanta, Ga 30303
(404)522-6741

A monthly city magazine that primarily serves a high demographic readership in the five counties that constitute metropolitan Atlanta. It addresses itself to politics, cultural trends, personalities of note, business, and social affairs. This fun magazine provides interesting browsing. Circulation: approximately 25,000.

The Banker
Bracken House, Common Street
London, England EC4 P4 B4
01-248-8000

A noteworthy little magazine, not of any particular general interest but informative for bankers and economists and those with a particular interest in international banking. About 150 pages per issue. Published monthly.

Banker's Monthly
601 Skokie Boulevard
Northbrook, IL 60662
(312)498-2580

A well-prepared magazine formerly connected with Rand McNally & Co., *Bankers Magazine* reviews banking thoughts, techniques, and ideas. Published every two months.

Banking
350 Broadway
New York, NY 10013
(212)966-7700

Banking is the monthly journal of the American Bankers Association, the trade journal of the commercial banking business (not mutual savings banks or savings and loan associations). *Banking* covers lending, trust, marketing, operations and automation, money and

market investment, as well as other subjects of interest to commercial bankers. Circulation: about 41,000.

Bay State Business World
734 Washington Street
Norwood, MA 02062
(617)762-7771

Publishes business news exclusively, with emphasis on manufacturing industries and small businesses. It offers a widely read and practical editorial comment on small business each month. The editorial department succeeds rather well in locating and featuring news of firms or products that will have impact on the commercial picture in Massachusetts. Published weekly; circulation about 6,500.

Bibliography of Publications of University
Business and Economic Research
Bureau of Business Research
West Virginia University
Morgantown, WV 26506
(304)293-5837

This yearly publication offers access to the latest research published by university business and research organizations. Many works listed—particularly monographs and working papers—are not indexed elsewhere. Contents of issues listed by subject, institution, author, and title. Back issues available. Circulation: approximately 1,200.

Boardroom Reports
500 Fifth Avenue
New York, NY 10036
(212)354-0005

A crisply written bimonthly publication which digests 300 business magazines and provides trends to subscribers ranging from top corporate executives to owners of small and medium-sized businesses. Mr. Martin Edelsta is the publisher and it is one of the most useful and widely read periodicals of interest to small business. Circulation: about 100,000.

British Journal of Industrial Relations
London School of Economics, Aldwych
London, England WC2AE

Carries original articles by academics and other experts. Some of the fields covered include psychological, economic, sociological, and political studies of management and labor in Britain and overseas. Book reviews and a chronicle of daily events and statistics regarding industrial relations in Britain are also included. Published three times a year; circulation about 3,000.

> *Bulletin of Public Affairs Information Service*
> 11 West 40th Street
> New York, NY 10018
> (212)736-6629

A selective subject list of the latest books, pamphlets, and government publications, this bimonthly journal also publishes reports of public and private agencies and periodical articles relating to economic and social conditions. Also covers public administration and business. Circulation: about 3,600.

> *Burroughs Clearing House*
> P.O. Box 418
> Detroit, MI 48232
> (313)972-7932

A monthly trade magazine serving the financial industry, *Burroughs Clearing House* is circulated to officers in banks, savings and loan associations, credit unions, and related financial services institutions. It is designed to help administrative management in the areas of operations, personnel development, credit administration, investment, and marketing, and is circulated throughout the free world. Circulation: about 63,000.

> *Business Horizons*
> Indiana University, School of Business
> Bloomington, IN 47401
> (812)337-5507

This academic journal publishes articles that are practical, rather than theoretical. Of considerable value to entrepreneurs. Published bimonthly; approximate circulation, 5,500.

> *Business Law Review*
> Bureau of Business Research
> West Virginia University
> Morgantown, WV 26506
> (304)293-5837

The official biannual journal of the National Association of Business Law Teachers, Inc., the review publishes scholarly research and writing in business law and other disciplines that apply business law as a collateral topic. Circulation: approximately 300.

The Business Lawyer
1155 East 60th Street
Chicago, IL 60637
(312)947-3860

A professional journal that touches on substantive and interpretive subjects in business law; deserving of attention from those in the field. Published quarterly; circulation: about 45,000.

Business Life
2023—2 Ave., S.E.
Calgary, Alb., Canada T2E 6K1
(403)273-8008

A monthly magazine presenting comprehensive coverage of the business scene in Western Canada. Emphasis is on construction and industry. Thorough regional reports on large and small centers showing outstanding growth and development. Circulation: about 35,000.

Business and Society
Roosevelt University
430 South Michigan Avenue
Chicago, IL 60605
(312)341-3822

An interdisciplinary biannual journal that publishes articles in areas of general interest to academicians and the business community. Articles with specific research in highly specialized fields are ordinarily not accepted. Circulation: about 2,000.

Business Week
1221 Avenue of the Americas
New York, NY 10020
(212)997-1221

Business Week is the Papa Bear magazine for readers with management responsibilities in business. It reports on and analyzes developments of significance to business and to the economy. Its coverage is worldwide and its contents of advantage to almost anyone concerned with the business world. Published weekly; approximate circulation of 765,000.

California Business
1060 Crenshaw Boulevard
Los Angeles, CA 90019
(213)937-1714

This biweekly newspaper features articles on business, finance, and investing. Also covers governmental actions relating to business regulations and restrictions. Circulation: about 42,000.

CAMagazine
250 Bloor Street East
Toronto, Ont., Canada M4W1G5
(416)962-1242

One of Canada's leading monthly magazines for professional accountants and financial managers. Major articles cover the broad range of accounting, auditing, and financial management topics of current concern. It is published by the Canadian Institute of Chartered Accountants. Circulation: approximately 40,000.

Canadian Business
59 Front Street East
Toronto, Ont., Canada M5E IR5
(416)364-4266

A good general monthly magazine reporting on the Canadian business scene. The editors take special interest in stories on innovation and entrepreneurship, and there's a regular back-of-the-book section devoted to small business. Approximate circulation: 53,000.

Canadian Business Review
Suite 100, 25 McArthur Road
Ottawa, Ont., Canada K1L 6R3
(613)746-1261

A quarterly business magazine put out by the Conference Board in Canada. Features articles on the Board's research and conference activities and articles by those in business, government, and educational institutions. Approximate circulation: 10,000.

Central New York Business Review
86 Maple Avenue
New City, NY 10956
(914)638-1414

This interesting little journal furnishes regional business and economic news for the businessperson in central New York communities. Approximate circulation: 10,000.

Challenge (The Magazine of Economic Affairs)
M.E. Sharpe, Inc.
901 N. Broadway
White Plains, NY 10603
(914)428-8700

A magazine that concerns itself with gathering the insights of some of the best-known economists in an attempt to provide a simply written, nontechnical source of information and opinion on current major economical issues. Published six times a year; circulation of about 8,000.

C L U Journal
P.O. Box 59
Bryn Mawr, PA 19101
(215)525-9500

A quarterly journal of note for those interested or involved in the life insurance business. CLU publishes articles that are original and focus on the nonselling problems of the life insurance business. The articles, in general, evidence research and have properly authenticated facts. Approximate circulation: 36,000.

Commercial and Financial Chronicle
120 Broadway, Suite 1515
New York, NY 10005
(800)225-4585

Lists over 4,000 stocks every week, including daily high, low, and closing prices. Also contains various weekly volume trading reports in addition to *Wall Street Report* summaries, Eliot Janeway articles, and more. A tool for professional investors, brokers, and bankers. Approximate circulation: 6,000.

The Commercial Record
750 Old Main Street
Rocky Hill, CT 06067
(203)563-3796

A business weekly containing a listing of real estate sales, mortgages, liens and attachments, foreclosures, bankruptcies, building permits, projects out for bids, new corporations, and trade names. Source of economic trends, business growth, credit information, and sales leads. Approximate circulation: 12,500.

Contents of Current Legal Periodicals
1105 N. Market St.
P.O. Box 552
Wilmington, DE 19899
(302)652-5636

A monthly publication that covers more than 300 legal periodicals. The contents page of every periodical covered is reproduced, there is a table of contents, and all articles, case notes, etc. are indexed by field of law. Of interest to those who do not wish to miss current legal articles.

Corporate Financing Week
488 Madison Avenue
New York, NY 10020
(212)832-8888

This magazine, published weekly by Institutional Investor Systems, is a valuable tool for commercial and investment bankers, corporate financial executives, and the like. It covers long-term financing, bank financing, money market trends, innovative financing, etc.

Cost and Management
154 Main Street East
Hamilton, Ont., Canada
(416)525-4100

The official publication of the Society of Management accountants, this is a limited-interest, albeit a good little bimonthly magazine. Approximate circulation: 25,000.

The CPA Journal
600 Third Avenue
New York, NY 10016
(212)661-2020

A professional magazine distributed monthly through U.S. and to some foreign countries with about 100 pages per issue. Of value chiefly to practicing accountants but also of interest to business attorneys and academic accountants. Approximate circulation: 34,000.

Credit and Financial Management Magazine
475 Park Avenue South
New York, NY 10016
(212)725-1700

A monthly magazine for business executives whose responsibilities include the extension of credit from one business to another. Covers business credit, corporate finance, and related areas. Special issues: insurance for business, new trends in finance, construction, and legislation. Approximate circulation: 44,000.

Credit Magazine
1000 16th Street, N.W.
Suite 601
Washington, DC 20036
(202)638-1340

Published bimonthly for persons professionally involved with consumer finance in areas such as direct cash lending, sales finance, installment and industrial banking, revolving credit, and credit insurance. Approximate circulation: 20,000.

Datamation
1801 S. La Crenega Boulevard
Los Angeles, CA 90035
(213)559-5111

A monthly computer trade magazine, one of the better ones, presenting articles and news on many aspects of the industry. Departments include coverage of the latest software and hardware, book and periodical reviews. Also carries a forward-reaching section of news-to-come. Approximate circulation: 150,000.

Decision Sciences
University Plaza
Atlanta, GA 30303
(404)658-4000

The quarterly journal of the American Institute of Decision Sciences and is a qualitative research-oriented academic journal. Approximate circulation: 4,000.

Defense Systems Management Review
Defense Systems Management College
Building 204
Fort Belvoir, VA 22061
(703)664-2817

A quarterly publication designed to disseminate program management information of fundamental importance aimed at the program management community. Not useful for the small-business owner. Approximate circulation: 7,000.

> *Delaware Today Magazine*
> 2401 Pennsylvania Avenue
> Wilmington, DE 19806
> (302)655-1571

A monthly regional magazine about Delaware, including news and information of business, commerce, and the professions. Approximate circulation: 8,000.

> *The Detroiter Business News*
> Greater Detroit Chamber
> 150 Michigan Avenue
> Detroit, MI 48226
> (313)964-4000

Covers chamber of commerce activities and business news of southeast Michigan. Also publishes an annual directory with classified and alphabetical listings of all current chamber members. Published monthly; circulation approximately 8,000.

> *Directors and Boards*
> Box 36
> McLean, VA 22101
> (703)534-7771

The semischolarly quarterly journal of corporate action. In general, articles examine legal, social, political, and other developments worldwide from the perspective of the evolving responsibilities of corporate boards with a view toward improving board performance. Circulation: about 3,000.

> *Downtown Ideas Exchange*
> 270 Madison Avenue, Suite 1505
> New York, NY 10016
> (212)889-5666

A semimonthly newsletter of data on subjects such as downtown malls, parking, traffic, transit preservation, etc. *Downtown Ideas Exchange* is circulated to individuals, organizations, institutions, and governments interested in revitalizing the cores of cities. Circulation figures unavailable.

Downtown Promotion Reporter
270 Madison Avenue, Suite 1505
New York, NY 10016
(212)889-5666

This monthly newsletter reports on marketing concepts, market research, retailing, advertising approaches, public relations techniques, budgeting, and organizing for action. It also concentrates on ways to improve downtown's image through events and institutional approaches. Circulation figures unavailable.

Dun's Review
666 Fifth Avenue, 9th Floor
New York, NY 10019
(212)489-2200

One of the most popular and successful business and financial publications, is directed at top-level executives. Interesting reading for those with concerns in the business world. Published monthly; circulation about 225,000.

Electronic News
7 East 12th Street
New York, NY 10003
(212)741-4260

A weekly newspaper supplying input to aid in decision making in all aspects of the electronics industry. Every Monday, its news columns report on the significant technical and business events of the preceding week in the electronics and computer markets. Approximate circulation: 72,000.

The Engineering Economist
25 Technology Park/Atlanta
Norcross, GA 30092
(404)449-0460

This quarterly journal concerns itself with the problems of capital investment. Of interest to those who must pay attention to the engineering economy. Approximate circulation: 1,500.

Estate Planning
125 East 56th Street
New York, NY 10022
(212)421-6740

A bimonthly journal devoted exclusively to the tax and non-tax aspects of estate planning. Articles suggest ways of accomplishing a client's objectives at lowest tax cost. Approximate circulation: 9,000.

> *Euromoney*
> 20 Tudor Street
> London, England EC4Y OJ5
> 353-0841 (606-12-34)

The monthly journal of the international money and bond markets. It contains articles by experts together with interviews, surveys, and the commentary of journalists. Circulation: about 8,000.

> *Finance Magazine*
> 8 West 40th Street
> New York, NY 10018
> (212)221-7900

A monthly magazine of money and banking, *Finance* serves an audience of executives with an editorial focus on the problems faced by its readers. Circulation: about 45,000.

> *Financial Management*
> Amos Tuck School of Business Administration
> Dartmouth College
> Hanover, NH 03755
> (603)646-2002

A vehicle for focusing the attention of the academic community on problems that confront financial managers at the level of the firm. Serves both executives and academicians with common interests in financial analysis and decision making. Published quarterly; circulation about 2,000.

> *Florida Trend*
> 13th Street & 8th Avenue
> P.O. Box 2350
> Tampa, FL 33601
> (813)247-5411

Publishes business and financial news and trends in Florida for business executives and others with vested interests in the state. Published monthly; circulation approximately 35,000.

> *Focus*
> 1015 Chestnut Street
> Philadelphia, PA 19107
> (215)925-8545

This business newsweekly pinpoints Philadelphia-area business trends and local sales opportunities through listings such as new business openings, bid opportunities, contract awards, personnel assignments, and local economic figures. Circulation: approximately 13,000.

Fortune Magazine
Time and Life Building
Rockefeller Center
New York, NY 10020
(212)586-1212

A biweekly magazine about and for leaders in business, finance, and government. Its editorial mission is to examine, explain, and broaden the views of business enterprise; *Fortune* succeeds well in this endeavor. Approximate circulation: 625,000.

Fur Age Weekly
127 West 30th Street
New York, NY 10001
(212)239-4983

Published since 1918, *Fur Age Weekly* covers news and fashions in the fur industry. Published weekly; approximate circulation: 5,000.

Greater Minneapolis Magazine
6601 West 78th Street
Minneapolis, MN 55435
(612)941-4800

A bimonthly magazine for the twin cities metropolitan area. Covers business and industry, with frequent special reports on specific industries such as trucking, real estate, and advertising. Approximate circulation: 5,000.

Harvard Business Review
Soldiers Field
Boston, MA 02163
(617)495-6800

This prestigious little bimonthly magazine is an educational arm of the Harvard Business School. The *Harvard Business Review* aims to develop a keener, more responsible sense of leadership among policy-making businesspeople and to increase the understanding of concepts and methods of professional management. Approximate circulation: 180,000.

Houston Business Journal
5314 Bingle Road
Houston, TX 77092
(713)688-8811

This weekly journal reports on the growth and new ideas relating to business in the seven-county Houston–Galveston statistical area. The publication covers many aspects of the area business. Circulation: about 15,000.

Houston Magazine
1100 Milam, 25th Floor
Houston, TX 77002
(713)651-1313

The monthly Houston Chamber of Commerce magazine, mainly distributed to members, though there is some newsstand distribution. Editorial content is directed toward the business community but covers nonbusiness aspects of that city as well. Circulation: about 15,000.

Houston Public Companies
5314 Bingle Road
Houston, TX, 77092
(713)688-8811

An annual guide to all Houston-based public companies, with complete listings on 138 firms. Additional firms included in appendix. Provides stock exchange information, offices and directors, financial data, background, and recent developments. Circulation: about 3,000.

Human Resource Management
Graduate School of Business Administration
University of Michigan
Ann Arbor, MI 48109
(313)763-0121

This is a quarterly semiacademic journal which contains no advertising and is based upon the belief that effective use of human resources is the key to success in any organization. Materials are chosen from research reports that are currently useful or that the editors think will be of future practical interest. Circulation: approximately 9,000.

Industrial Engineering
25 Technology Park/Atlanta
Norcross, GA 30092
(404)449-0460

Industrial Engineering attempts to alert its readers to developments in procedures and equipment throughout the profession of industrial engineering. It succeeds rather well in providing specific guidelines for the application of both new and old procedures or equipment to the problems in manufacturing, service industries, and government. Published monthly; circulation about 32,000.

Industrial and Labor Relations Review
Cornell University
Ithaca, NY 14853
(607)256-3295

An interdisciplinary quarterly journal containing articles exploring major aspects of industrial relations, such as labor law, manpower, public employment, etc. Also contains a bibliography listing current books as well as book reviews and reports of research currently in progress at major universities, government agencies, and research institutes. Approximate circulation: 4,500.

Industrial Marketing Management
52 Vanderbilt Avenue
New York, NY 10017
(212)986-5050

A bimonthly written for the decision-makers dealing with problems common to all industrial marketing managers. Each issue contains a unique blend of industry case studies, analytical methods, and information on the kinds of problems faced by these executives.

Industrial Relations
Institute of Industrial Relations
University of California
Berkeley, CA 94720
(415)642-5452

A source of ideas and information on various aspects of the employment relationship. This interdisciplinary journal, published three times a year, draws from the work of a variety of scholars and practitioners.

Industrial Relations Journal
Mercury House, Waterloo Road
London, England S61 8UL
01-928-3388

The quarterly *Industrial Relations Journal* covers industrial relations defined in a broad way, including styles of managerial behavior, in-

dustrial sociology, psychology, and labor economics. It studies the international, national, regional, and local labor markets. Approximate circulation: 2,500.

Industrial Research Magazine
222 South Riverside Plaza
Chicago, IL 60606
(312)648-5820

A monthly international journal which serves the applied science industry, including industrial, government, university, and independent laboratories, primarily in the physical sciences and engineering. Approximate circulation: 95,000.

Industry Week
1111 Chester Avenue
Cleveland, OH 44114
(216)696-7000

An excellent biweekly magazine providing analytical news coverage and problem-solving feature coverage to middle and upper management in manufacturing and related fields. Reaches administration, sales, marketing, engineering, production, and financial management in all plants having 100 or more employees. Circulation: about 250,000.

Institutional Investor
488 Madison Avenue
New York, NY 10023
(212)832-8888

Provides a monthly in-depth look at money management, including pensions, real estate, research, investment banking, corporate financing, trading, and international finance. In short, deals with the world of professional money. Circulation: about 34,000.

The Internal Auditor
249 Maitland Avenue
Altamonte Springs, FL 32701
(305)830-7600

A biannual journal for those in the internal auditing profession as well as business managers. Articles are technical in nature, dealing with the various aspects of internal control, operational and managerial auditing. Circulation: approximately 18,000.

The International Executive
64 Ferndale Drive
Hastings-on-Hudson, NY 10706
(914)478-0193

A reading service for international business. Books and articles useful for international business are listed in a classified annotated bibliographic section. The most significant items are described in short summaries, typically around 400 words. Published three times a year; circulation approximately 500.

International Journal of Social Economics
198/200 Keighley Road, Bradford
West Yorkshire, England BD9 4JQ
43823

A digest of reports on the major aspects in the area of social economics. This journal provides an international forum for the discussion of the economic implications of social theories and policies. Published three times a year; circulation approximately 600.

International Management
McGraw-Hill House
Shoppenhangers Road
Maidenhead, Berkshire
England SL6 2QL
Maidenhead 23431

Published monthly in four languages—English, Spanish, Arabic, and Farsi—and is written for directors and senior executives of major industrial, commercial, and financial firms outside North America. Articles concentrate on management systems, philosophies and styles of outstanding companies and their executives. Approximate circulation: 140,000.

International Review of Administrative Sciences
25 rue de la Charité
B1040 Brussels, Belgium

Circulated quarterly in 105 countries, this international journal aims at formulating and disseminating the general principles of public administration, comparing the experience of different countries in this field. Also studies adequate methods for the improvement of administrative science and practice. Circulation figures unavailable.

International Studies of Management & Organization
M. E. Sharpe, Inc.
901 North Broadway
White Plains, NY 10603
(914)428-8700

Publishes translations drawn from scholarly journals and books published throughout the world. A quarterly journal; approximate circulation of 365.

Investment Dealers' Digest
150 Broadway
New York, NY 10038
(212)227-1200

A professional newsweekly magazine of finance serving investment and commercial bankers and institutional and other investors. Approximate circulation: 5,000.

Journal of Accounting Research
Graduate School of Business
University of Chicago
5836 South Greenwood Avenue
Chicago, IL 60637
(312)753-4248

Reports on new developments in accounting occasioned by similarly new developments in management science. Not of particular value to the small-business owner or entrepreneur. Published three times a year; approximate circulation 2,500.

Journal of Advertising
Henry W. Grady School of Journalism
   and Mass Communication
University of Georgia
Athens, GA 30602
(404)542-1704

The *Journal of Advertising,* published quarterly, encourages the discovery and development of valid theory and relevant facts regarding the psychological and philosophical aspects of communication as well as the relationship between these and other components of the advertising process. Approximate circulation: 1,000.

Journal of Advertising Research
3 East 54th Street
New York, NY 10022
(212)751-5656

An open-forum journal that solicits original papers. Reports of findings are favored over theoretical discussion, and publication in the journal implies no endorsement of the writer's purpose, methods, or views by the Advertising Research Foundation. An interesting and fairly open little magazine. Approximate circulation: 4,500.

The Journal of Applied Behavioral Science
P.O. Box 9155, Rosslyn Station
Arlington, VA 22209
(703)527-1500

A quarterly journal that publishes articles and case studies that analyze the interplay of theory, practice, and values in the domain of planned change. Emphasis on strategies of social intervention, small-group theory, innovations in organization development, and application of social science to public policy. Approximate circulation: 6,000.

Journal of Business
Graduate School of Business
University of Chicago
5836 Greenwood Avenue
Chicago, IL 60637
(312)753-3660

This journal is too academic to be of value to the small-business owner or entrepreneur. Published quarterly; approximate circulation 4,500.

Journal of Business Administration
Faculty of Commerce and Business Administration
University of British Columbia
Vancouver, B.C., Canada V6T 1W5
604-228-2144

Publishes biannual articles on studies in areas of business. Approximate circulation: 400.

Journal of Business Research
College of Business Administration
University of South Carolina
Columbia, SC 29208
(803)777-6074

Prints manuscripts testing theory or studying environments within actual business-related settings. Published quarterly; circulation about 800.

Journal of Consumer Affairs
Stanley Hall, University of Missouri
Columbia, MO 65201
(314)882-4450

A multidisciplinary journal dealing with topics and issues of consumer education, protection, and behavior. Published biannually; approximate circulation 3,500.

Journal of Consumer Research
University of Illinois
Chicago Circle, Box 6905
Chicago, IL 60680
(312)996-5312

A quarterly interdisciplinary journal that publishes articles on consumer behavior from the various social sciences. Includes articles directly or closely related to the purchase, consumption, or usage of goods and services. Circulation about 3,800.

Journal of Contemporary Business
Graduate School of Business Administration
University of Washington
Seattle, WA 98195
(206)543-4598

Examines problems of imminent concern to business from both academic and professional viewpoints. Most articles are solicited from recognized scholars and professional specialists, with commentaries from executives involved in the problem or issue under scrutiny. Published quarterly; circulation about 2,500.

The Journal of Corporate Taxation
870 Seventh Avenue
New York, NY 10019
(212)977-7406

In-depth analysis of important developments, practical guidance, and a general review of corporation tax law. Published quarterly; approximate circulation 5,000.

Journal of Economics and Business
Temple University School of
   Business Administration
Philadelphia, PA 19122
(215)787-8101

Emphasizes general business and management with specialization in
economics and finance. Published three times a year; approximate
circulation 3,000.

Journal of International Business Studies
Rutgers University—GSBA
92 New Street
Newark, NJ 07102
(201)648-5074

A scholarly journal that publishes articles in the fields of international
or comparative business. These articles represent basic or applied
research, conceptual contributions, or important contributions to
educational methodology. Published three times a year; circulation
about 1,200.

Journal of Management Studies
Basil Blackwell & Mott, Ltd.
5 Alfred Street
Oxford OX1 4HB, England

A scholarly journal combining high academic standards with coverage
of a wide range of disciplines and subject areas. Many contributors are
actual practitioners in various areas of management. Published three
times a year; approximate circulation 1,400.

Journal of Retailing
New York University
Institute of Retail Management
New York, NY 10003
(212)598-2287

This wide-ranging journal fulfills two basic needs in the field of retailing: to serve as a medium for the exchange of information on new
and evolving concepts by retail practitioners and researchers; and to
aid in disseminating information on future management opportunities and techniques presently being tested in the marketplace.

Often includes research articles, book reviews, abstract of pertinent magazine articles, and summaries of recent Ph.D. dissertations. Also a "Special Issue" section reserved for articles on such subjects as store image of retailing in the next ten years. Published quarterly; circulation about 3,000.

Journal of Risk and Insurance
One State Farm Plaza
Bloomington, IL 61701
(309)662-2614

A scholarly quarterly journal reserved primarily for articles on theory and practice relevant to insurance and related areas. Articles cover both research that expands the knowledge of risk and insurance and method and procedures related to risk managers and various segments of the insurance business. A forum for manuscripts devoted to theoretical concepts pertinent to risk and insurance, book reviews, and communications. Approximate circulation: 2,100.

Journal of Systems Management
24587 Bagley Road
Cleveland, OH 44138
(216)243-6900

A unique monthly publication that seeks to fulfill the journalistic needs of the business systems community. Geared toward reporting, interpreting, and forecasting developments and techniques in administrative planning and systems, both automated and nonautomated. Publishes original manuscripts by authorities in the business systems discipline. Circulation: about 12,000.

Kiplinger California Letter
1729 H Street, N.W.
Washington, DC 20006
(202)298-6400

A monthly newsletter for the California businessperson, *Kiplinger California Letter* is concerned with developments, at the federal and state levels, that affect California's business and economic climates. Reports on federal and state legislation, government regulations, and business-related trends in California communities. Circulation: approximately 18,000.

Lloyd's Bank Review
71 Lombard Street
London, England EC3P 3BS
01-626 1500

Covers a wide range of topics dealing both with British and international major economic problems. Articles stimulate discussion and encourage full inquiry into the subjects presented. Recent articles have included discussions of debt problems of developing countries, the future of European monetary union, lessons from the oil crisis, the debate between Keynesians and monetarists, the effect of President Carter's energy plans on the European community's energy policy, etc. Published quarterly; approximate circulation 50,000.

Long Island Business Review
303 Sunnyside Boulevard
Plainview, NY 11803
(516)681-8000

A weekly newspaper geared toward and read by the top and middle management of the Long Island business area. Circulation about 8,000.

Manage
2210 Arbor Boulevard
Dayton, OH 45439
(513)294-0421

An educational magazine published by the National Management Association for members. Content directed toward the advancement of management status and the encouragement of the free enterprise system. Material is management-oriented and reflects a balance of appeal to first-line supervision, middle management and scientific/technical/professional management. Published six times a year; circulation approximately 55,500.

Management Accounting
63 Portland Place
London, England WIN 4AB
01-637 2311

A monthly professional journal oriented toward accountants and managers in industry and commerce. The official journal of the Institute of Cost and Management Accountants. Approximate circulation: 50,000.

Management Accounting
919 Third Avenue
New York, NY 10022
(212)754-9718

A monthly journal designed to keep professional management accountants current and topical in their profession. Offers a compen-

dium of information on all facets of accounting. Subscriptions restricted to members of the National Association of Accountants and libraries. Approximate circulation: 86,000

Management Contents
P.O. Box 1054
Skokie, IL 60076
(312)982-7380

A biweekly magazine created for individuals in business, consulting firms, educational institutions, government agencies or bureaus, and libraries. Presents an economical approach to current information on a variety of business and management topics. Each issue contains the tables of contents of the latest issues of the finest business/management periodicals available, familiarizing readers with what is new in the field and related areas and with new publications. Circulation: approximately 50,000.

Management Focus
Peat, Marwick, Mitchell & Co.
345 Park Avenue
New York, NY 10022
(212)758-9700

A bimonthly journal widely distributed in the business and academic worlds. Content focuses on management topics of interest to executives in business, industry, government and nonprofit organizations. Distributed, upon request, to college and university libraries and faculty members. Circulation: about 45,000.

Management Research
School of Business Administration
Room 357
University of Massachusetts
Amherst, MA 01002
(413)545-2004

Management Research is the official publication of the School of Business Administration, University of Massachusetts at Amherst. It is a comprehensive research and reference journal. Published bimonthly; circulation about several thousand.

Management Services in Government
Civil Service Department
15 Whitehall
London, England SW1A 2AZ
01-273 3780

Covers a wide range of topics in the management services and personnel management fields. Of special interest to those connected with operation and management, computers, operational research and training, and to line managers. All articles are related to situations in the central government of the United Kingdom. Published quarterly; approximate circulation about 6,500.

Marketing
Regent House
54-62 Regent Street
London, England W1A4Y5
01-439 4242, ext. 20

The journal of the Institute of Marketing, this monthly publication provides informative and practical articles of use to marketing directors and executives. Utilizes in-depth case studies as well as a regular series of indexes which provide a valuable reference source to practitioners in the marketing field. Approximate circulation: 21,000.

Marketing Executive's Digest
466 Central Ave. Suite 50
Northfield, Ill. 60093
(312)446-0709

An exclusive monthly business information newsletter for marketing, sales and advertising executives. Scans approximately 300 business publications to ascertain important and interesting news items. These are then summarized into about 70 succinct digests. Also offered is a bimonthly supplement, "Report on Reports," which summarizes market studies from private and government sources. Circulation about 600.

Market Research Society Yearbook
15 Belgrave Square
London, England SW1X 8PF
01-235 4709

Contains listings of all full and associate members of the Market Research Society as well as their organizations. Also includes a listing of companies practicing market research in Great Britain which have among their staff someone qualified as a full member of the Society. Also available are various publications such as *Market Research Abstracts,* covering all fields of marketing and advertising research as well as relevant papers in statistics, psychology, and sociology; and *The International Research Directory,* which contains details of over 900 market research organizations related to over 60 countries. Published yearly; circulation about 3,000.

Marketing Times
380 Lexington Ave.
New York, NY 10017
(212)986-9300

A bimonthly journal geared toward sales and marketing executives. Approximate circulation: 25,000.

Massachusetts Business and Economic Report
School of Business Administration, Room 357
University of Massachusetts
Amherst, MA 01002
(413)545-2598

A quarterly publication of the School of Business Administration of the University of Massachusetts at Amherst, this report contains the only econometrics projections for the state of Massachusetts, the *Massachusetts Economic Policy Analysis* model. Also features articles by regional business and political leaders. Approximate circulation: 2,400.

The Media General Financial Weekly
Box 26991
Richmond, VA 23261
(804)649-6586

A weekly compendium of information on the stock market; consists mainly of tables and charts, and updated weekly. Circulation: about 3,000.

Medical Economics
680 Kinderkamack Road
Oradell, NJ 07649
(201)262-3030

The emphasis of this magazine is on business; tells the doctor how to manage the practice, how to handle personal finances, and how to cope with problems in professional life. Major subject content includes medicolegal matters, health legislation, investments, fees, hospital problems, insurance, taxes, cars, and doctor-patient relationships. Published every two weeks; approximate circulation: 165,000.

Mergers and Acquisitions
Box 36
McLean, VA 22101
(703)534-7771

A quarterly journal, thorough in its coverage of the merger/ acquisition, joint venture, and divestiture processes. Covers the economics, business, management, accounting, and legal aspects of these processes and reports details on approximately 1,500 major deals per year. Circulation: about 3,200.

Metro-Newark! Magazine
50 Park Place
Newark, NJ 07102
(201)624-6888

Published bimonthly by the Greater Newark Chamber of Commerce; circulation of about 15,500 includes not only local New Jersey–New York businesspeople but also their national counterparts. Projects metropolitan Newark area's heritage as one of the nation's leading business centers. Covering a wide range of information, the magazine features timely and thought-provoking articles on local and regional issues.

The Milwaukee Journal Consumer Analysis
c/o The Milwaukee Journal
Milwaukee, WI 53201
(414)224-2116

An annual journal that reports on the annual product use study of the Milwaukee Standard Metropolitan Statistical Area. Includes an annual population study with household updates. Approximate circulation: 50,000.

Mini-Micro Systems
5 Kane Industrial Drive
Hudson, MA 01749
(617)562-9305

Every issue features an entire section on minicomputers, microcomputers, microprocessors, and miniperipherals; also includes "Product Profiles," a buyer's reference guide to the latest types of computers and related input/output equipment. Often includes comparison tables and diagrams, as well as a section on conferences and shows. This monthly magazine is aimed at subjects engineers, sophisticated computer end users, data communication planners, and related technical and general management personnel. Approximate circulation: 85,000.

Monograph Series in Finance and Economics
New York University
Graduate School of Business Administration
Center for the Studies of Financial Institutions
90 Trinity Place;
New York, NY 10006
(212)285-6103

Economists' Bookshop
Portugal Street
London, England WC2

This series includes original studies in the fields of economics and finance, presenting and analyzing data on current economic and financial conditions in the United States and other nations. *Monographs* are available either out of New York or England. Published four to six times a year; approximate circulation 4,000.

Mortgage Banker
1125 15th Street, N.W.
Washington, DC 20005
(202)785-8333

A monthly publication serving the entire mortgage industry; provides up-to-date information on economic conditions, legislation, government regulations, market innovations, financing techniques, and internal management of mortgage companies. Published primarily for the mortgage banking industry, and of major interest to mortgage bankers, commercial banks, savings and loans banks, builders, developers, title insurers, appraisers, investors, and related government officials. Approximate circulation: 11,000.

Mountain States Banker
1150 First National Bank Building
Denver, CO 80293
(303)825-5359

The only journal primarily serving the Rocky Mountain States of Colorado, Utah, New Mexico, and Wyoming. Aimed at the upper-level management of the commercial banking industry in these states and includes, among other information, a listing of all state and federal banks. Published monthly; circulation about 1,000.

The National Public Accountant
1717 Pennsylvania Avenue, N.W.
Washington, DC 20006
(202)298-9040

A monthly magazine that is the official publication of the National Society of Public Accountants. Covers a spectrum of up-to-date information valuable to the accountant. Includes monthly features on such items as how regulations affect tax preparers, guides to auditing, surveys concerning the accountant's opinion about government policies, and editorials concerning the accountant's problems. Approximate circulation: 20,000.

National Retail Merchants Association
100 West 31st Street
New York, NY 10001
(212)244-8780

A non-profit corporation representing 35,000 leading department, chain, and specialty stores in the United States, Canada, and 50 other countries, the National Retail Merchants Association offers many services and materials to merchants. These include films, periodicals, newsletters, calendars of seminars and workshops, and other valuable information. Most of this information is available to both members and non-members but on many items, members receive a discount. The corporation has various divisions specializing in specific phases of retail operations. Each division provides information exchange, research facilities and individual services to NRMA members. The combined annual volume of NRMA is $80 billion.

Nebraska Journal of Economics and Business
200 CBA
University of Nebraska–Lincoln
Lincoln, NE 68588
(402)472-2334

A quarterly journal covering economic and business topics of local, national, and international interest. Offers stimulating and readable articles on a wide range of subjects applicable to the needs and demands of both the economist and the member of the more general business community. Approximate circulation: 800.

The New Englander
New England Business
Suite 420
120 Tremont St
Boston, MA 02108
(617)482-7040

Of primary interest to New Englanders, this is a monthly publication of business and public affairs. Its aim is to chronicle the way people

live and work in New England. Subject matter ranges from articles on the success (or failure) of New England firms to the fortunes (or misfortunes) of interesting New Englanders. Traces trends in economic, political, and social issues affecting New England business. Approximate circulation: 15,000.

> *New Jersey Banker*
> P.O. Box 573
> Princeton, NJ 08540
> (609)924-5550

Of primary interest to people involved in the New Jersey banking community. Approximate circulation: 3,000.

> *Optimum*
> 365 Laurier Avenue West, Room 636
> Ottawa, Ont., Canada K1A D55
> (613)996-3255

Printed in both English and French, this quarterly Canadian publication provides a forum in which a wide range of views on management are presented. Purpose is to serve as an aid for the busy executive. Circulation: about 2,000.

> *Organization and Administrative Sciences*
> Comparative Administration Research Institute
> Graduate School of Business
> Kent State University
> Kent, OH 44242
> (216)672-2094

A distinctive monthly journal devoted to research in organization theory and cross-cultural comparative studies. This international publication features full-length intensive studies in almost every issue. Circulation: over 600.

> *Over the Counter (OTC) Review*
> Box 110
> Jenkintown, PA 19046
> (215)887-6313

Over-the-Counter securities comprise the biggest securities market, and the monthly *OTC Review* is devoted exclusively to this market. Provides valuable information on such opportunities as the "special situation," the takeover that can mean profits to shareholders, regardless of market conditions. Includes coverage of acquisitions, new

products, dividends, earnings (with p/e ratios), a monthly review of the OTC market, etc. Approximate circulation: 4,000.

Pensions and Investments
708 Third Avenue
New York, NY 10017
(212)986-5050

Pensions and Investments, published biweekly, has a specific purpose— to assist employers in their management, administration, and investment of pensions and other employee benefit assets. Aimed at corporate financial executives and others responsible for these funds. Circulation: about 27,000.

Personnel Journal
1131 Olympic Boulevard
Santa Monica, CA 90404
(213)451-8724

The material presented in this monthly journal is aimed at the practicing professional person in the fields of personnel management, human resources, compensation, benefits, motivation, workforce planning, and related fields. Approximate circulation: 14,500.

Personnel Management
Mercury House
Waterloo Road
London, England SE1 8UL

The official monthly journal of the Institute of Personnel Management. Provides timely news on various aspects of personnel management, featuring in-depth articles on such subjects as research, new techniques, legislation, and practice in personnel training and industrial relations. Approximate circulation: 27,000.

Personnel Management Abstracts
Graduate School of Business Administration
University of Michigan
Ann Arbor, MI 48109
(313)763-0121

Valuable as a reference guide, this quarterly index lists all the articles from about 70 academic and trade journals dealing with personnel management and organizational behavior. Each listing is categorized by subject, author, and title; subject index includes a brief description of the article's thesis and conclusions and reference information con-

cerning the journal in which it appears. About 60 articles per issue are described at greater length and 15 books that have more intensive treatment of the same subjects are abstracted. The index can be used to locate recent material published in any of about 40 categories (e.g., absenteeism, communication in organizations, compensation, consultants, creativity, employee health and security, equal opportunity, human resources, accounting, etc.). Approximate circulation: 1,500.

Personnel Psychology
Box 6965
College Station
Durham, NC 27708
(919)477-7973

A quarterly magazine for the writer/researcher and the concerned employer in the field of personnel. Publishes manuscripts reporting research methods and results and the application of these results to the solution of personnel problems in business, industry, and government. Also includes critical surveys of current literature concerning the status of knowledge and research on various phases of contemporary personnel psychology (e.g., aspects of training, job and worker analysis, employee relations, morale, etc.). Each issue also contains a section with comments on research methods, findings, and related ideas. Circulation: about 3,000.

Planning Review
c/o Bell PubliCom
1406 Third National Building
Dayton, OH 45402
(513)223-0419

A bimonthly journal dealing with mainly global issues. Articles concentrate on such subjects as long-range planning and business strategy, often including information on behavioral and management sciences, economic and financial planning, and issues that will be important in the 1980s. Approximate circulation: 5,000.

The Practical Accountant
964 Third Avenue
New York, NY 10022
(212)935-9210

Of interest to persons practicing any aspect of accounting, this bimonthly journal is published by the Institute for Continuing Professional Development. Regular features include a wide range of subjects

dealing with problems and solutions in accounting and taxes in everyday practice.

Public Administration
Hamilton House
Mabledon Place
London, England WC1
01-388 0211

A quarterly journal dealing primarily with the administration of public services in the United Kingdom. Also includes articles about other countries and information applicable to public administration regardless of national boundaries. Approximate circulation: 8,000.

Public Administration Review
1225 Connecticut Avenue N.W.
Washington, DC 20036
(202)785-3255

The goal of this informative bimonthly journal is to further the goals of the American Society for Public Administration: "to advance the sciences, processes and art of public administration." The *Public Administration Review* seeks to increase communication and promote understanding among practitioners, teachers, researchers, and students. Circulation: about 21,000.

Public Relations Journal
845 Third Avenue
New York, NY 10022
(212)826-1757

A monthly magazine of interest to public relations practitioners. Content consists of opinion and news concerning public relations and related issues. Circulation: about 12,000.

Real Estate Review
P.O. Box 1019
Manhasset, NY 11030
(516)627-4810

Real Estate Review is a quarterly publication directed at real estate investors, developers, brokers, attorneys, accountants, lenders, and corporate real estate executives. It provides professional reports on current trends in all phases of real estate. Approximate circulation: 15,000.

Research Management
100 Park Avenue
Suite 2209
New York, NY 10017
(212)683-7626

A bimonthly magazine designed to bring new ideas to the field of research and development. Articles concern planning and budgeting, personnel and administration, innovation, project selection and management, organization, communications, science policy, etc. Every issue also carries two special features: "Perspectives," which has reports on the current science and technology policies, "Pertinent Literature," devoted to reviews of the latest books, reports, and other publications in a broad range of management subjects. Approximate circulation: 4,000.

Review of Economics and Literature
211 Littauer Center
Cambridge, MA 02138
(617)495-2113

North-Ho Mand Publishing Company
P.O. Box 211
Amsterdam, The Netherlands

A quarterly economic journal distinguished by its emphasis on empirical research. Articles have a sound theoretical basis, meaningful data, and appropriate statistical methods. Many articles have immediate policy implications. Circulation: about 5,000.

Salesman's Opportunity Magazine
1460 John Hancock Center
875 North Michigan Avenue
Chicago, IL 60611
(312)337-3350

A nationwide monthly magazine aimed at salespeople at all levels of distribution, from the independent salesperson to distributors and agents. Provides information concerning products and lines as well as about companies offering opportunities for mutually profitable affiliations. Each issue includes data about opportunities in various sales fields. Approximate circulation: 180,000.

Society for Advanced Management Journal
S.A.M.
135 West 50th Street
New York, NY 10020
(212)586-8100

A quarterly publication of interest to those seeking advancement in management. Offers practical information, a wealth of solid management sense, exciting ideas, and thought-provoking suggestions for dealing more effectively with every phase of a business career. One special department offers articles to help the new manager get started; another focuses on summaries of timely books to help the manager at any stage. Circulation: about 12,000.

Savings and Loan News
111 E. Wacker Drive
Chicago, IL 60601
(312)644-3100

The editorial objective of this monthly magazine is to assist management and supervisory personnel in all functions and areas of savings and loan associations. Articles help people in this field perform more effectively both in their specific job assignments and as members of a business serving the financial needs of the public. Circulation: about 75,000.

Sloan Management Review
Massachusetts Institute of Technology
50 Memorial Drive E52-062
Cambridge, MA 02139
(617)253-7170

Serves as a link between the academic and the business world; the professional management journal of the Alfred P. Sloan School of Management at the Massachusetts Institute of Technology. Principle goal is the exchange of information between the academic and business communities. Articles are selected to inform readers of analytical, application-oriented approaches to managerial problems. Published three times a year; approximate circulation 10,000.

The South Magazine
P.O. Box 2350
Tampa, FL 33601
(813)247-5411

A monthly journal specifically edited to meet the informational needs and interests of Southern business and community leaders and decision-makers. Circulation: about 50,000.

The Southern Banker
6364 Warren Drive
Norcross, GA 30093
(404)448-1011

A monthly regional trade journal directed toward commercial bankers. Each issue covers a broad range of topics and there are several regular departments under such headings as "Equipment and Supply News," "State News," etc. Subject matter treats the activities of banks and bankers within a twelve-state region of the Southeastern United States. Circulation: approximately 4,300.

Southern California Business
404 South Bixel
Los Angeles, CA 90017
(213)629-0653

A weekly business newspaper that offers up-to-date coverage of business affairs in the southern California area. The official publication of the Los Angeles Area Chamber of Commerce. Approximate circulation: 16,000.

State Government News
Box 11010
Lexington, KY 40578
(606)252-2291

Each issue of this monthly magazine highlights developments within state governments. Other information includes a summary of each state's legislative session. Circulation: about 12,000.

Success Unlimited
6355 Broadway
Chicago, IL 60660
(312)973-7650

A monthly magazine that attempts to guide motivated businesspeople and help them set and achieve new goals. Articles are often written by famous personalities who have obviously succeeded, or not-so-famous people who have made their million(s) quietly. Several regular sections include commentaries by people like W. Clement Stone and Paul Harvey; also a book review section. Circulation: approximately 186,500.

Survey of Business Attitudes
The Conference Board of Canada
25 McArthur Road, Suite 100
Ottawa, Ont., Canada, K1L 6R3
(613)746-1216

Aimed primarily at Canadian businesspeople, this quarterly report contains a survey of Canadian businesses and business attitudes. Con-

tains graphs and charts and written articles based on these diagrams; based on a questionnaire designed to reveal as much information as possible concerning senior executives' perspectives of the overall economic environment and the factors influencing the investment spending decision. Circulation: about 4,000.

Survey of Consumer Buying Intentions
The Conference Board of Canada
25 McArthur Road, Suite 100
Ottawa, Ont., Canada K1L 6R3
(613)746-1216

A quarterly report that shows the relationship of consumer confidence to current developments in the Canadian economy, particularly concerning labor market conditions. Contains graphs, charts, and written statements based on a questionnaire sent to a cross-section of Canadian consumers. Circulation: approximately 4,000.

The Tarheel Banker
P.O. Box 30609
Raleigh, NC 27612
(919)782-6960

A monthly magazine that gives thorough coverage to North Carolina banking news. Editorial content includes reports and photo coverage of association conventions, meetings and activities, editorials, actions by the Comptroller of the Currency regarding North Carolina banks, actions of the North Carolina State Banking Commission, new banks and branches, and more. It is the official monthly publication of the North Carolina Bankers Association. Approximate circulation: 4,000.

The Tax Adviser
1211 Avenue of the Americas
New York, NY 10036
(212)575-6200

A monthly publication of the American Institute of Certified Public Accountants, *The Tax Adviser* includes thorough articles on subjects of interest to persons employed in the field of accounting. Each issue includes several detailed articles on tax-related subjects and/or problems. Also included are several regular departments such as "Tax Clinic" and "Tax Trends" and a subject and author index for the previous twelve months. Approximate circulation: 11,000.

Taxation for Accountants
125 East 56th Street
New York, NY 10022
(212)421-6740

A monthly magazine especially valuable to the accountant who is not a specialist in taxation. Focuses on tax articles for the accountant in general practice with an emphasis on tax problems of small corporations and individuals. Includes information on estate planning. Regular departments include "Tax Newsletter," "CPA Questions," "Tax Quiz," etc. There is also a section on technical matters which includes comments. Circulation: about 17,000.

Taxation for Lawyers
125 East 56th Street
New York, NY 10022
(212)421-6740

A bimonthly magazine focusing on tax articles for the lawyer in general practice. The main emphasis is on tax problems of small corporations and individuals, including estate planning. There are regular departments such as "Landmark Tax Cases," "Tax Literature," "Test Your Knowledge," etc. There is also a detailed section concerning technical notes and comments. Approximate circulation: 6,000.

Teens and Boys Magazine
71 West 35th Street
New York, NY 10001
(212)594-0880

A nicely illustrated monthly magazine; the only trade publication in the United States devoted exclusively to the male youth apparel market. It has nationwide reach and its readers include retailers and manufacturers serving the clothing and furnishing needs of boys and male teenage students. Each issue includes fashion features such as "Retail News," "Trade Associations," "Fabrics, Fibers, Finishes, Findings," and a section concerning people and events of interest in the world of young male fashion. Approximate circulation: 8,500.

Trenton
P.O. Box 8307
Trenton, NJ 08650
(609)586-2056

A monthly publication of the Mercer County Chamber of Commerce. Feature articles explore and attempt to explain the social, business,

and governmental fabric of the area. They are written with the goal of furthering the interests of the businessperson in Mercer County. Circulation: about 10,000.

Trusts and Estates
461 Eighth Avenue
New York, NY 10001
(212)239-6200

A specialized monthly financial magazine that serves trust, pension, and investment officers of banks, as well as attorneys, life underwriters, accountants, institutional investors, and practitioners in related fields. Articles, features, and columns deal with the practical aspects of estate and trust administration, planning, investments, charitable giving; and current legal, tax, and financial developments. Circulation: about 15,100.

United States Banker
286 Congress Street
Boston, MA 02210
(617)426-3860

An independent voice to the U.S. financial community since 1891, this biweekly magazine is written principally for chief executive officers and marketing directors in financial institutions. It is of value to persons with many responsibilities in banks, investment firms, insurance companies, various types of credit firms, legal firms, management consultant firms, research firms, and related areas of business. Approximate circulation: 12,500.

University of Michigan Business Review
Graduate School of Business Administration
The University of Michigan
Ann Arbor, MI 48109
(313)763-4510

A bimonthly journal offering current reviews and research in the areas of management, finance, marketing, economics, and accounting. Circulation: about 4,500.

Vision
52, rue Taibout
Paris, France 75009
285-71-75

This free monthly journal is aimed at the European businessperson.

It is unique in that it publishes identical material in four different language editions—English, French, German, and Italian. Circulation: about 125,000.

The Voice of Small Business
1225 19th Street, N.W.
Washington, DC 20036
(202)296-7400

A monthly newsletter that offers articles of interest to small-business owners in all industries, trades, and professions. Deals with news relating to legislative and governmental activities in Washington. It is the membership newsletter of the National Small Business Association, a nonprofit organization dedicated to the preservation and expansion of the small-business sector of the economy. Circulation: about 50,000 members and 5,000 nonmembers.

Wall Street Review of Books
430 Manville Road
Pleasantville, NY 10570
(914)769-3629

A quarterly journal devoted exclusively to reviewing publications of interest to the business and financial communities. The reviews cover trade and professional books in the areas of economics, finance, banking, and economic and social services. Approximate circulation: 400.

What's Ahead in Personnel
20 N. Wacker Drive
Chicago, IL 60606
(312)332-3571

A fast-moving bimonthly newsletter covering personnel problems employers are likely to have in the near future. Comprehensive news of trends, ideas, research, key government rulings, and career opportunities; covered through reports on surveys, forecasts, and developments within the business world. Approximate circulation: several thousand.

Wigs, Hats, and Accessories
22 East 42nd Street
New York, NY 10017
(212)986-8290

A biweekly publication of primary interest to retailers of wigs and other fashion accessories and to the manufacturers, wholesalers, dis-

tributors, and importers of these items. Deals with current fashions, trend reports, industry personalities, new merchandise, and personnel and management changes within the industry. Approximate circulation: 4,400.

The Woman CPA
P.O. Box 389
Marysville, OH 43040
(513)644-5416

A quarterly joint publication of the American Woman's Society of Certified Public Accountants and the American Society of Women Accountants; features technical articles in all fields of accounting. One regular department is devoted to the problems and needs of the small business. Circulation: approximately 8,000.

Yale Law Review
401-A Yale Station
New Haven, CT 06520
(203)436-8243, 8244, 8245

An academic journal specializing in articles written by judges, lawyers, and professors. Notes by students are often included. There is also a section containing reviews of books of current interest. Published November through July, excluding February; circulation about 4,500.

Index